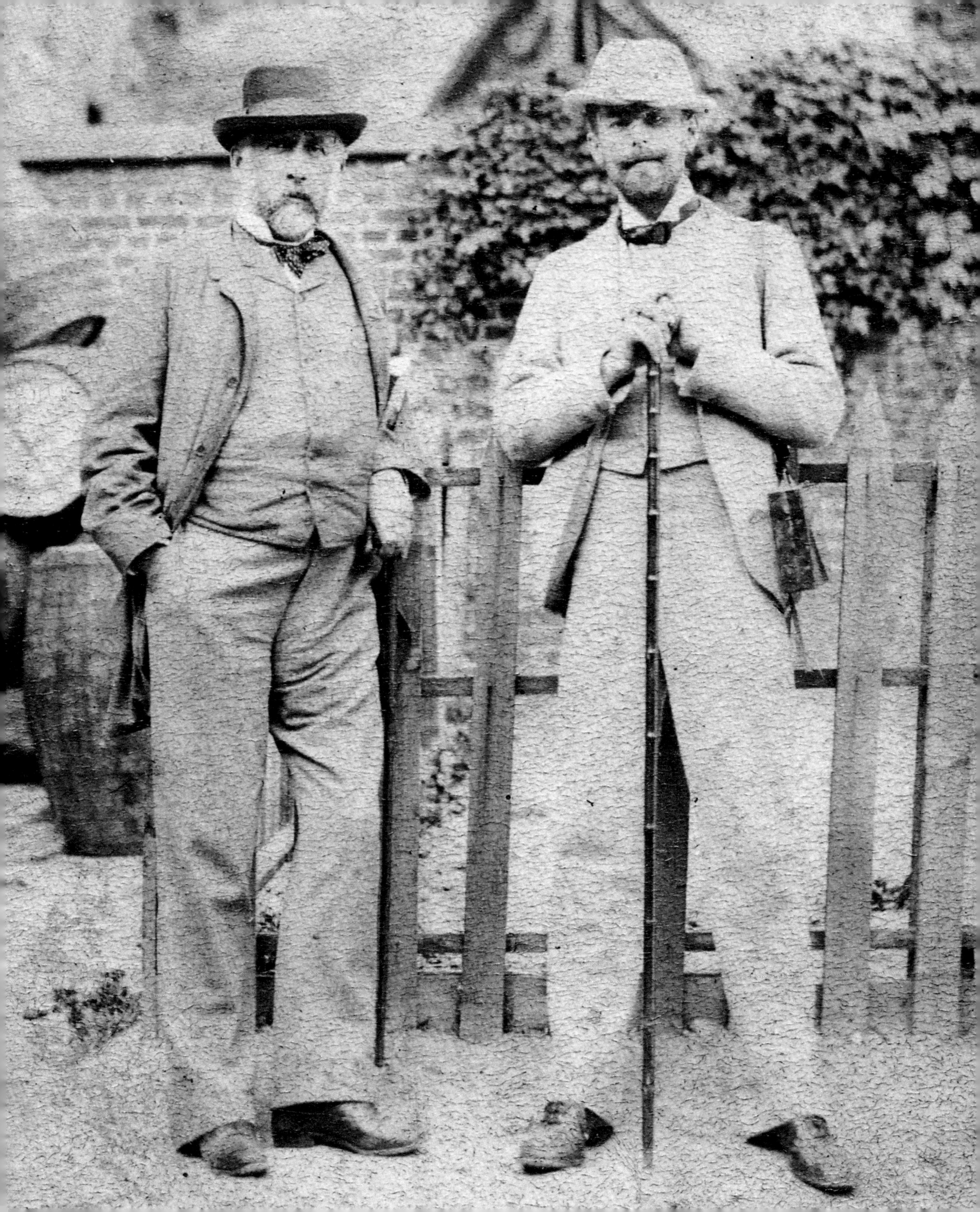

**IN MEMORY OF
DELPHINE LÉVY
(1969–2020)**

WALTER SICKERT

**EDITED BY
EMMA CHAMBERS**

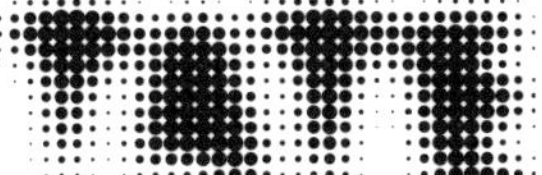

First published 2022 by order of the Tate Trustees
by Tate Publishing, a division of Tate Enterprises Ltd,
Millbank, London SW1P 4RG
www.tate.org.uk/publishing

on the occasion of the exhibition
Walter Sickert

Tate Britain, London
28 April – 18 September 2022

Petit Palais, Paris
14 October 2022 – 29 January 2023

The exhibition at Tate Britain is supported by

The Walter Sickert Exhibition Supporters Circle:
Robert and Matthew Travers, PIANO NOBILE, London

and Tate Patrons

A catalogue record for this book is available from the
British Library

ISBN 978-1-84976-821-4

Distributed in the United States and Canada by
ABRAMS, New York

Library of Congress Control Number applied for

Senior Editor: Alice Chasey
Production: Juliette Dupire
Picture Researchers: Roz Hill and Emma O'Neill
Designed by Sandra Zellmer
Colour reproduction by DL Imaging
Printed and bound in Italy by Graphicom

Wendy Baron is an independent scholar and former
Director of the Government Art Collection. She is the
author of numerous texts on Walter Sickert and the
Camden Town Group.

Emma Chambers is Curator, Modern British Art,
Tate Britain.

Caroline Corbeau-Parsons is Curator of Drawings
at Musée d'Orsay.

Somaya Critchlow is an artist who lives and works
in London.

Kaye Donachie is an artist who lives and works
in London.

Anna Gruetzner Robins is a Professor at the
University of Reading.

Martin Hammer is the author of *Bacon and
Sutherland* (2005), *The Naked Portrait* (2007) and
Francis Bacon and Nazi Propaganda (2012).

Thomas Kennedy is Assistant Curator, Modern British
Art, Tate Britain.

Patricia de Montfort is Lecturer in Art History at the
University of Glasgow.

Katy Norris is a curator and PhD candidate with
Tate and Bristol University. Her publications include
Sickert in Dieppe (2015), *Christopher Wood* (2016)
and *Sylvia Pankhurst* (2019).

Clara Roca is Curator of 19th- and 20th-Century
Graphic Arts and Photography at the Petit Palais.

Sam Rose is an art historian and academic.

Dr Billy Rough is an art historian at the University of
St Andrews. His research focuses on the relationship
between British painting and the theatre.

Lisa Tickner is Honorary Professor, Courtauld
Institute of Art, and Professor Emerita of Art History,
Middlesex University.

Front cover: Walter Sickert, *Little Dot Hetherington
at the Bedford Music Hall* c.1888–9 (see no.40)
Back cover: Walter Sickert, *Nuit d'Amour* c.1920
(see no.99)
Frontispiece: Walter Sickert (right) and Edgar Degas
(left), Dieppe, c.1885, Tate
Page 223: Portrait of Walter Richard Sickert
c.1934–42, Tate Archive

Measurements of artworks are given in centimetres,
height before width, before depth.

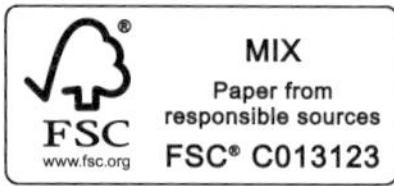

CONTENTS

In this exhibition, Tate Britain presents the most extensive retrospective of Walter Sickert (1860–1942) in almost thirty years. Sickert's multifaceted production and wide artistic networks, both in Britain and Europe, make him a key figure in understanding the development of British art in the late nineteenth and early twentieth centuries. A master of self-invention and theatricality, Sickert took a radically modern approach to painting, transforming how everyday life was captured on canvas. The exhibition features over 150 of his works from over seventy public and private collections, from scenes of rowdy music halls to ground-breaking nudes and narrative subjects. Spanning Sickert's six-decade career, it uncovers the people, places and subjects that inspired him, and explores his legacy as one of British art's most distinctive, provocative and influential artists.

The exhibition examines how Sickert's interaction with the French art world inspired him to transform key genres of British art, such as the nude and the conversation piece, in a way that both inspired his contemporaries and left a legacy for subsequent generations of British artists, including Francis Bacon and Lucian Freud, as well as contemporary artists working today. Sickert was always fascinated by the materiality of paint and this inspired him to constantly explore new methods of working, from impressionist handling in his early career to the pioneering use of photography as source material for his paintings in his late work. The exhibition considers these technical developments and also examines the performative nature of his practice, both through his depictions of popular culture and celebrity, and his own changing self-presentation in self-portraiture.

The exhibition was conceived from the beginning as a partnership between Tate Britain and the Petit Palais, Paris. One of the major aims of the exhibition was to reintroduce Sickert to French audiences and to remind British audiences of the importance of France to his work. The interest of the late Delphine Lévy (former Executive Director, Paris Musées) in this French connection was of central importance to the conception of the exhibition and profoundly shaped its development and the selection of works. We would like to dedicate the exhibition to her memory and thank her partner David Azéma and her daughter Lila Wickers-Lévy for their help with the exhibition and catalogue.

Walter Sickert is organised by Tate Britain in collaboration with the Petit Palais, Paris. We thank our colleagues at the Petit Palais for sharing our enthusiasm for the project, led by their former Director Christophe Leribault, who recently became Director, Musée d'Orsay, and curator Clara Roca. We look forward to working with Annick Lemoine, Christophe Leribault's successor, in the coming months.

The exhibition is curated by Emma Chambers (Curator, Modern British Art, Tate Britain), Caroline Corbeau-Parsons (Curator of Drawings / Conservatrice des Arts Graphiques at Musée d'Orsay, and former Curator, British Art, 1850–1915 at Tate Britain), the late Delphine Lévy (former Executive Director, Paris Musées) and Thomas Kennedy (Assistant Curator, Modern British Art, Tate Britain).

The catalogue contributors, who include both distinguished writers on Sickert's oeuvre and a new generation of writers and artists inspired by his work, have enriched the understanding of Sickert's practice with their thoughtful contributions.

The curators' acknowledgements detail the many debts we owe to colleagues and lenders of work to the exhibition. I would like to reiterate our thanks to the lenders who have supported the exhibition with enthusiasm and generosity, and without whom exhibitions such as this would not be possible.

The exhibition has greatly benefitted from the support of the Walter Sickert Exhibition Supporters Circle. We are also grateful to Tate Patrons for their support towards the presentation of the exhibition.

The exhibition has been made possible by the provision of insurance through the Government Indemnity Scheme. Tate Britain would like to thank HM Government for providing Government Indemnity, and the Department for Digital, Culture, Media and Sport for arranging the indemnity.

Alex Farquharson
Director, Tate Britain

CURATORS' ACKNOWLEDGEMENTS

Our first and greatest debt is to the many lenders to this exhibition, whose generosity has allowed us to do justice to Walter Sickert's vision by showing his most important and innovative works. Many of these are held in British public collections, and we are very grateful to colleagues in these institutions for their enthusiasm for the show and their readiness to lend these key objects from their collections. We are also extremely grateful to the many private lenders to the exhibition who have temporarily parted with the Sickert works on their walls. Colleagues in the commercial sector have also been incredibly helpful in tracing key works in private collections and we would like to thank: Guy Agazarian, Lukas Baumann, Richard Calvocoressi, Jason Carey, Grant Ford, James Holland-Hibbert, Daniel Katz, Robert Travers, Stella Vasileiadou, and others for their assistance with this.

Any curator of a Walter Sickert exhibition owes a huge debt to the work of Wendy Baron, whose deep and perceptive scholarship over many decades has shed light on all aspects of Sickert's work, and whose 2006 catalogue raisonné is still the primary publication on Sickert's work, in addition to the invaluable catalogue for the *Sickert Paintings* exhibition curated by Baron and Richard Shone at the Royal Academy of Arts in 1992–3. Other more tightly focused shows, such as *Sickert in Dieppe* curated by Katy Norris at Pallant

House Gallery in 2015 and *Walter Sickert: The Camden Town Nudes* curated by Barnaby Wright at the Courtauld Gallery in 2008, have also contributed greatly to our understanding of his multifaceted work. Anna Gruetzner Robins's *Walter Sickert: The Complete Writings on Art* (2000) has illuminated Sickert's wide-ranging opinions on the art of his time, allowing his work to be seen in its intellectual context. Rebecca Daniels's research on the photographic sources for Sickert's late work has been invaluable in increasing understanding of his practice. We would particularly like to thank Wendy Baron and Anna Gruetzner Robins, who were generous with their expertise in conversations which helped to shape the direction of the show in its early stages, and have been helpful in answering questions throughout. We are also grateful to the catalogue authors, who have expanded our understanding of Sickert's work and its legacy in their thoughtful contributions. We are also indebted to many individuals who generously shared their knowledge of Sickert's work and its wider context, or helped with archival research during the development of the show, and would like to thank: Rebecca Daniels, Marlin Khondoker, Robert Upstone, Taylor Zakarin, and others who have helped with research questions.

At Tate we would particularly like to thank Andrew Wilson for his invaluable assistance in steering the project through its early stages and his advice throughout. The input of Elena Crippa and Andrea Schlieker was also invaluable in the latter stages of the exhibition process. We are also extremely grateful to Sarah Bashir, Tim Batchelor, Darren Beament, Zoe Bromberg-McCarthy, Soraya Chumroo, Oliver Cowling, Angie De La Puente Cuya, Sionaigh Durrant, Adrian Glew, Juleigh Gordon-Orr, Abigail Granville, Lauren Greenwood, Amy Griffin, Figgy Guyver, Christopher Higgins, Duncan Holden, Victoria Jenkins, Carolyn Kerr, Caitlin Lambert, Abi Laughton, Margot Lombaert, Wendy Lothian, Gabriella Macaro, Kathy Maniura, Rosie Marshall, Caroline McCarthy, Jane McCree, Jennifer McShane, Tori Miller, Dana Mokaddem, Jacqueline Moon, Adrian Moore, Hannah Murray, Camille Polkownik, Catherine Poust, Adriana Rojas-Viquez, Alyson Rolington, Sophie Sarkodie, Alessandra Serri, Andy Shiel, Gates Sofer, Enrico Tassi, Liam Tebbs, Dale Wilson, Gillian Wilson, and others including the Tate art handlers.

After being shown at Tate Britain, the *Walter Sickert* exhibition will travel to the Petit Palais in Paris, and we would also like to thank: the Paris Musées team, its Executive Director Anne-Sophie de Gasquet, and particularly Mélanie Adicéam, Emilie Augier, Céline Boudot and Adeline Souverain; and the Petit Palais team, particularly Agnès Faure, Cécile Maisonneuve and Clara Roca, who have made this partnership a reality.

This catalogue has been beautifully designed by Sandra Zellmer. Alice Chasey at Tate Publishing skilfully steered the catalogue through the editorial and production stages. Roz Hill and Emma O'Neill brought characteristic thoroughness to the picture research.

Emma Chambers
Curator, Modern British Art, Tate Britain

Thomas Kennedy
Assistant Curator, Modern British Art, Tate Britain

EMMA CHAMBERS

INTRODUCTION

One of Walter Sickert's most famous statements was that: 'The plastic arts are gross arts, dealing joyously with gross material facts … and while they will flourish in the scullery, or on the dunghill, they fade at a breath from the drawing-room.' [1] It was Sickert's embrace of this materiality – both in his handling of paint and in the exploration of the hidden lives of ordinary people and simply furnished settings in his work – that was pioneering in his time, and that would influence generations of younger artists.

Sickert was one of the most significant British artists of the late nineteenth and early twentieth centuries. Born in Munich, he moved to England with his family at the age of eight. His father was an artist and introduced him to the work of prominent artists in France and in Britain, but Sickert's focus in his early years was on becoming an actor, something he pursued working in theatre for four years. He switched to art in 1881, studying briefly at the Slade School of Fine Art and becoming a pupil of James Abbott McNeill Whistler in 1882 after leaving the school. He was one of the central figures in avant-garde artistic groupings in late nineteenth- and early twentieth-century Britain, gathering together groups of like-minded artists, and he was also a prolific contributor to artistic journals as a critic. [2] His work was particularly important for links

between Britain and France. He spent significant periods of his working life in France, and exhibited in both London and Paris throughout his career. [3] He was a founder member of the New English Art Club, formed as a French-influenced alternative to the Royal Academy. He also inspired groups of younger artists interested in the development of post-impressionist ideas, such as Spencer Gore, Harold Gilman and other members of the Camden Town Group.

The major aims of this exhibition are to reintroduce Sickert to French audiences and to remind British audiences of the importance of French sources to his work and to the British artists he influenced. The late Delphine Lévy's interest in this French connection was crucial in shaping the exhibition and is looked at in detail in her essay (see p.126). Sickert had a significant audience in France, exhibiting there and selling to French patrons. His primary dealers Bernheim-Jeune and Durand-Ruel were based in Paris. His nudes were first exhibited in the 1900s in Paris, where there was already a tradition of depicting nudes in everyday settings. They were seen by French critics as distinctively British in their composition and palette, while British critics remarked disapprovingly on the French influences in Sickert's work. Lévy draws out these different responses with a judicious use of quotations from the French critical press at the time, which complements Lisa Tickner's analysis of British responses later in the catalogue (see p.144).

The exhibition begins with a series of self-portraits ranging from the start of Sickert's career to the end. His theatrical background meant that he was skilled at adopting different personas in his images of himself, depending on his preoccupations at the time. The works range from intense self-portraits to studies of the artist in his studio, and later Sickert playing the role of biblical figures such as Lazarus. Anna Gruetzner Robins's essay 'The Look of Sickert: Painting the Self' (p.16) examines some of the identities the artist adopted over his long career.

After a brief spell at the Slade School, Sickert began his artistic career in 1882 in Whistler's studio, assisting with printing etching plates. His own etchings were close in style to Whistler's and often represented urban scenes with a deliberate economy of line. Whistler's other influence on Sickert in this period was in the painting of small oil panels from life. Panels painted by Sickert and Whistler in Dieppe and London show the importance of Dieppe as a location for Sickert from his earliest days and demonstrate Sickert's adoption of Whistler's tonal approach to painting, learned from his preparation of Whistler's palette before sketching trips. In 1885 Sickert came under the influence of Degas, whom he had first met in 1883, and began to use bolder colours and to plan his compositions with preliminary drawings. It is likely that Sickert's fascination with the music hall also stems from Degas's influence, as Patricia de Montfort's essay on Sickert's apprenticeship years demonstrates (see p.32).

The music hall was one of the most important themes for Sickert throughout his career, as outlined by Thomas Kennedy in his essay for this catalogue (see p.54). Inspired by Degas's ballet paintings and pastels, Sickert explored the music hall's performers, audiences and architecture between the 1880s and the 1920s. He sat in the audience to make his studies and adopted unusual viewpoints, which showed artist, orchestra and audience together, as well as mirrors, which created trompe-l'oeil perspectives on the scene. Sickert's unusual focus on the popular culture of the music hall was unique in Britain in this period and drew on the subject matter of the café-concerts depicted by Manet and Degas in Paris, but this was seen as inappropriate subject matter in Britain outside independent exhibiting societies and galleries. His early music hall paintings focus on the performers such as Minnie Cunningham, Little Dot Hetherington, Vesta Victoria and Ada Lundberg whose performances offered a degree of public attention to female concerns not usually available to women in the period, as Billy Rough's essay examines (see p.80). In later music hall works, Sickert became more interested in the audience and their reaction to the spectacle. As well as music halls in London, he depicted halls in France such as Gaîté Montparnasse in Paris and Vernet's in Dieppe.

Since the 1970s, Sickert's passion for the theatre, his forays into acting and his love of role playing have also contributed to speculation about him being a key suspect in the Jack the Ripper murders of 1888. From at least around 1896, Sickert had a long-standing interest in Jack the Ripper, which lasted until the end of his life. According to the artist Marjorie Lilly, he also dressed up in the role of this notorious killer, an activity that was consistent with his fascination with performing different identities in his portraiture. Lilly's 1971 book sparked unfounded speculation that Sickert was the murderer, including most comprehensively in Patricia Cornwell's recent book on the subject.[4] The identity of Jack the Ripper probably will never be proven, but nevertheless Sickert remains on a list of key suspects in the public imagination, and once stated these associations are difficult to disprove despite the tenuous links between Sickert and the murders. Anna Gruetzner Robins reviews the evidence in her catalogue essay 'Catch Me If You Can: Sickert and Jack the Ripper' (see p.220).

Although Sickert is primarily known as a figure painter, portraiture occupies a minor role in his oeuvre. His portraiture, discussed in Caroline Corbeau-Parsons's essay for this catalogue (see p.92), included both formal commissions and informal portraits of friends and regular models. The vast majority were not commissions, so did not earn him the steady income he hoped for, but his sitters, many of them well-known personalities, show the extent of his connections within cultural circles and high society in England and in France. Contemporary painter Kaye Donachie explores Sickert's formal portraiture in her text, showing how the artist's narrative paintings have influenced her practice (see p.95). In more informal portraits, painted in London and Venice, Sickert's work became closer to genre painting, and the interiors in which the figures were placed became equally important in suggesting a narrative and an emotional connection, as Wendy Baron examines in her essay on Sickert's narrative paintings (see p.166).

Landscape painting also occupies a defined niche in Sickert's output, but it was his most successful genre in terms of sales, especially Dieppe and Venice views sold through his Paris dealers Bernheim-Jeune and Durand-Ruel. As Katy Norris examines in her essay, '"Full of Appeal – Sad – Wan – Touching": Sickert's "Picturesque" Work' (see p.110), Sickert returned to favourite painting locations such as Dieppe (where he lived between 1898 and 1905) and Venice (which he visited regularly from 1895), repeatedly painting their buildings and streets, developing source material sketched on the spot into finished paintings in his studio. He frequently focused on the façades of two famous buildings: St Mark's in Venice and St Jacques in Dieppe, where he explored the effect of light on the architecture at different times of day. Although this approach to the effect of shifting light on architecture drew its initial inspiration from Monet's Rouen Cathedral series, in Dieppe Sickert remained interested in the human aspect of the urban scene and often included scenes of everyday life in the foreground of his paintings, inspired by Camille Pissarro's views of Dieppe. His street scenes evolved from small formats that were relatively dark to bigger paintings that were brighter and more colourful under the influence of the French impressionists, the Fauves and the Nabis, and with the encouragement of his dealers who viewed these works as more commercially attractive.

Nude subjects in contemporary interiors were popularised by French realist and impressionist painters as a way of connecting the genre with modern urban life. These located the nude within domestic spaces, engaged in intimate activities and unaware of being looked at, giving the viewer the illusion of access to a private world. Sickert was inspired by French artists such as Bonnard and Degas to place the nude in contemporary interiors in explicit poses and to employ 'keyhole' viewpoints which offered the viewer a voyeuristic partial view. Sickert was also interested in the aesthetic qualities of the nude, in particular the patterns of light and shade on flesh created by light from a window streaming into a dimly lit room. He specialised in urban working-class subjects and wanted to show the naked female form without idealisation in a contemporary setting. He first exhibited his nudes in

1905 in Paris, where they were seen in the context of French painting, but in London, where they were first shown in 1911, they became associated with Camden Town, the seedy area of London where Sickert had several studios between 1905 and 1914. In Britain, his subject matter of a naked woman on an iron bedstead with crumpled sheets in a dimly lit room created a scene that suggested poverty and prostitution. Although admired by French critics, the explicit poses and bedroom interiors were strongly disapproved of by British critics, as Lisa Tickner shows in her essay. Somaya Critchlow brings a contemporary lens to Sickert's nudes in her text, examining the psychological tension between artist and model in *The Studio: The Painting of a Nude* c.1906 (see p.149).

Although nude subjects represented a tiny fraction of his oeuvre, Sickert created a major innovation in British paintings of the nude by showing unidealised female bodies in everyday interiors, and this has gone on to influence later painters such as Francis Bacon and Lucian Freud in their treatment of the nude, as Martin Hammer examines in his essay (see p.216). Tickner also suggests that artists such as Jenny Saville and Alice Neel provide examples of Sickert's impact on the late twentieth-century nude. However, the topic of the female nude, always a subject of controversy for feminist art historians focused on the nature of the male gaze, has become even more contested in recent years, with questions asked about the power relationships between model and artist. Like most artists of his generation, Sickert worked from regular models, some of whom would become close friends and lovers or employees, but more often the relationship was a business transaction with the model being paid for her time. We know the identity of some models – Augustine Villain in Dieppe, Carolina dell'Acqua and La Giuseppina in Venice, Blanche and Adeline in Paris, Hubby and Marie in London – but not of others. Wendy Baron examines Sickert's relationship with his models in her catalogue essay.

Sickert's fascination with narrative painting led to his radical reinvention of the tradition of the 'conversation piece', following

Hogarth and other eighteenth-century British artists. Baron's essay traces Sickert's transformation both of this historical tradition and of paintings of figures in interiors by French artists such as Bonnard into a uniquely British twentieth-century version that concentrated on everyday life. The combination of two figures in an interior began with his Venetian scenes of nude and clothed women in conversation seated on a bed. From these, back in London, he developed a series of paintings of a clothed man and nude woman, in the same dingy rooms that he used for his nudes, which became known as the Camden Town Murder series. Associating with a real murder that had occurred in Camden Town in 1907 and attracted huge press attention, Sickert deliberately took advantage of the controversy and popular interest in the murder with his use of the 'Camden Town Murder' titles for his works. However, he also reworked the same compositions with both male and female figures, and exhibited them under alternative titles, allowing the viewer to create different narratives from the same composition. As Baron argues, Sickert was interested in the emotional connection between the figures in their different configurations, rather than in any illustration of the murder. Other, less controversial narrative paintings such as *Ennui* explored the claustrophobic environments and conflicted emotions of everyday relationships in stage sets created by Sickert in his studio. Baron posits that the shifting configurations of figures and alternative titles allowed the viewer the opportunity to interpret these relationships, with the serious purpose of demonstrating the overwhelming importance of the visual content of the painting over any verbal interpretation.

In the 1930s Sickert's fascination with popular culture continued, and he began to paint on a larger scale and to use a brighter palette. Theatre scenes and subjects from the popular press dominated his output. The majority of these had black and white photographs as their source, which were then translated into vivid colour. Sickert was fascinated by the way that the flattened perspective and stark tonal contrasts of black and white photography resulted in simplified forms which he retained as

almost abstract effects in the final painting. He also produced a series of works based on Victorian engravings, which he titled 'Echoes'. Sickert had favourite performers such as Peggy Ashcroft and Gwen Ffrangcon-Davies, whom he painted repeatedly, and his theatrical scenes were based on photographs taken by himself or by his assistants during rehearsals, or on press cuttings. He also used press cuttings as the source for images of royalty or historic events, such as Amelia Earhart's solo flight across the Atlantic in May 1932.[5] Sam Rose (see p.194) examines the method Sickert used for his late paintings and the mediation of their sources, arguing for their significance in addressing issues of authorship and contemporary culture. Sickert's use of photography is now recognised as a significant precursor of subsequent developments in the transmutation of found popular images and the employment of photography as source material by artists in the late twentieth century. Martin Hammer's essay explores the role of the Beaux-Arts Gallery in promoting Sickert's work in conjunction with a younger generation of 'Kitchen Sink' and 'School of London' artists, and in particular his impact on the work of Auerbach, Bacon and Freud.

Sickert is often described as a 'painter's painter' because of his fascination with different approaches to manipulating paint to create almost abstract effects as he depicted the figure. He remained devoted to figurative painting but the genres he explored and his approach to his subject matter shifted throughout his career, creating a rich and varied oeuvre where he was always at the forefront of developments in British art. His interest in popular culture was pioneering for the early twentieth century and inspired many of his contemporaries, such as members of the Camden Town Group. His work continues to be discovered by new generations of contemporary artists, emphasising his relevance now as well as at the time he was working.

SICKERT'S IDENTITIES

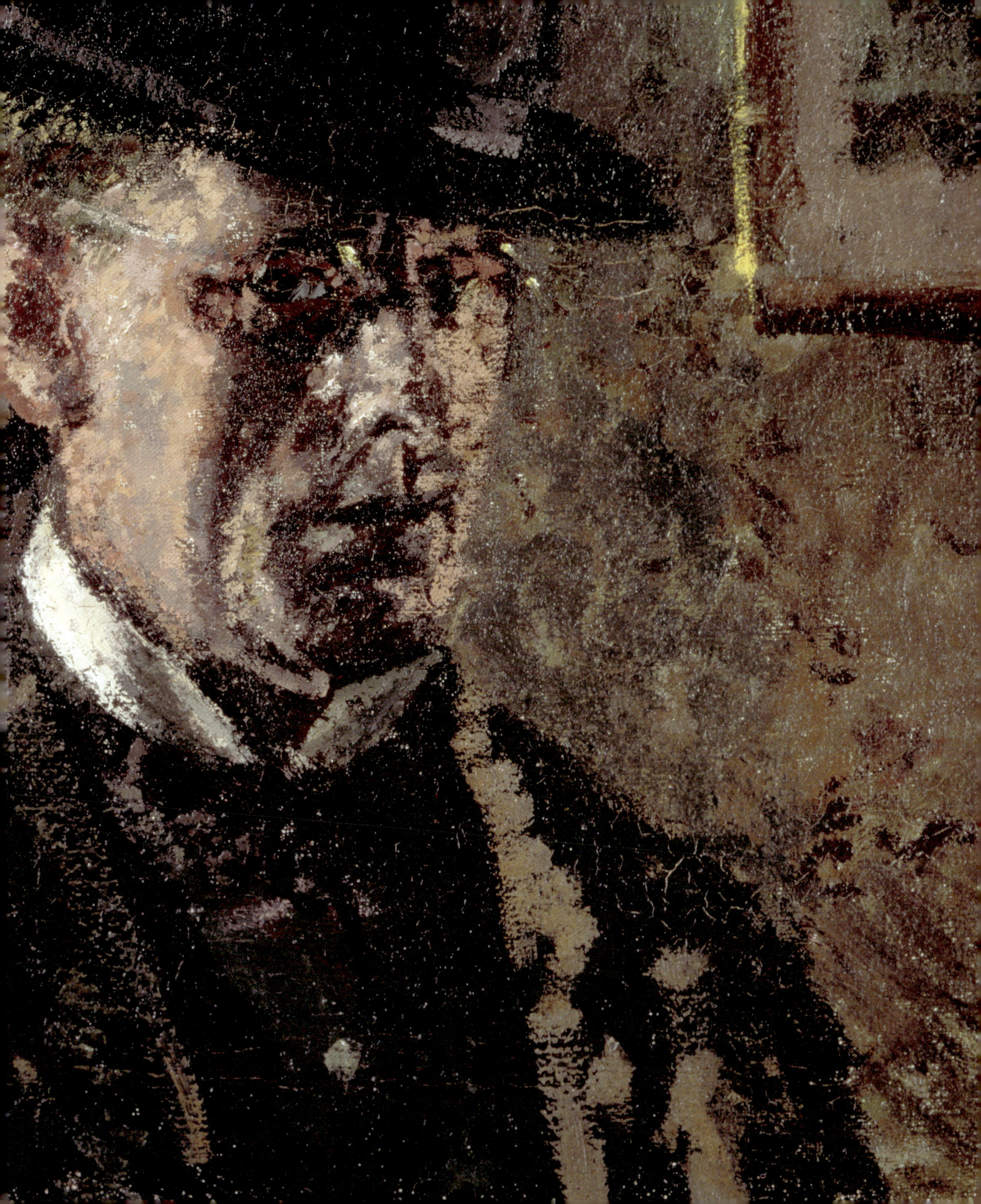

ANNA GRUETZNER ROBINS

THE LOOK OF SICKERT: PAINTING THE SELF

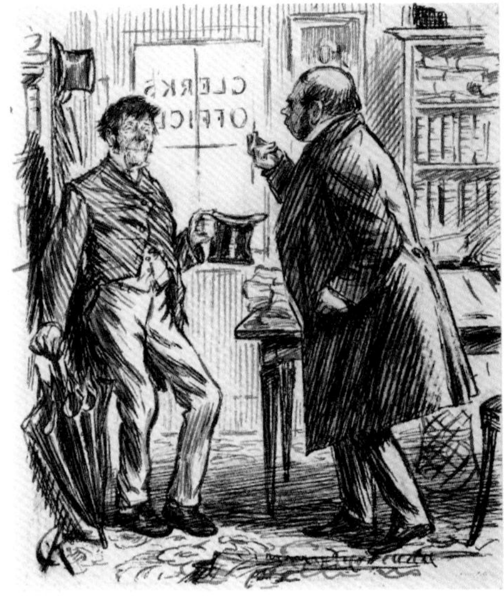

Fig.1
Charles Samuel Keene,
'Incorrigible!' 1883,
ink on paper, 17.5 × 14.6,
Tate

Sickert looks up from a bowed head in *Self-Portrait* 1882 (see no.1). The young would-be artist and former actor has portrayed himself in a favoured pose of Sir Henry Irving (see, for example, fig.2), the actor and manager whom he hero-worshipped, and whose theatre company he joined in 1879. Although he acted with several companies, Sickert never had any real success, and he soon left the stage to enrol at the Slade School of Fine Art before joining Whistler as his pupil, where he painted Whistlerian-like pictures and emulated Whistler's dandyism in dress and behaviour. Until his old age he continued to be a consummate performer who loved to appear in fresh disguises, made kaleidoscopic changes to his way of dress, and had a bewildering number of ways of speaking and behaving. Those who knew him claimed that it was impossible to discover the man behind his many personas and egos. 'Is there ... no fixed point, no common denominator, that we may take hold of and say "this is the real man"?', asked his first biographer, who decided that the work was the best way of knowing him.[1] If that is the case, then how do we interpret his self-portraits? Nearly all of them tell us something about Sickert and his art, and the richly rewarding and fascinating changes in his practice over nearly sixty years, but they hardly reveal the man behind the mask.

The fine unbroken line and cross-hatching in *Self-Portrait* 1882 compares to the drawings of another, less known, early hero of Sickert's, the *Punch* illustrator Charles Keene, whom Sickert considered to be 'one of the master draughtsmen of the world' (see, for example, Keene's 1883 pen and ink drawing, *'Incorrigible!'*, fig.1).[2] In 1896, Sickert paid one of his many tributes to Keene when he observed that he was a great artist because he drew what he observed around him, and believed that 'the somewhat embarrassed grace of a burgess's wife ... dressed without taste, is as interesting and as beautiful ... as the good-breeding of a lady'.[3] The educated, middle-class Keene ignored the fashion among successful English artists to dress and live like gentlemen. Instead he wore 'the loose-fitting jacket, corduroys and billycock of the countryman',[4] and worked in 'two or three scruffy studios and lodgings in and around the King's Road' in Chelsea.[5] His refusal to follow convention in his dress and his choice of accommodation would be a lasting role model for Sickert. In 1893 he gave up his luxurious studio with living accommodation at 24 Glebe Place, Chelsea, and took a 'small room to work in' at 127 Cheyne Walk, one of six artisans' dwellings in Milton Chambers.[6] He was making a life choice, and he would seek out this kind of humble workspace for the rest of his life.

Self-Portrait c.1896 is masked in darkness (see no.2): Sickert's head turns towards a mirror on his left, and an almost black anxious eye, not a reportedly wonderful blue one, looks tentatively back at us. The dark tonal brownish colour enlivened by the whitish colour of his eye, which is repeated in the scarf, together with the dark reddish ground, is a more subdued version of the palette of the controversial early music hall pictures. Sickert suffered from depression, and it is tempting to blame his morose haggard expression in *Self-Portrait* c.1896 on his lack of financial success and other personal difficulties, but it also speaks of a recent life choice. The business of making art was difficult, especially if you were challenging just about every social and artistic convention in the London art world. The man with tousled hair and a carelessly knotted scarf around his neck had left the self-styled Whistlerian dandy behind.

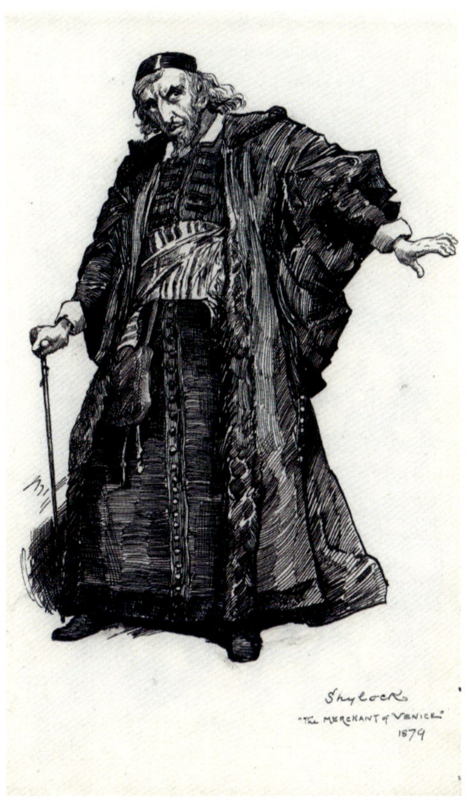

Fig.2
Harry Furniss, *Sir Henry Irving as Shylock* 1879, pen and ink on paper, 33.7×22.7, National Portrait Gallery, London

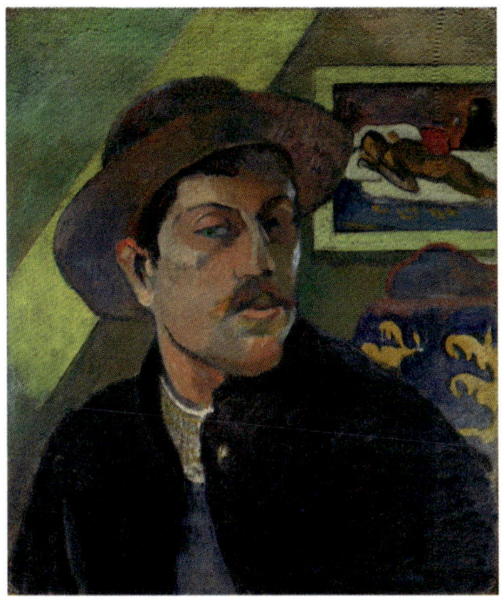

Fig.3
Paul Gauguin, *Autoportrait au chapeau* 1894, oil paint on canvas, 46×38, Grand Palais (Musée d'Orsay)

From 1898, Sickert lived largely in France, until he took a London address in 1905, though he continued to take part in the Paris exhibition circuit. He was in Paris in autumn 1906 when he exhibited at the Salon d'Automne which staged a comprehensive Gauguin posthumous exhibition[7] with a number of Gauguin's self-portraits (see, for example, fig.3), each of which represented one of the artist's carefully constructed identities.[8] These may have been an inspirational model for a number of Sickert's self-portraits, including nos.3 and 4, each of which represents a different self. While living in France, Sickert thought of taking out French citizenship, and told his friend and patron Jacques-Émile Blanche that 'I am a French painter',[9] but French critics were keen to point out his English connections. They associated his palette with the grimy London atmosphere, and in one instance wrote that his female figures were 'poor wretches who wander in the Whitechapel alleyways, stupefied with gin'.[10] He answered these claims about the Englishness of his painting by exhibiting a 'punching ball', *L'Homme au chapeau melon* (The Man with the Bowler Hat – the original title of *Self-Portrait. Juvenile Lead*; no.4), at the 1907 Salon d'Automne.[11] It is as good an advertisement as any for his Englishness. Bowler hats were invented by a British hatmaker around 1850 and were only taken up by bankers and other city men later, in the twentieth century. The young fashionable clerks or 'mashers' ogling the music hall performer Ada Lundberg wear them (see no.34). Sickert wears one in an 1880 photograph, in a pen and ink drawing where he poses against a Venetian background, and in a late self-portrait (see no.10).

At the same time that he was exhibiting in Paris, Sickert was gaining a new foothold in the London art world. *Self-Portrait. The Painter in his Studio* (see no.3) was exhibited in 1907 at the New English Art Club, which Sickert had spearheaded as a young man, turning it into a showcase for the 'New Painting'. Sickert portrays himself at a crossroads in this self-portrait, which brings together a reflection of him holding a palette in the mirror with the painting *Théâtre de Montmartre* (see no.44) on the wall behind him. Casts of a variant of the Cnidian Venus, Michelangelo's *Dying Slave* and an écorché

(literally, 'flayed'; a model of the body with the skin removed – an age-old source for study, which artists frequently included in self-portraits)[12] are arranged in 'real space' on the mantelpiece below the mirror. *Self-Portrait. The Painter in his Studio* is about choices: to relaunch himself as a painter of popular entertainment or to rethink some of the sources that his French associates used when representing the female nude, and to disrupt these existing models with something far more explosive. His solution was the Camden Town nudes.

'What beard were I best to play it in?'[13] Sickert certainly knew *A Midsummer Night's Dream* – he acted as Demetrius in the play – but whether he was thinking of Bottom's question about changing his beard or not, he certainly changed his beard (and his hair) often enough. These different guises and personas 'had the power to surprise, confuse, even shock', and each change in his hair and beard, his costume and his character is part of a lasting self-mythologising of his appearance, class, speech and behaviour that were designed to keep even those closest to him at a distance.[14]

Beards were fashionable in the mid-Victorian period, but by the late 1880s they were rather passé. Fashionable or not, the beard that Sickert sports in *Self-Portrait: The Bust of Tom Sayers* 1913 is decidedly odd (see no.5). In summer 1913 he grew what he described as a 'hoary' (grey-white) beard, which he shaved off in December.[15] His beard is fuzzy brown (not grey) in the self-portrait of 1913, his untrimmed bushy eyebrows fall over his spectacles, and his naturally curly hair is flattened in short tufts against his head. Did he dye his facial hair and leave his bushy eyebrows untrimmed, or has he pasted on a false beard and eyebrows for a bit of make believe? Marjorie Lilly remembered that Sickert 'produc[ed] a vast square beard … which seemed to grow as fast as Jack's beanstalk'.[16] His facial hair does seem to have grown with remarkable speed. The inclusion of the marble bust of Tom Sayers (1826–65), a mid-Victorian heavyweight champion, may explain Sickert's disguise. After Sayers won a notoriously brutal fight against Tom Heenan in 1860, *Punch* ran a series of John Leech

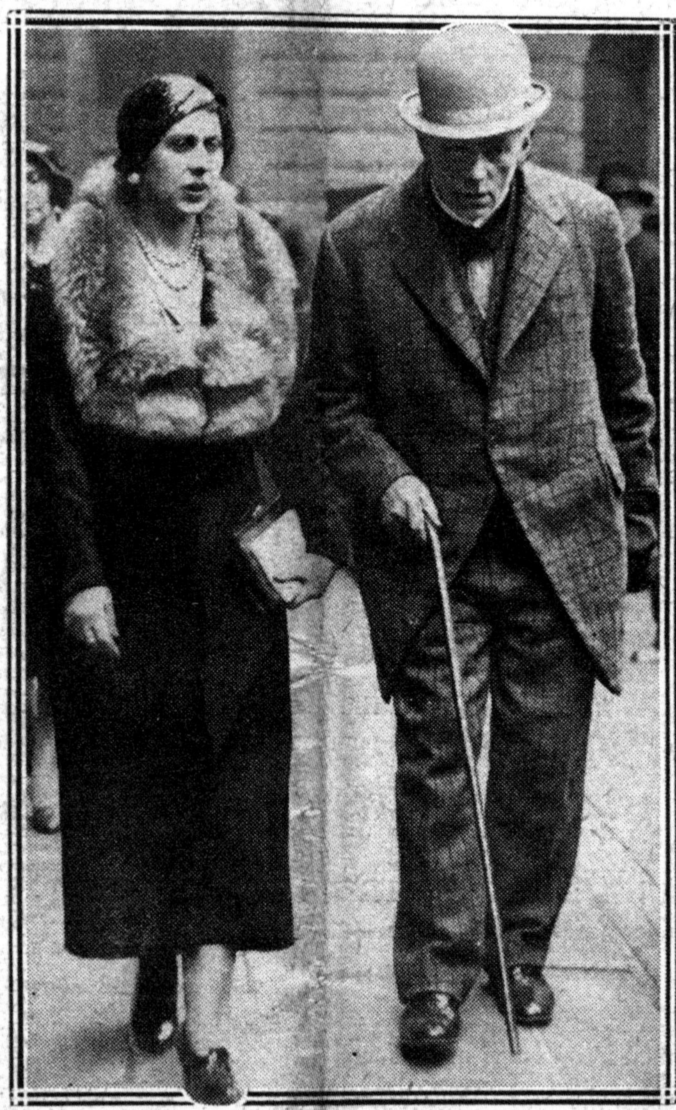

Richard Sickert arriving at the Royal Academy with Gwen ffrangcon Davies, the actress, for yesterday's private view. His picture, " The Raising of Lazarus " (right), is generally regarded as the picture of the year.
—(Copyright reserved for owner by " Royal Academy Illustrated.")

cartoons about 'extremely proper-looking personnages' who went to great lengths to disguise their interest in Sayers.[17] Sickert would have enjoyed the widespread duplicity of these 'respectable' Victorian men who covertly admired Sayers, and he cannot have been unaware of the 1890s nostalgia for the prize fighter and what increasingly came to be regarded as a great moment in English boxing. On the other hand, the large blue and white vase would not be out of place in one of Whistler's 'Aesthetically' arranged figure pictures, such as *Symphony in White, No. 2: The Little White Girl* 1864 (Tate), which teasingly refers to a far more refined world. The two objects make strange bedfellows, but a love of popular local culture together with his early training in the Aesthetic theory of art for art's sake were at the heart of Sickert's art-making.

Sickert started a new group of self-portraits in 1927, and together they mark another significant moment in his art-making. He was unwell during the winter of 1926–7, and while the exact nature of his illness is unknown, he appears to have had a serious physical illness, possibly a stroke, and the mental health issues of the early 1920s, when 'he was evidently depressed' with 'morbid' thoughts, may have returned.[18] After 'resting' off stage, away from the public eye, he emerged as Richard Sickert with the long white beard of a patriarchal Victorian and took on his greatest performative roles as the biblical figures of Lazarus and the servant of Abraham, and finally Christ, in three extraordinary self-portraits that share a new, bolder painterliness.

Portraying himself digging into what looks like a bowl of cereal in an ordinary domestic setting is an audacious response to the title of *Lazarus Breaks his Fast* (see no.6). His choice of the subject of Lazarus, who was brought back from the dead by Christ, is an obtuse reference to Sickert's own rejuvenation after a long illness. Everything about this painterly portrait – the exuberant, vigorous handling of paint, the contrast of the yellow bib against the purple sleeve, and the boldly worked patches of colour on his face – celebrates his rejuvenation. Sickert was sixty-nine when he painted *The Servant of Abraham* (see no.8). Like *Self-Portrait.*

Lazarus Breaks his Fast (see no.7), it was painted from a squared-up photograph (no.9), which freed Sickert from the tyranny of the mirror and opened up new possibilities for portraying the self at close range. Following his life-long belief that an artist should work to scale, he used photography to adjust his range of vision to the size of the canvas. In *The Servant of Abraham*, Sickert's ageing face dissolves into patches of brownish tonal colour that nearly obliterate his features, except for the two darker blobs of his eyes on the pale crumbling surface. The painting's biblical title is telling. Like the servant of Abraham who single-mindedly followed his master's wishes to find a wife for his son Isaac, Sickert was singularly devoted – but to his art, which was the one constant in his complicated life.

The photographs of Sickert in the last years of his life conceal as much as they reveal. *Self-Portrait in Grisaille* 1935 (see no.10) is based on a 1932 photograph of a clean-shaven Sickert, wearing the kind of window-paned check suit he favoured for a large part of his life (see fig.4). In the painting, he looks up from a bowed head, and plays the part of a shrunken, disillusioned old man arriving at the Royal Academy of Arts on Piccadilly.[19] In 1935 the Royal Academy had refused to stand up for Jacob Epstein when his sculptures were attacked and Sickert resigned in protest, so it is reasonable to refer to *Self-Portrait in Grisaille* as a picture about protest. If he had emblazoned it with part of his impassioned published defence of the Epstein reliefs that the Royal Academy had refused to defend, there would be no argument.[20]

Sickert's role-playing fantasies increased in the 1930s, or at least he was more likely to air them in public spaces. There are no self-portraits of him as a shepherd or a cook, but he did insert himself and also his third wife Thérèse Lessore into what are more broadly speaking 'conversation pieces', or portrait interiors for which he used photographs to set up scenes of their life together. The bearded old man is recognisable as Sickert in *The Front at Hove (Turpe Senex Miles Turpe Senilis Amor)* (see no.11 and fig.39), and the younger woman on the bench beside him may be his wife, but the Latin quotation from Ovid – 'An old soldier is a wretched thing, so also is senile love' – makes the picture more broadly speaking closer to his earlier 'conversation pieces' (see nos.133, 134 and 135) which explore the psychology of human intimacy. There is no mistaking the couple in *Reading in the Cabin* (see no.12), which was based on another cropped newspaper photograph, but Sickert added a row of carefully arranged books in the background of the picture.[21] During Sickert's last years, his mind would wander, and he would confuse places and things. The Sickerts were photographed at home in Bathampton so the title of the picture, and Sickert's jaunty nautical peaked cap, are fanciful additions. Perhaps he imagined that he was making one last Channel crossing to Dieppe. We can allow him that moment of fantasy.

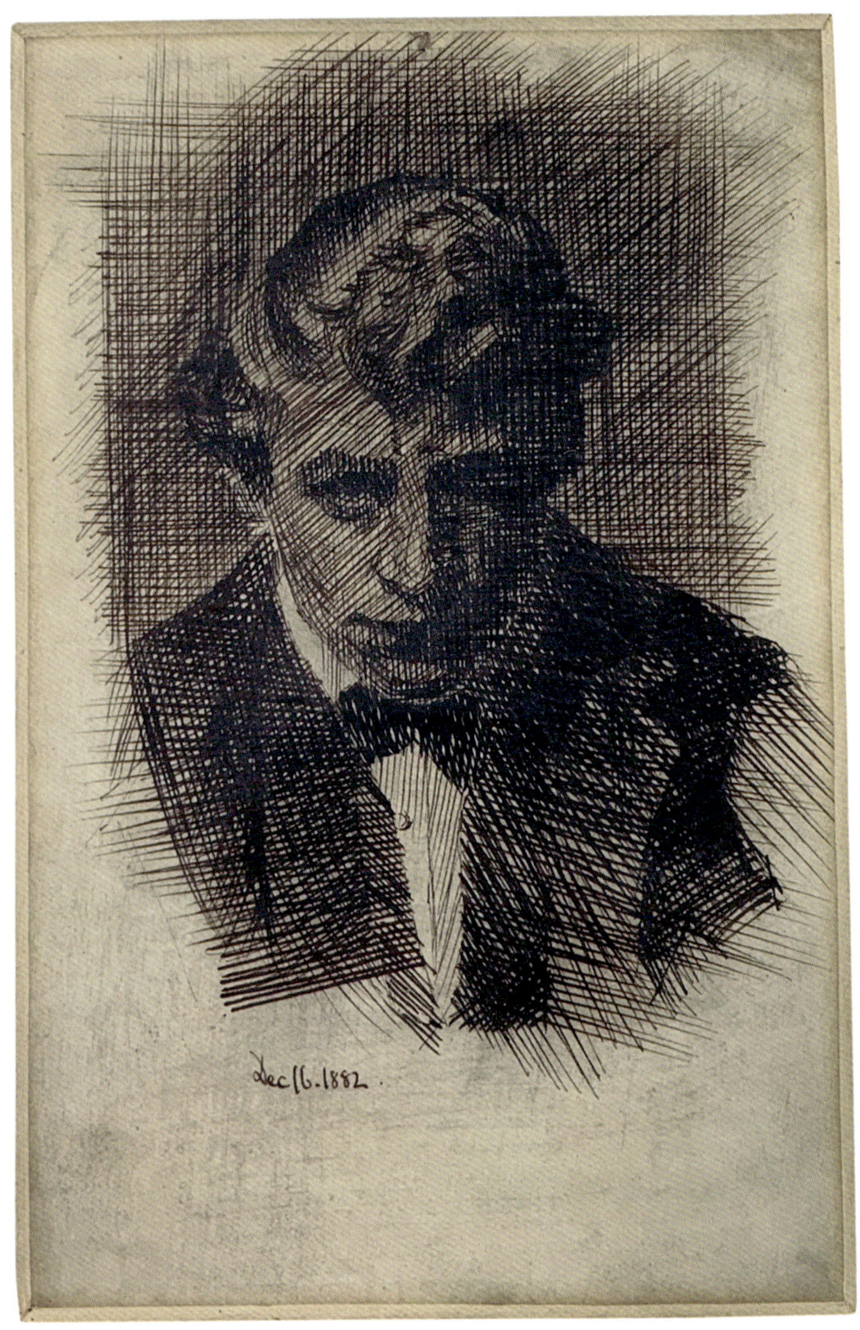

1
Self-Portrait 1882
Pen and ink on paper
Islington Local
History Centre

2
Self-Portrait c.1896
Oil paint on canvas
Leeds Museums
and Galleries

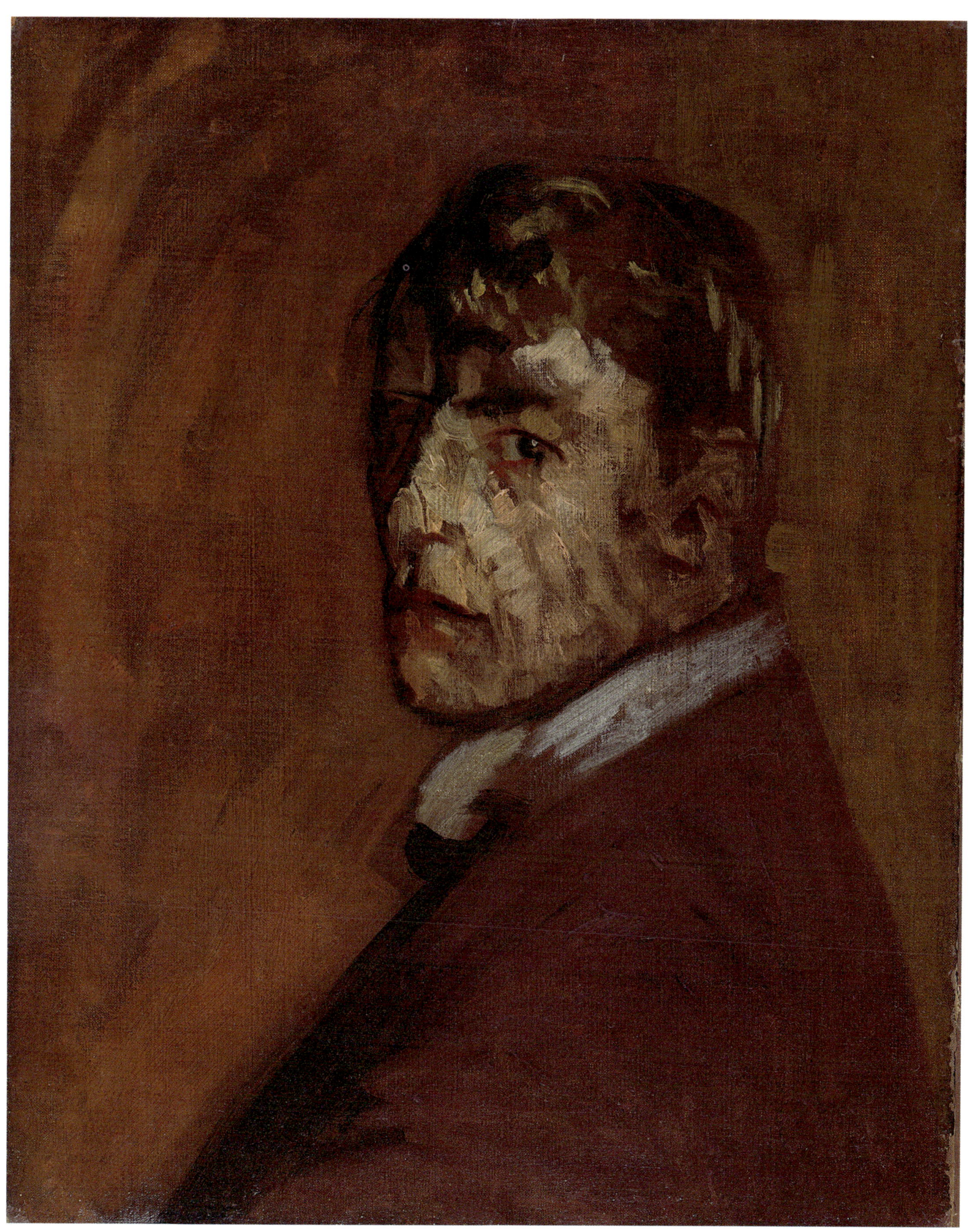

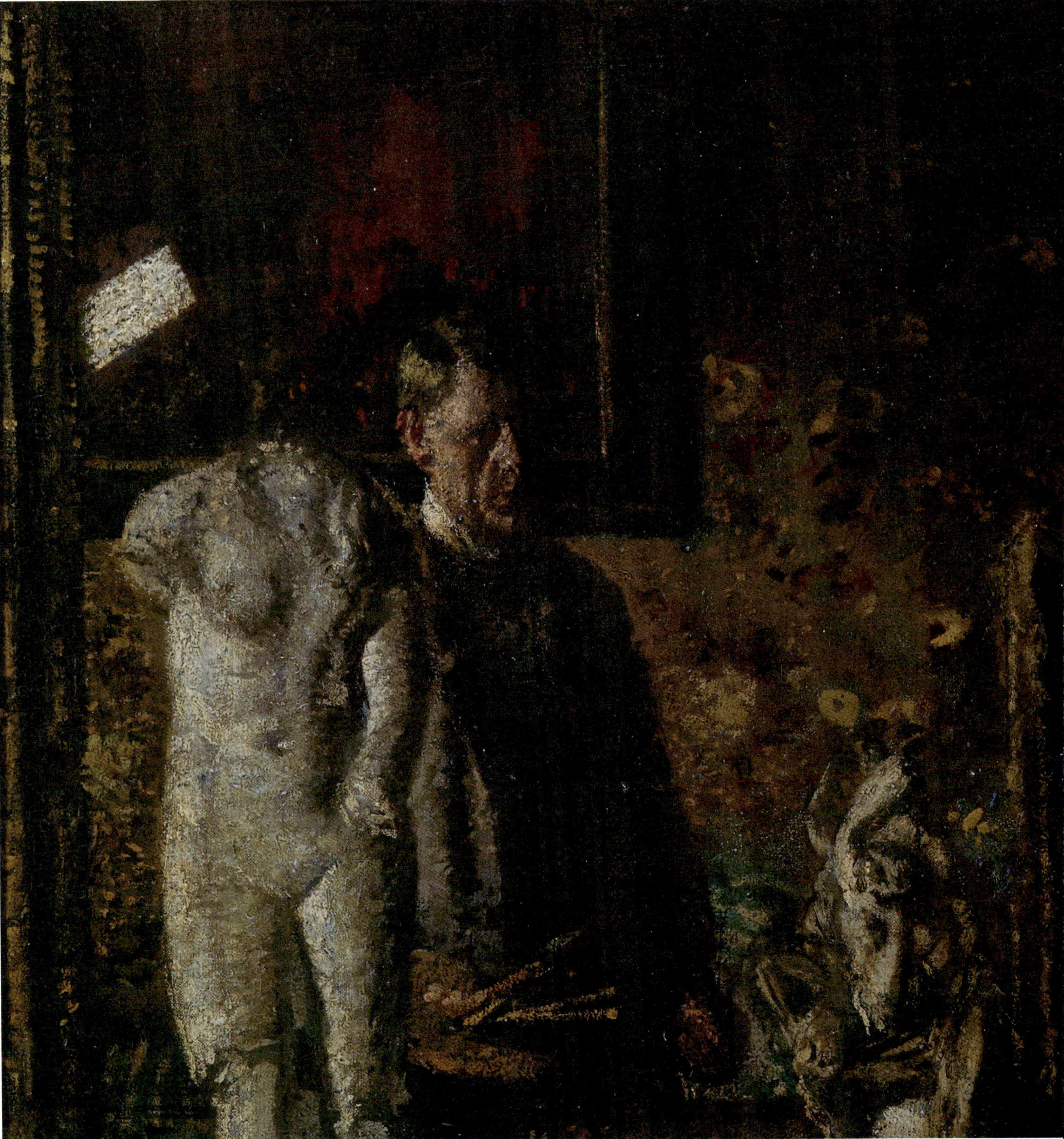

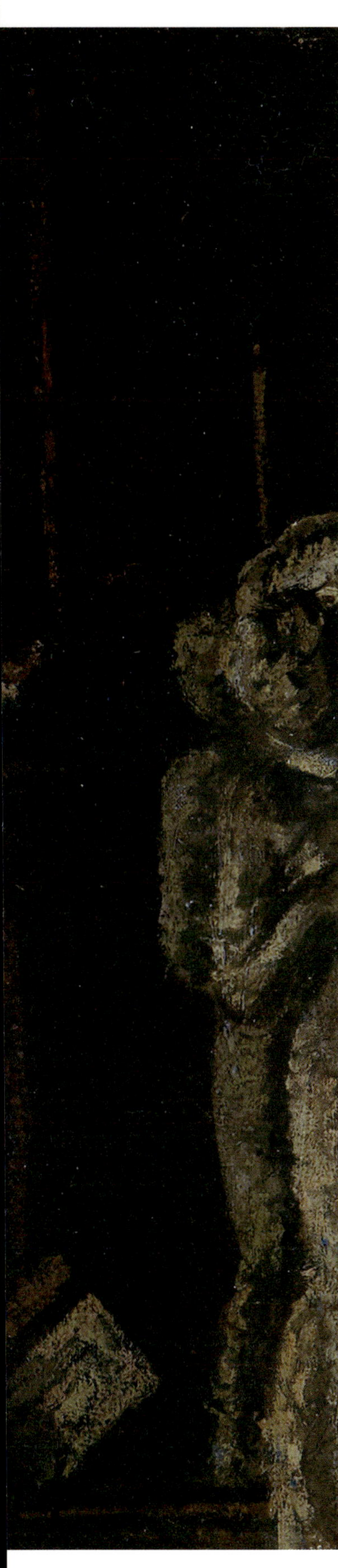

3
*Self-Portrait. The Painter
in his Studio* 1907
Oil paint on canvas
Art Gallery of Hamilton,
Ontario, Canada

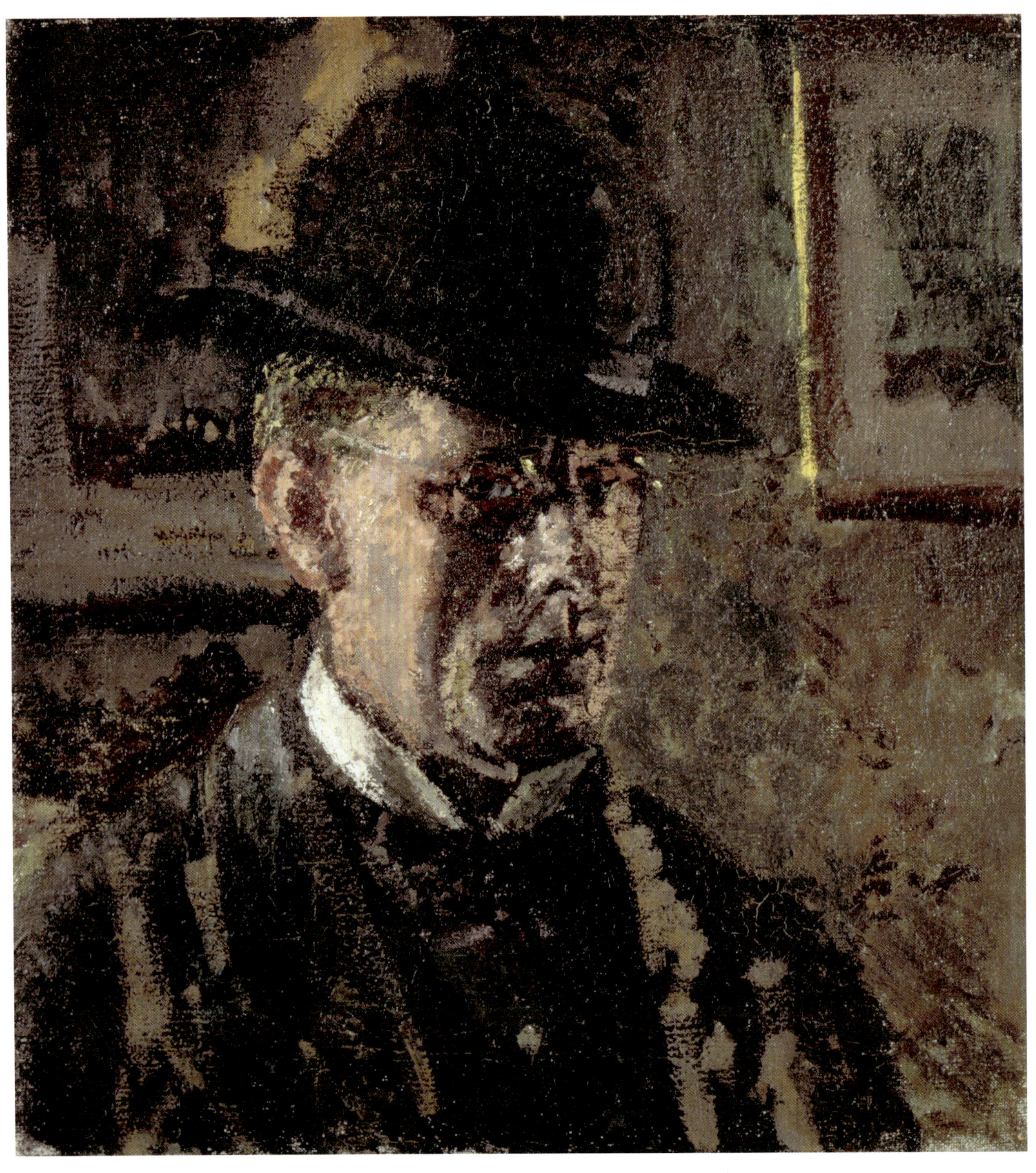

4
Self-Portrait. Juvenile Lead
1907
Oil paint on canvas
Southampton City
Art Gallery

5
*Self-Portrait: The Bust
of Tom Sayers* 1913
Oil paint on canvas
The Ashmolean Museum,
University of Oxford

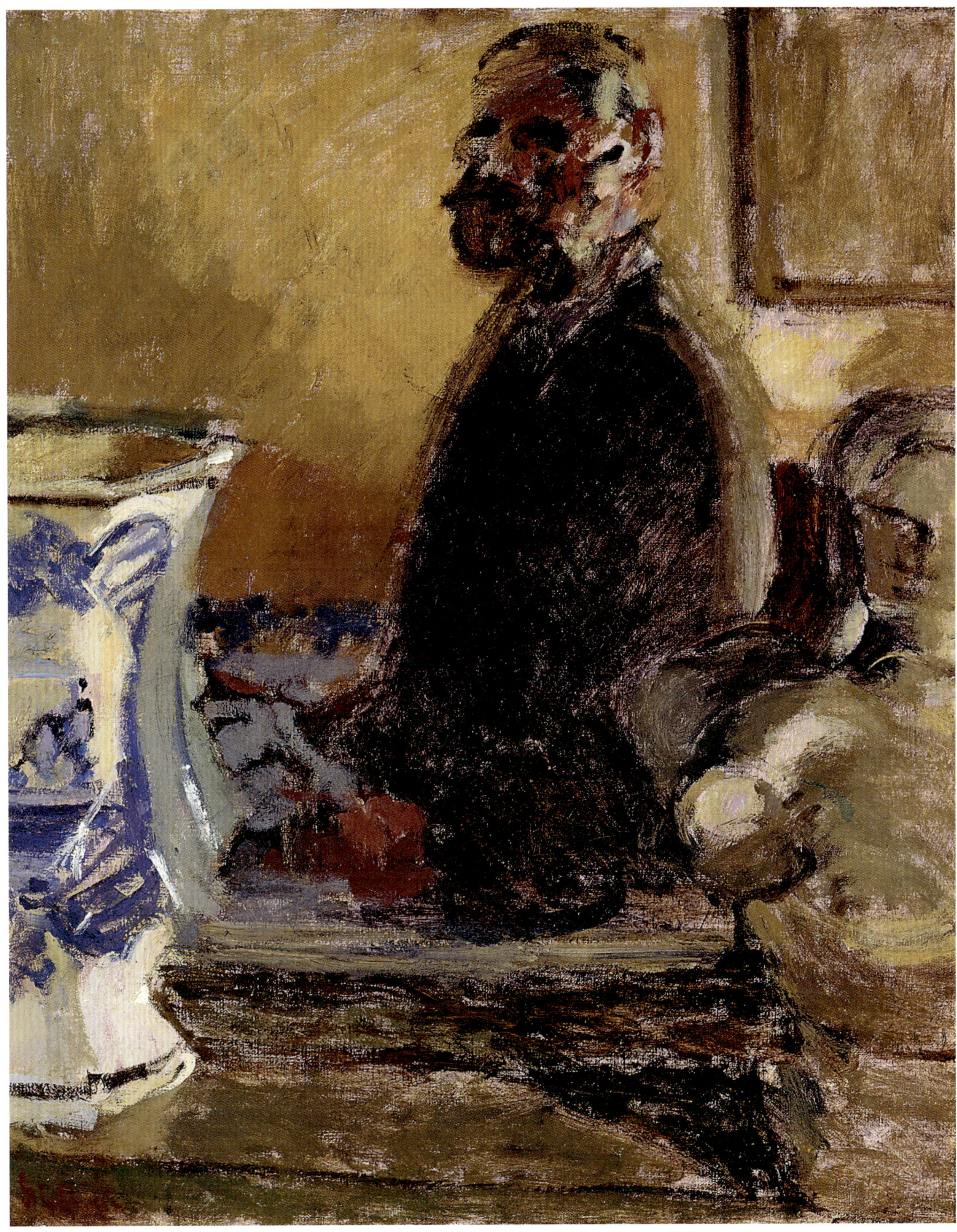

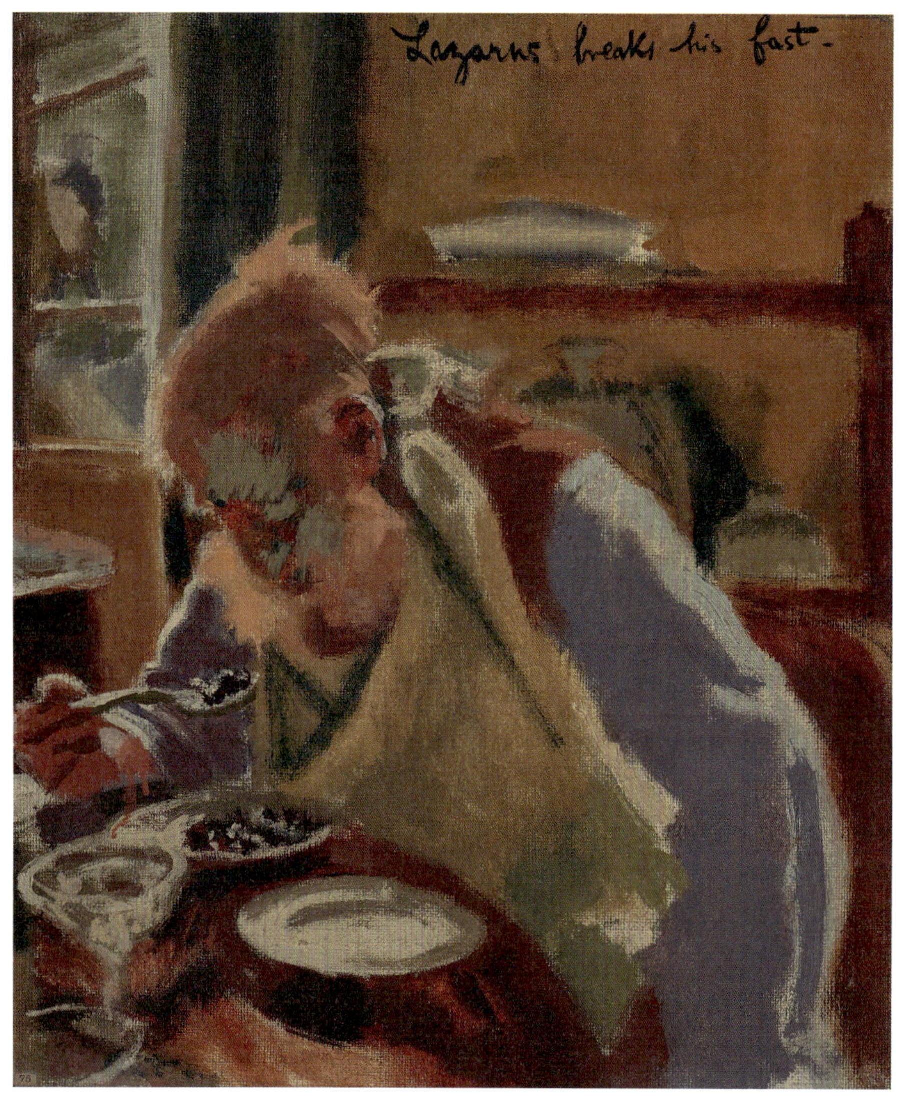

6
*Self-Portrait. Lazarus
Breaks his Fast* c.1927
Oil paint on canvas
Private collection

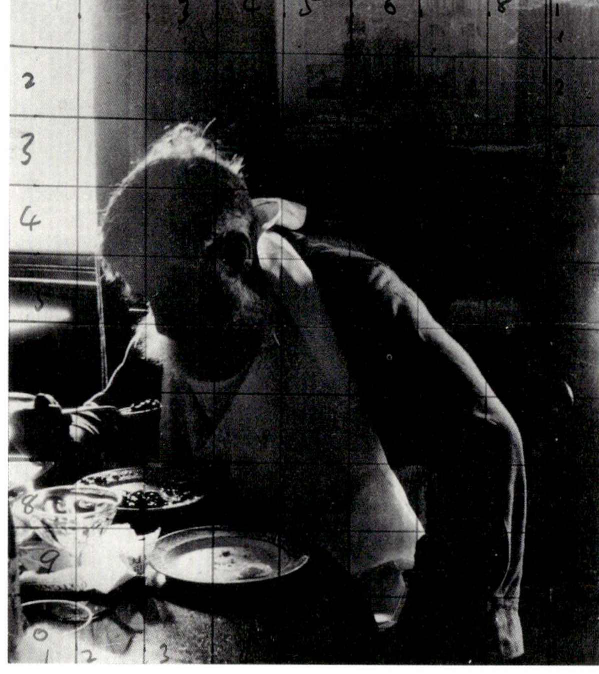

7
Thérèse Lessore,
photograph of Walter
Sickert

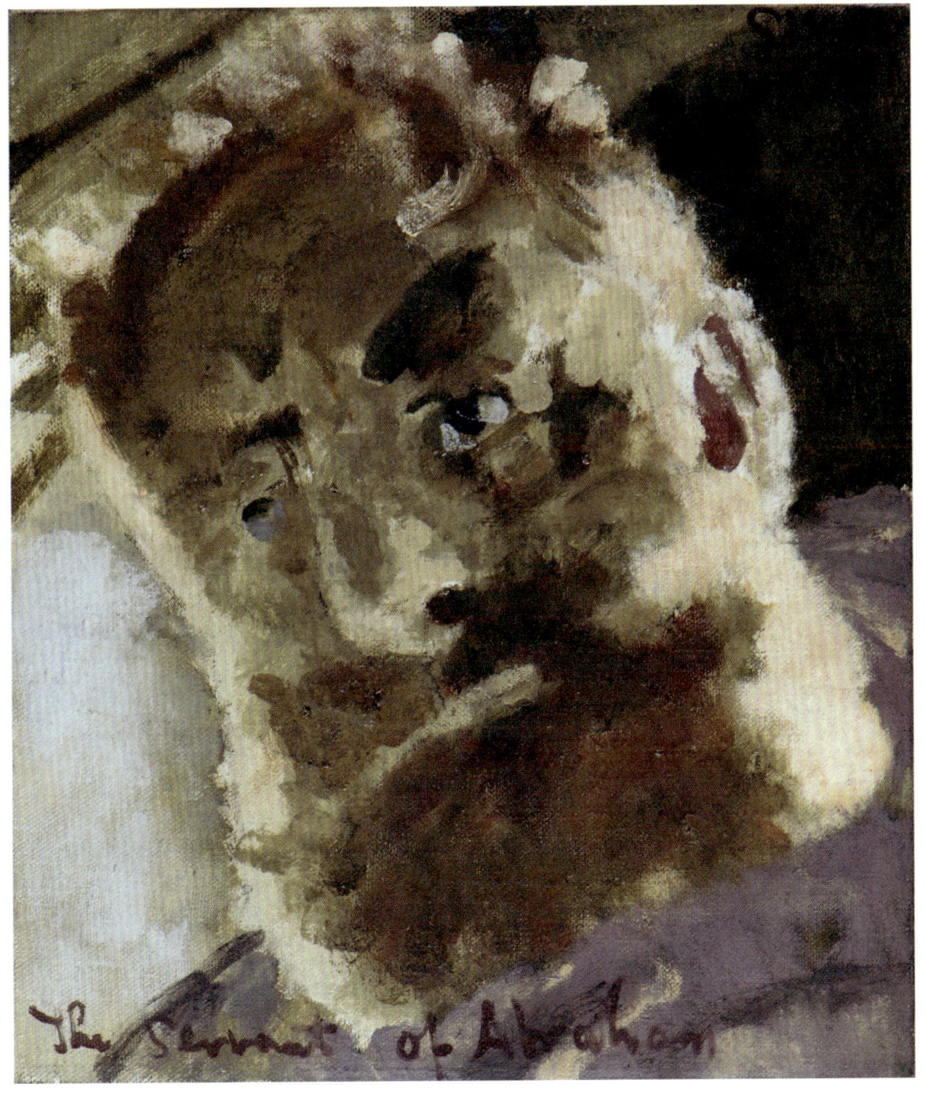

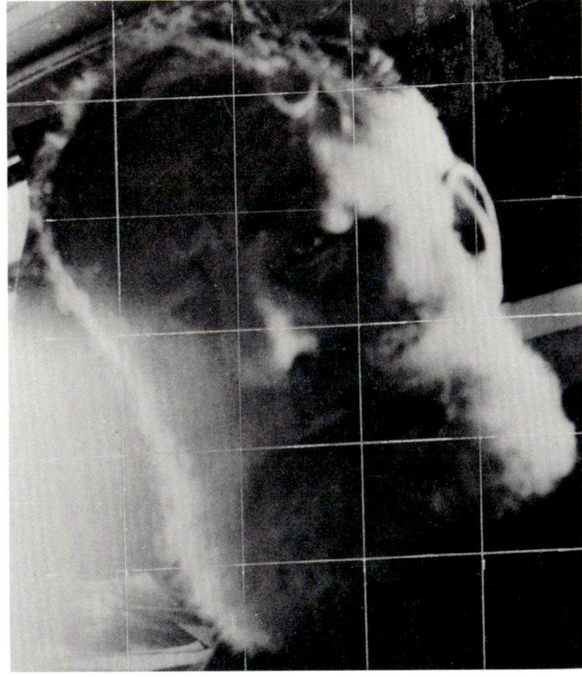

8
The Servant of Abraham
1929
Oil paint on canvas
Tate

9
Thérèse Lessore,
photograph of Walter
Sickert

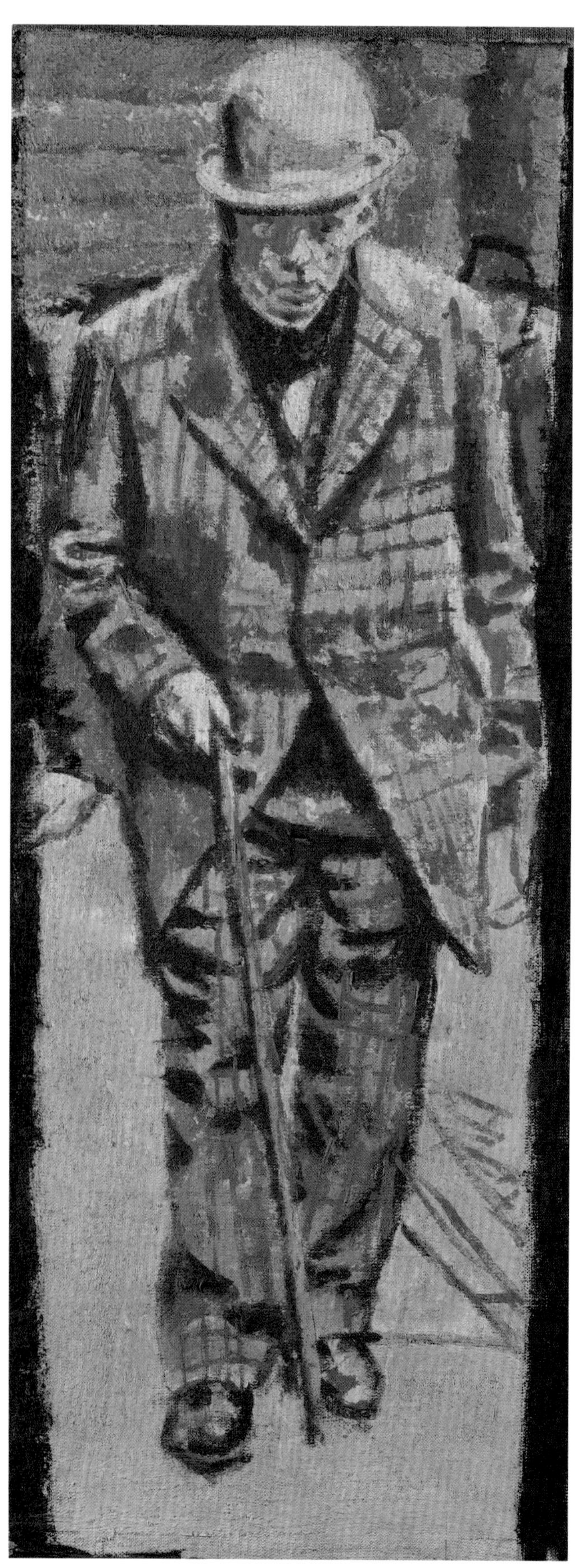

10
Self-Portrait in Grisaille
1935
Oil paint on canvas
National Portrait Gallery,
London

11
*The Front at Hove
(Turpe Senex Miles Turpe
Senilis Amor)* 1930
Oil paint on canvas
Tate

12
Reading in the Cabin 1940
Oil paint on canvas
Corsham Court Collection

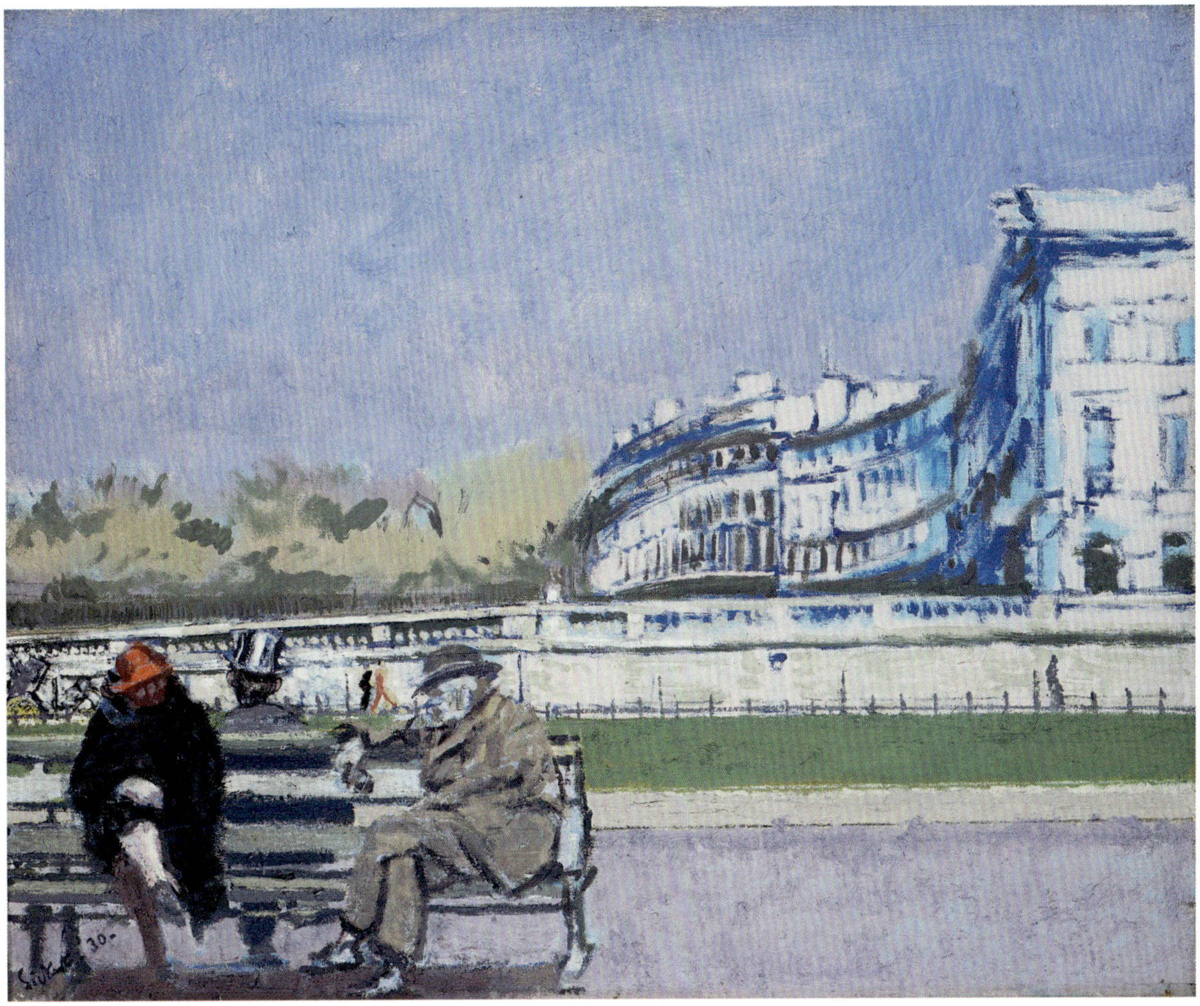

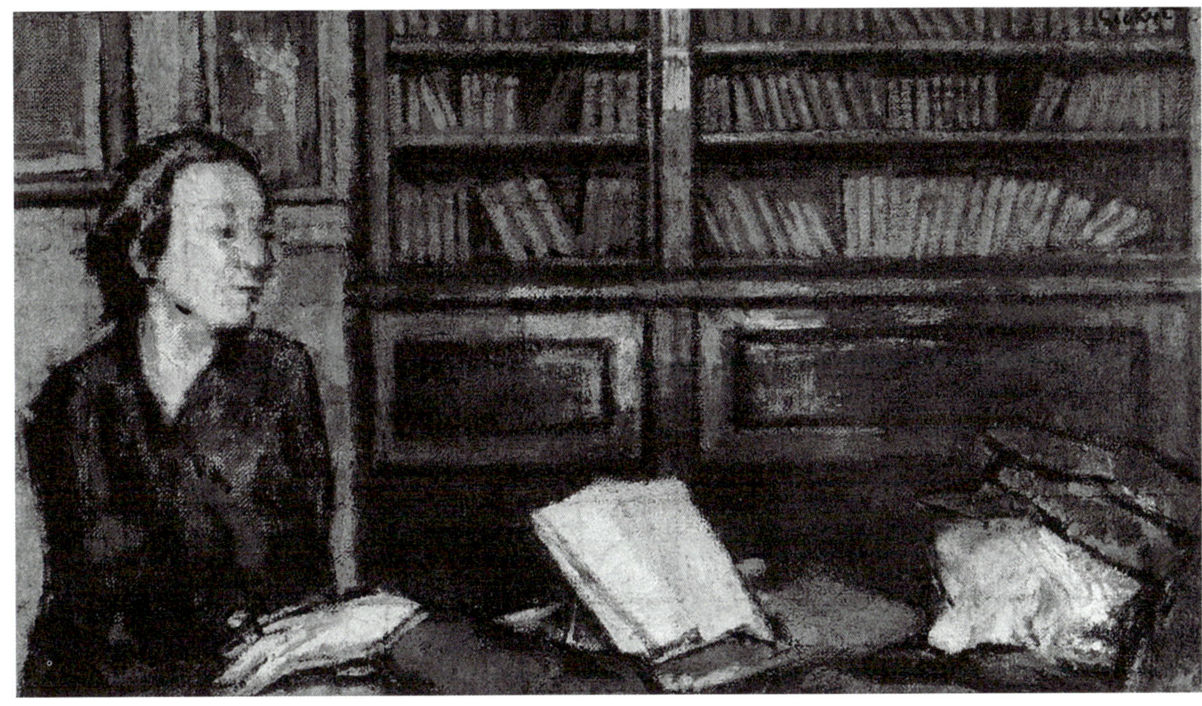

THE APPRENTICESHIP YEARS

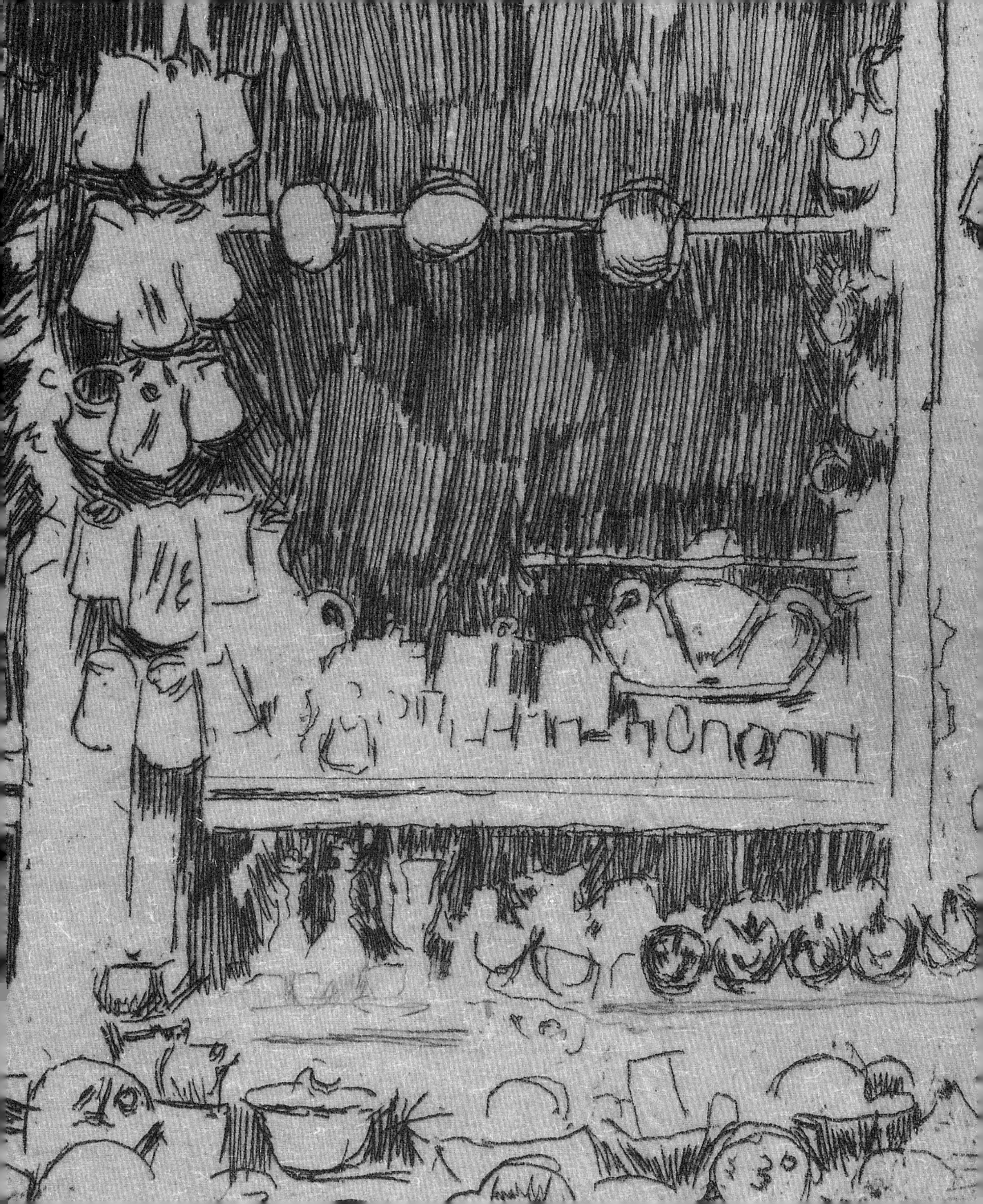

PATRICIA DE MONTFORT

THE APPRENTICESHIP YEARS: FROM WHISTLER TO DEGAS

'[D]on't attempt to repaint the whole picture to the boy's present condition but merely touch details. The picture is finished.'[1] Sickert wrote this strongly worded plea to Whistler during the spring of 1885, having abandoned a brief period of study at the Slade School of Fine Art three years previously for a life as Whistler's studio assistant and informal pupil. He was concerned that Whistler's attempts to repaint the picture in question, *Arrangement in Grey: Portrait of Master Stephen Manuel*, might ruin it, for he thought Whistler 'not quick enough for the child, who was wearied with the number of sittings'.[2] The reference can be traced to a letter that survives only as a fragment, yet, along with the rest of its contents, it offers useful insights into the pair's complex artistic relationship.

Sickert was drawn to a Whistlerian aesthetic that centred upon the visual poetry of modern life subjects and was expressed through supreme economy of means. This led him to occupy variously the roles of pupil, cheerleader and critic. He assisted Whistler in the studio, ran errands, and accompanied him on painting excursions. He also defended his master in the press, beginning in June 1882 when, under the guise of 'An Art Student', he published a rejoinder to a review of Whistler's *Scherzo in Blue: The Blue Girl*, which had charged it with

being 'sketchy'.[3] In addition, Sickert was as loyal a patron as his modest means allowed: Whistler painted at least three portraits of him, including *Sketch Portrait of Walter Sickert* 1894–5 (see no.13), and two of his first wife Ellen.

As Sickert grew in artistic independence, he became more critical of Whistler, however – a process that began with his first meeting with Degas in 1883 while delivering *Arrangement in Grey and Black No. 1*, Whistler's celebrated portrait of his mother, to the Paris Salon exhibition. He was captivated by Degas and is considered to have taken up music hall and other subjects from popular entertainment under his influence. At the same time, he came to regard Whistler as over-dependent on *alla prima* (or wet-on-wet) technique, in which the pigments are laid on in a single session: Whistler, he declared years later, 'why I have never understood', had allowed himself to take on 'the very limited and subaltern position of a prima painter'.[4] Moreover, their personal relationship broke down in 1897 when the two men found themselves on opposite sides of a legal case brought by the American printmaker Joseph Pennell against Sickert.[5] Yet he remained loyal to Whistler in many respects, and continued to acknowledge his artistic debt to him. What, then, do we make of their relationship during this period of Sickert's apprenticeship in the 1880s, as Whistler fought to rebuild his career in the aftermath of his libel case against the critic John Ruskin?[6]

Whatever the circumstances that accompanied the ending of their relationship, Sickert's knowledge of and feeling for Whistler's art is unrivalled for the period. His fellow pupil, Australian-born artist Mortimer Menpes, claimed that they received little formal training from Whistler and rarely questioned him about his work, but, as a studio assistant, Sickert would have been required to lay out Whistler's sequence of colours on the palette. He would also grind up Whistler's lead white paint pigment and 'mix it with linseed oil'.[7] On sketching trips, such as their stay in St Ives in January 1884, Whistler would rise at dawn, impatient to start work, and, according to Menpes, bawl a list of demands: 'Have you got my

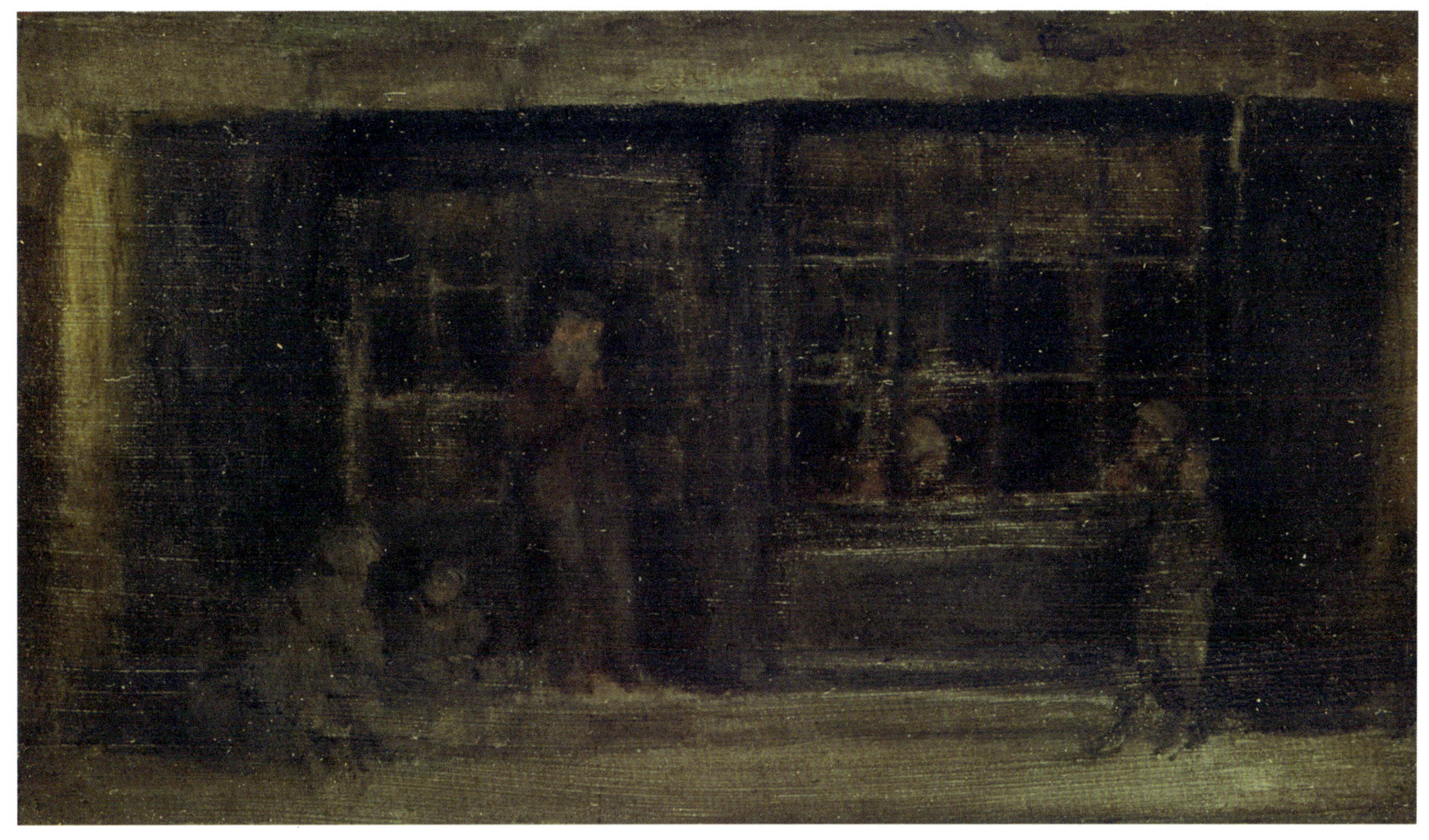

panels prepared? Did you mix that grey tone and put it in the tube?' In addition, they drew from the same models (who included Manuel) on occasion. Sickert's knowledge thus encompassed an understanding of the full range of Whistler's materials (for example, he helped print Whistler's Venice etchings), and it seems likely that some level of technical dialogue took place between the two men as to the merits of different types and their potential effects. Elsewhere in his letter to Whistler (alongside flattering praise of Whistler's recent delivery of his aesthetic manifesto, the 'Ten O'clock Lecture', at Cambridge University), Sickert confides in him in specific terms: 'I have tried the Petroleum oil on a lifesized canvas: it is perfect: not sticky like turps: keeps wet: doesn't sink in: works quicker somehow, and fresher: five of it to one of burnt oil: I wish you would try it.'

While it is unclear from this quote whether he is referring to a completed picture, the approximate date of the letter, 1885, ties in with Sickert's growing interest in shopfronts and figures in doorways, first manifested in 1884 through etchings made in emulation of Whistler, like *Six Pence Three Farthings* (see no.17). This was developed during a visit to Dieppe in 1885 through works such as *A Shop in Dieppe* (see no.23), *The Laundry Shop* (no.22) and *The Butcher's Shop* (no.18). While Katy Norris points towards Degas's increasing impact on Sickert that summer through a 'new emphasis on architectural detail' in *A Shop in Dieppe*,[8] his palette and loose handling of the paint can be more closely aligned to Whistlerian shopfront examples from this period, like *A Shop* 1884–90 (fig.5 and no.19). However, the second picture, *The Laundry Shop*, represents a more visible departure in favour of Degas. Although Sickert's comments in his letter to Whistler broadly confirm a continuing allegiance to his master, he was increasingly taken with Degas's essentially traditional oil painting technique, in which the paint layers were built up over a preparatory drawing. This process, as Sickert writes elsewhere, enabled the picture to be 'brought about by conscious stages', each layer being allowed to dry between coats.[9] His experimental fervour at this time is present in the sharply delineated, grid-like composition of *The Laundry Shop*, in which close attention is given to its individual components, contrasting with the flatter, more blurred outlines of Whistler's *A Shop*. It is intensified by the presence of a squared-up preparatory drawing of *The Laundry Shop* (incorporating more of the window; see no.21), and a larger version in oil (Brighton and Hove Museums) which focuses more strongly upon the figure in the doorway. Sickert also made a related etching, *Dieppe, The Laundry, rue de la Barre*, plus two etchings of Juliette Lambert shopping on the rue de Clieu, which, as Norris notes, share the same visual format.[10] Alongside this, Sickert's comments to Whistler in his letter hint at an increased prioritisation of surface richness and freshness of colour. This finds expression to vivid effect in the brown-ochre-gold colour scheme of *The Red Shop (or The October Sun)* c.1888 (see no.26), with its vermilion contrasts; this kind of scheme also, as Wendy Baron has highlighted, typifies his music hall pictures of this period.[11]

Arguably, the range of these experiments suggests not only the buoying influence of Degas but also Sickert's apprehension at the prospect of a departure from the Whistlerian aesthetic that had so long dominated his thinking. Certainly, Sickert was slow to cut ties with Whistler. While, in an exhibition review published in 1889, he places both Whistler and Degas at the forefront of modern drawing – 'the torch of pure draught[s]manship burns brighter every day, fed by such votaries'[12] – it is Whistler he has in mind when he claims later in the piece that to draw is to capture 'the time of day … life and air and movement … space and rhythm. That is imagination. That is poetry.'[13] Sickert's technical intimacy with Whistler's

work, acquired during the early 1880s, was difficult to shed, and was doubtless a factor in his continuing study of Whistler's small oil panels (which he referred to as '*pochades*' – meaning rapidly executed sketches or studies), and his eagerness to promote seascape subjects like *The Bathing Posts, Brittany* 1893 (see no.27) as the epitome of Whistler's artistic genius:

> He will give you in a space nine inches by four an angry sea, piled up, and running in, as no painter ever did before. The extraordinary beauty and truth of the relative colours, and the exquisite precision of the spaces, have compelled infinity and movement into an architectural formula of eternal beauty. Never was instrument better understood and more fully exploited than Whistler has understood and exploited oil paint in these panels.[14]

'[A]ll the disadvantages' of Whistler's prima technique, Sickert concluded, 'became advantages' in these works.[15]

Moreover, despite personal divisions by the 1890s and a narrowing of Sickert's regard for Whistler's art, both shared an aesthetic cosmopolitanism by background and temperament. This continued to breed an art in both men that, as David Peters Corbett has remarked of Sickert, 'was changeable, rapid, hard to pin down' (a description that might also be applied to Whistler).[16] It also led them to return on occasion to the same shopfront and seascape subjects, far into the late 1890s. Arguably, Sickert's presence as pupil, patron and critic over a long period, in which he witnessed (and on occasion participated in) Whistler's attempts to interrogate the laws of his materials helped maintain his master's progress towards a rhythmic art that was about light, space and air.[17]

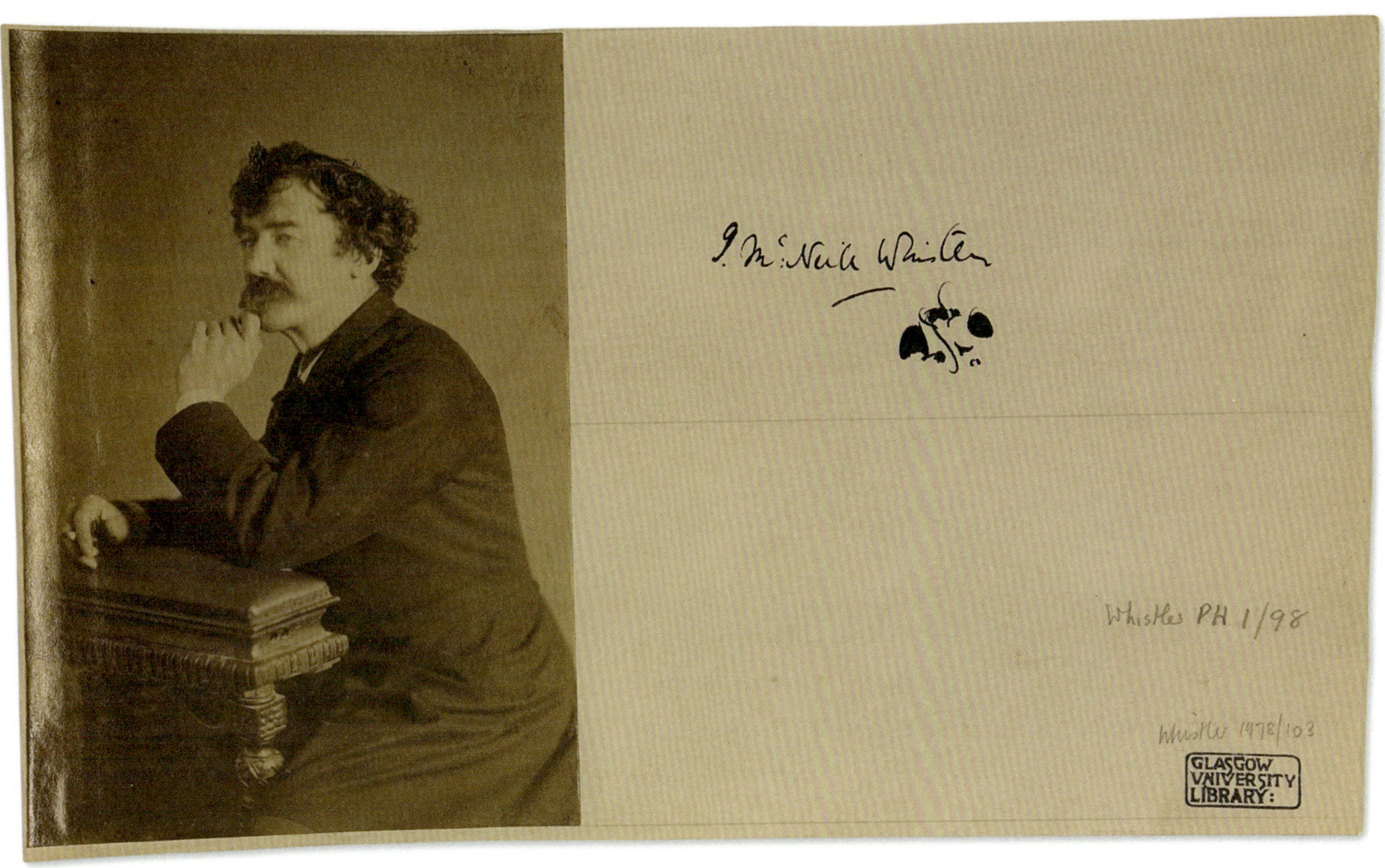

Fig.6
Photograph of James
Abbott McNeill Whistler
in his Fulham Road studio,
1886, albumen print

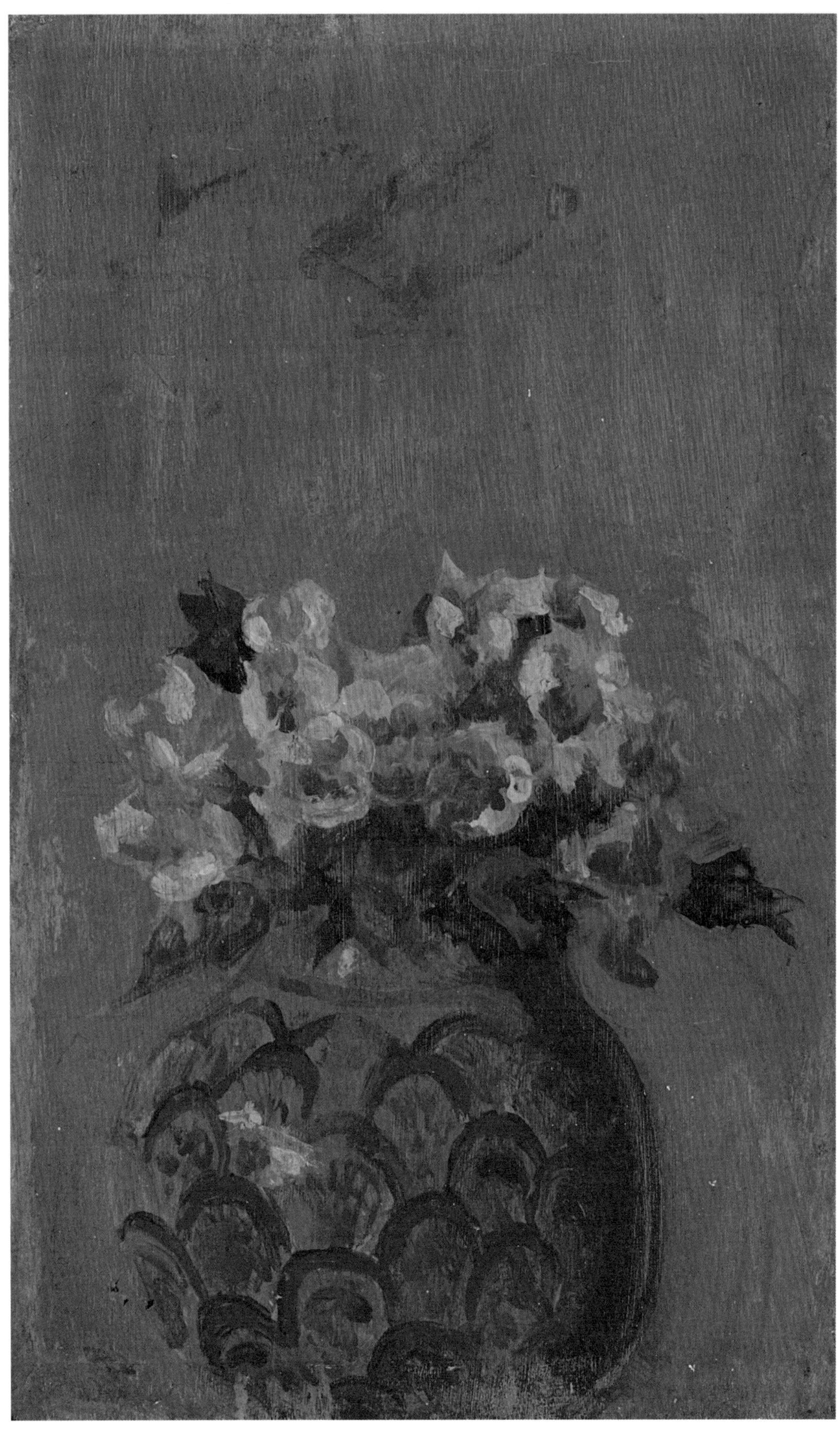

13
James Abbott
McNeill Whistler
*Sketch Portrait of
Walter Sickert* 1894–5
Oil paint on canvas
Hugh Lane Gallery

14
White Violets
c.1884
Oil paint on panel
The Courtauld,
London (Samuel
Courtauld Trust)

15
*Venice, The Little Lagoon,
after Whistler* c.1884
Drypoint, black carbon
ink on paper
The Syndics of the
Fitzwilliam Museum,
University of Cambridge

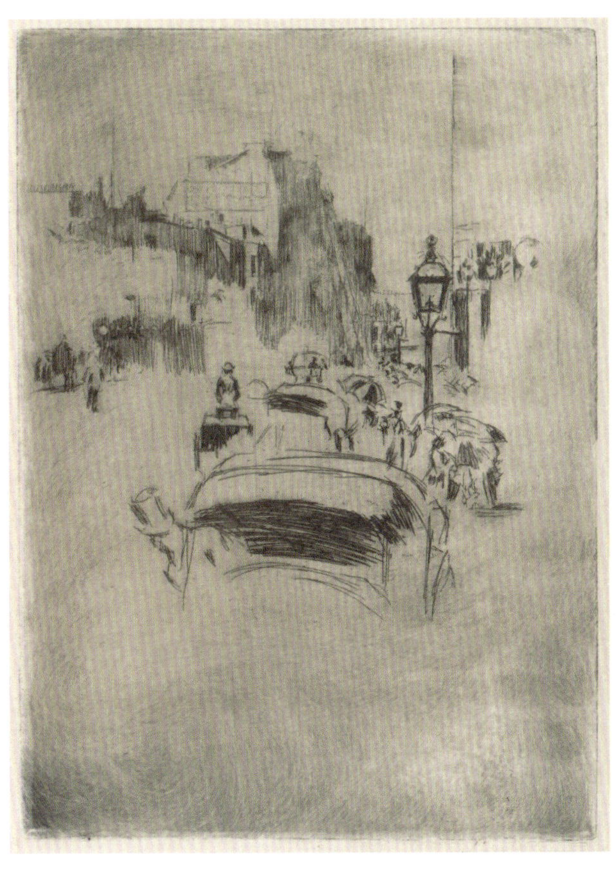

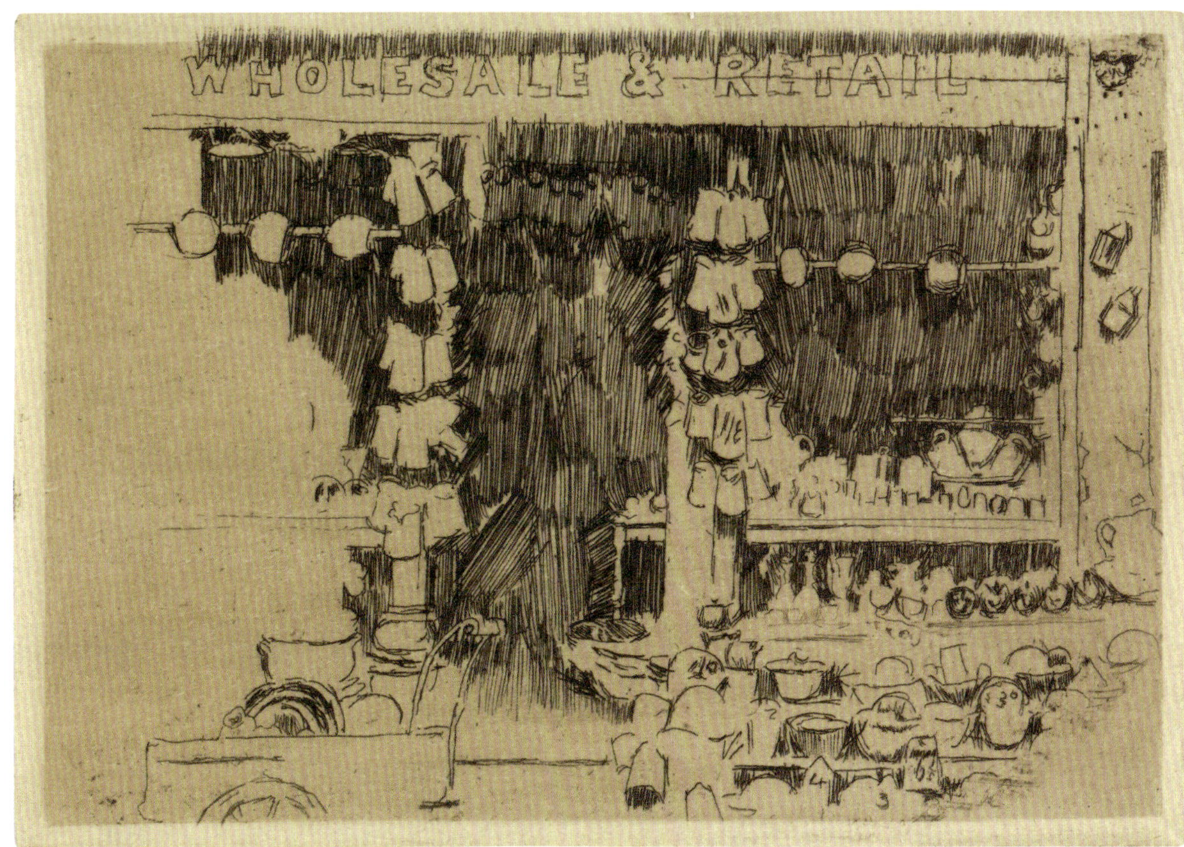

16
*The Burning of the
Japanese Exhibition* 1885
Etching, black carbon
ink on paper
The Syndics of the
Fitzwilliam Museum,
University of Cambridge

17
*Six Pence Three
Farthings* 1884
Etching, brown ink on paper
The Syndics of the
Fitzwilliam Museum,
University of Cambridge

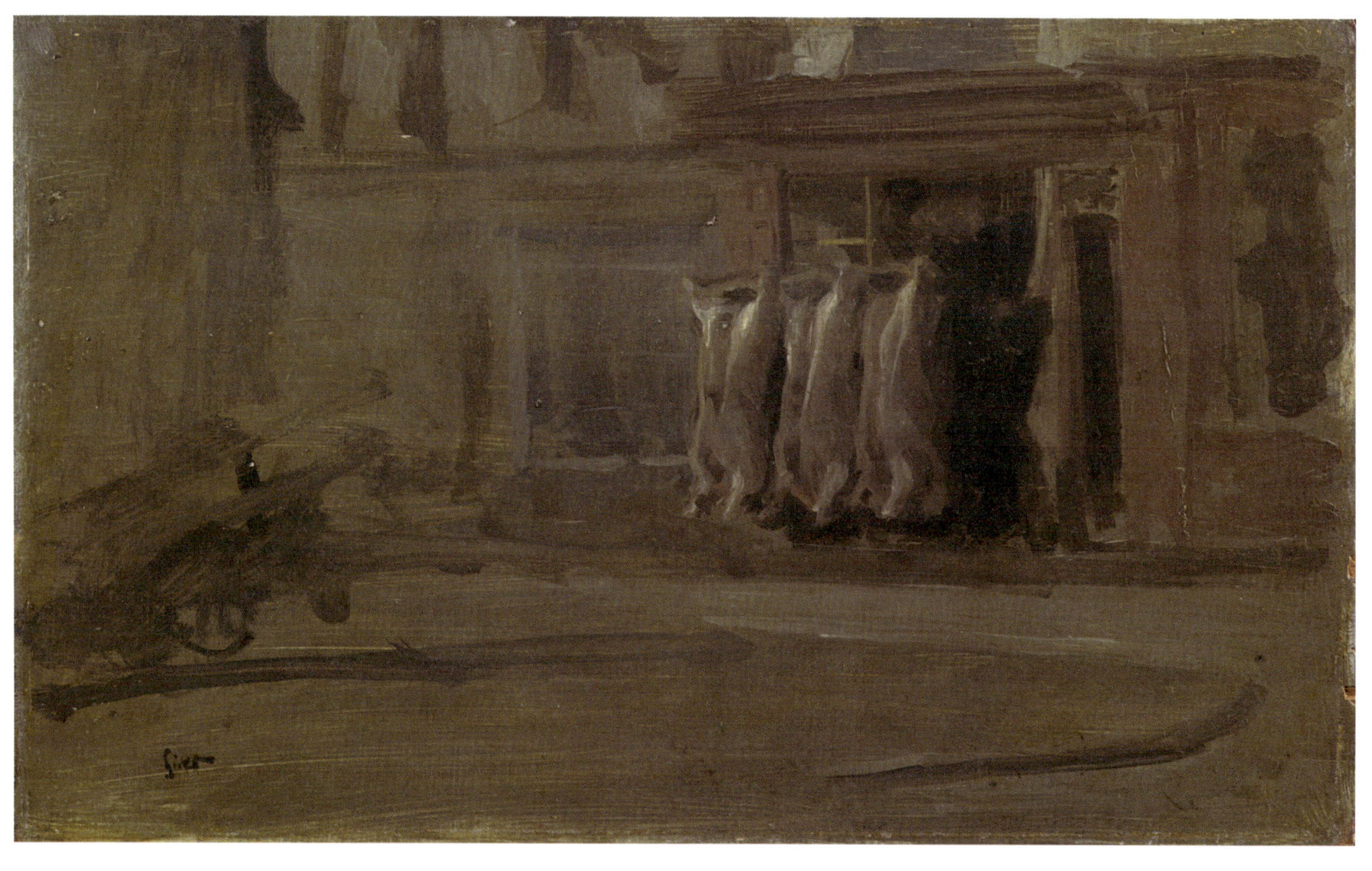

19
James Abbott McNeill Whistler
A Shop 1884–90
Oil paint on wood
The Hunterian,
University of Glasgow

18
*The Butcher's Shop,
Dieppe* 1885
Oil paint on panel
York Museums Trust
(York Art Gallery)

20
James Abbott McNeill Whistler
The Priest's Lodging, Dieppe
1897
Oil paint on wood
The Hunterian,
University of Glasgow

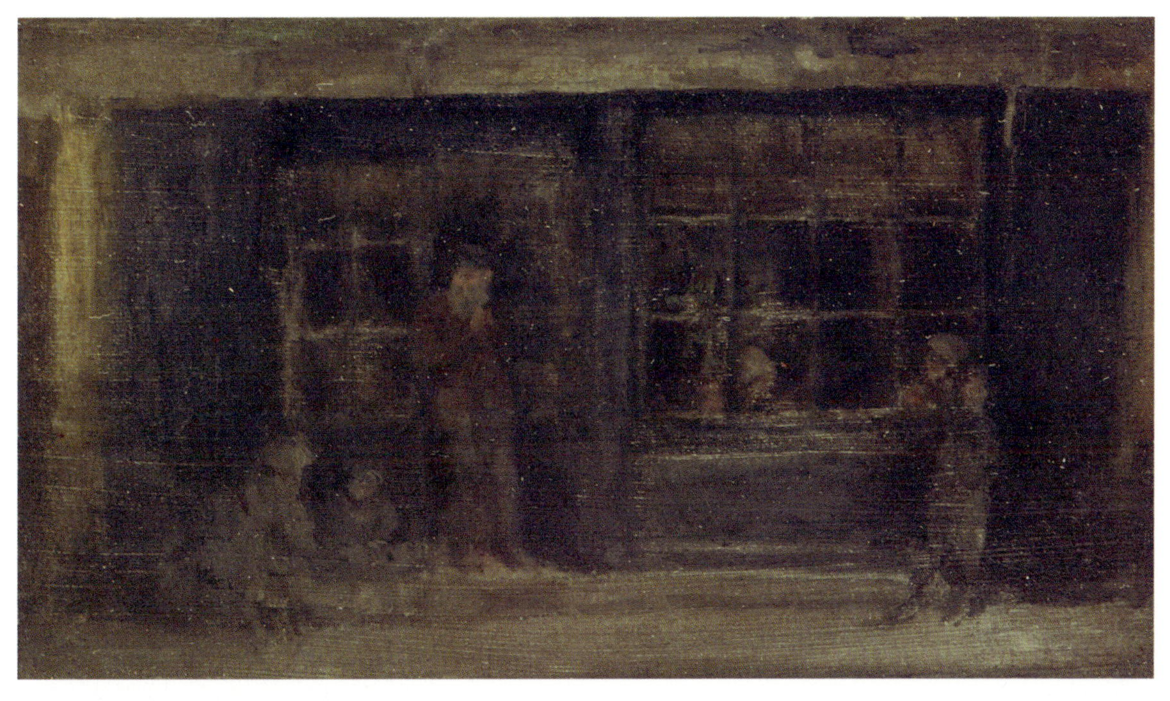

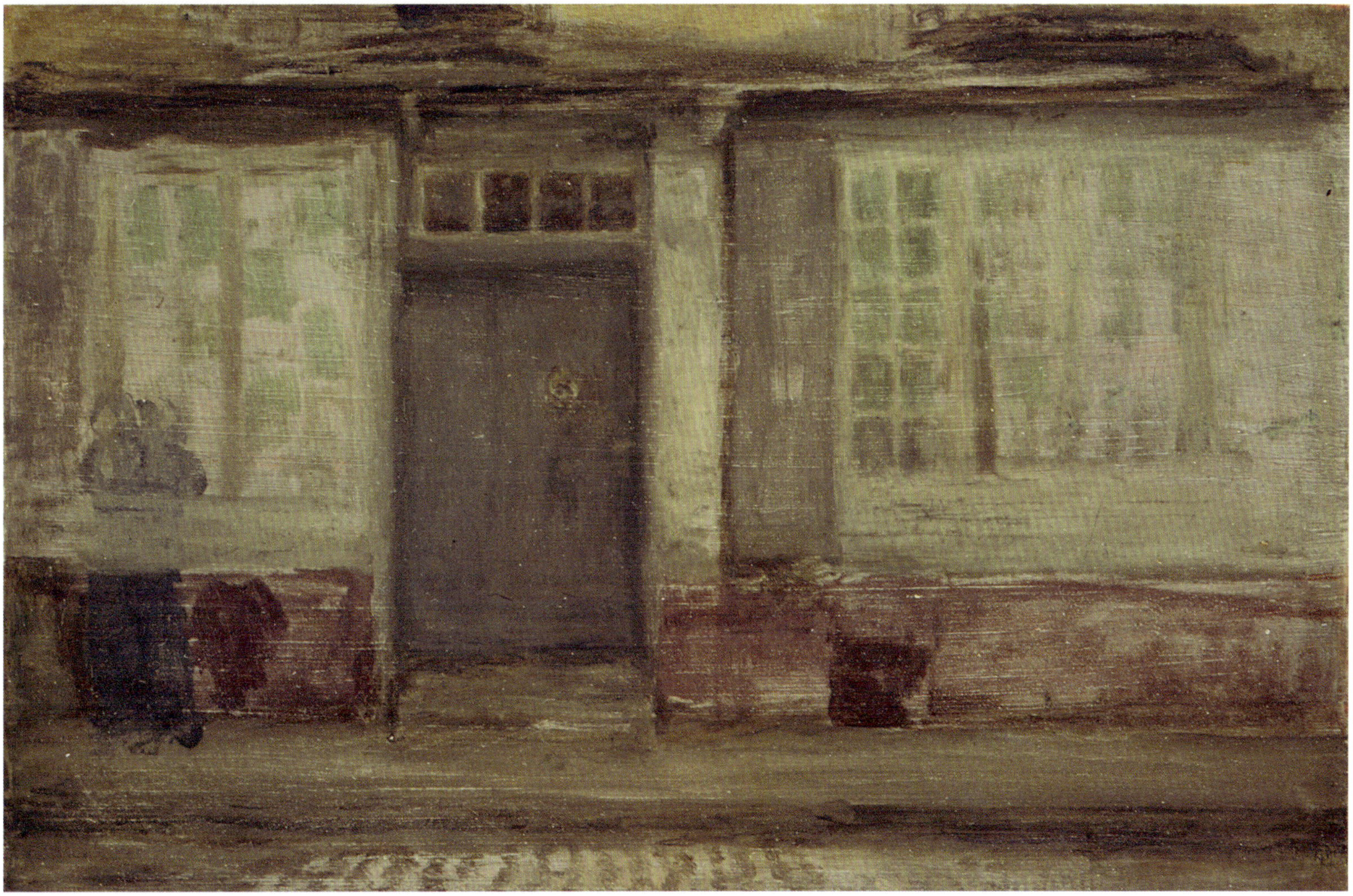

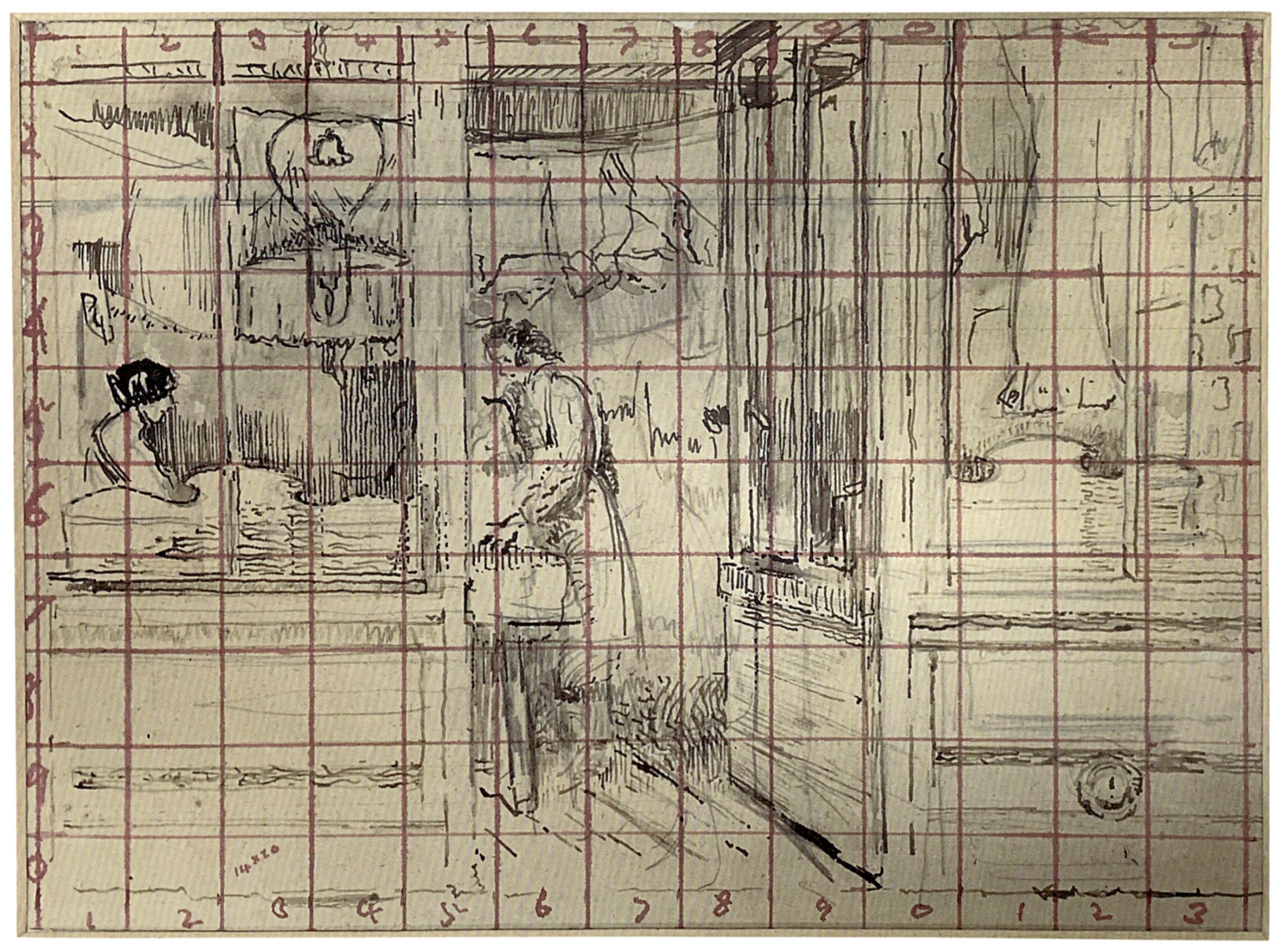

21
Shop Front, The Laundry 1885
Pencil, pen and ink on paper
Islington Local History Centre

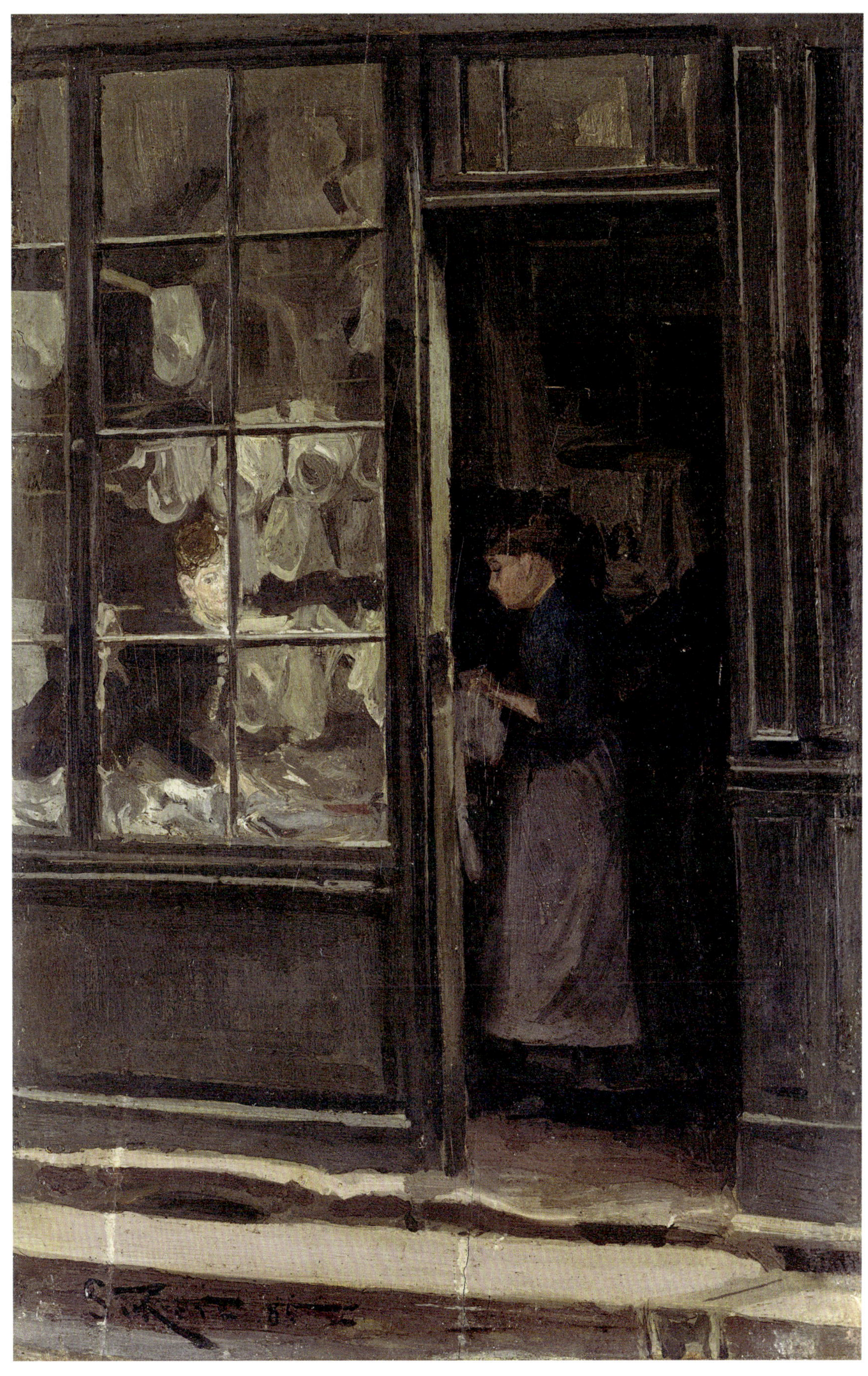

22
The Laundry Shop 1885
Oil paint on panel
Leeds Museums and Galleries

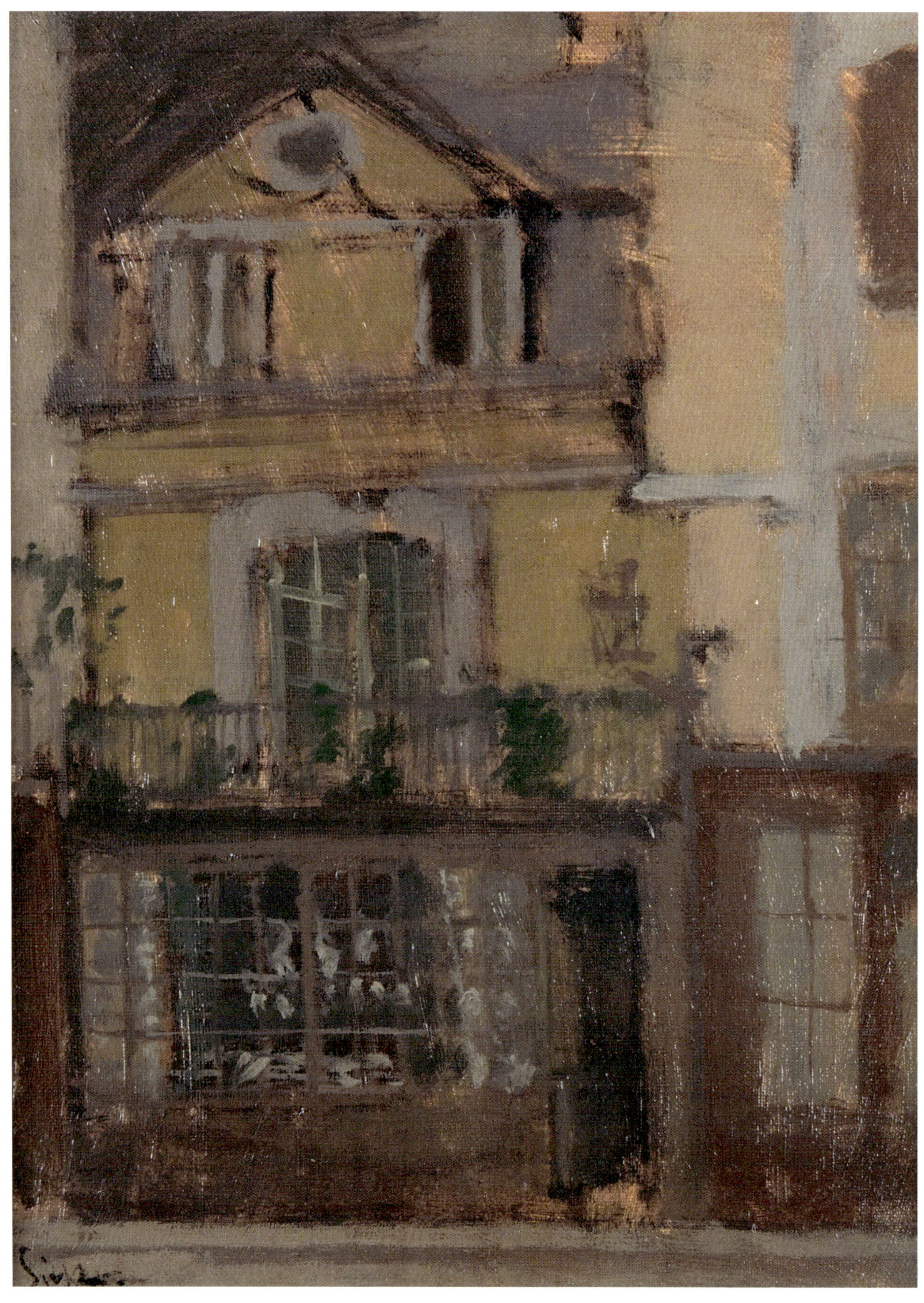

23
A Shop in Dieppe 1885–9
Oil paint on canvas
The Hunterian,
University of Glasgow

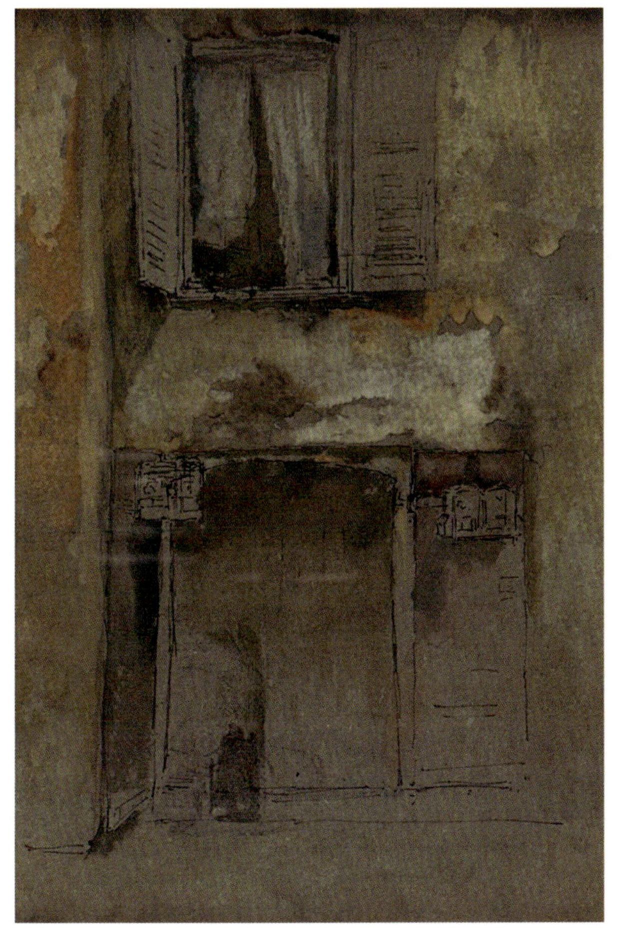

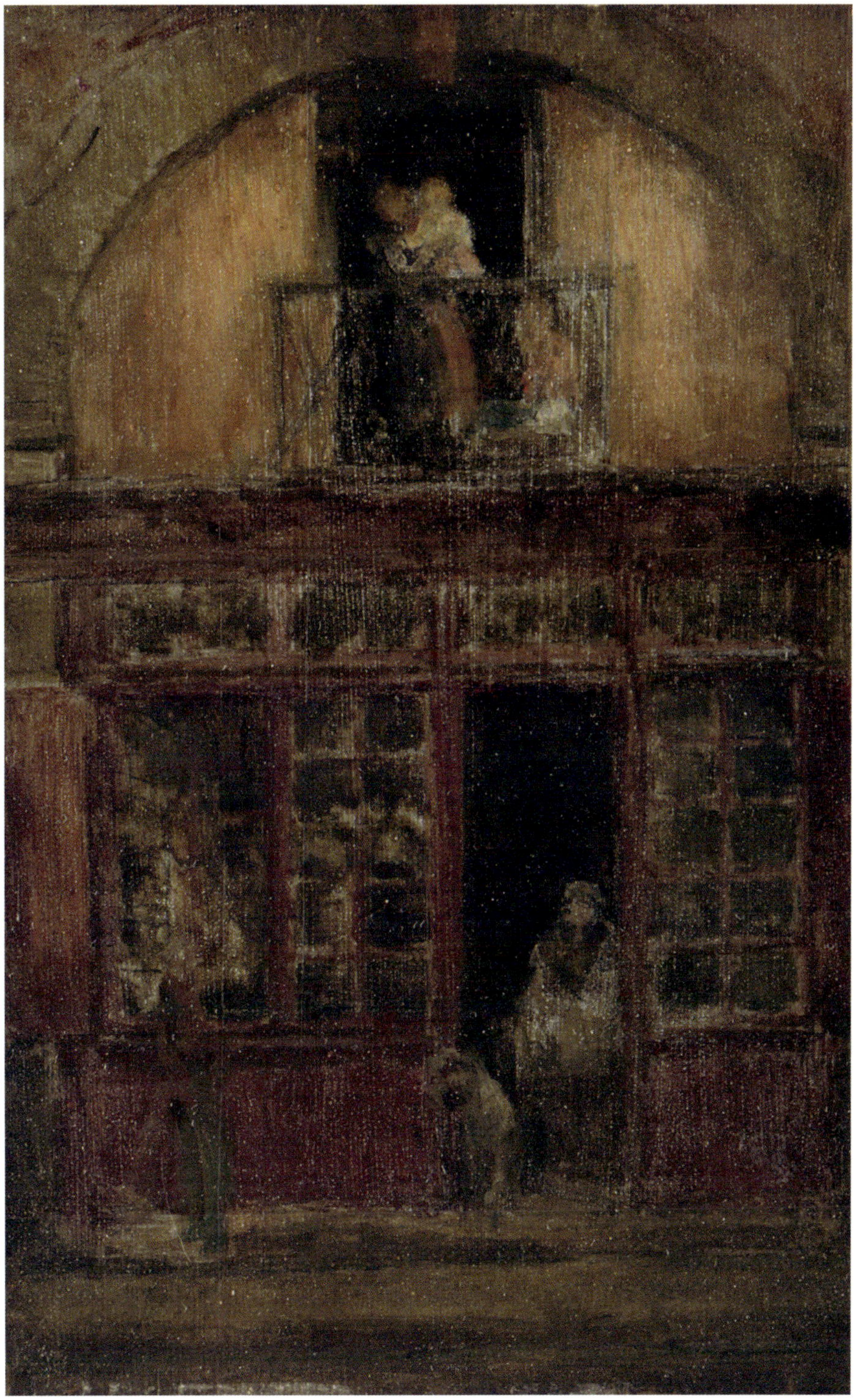

24
James Abbott McNeill Whistler
Shop Front: Dieppe 1897–9
Pen, brown ink, chalk,
watercolour and gouache on
brown paper laid down on card
The Hunterian,
University of Glasgow

25
James Abbott McNeill
Whistler *A Shop with a Balcony*
1897–9
Oil paint on wood
The Hunterian,
University of Glasgow

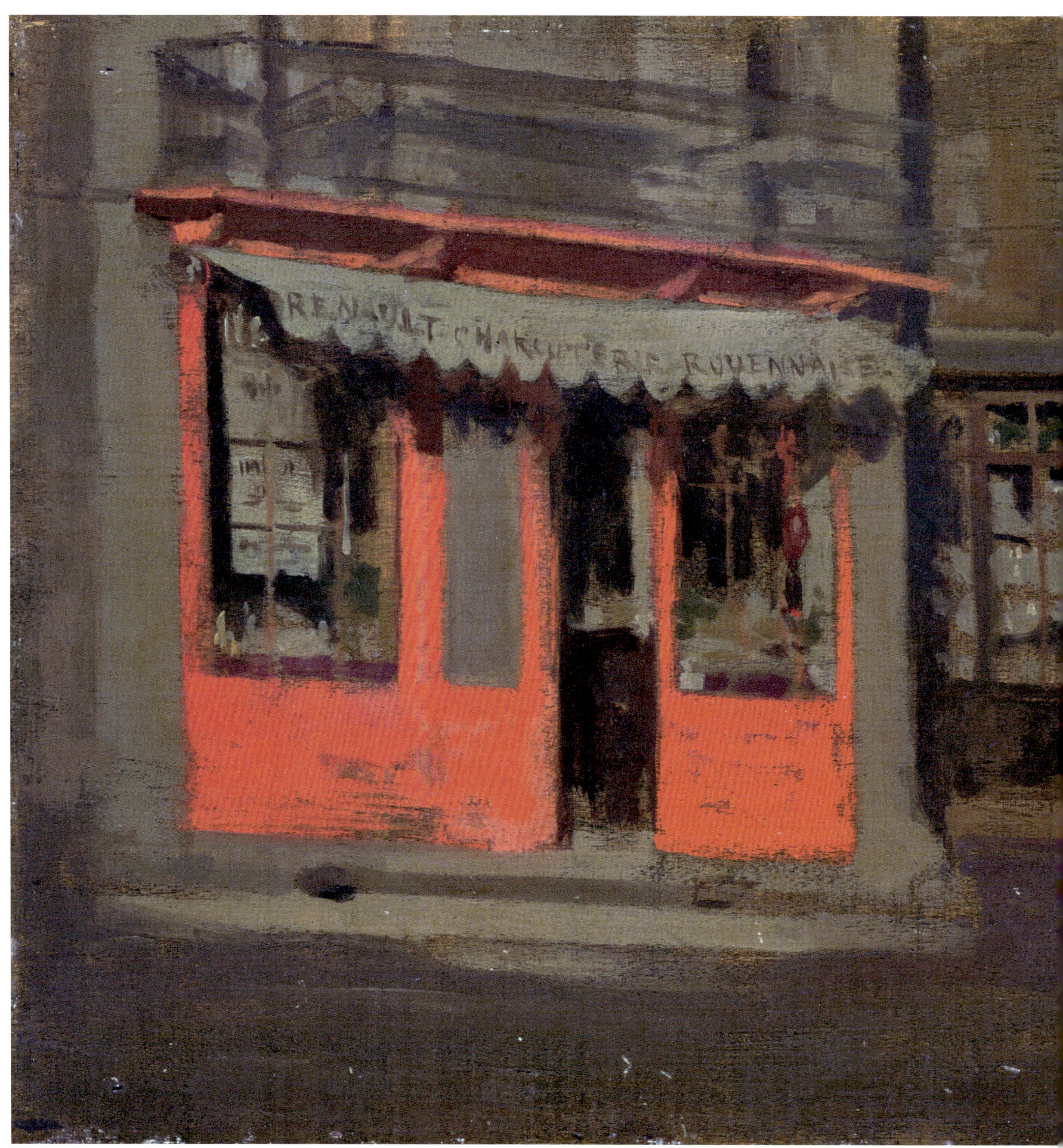
RENAULT CHARCUTERIE ROUENNAISE

26
The Red Shop (or The October Sun) c.1888
Oil paint on panel
Norfolk Museums Service
(Norwich Castle Museum &
Art Gallery)

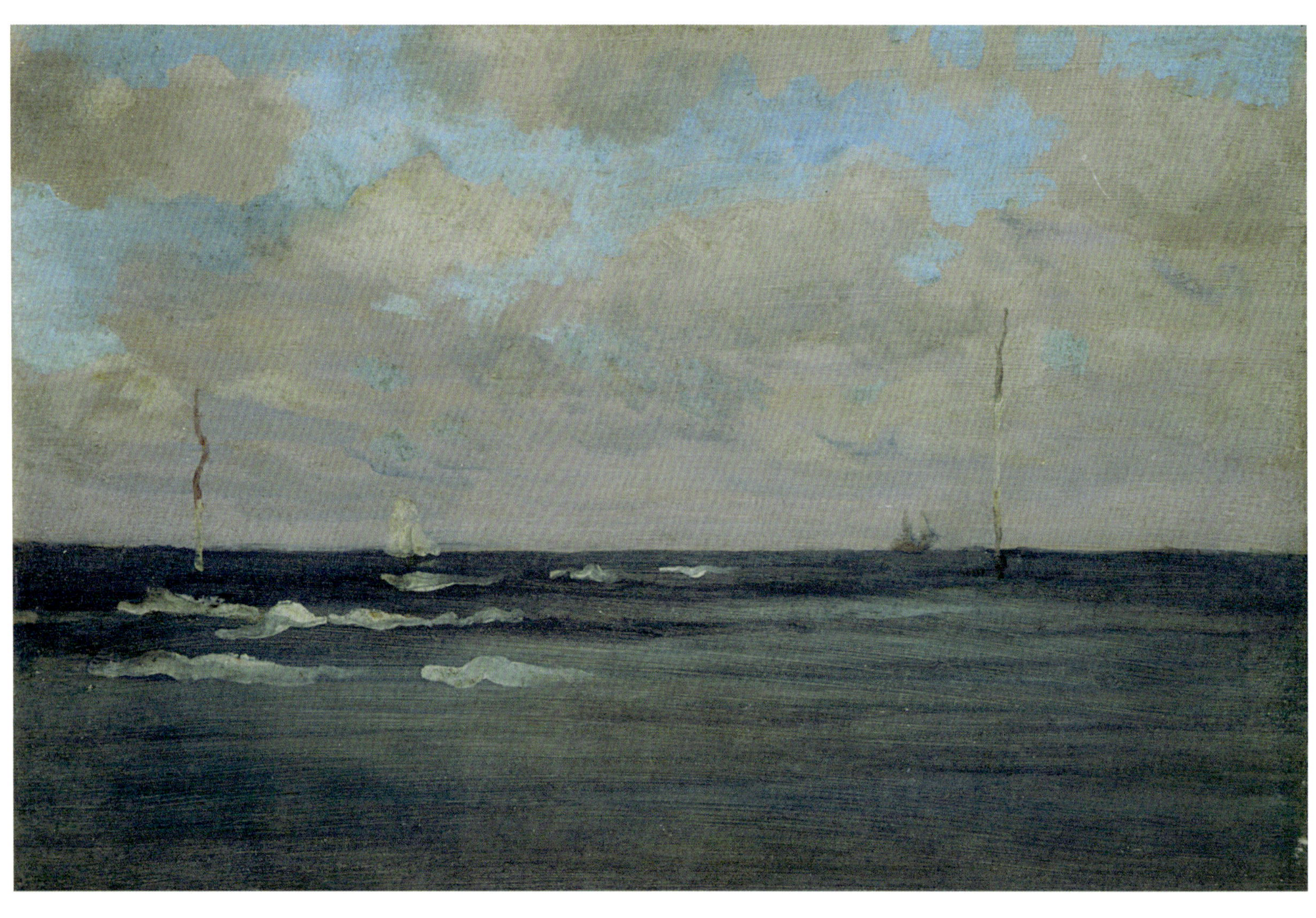

27
James Abbott McNeill Whistler
The Bathing Posts, Brittany
1893
Oil paint on wood
The Hunterian,
University of Glasgow

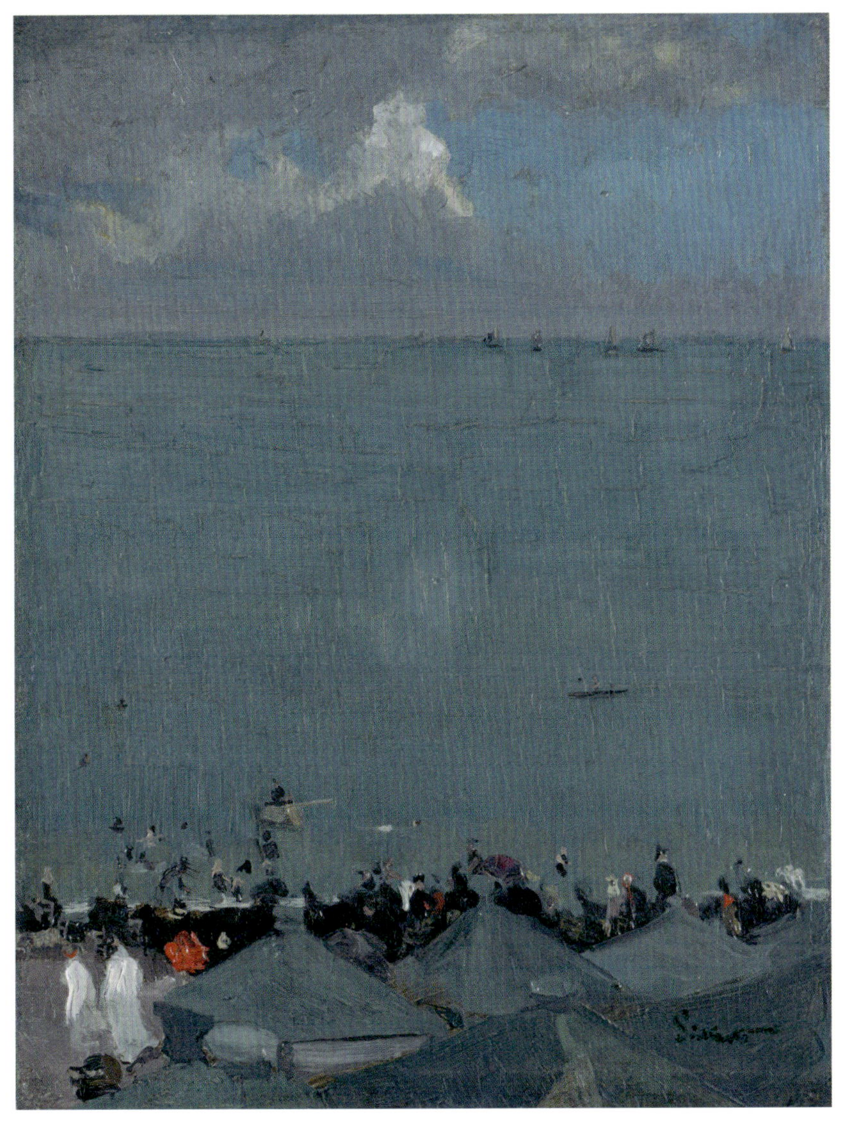

28
*La Saison des Bains,
Dieppe* 1885
Oil paint on panel
Brooklyn Museum

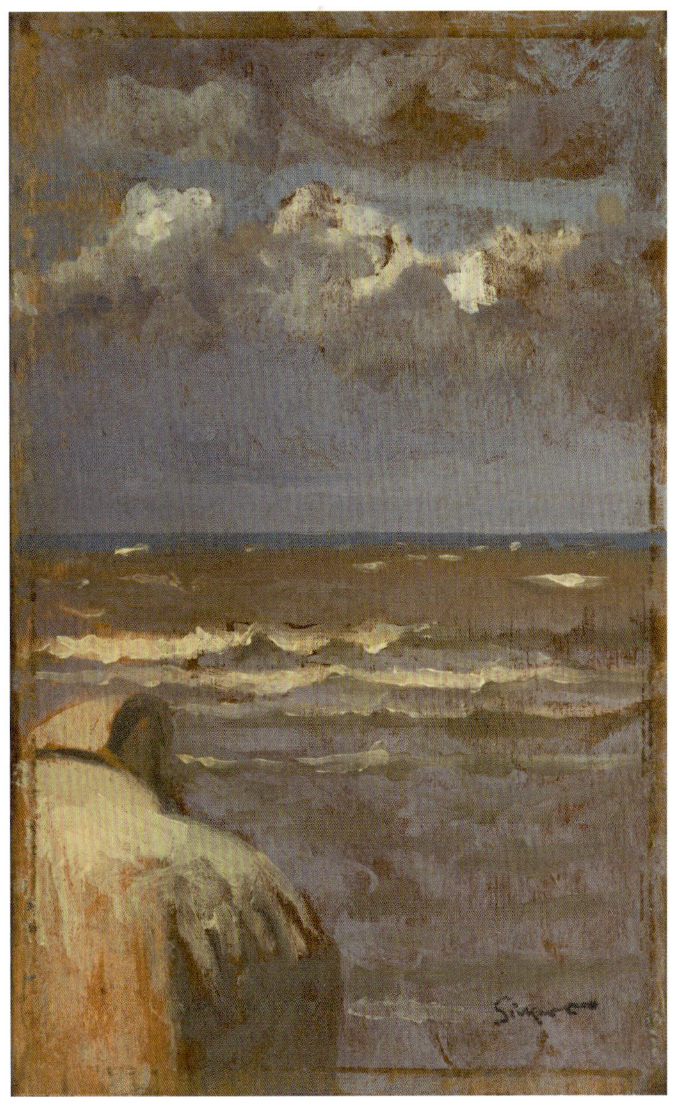

29
Seascape c.1887
Oil paint on wood
National Galleries of Scotland

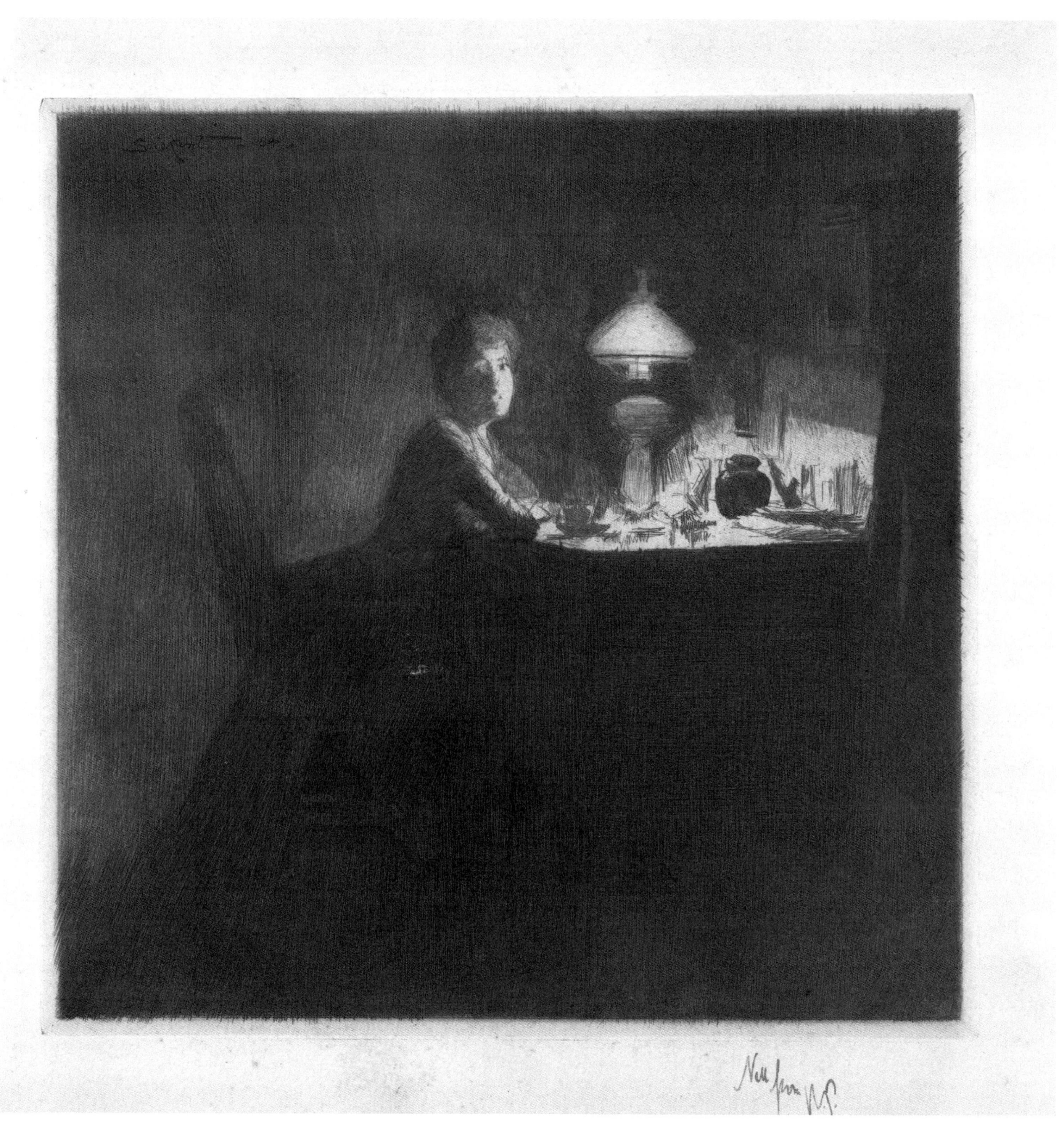

30
The Acting Manager 1884
Etching, printed in black-
brown ink on wove paper
The Ashmolean Museum,
University of Oxford

31
*The End of the Act,
or The Acting Manager*
c.1885–6
Oil paint on canvas
Private collection

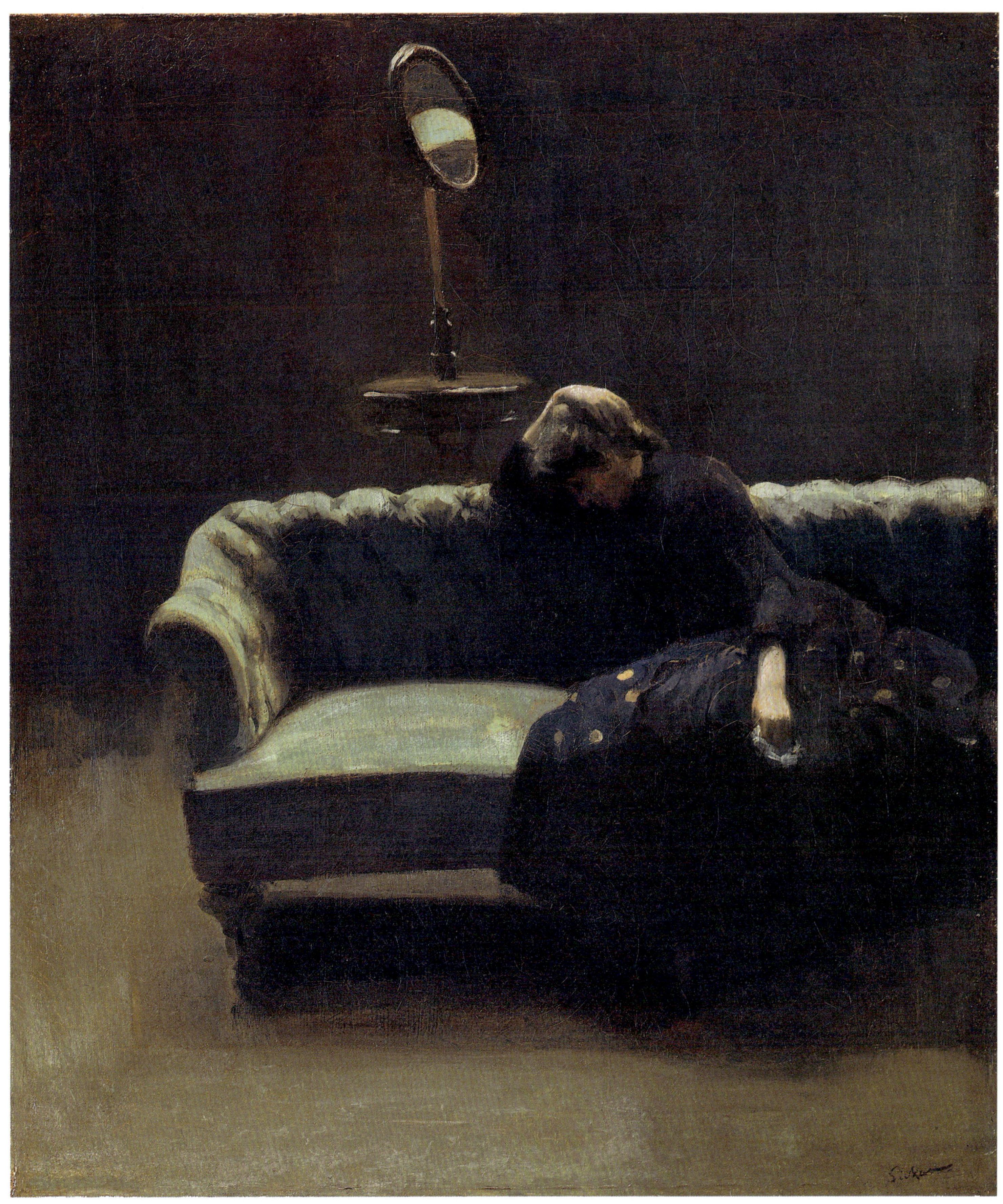

THE MUSIC HALL

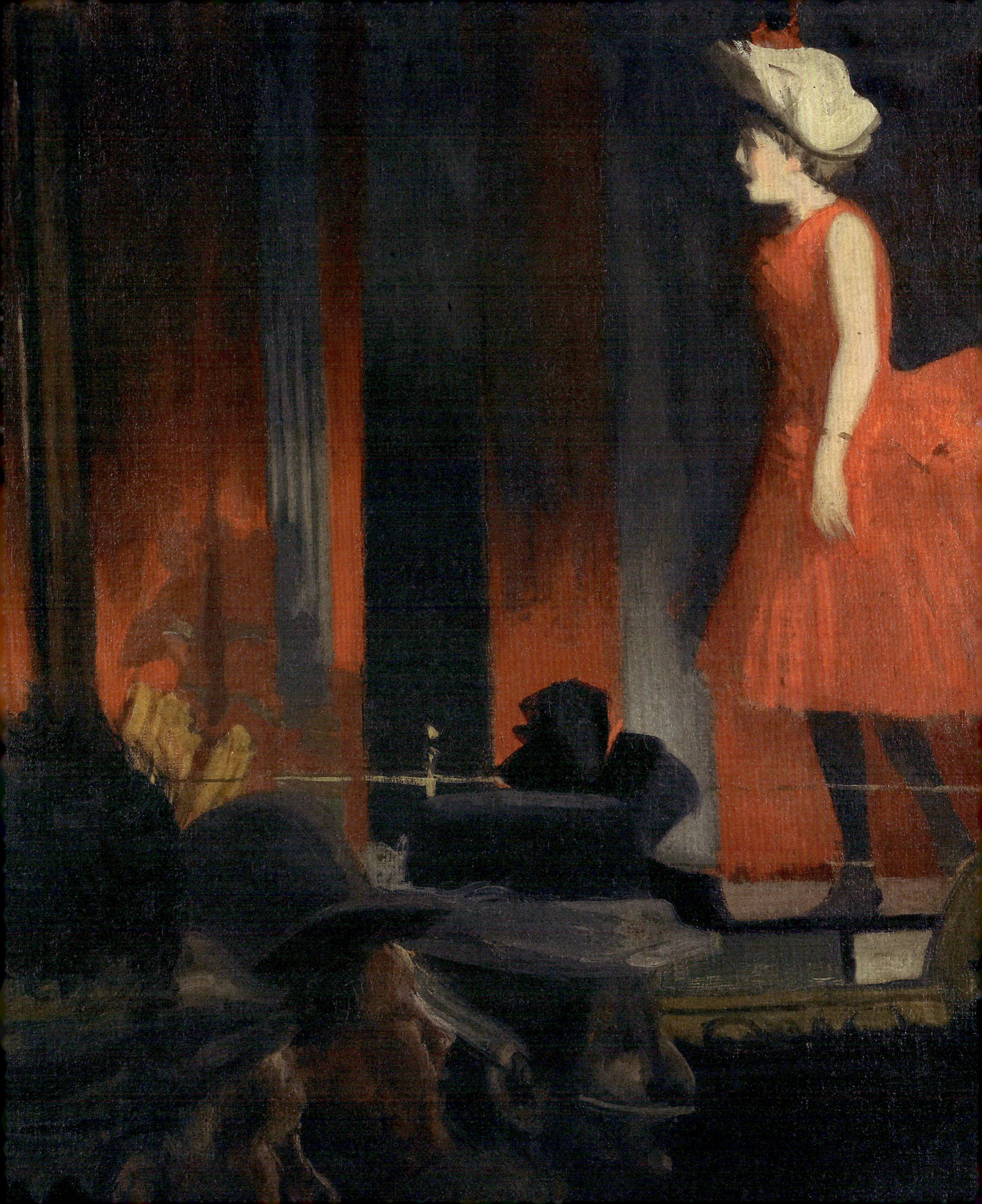

THOMAS KENNEDY

THE MUSIC HALL AND THE 'STAGE-STRUCK' ARTIST

Music halls were popular venues in the Victorian era, showcasing nightly entertainments – from singing and dancing to acrobatic and comedic performances. There were more than three hundred performative venues in London around the turn of the twentieth century, reflecting their huge popularity.[1] Some of the largest and most famous in London included Bedford Music Hall in Camden, Oxford Music Hall on Oxford Street, Collins' Music Hall in Islington, and Middlesex Music Hall on Drury Lane. Walter Sickert visited these venues regularly, and composed studies that captured not only the infectious thrill of seeing performers onstage but also the incidental performativity of the audience, as well as the decorative theatricality of the architecture. His studies were used to develop sophisticated paintings which experimented with form and colour in a new way. Sickert's paintings of music halls in London, but also Paris and Dieppe, show the boisterous, social atmosphere in these venues, full of raucous people from differing social classes. However, critics viewed his paintings of music halls as an improper subject matter due to a growing social conservatism in Britain.[2] They were initially scorned outside independent exhibiting societies and galleries, but nevertheless launched his career in Britain.[3]

From a young age, Sickert was described as 'stage-struck'.[4] His maternal grandmother Eleanor Henry had been a performer at The Princess in Shoreditch, and his mother Nelly was also inherently musical. She regularly sang to Walter and his siblings, and composed songs with her artist husband Oswald Sickert.[5] They discussed operas and stage shows (particularly Shakespeare) together as a family, developing the children's knowledge of plays.[6] A young Walter Sickert was also an avid theatre-goer, regularly attending shows with his great-aunt Anne Sheepshanks.[7] After leaving King's College school at the age of eighteen, he listened to his father's advice about the instability of being an artist and sought a career instead as an actor, owing to his knowledge of theatrical productions.[8]

By 1880, Sickert had a career on the stage. He was associated with Sir Henry Irving at the Lyceum Theatre, becoming one of the 'Lyceum young men' who had small walk-on roles on stage but also crowded into the audience and devotedly met actors and actresses at the stage door.[9] During his short career Sickert also acted in William and Madge Kendal's company, and toured with George Rignold's company.[10] Though he never progressed beyond minor roles, he appeared in a variety of productions, from *Henry V*[11] and *The Lady of Lyons*[12] to *Othello*[13] and *A Midsummer Night's Dream*,[14] demonstrating his knowledge and versatility in dramatic roles. Sickert opted to pursue a career as an artist, joining the Slade School of Fine Art in 1881, but the stage remained a significant part of his life. He continued to visit theatres and music halls frequently, and before long they became an artistic subject which defined his career.[15]

Sickert became an apprentice to Whistler in 1882. The following year, he carried his master's painting, popularly known as *Portrait of the Artist's Mother*, to an exhibition in Paris, where he met the impressionist Edgar Degas for the first time.[16] Degas's intersectional view of both the performer and orchestra in Parisian café-concerts soon came to be a significant influence on Sickert's own practice, reflected in early paintings *The Pit at the Old Bedford* (see no.38), *Bonnet et Claque. Ada Lundberg at*

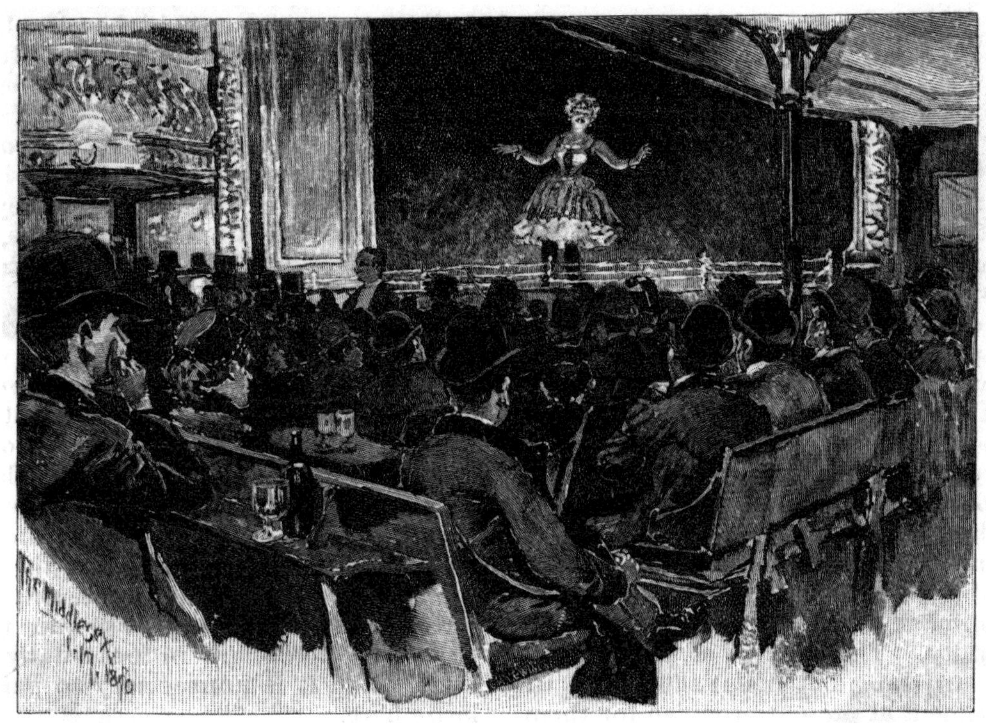

Fig.7
A serio-comic song and dance
artiste at the Middlesex,
a London music hall, 1890

the *Marylebone Music Hall* (no.34) and *The P.S. Wings in the O.P. Mirror* (no.36), which abandon the boundary between an onstage performance and its audience. However, Sickert downplayed the significance of any such influence, responding to a critic: 'It is surely unnecessary to go so far afield as Paris to find an explanation of the fact that a Londoner should seek to render on canvas a familiar and striking scene in the midst of the town in which he lives.'[17]

Some of Sickert's first paintings were of performers on stage. Music hall singers, like the famous Marie Lloyd, were known for performing rowdy, comical songs, usually including sexual innuendos. All too often protested against or censored, the songs were named 'vile' by critics, 'vomited by the lowest grade of public singer'.[18] However, in 1922 T.S. Eliot expressed the scale of Marie Lloyd's popularity by arguing that she was 'the greatest music hall artist of her time in England', and that her death constituted a decisive crisis for both the working classes and England itself.[19] Sickert painted well-known performers but also immortalised singers who may have otherwise been forgotten. He particularly admired Minnie Cunningham and invited her to his studio to pose for him in 1892 (see no.39), a work which incorporates the influence of café-concerts from Degas with an artistic treatment akin to Whistler – a sombre profile figure set against a shallow, non-receding background.[20] Other performers painted by Sickert include Ada Lundberg (see no.34), Rosie Lloyd and Bella Orchard (known collectively as the Sisters Lloyd; no.35), and Florence Louise Hetherington (or Little Dot Hetherington; no.40). Sickert's paintings not only convey his affection for those on stage but also express what it feels like to perform on stage. His works are not necessarily composed from his viewpoint in the audience, but channel evocative memories of his time as an actor.[21]

Turning his attention to the audience, Sickert created realistic representations of people who visited music halls. Akin to the dramatised illustrations found in *The Graphic, The Illustrated London News* or *Harper's Magazine* newspapers (see also fig.7), Sickert's paintings showed authentic views of people who populated the musical venues.[22] *Gallery of the Old Bedford* (see no.41) and *Noctes Ambrosianae* (no.43) were among his first paintings of lofty music hall galleries, showing crowds of young men vying to see the stage. Music halls were communal spaces which eroded entrenched British concepts of class, one observer calling them a place where 'the middle classes and working classes got drunk like brother and sister'.[23] However, moral purists viewed music halls as spaces which encouraged alcoholism, obscenity and aggressive nationalism, filled with lewd spectators who were 'too susceptible of evil example and demoralising values'.[24] They particularly disapproved of sex workers, frequently complaining to the police and attempting to close venues where prostitution was tolerated.[25] Though there were differing perceptions of music halls, Sickert's paintings depict his experience of visiting them as well as showing undramatic, truthful observations of everyday people enjoying popular entertainments in their leisure time.[26] His works show how people unconsciously engage with the social performative act of being part of an audience. Whether actively or passively interacting with performers on stage, or in their own interactions with one another as a crowd, they reveal the spectrum of human engagement in Victorian music halls.

As well as observing the attendees, Sickert created paintings which documented interiors of several music halls. The Bedford Music Hall, often referred to by locals as the Old Bedford, would become the subject of several compositions, including *Gallery of the Old Bedford*, *Little Dot Hetherington at the Bedford Music Hall* and *The Pit at the Old Bedford*. It would undergo a transformation in 1899. Renamed the Bedford Palace of Varieties (or colloquially the New Bedford), it was rebuilt to include modern amenities such as plush-covered seating, electric lighting and heating, as well as a motorised fireproof stage curtain and sliding roof to aid ventilation.[27] *The New Bedford* (see no.49) shows the lavish design of the new space. The gilded walls, decorated with ornate plasterwork and majestic caryatids, preside above a well-dressed crowd of spectators seated in the stalls below, reflecting the

increased glamour found in late Victorian music halls. Another work shows one of the earliest ever depictions of a cinematic screening. Composed in 1906, *Gallery of the Old Mogul* (see no.42) shows a crowd of patrons at the Mogul Tavern scrambling to see one of the first ever Westerns in Britain.[28] Early moving pictures were initially shown in music halls as part of the evening programme before the creation of purpose-built cinemas, the venues ultimately contributing to the decline of these spaces.

Sickert's music hall paintings signal the decline of performance spaces and the rise of popular culture in Britain, acting as fond memorials to entertainments at the turn of the century before the advent of new technologies. Due to radio and phonographic recordings, as well as cinemas and eventually television, music halls faded in popularity with interwar and postwar generations. Most music halls had closed by the 1960s, and few remain to this day. In 1888, Sickert's paintings of music halls were thought to be 'the lowest degradation of which the art of painting is capable', but were later lauded and considered to be some of his foremost works, influencing the practices of many artists, including Camden Town Group painter Spencer Gore.[29] Despite the waning popularity of music halls in his lifetime, Sickert never relinquished his love of theatrical subjects and continued to explore the development of other entertainments – music and theatre, cinema and popular news, as well as the early notion of the celebrity (see pp.82–3) – for the rest of his career.

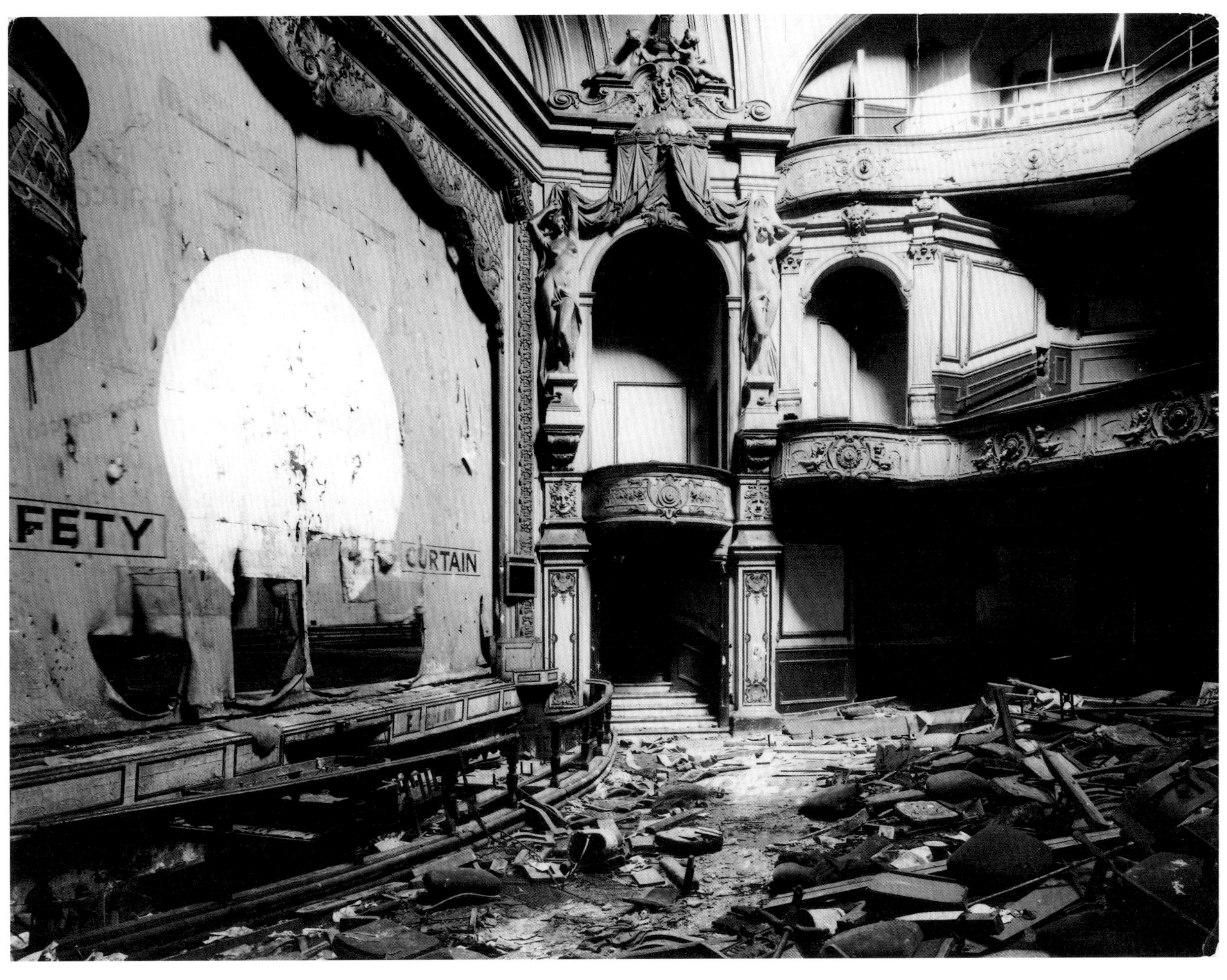

Fig.8
The Bedford Palace of
Varieties after it closed
in 1959

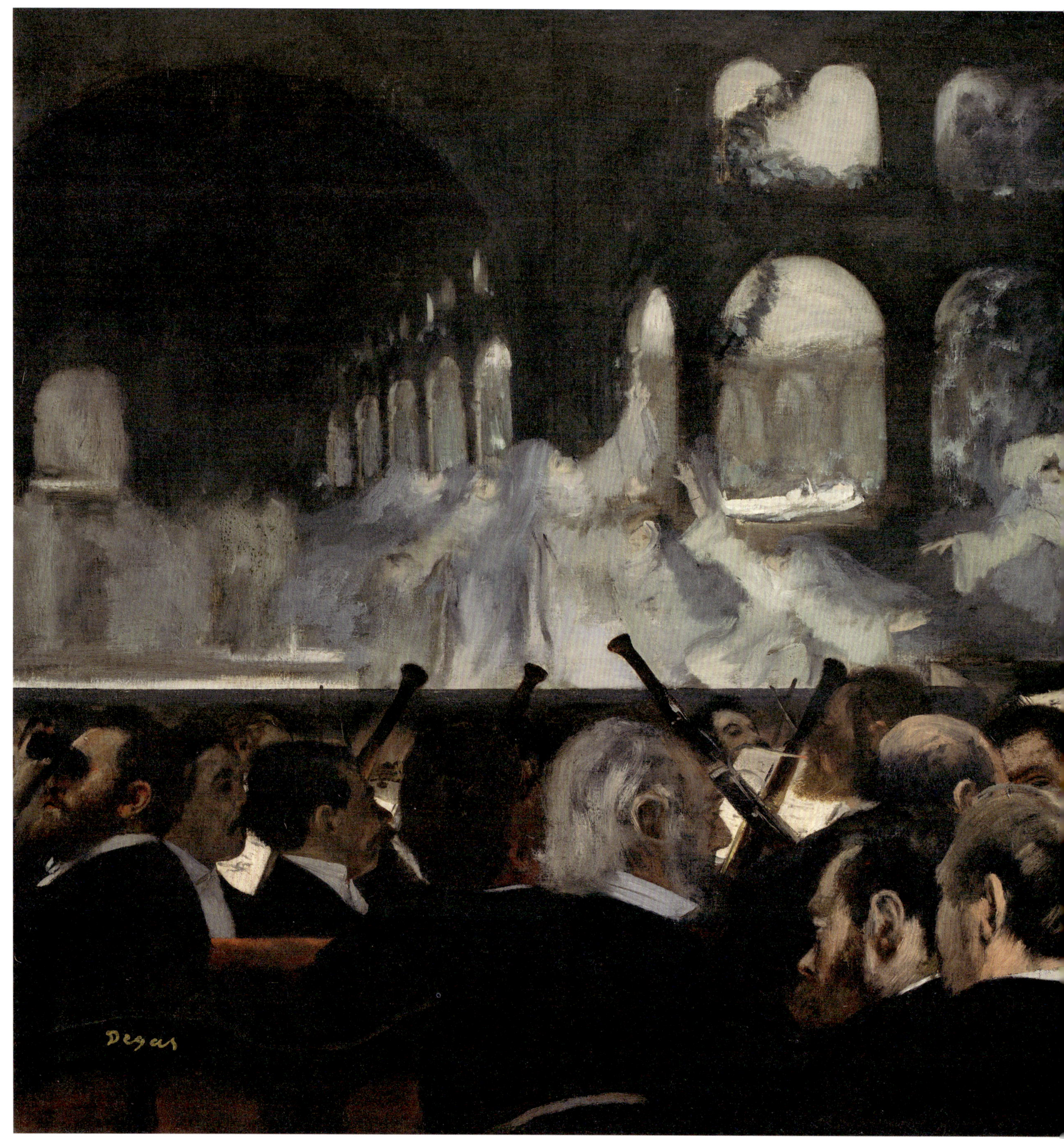

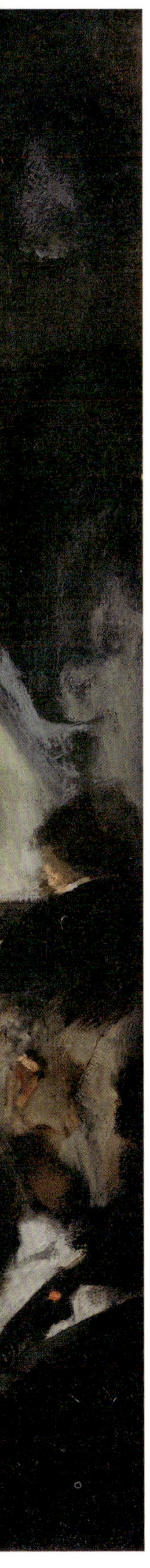

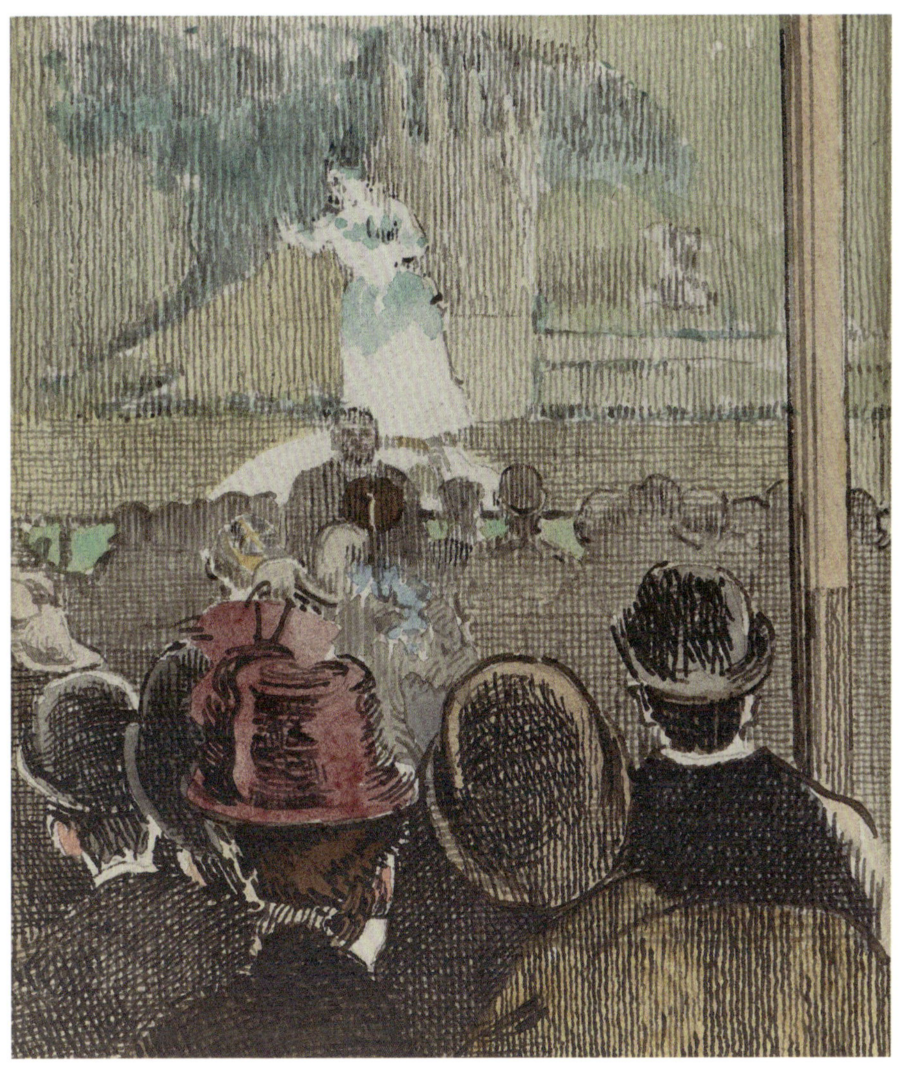

32
Edgar Degas
*The Ballet Scene from
Meyerbeer's Opera
'Robert Le Diable'* 1876
Oil paint on canvas
Victoria and Albert
Museum, London

33
*Sam Collins's Music Hall,
Islington Green* 1888
Pencil, pen and
ink on paper
Lord and Lady Irvine
of Lairg

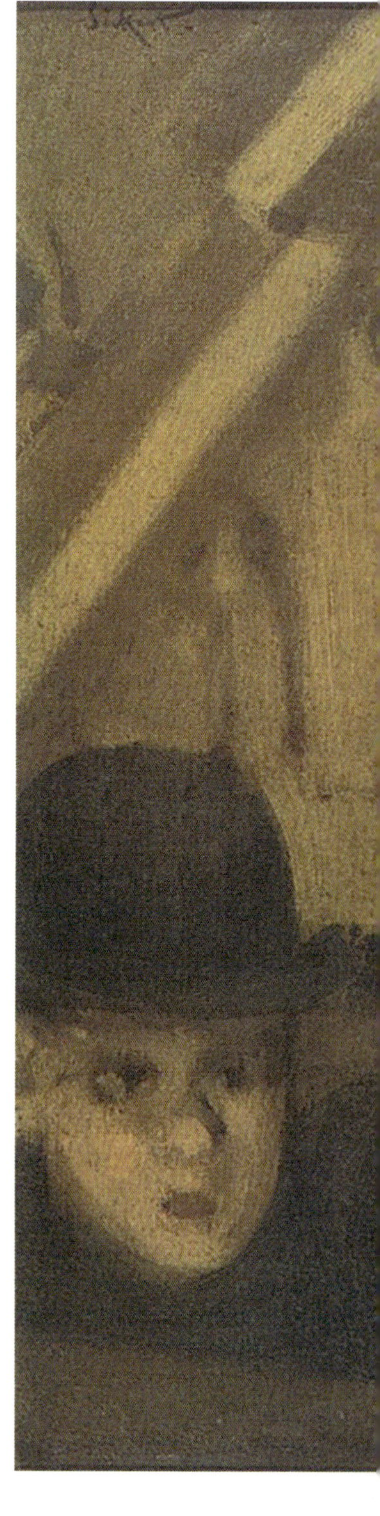

34
Bonnet et Claque. Ada
Lundberg at the Marylebone
Music Hall c.1887
Oil paint on canvas
Private collection

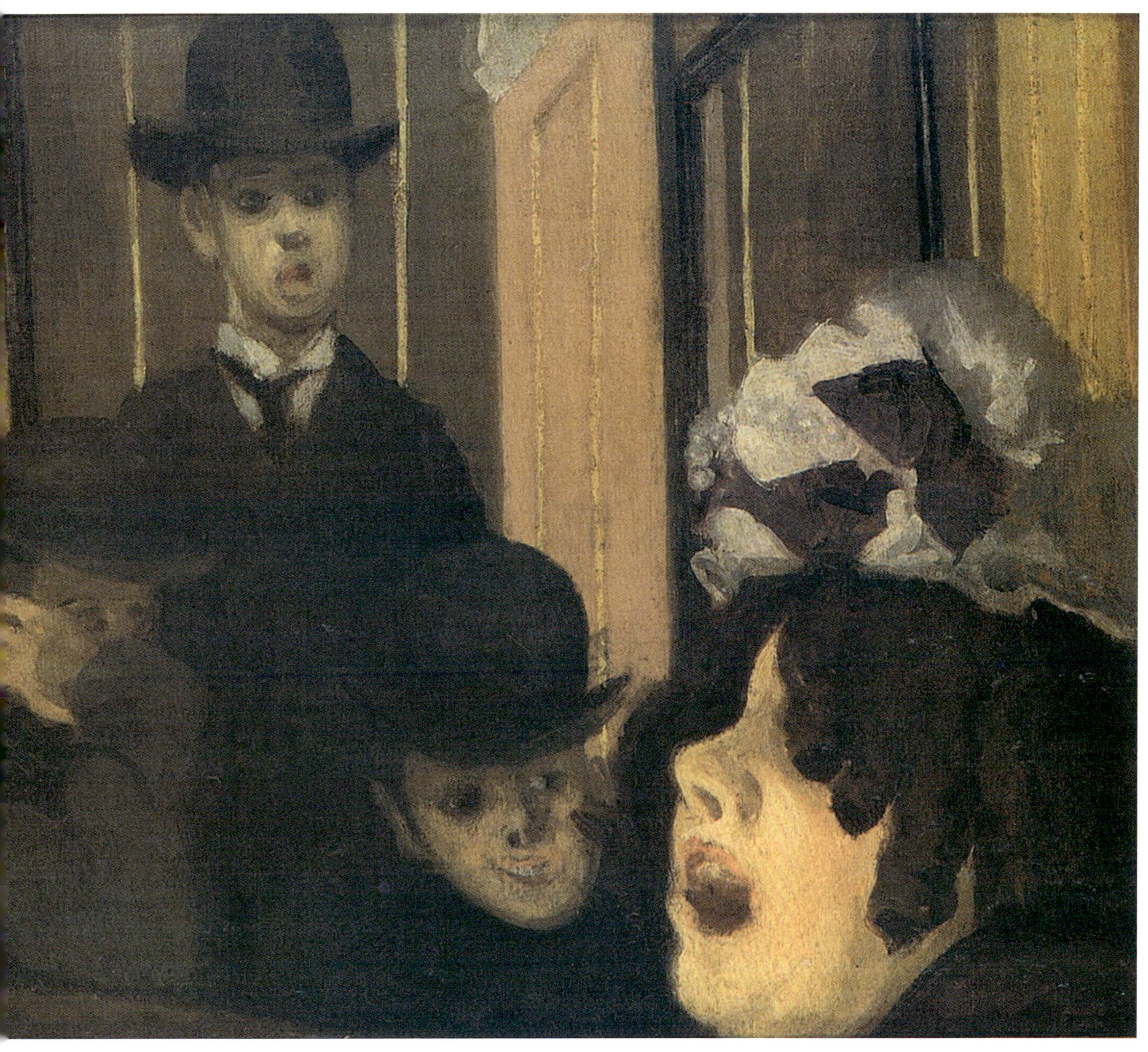

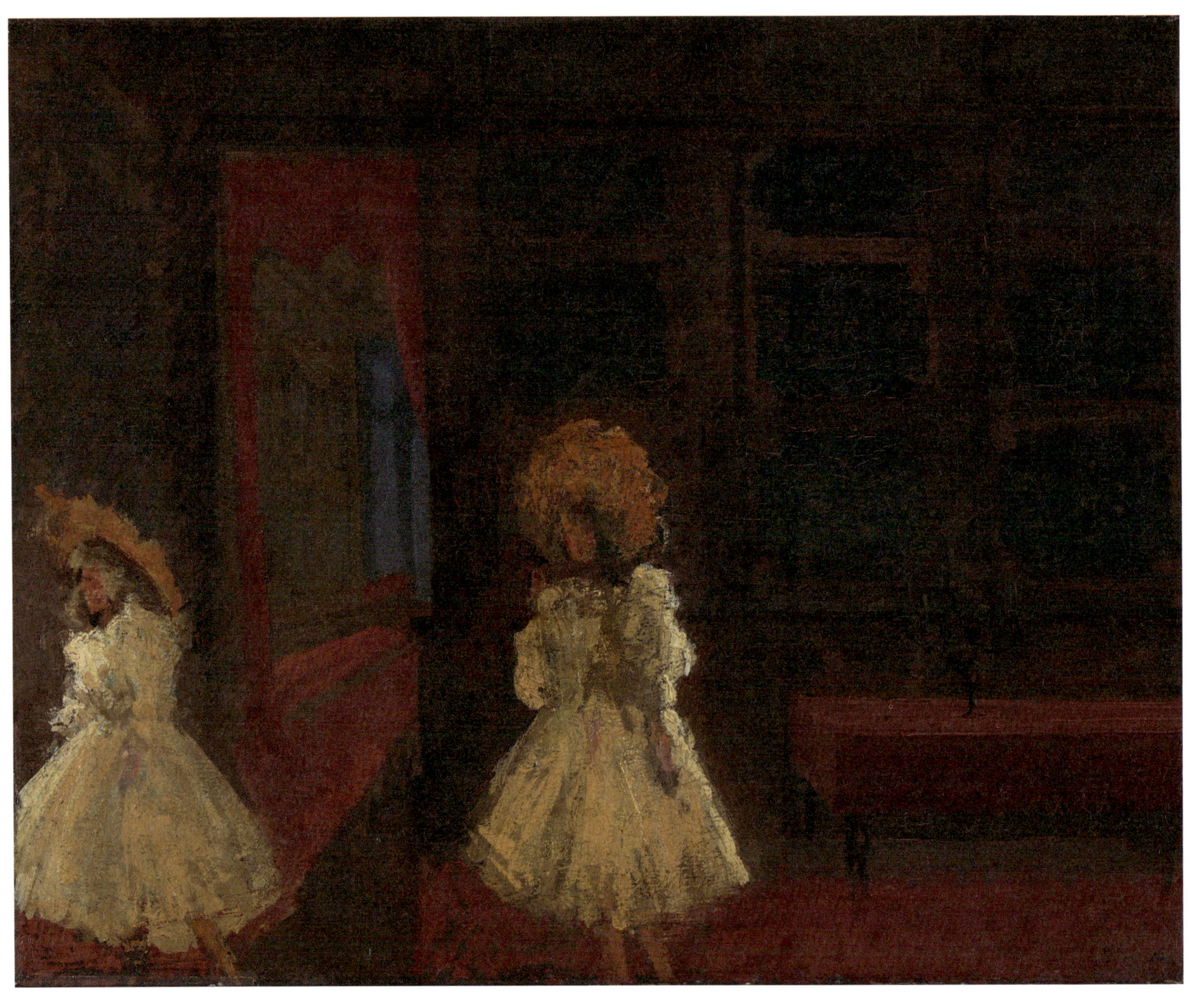

35
The Sisters Lloyd c.1889
Oil paint on canvas
Government Art
Collection

36
*The P.S. Wings in the
O.P. Mirror* c.1888–9
Oil paint on canvas
Rouen, Musée des
Beaux-Arts

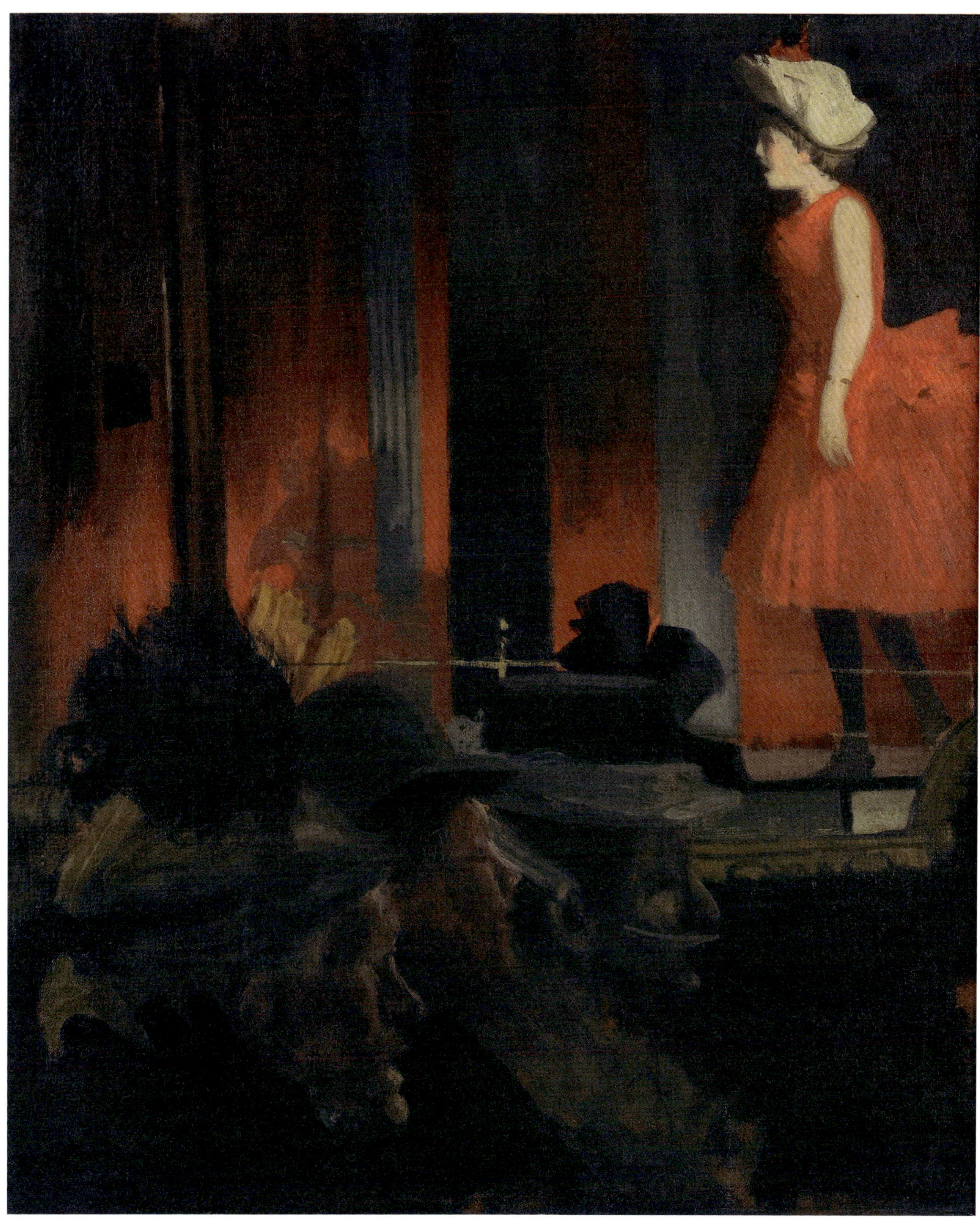

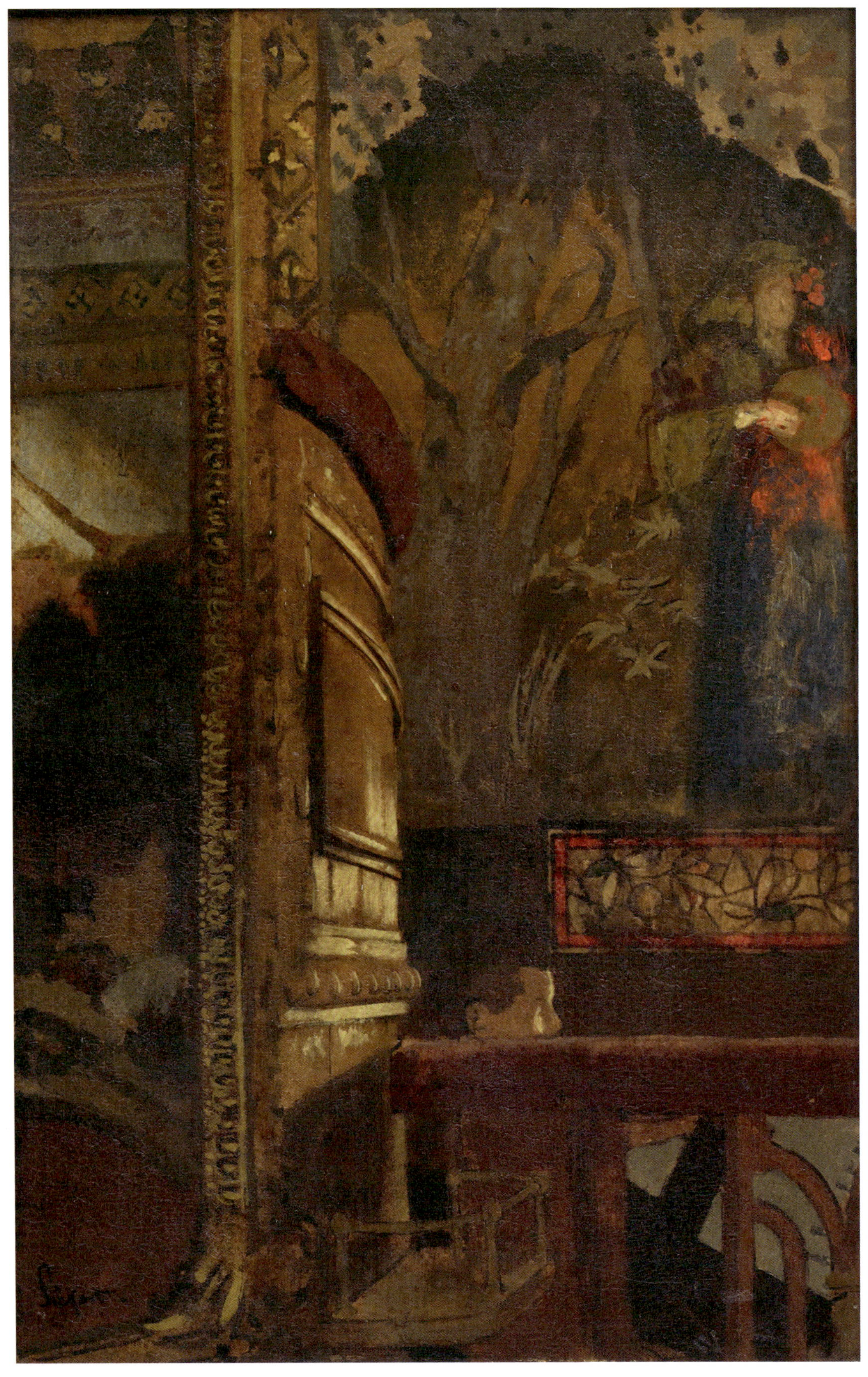

37
Vesta Victoria at the Old Bedford c.1890
Oil paint on canvas
Burrows Family

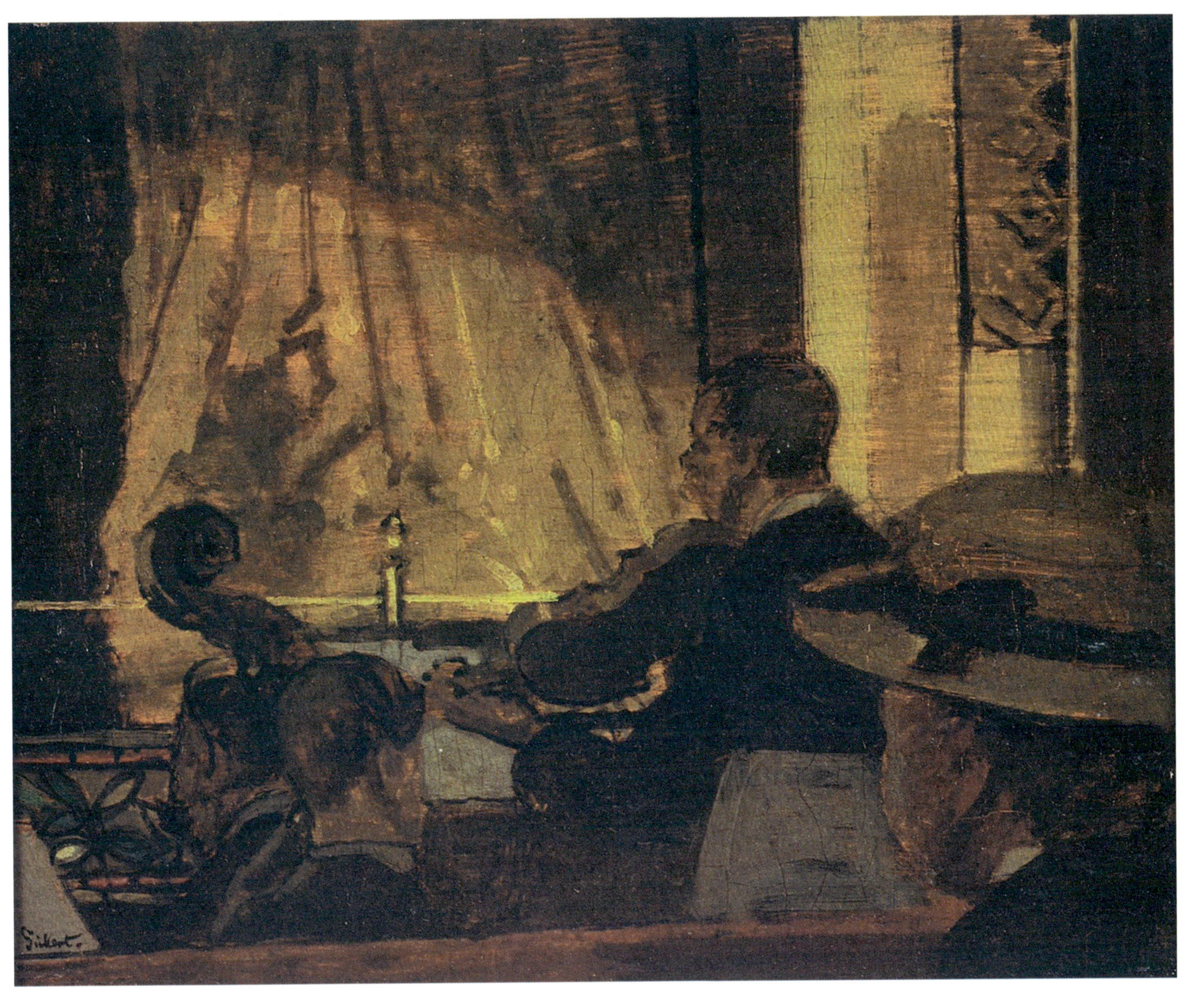

38
The Pit at the Old Bedford
c.1889
Oil paint on canvas
Fondation Bemberg, Toulouse

39
*Minnie Cunningham at the
Old Bedford* 1892
Oil paint on canvas
Tate

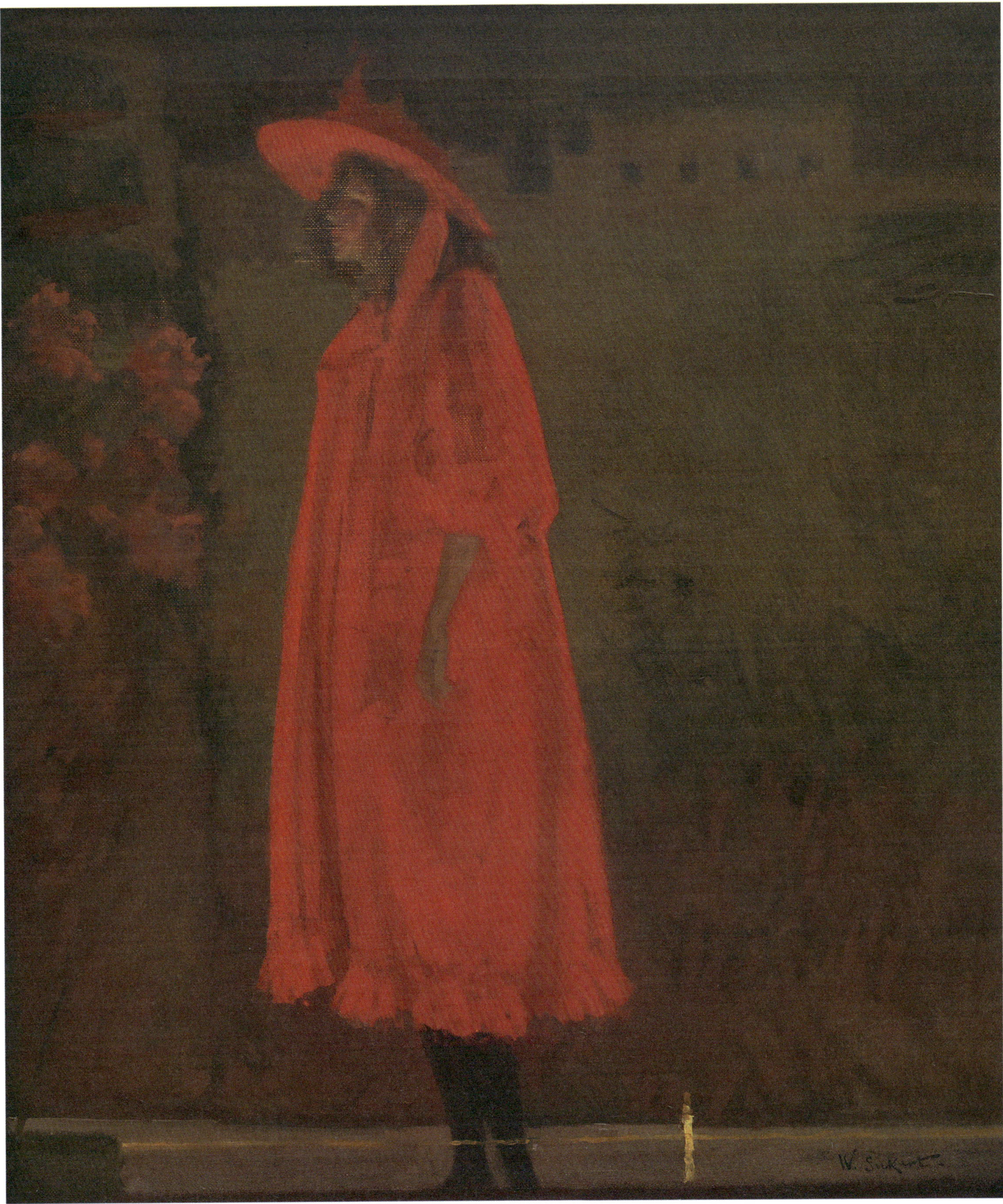

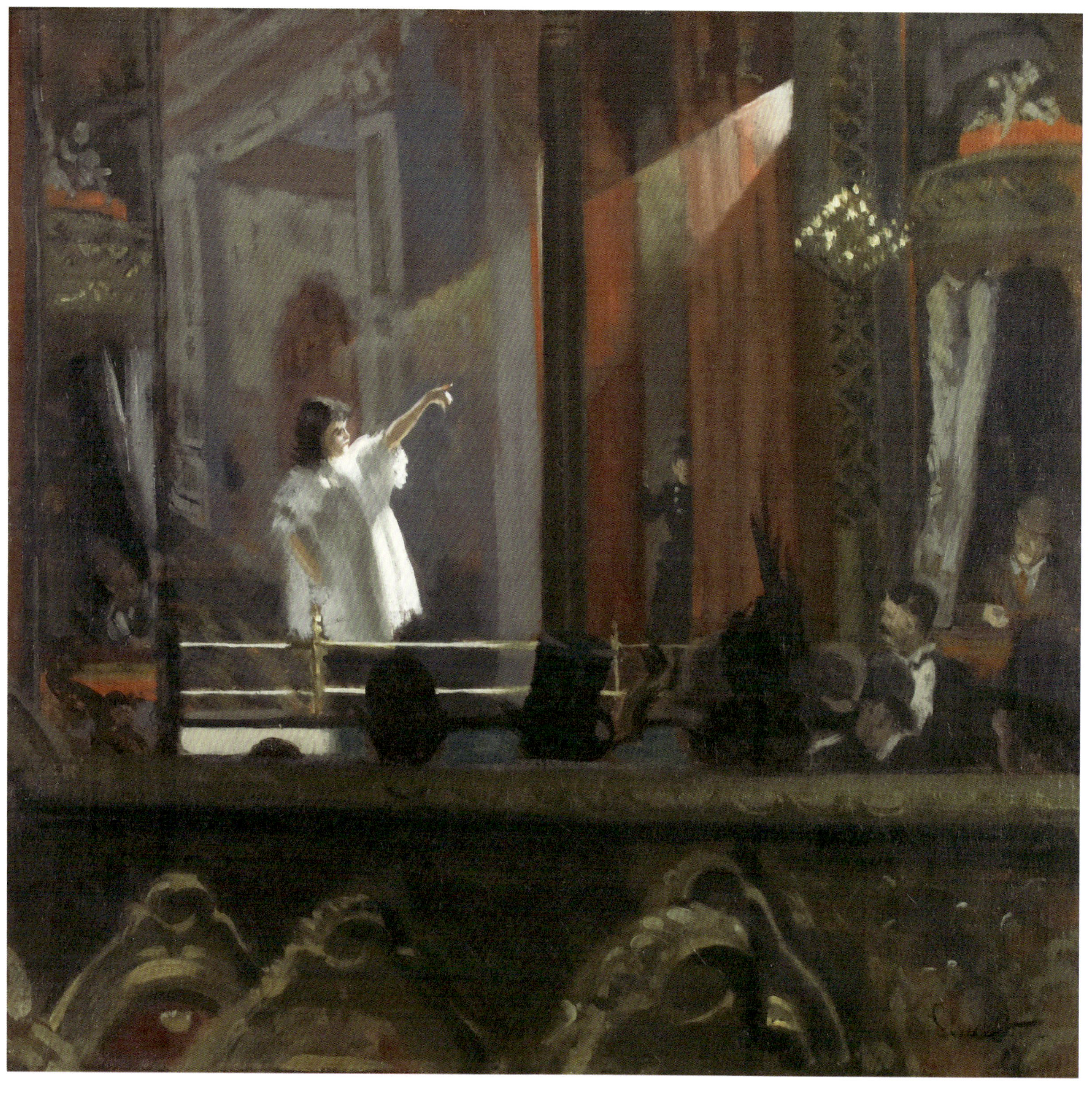

40
*Little Dot Hetherington at
the Bedford Music Hall*
c.1888–9
Oil paint on canvas
Private collection

41
Gallery of the Old Bedford
c.1894–5
Oil paint on canvas
National Museums
Liverpool, Walker Art Gallery

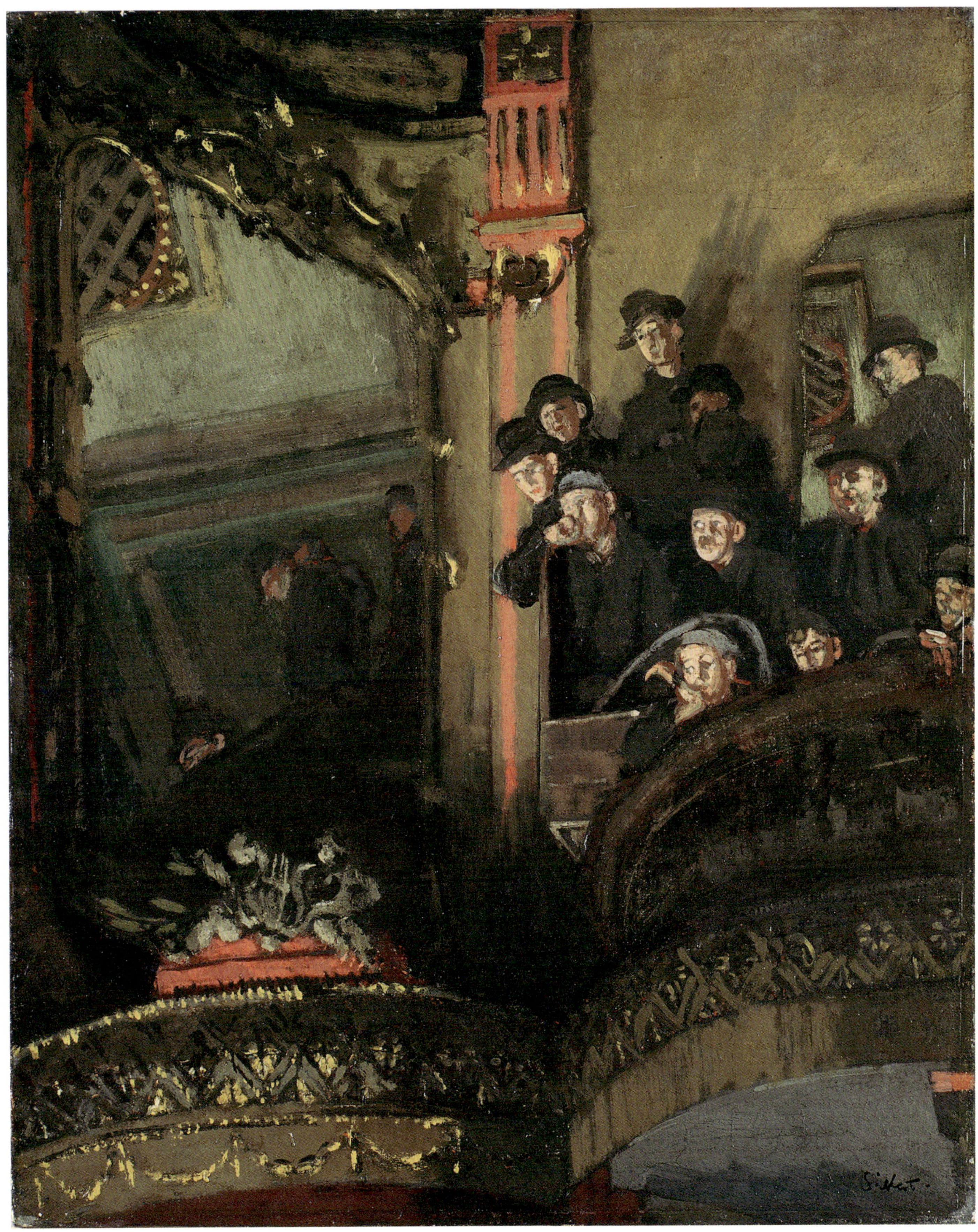

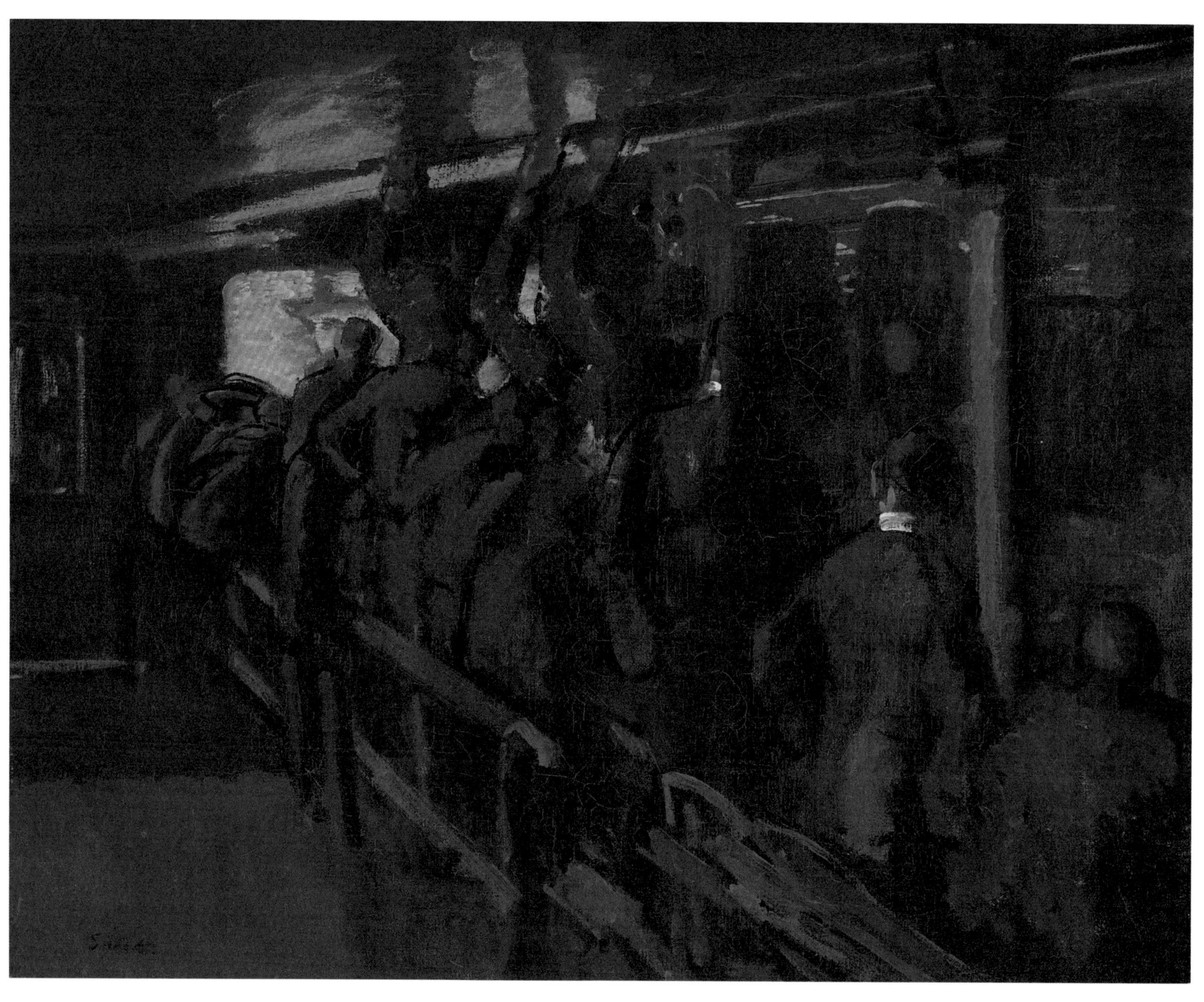

42
Gallery of the Old Mogul
1906
Oil paint on canvas
Private collection

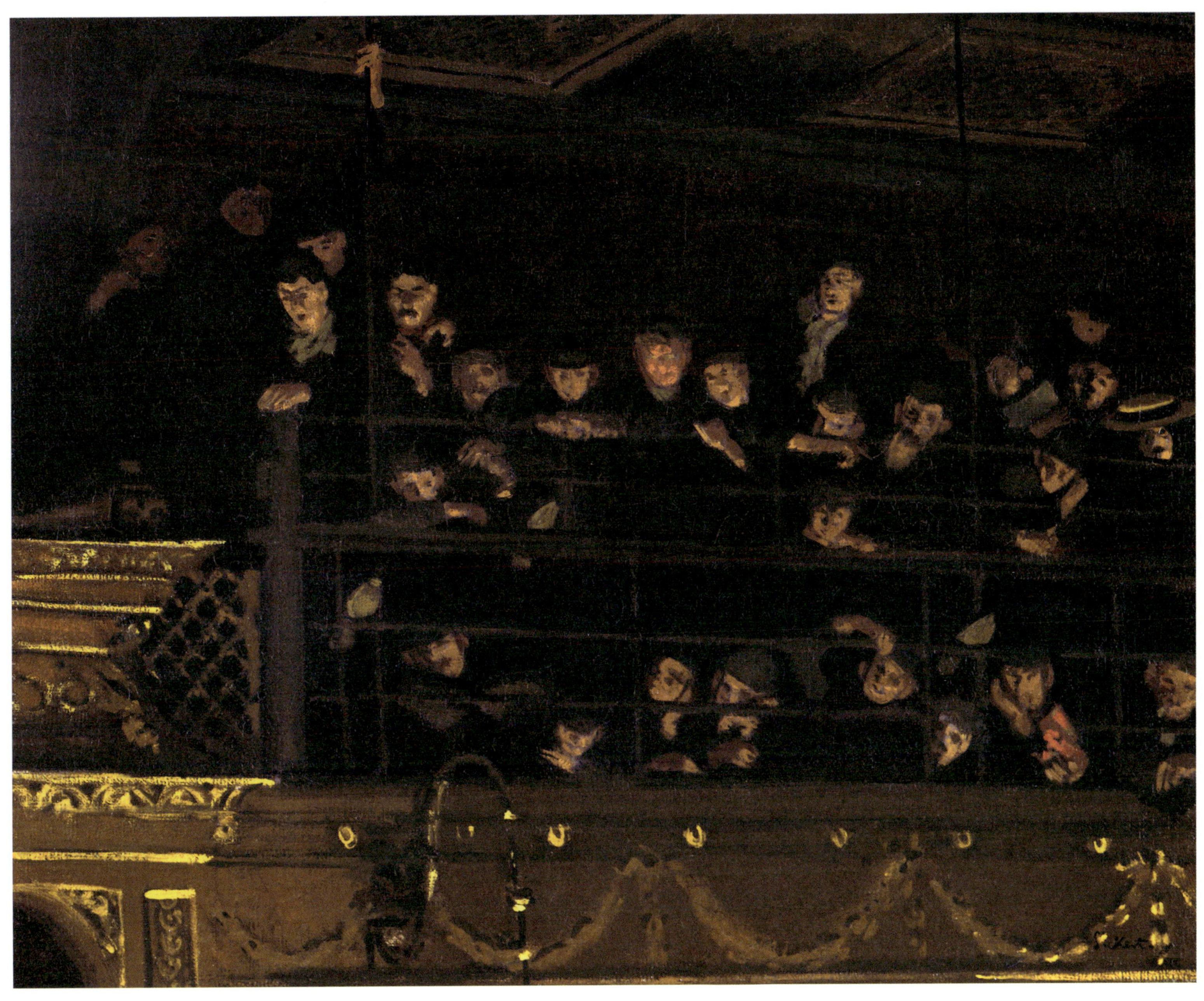

43
Noctes Ambrosianae
1906
Oil paint on canvas
Nottingham City
Museums & Galleries

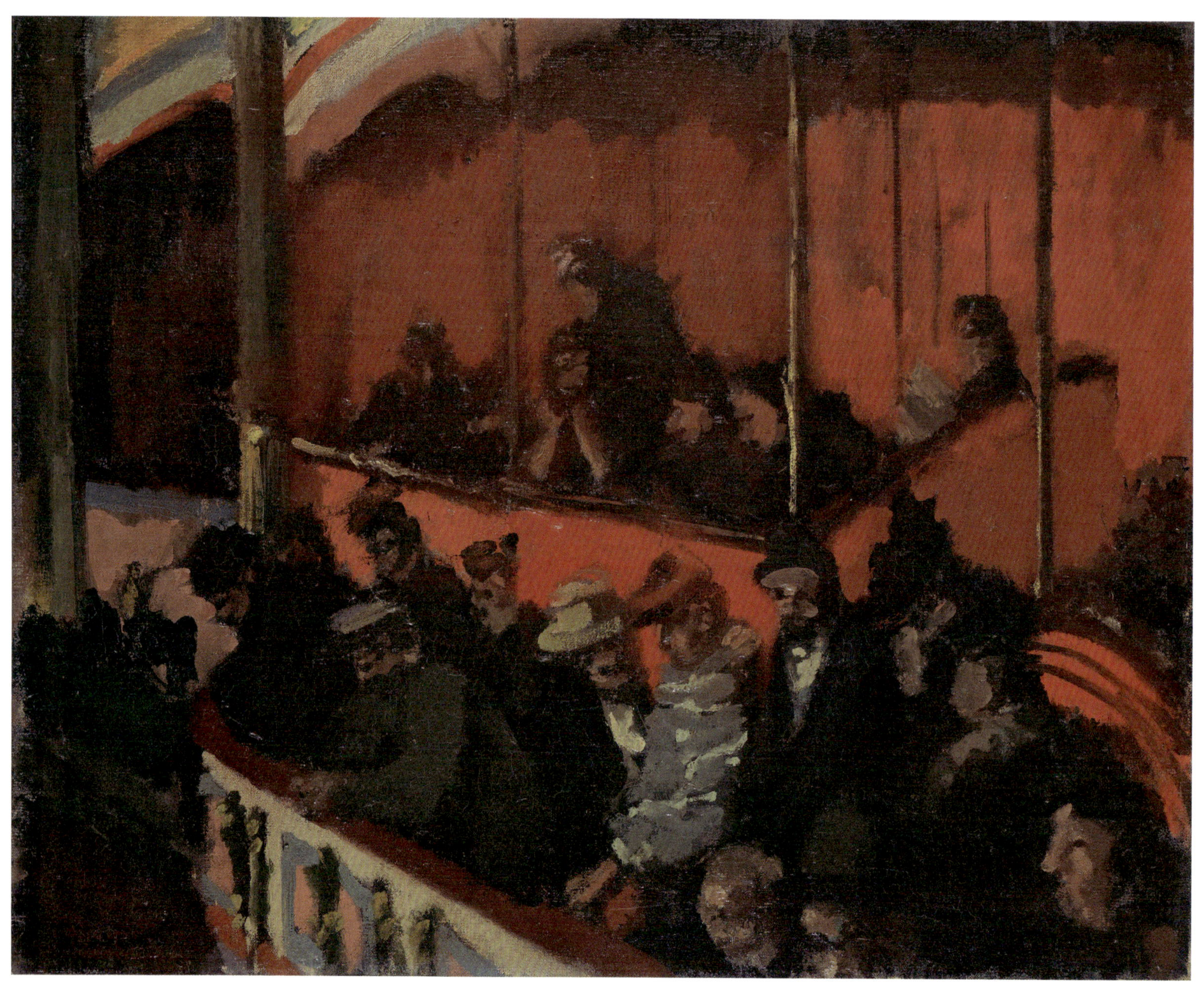

44
Théâtre de Montmartre
c.1906
Oil paint on canvas
King's College, University
of Cambridge

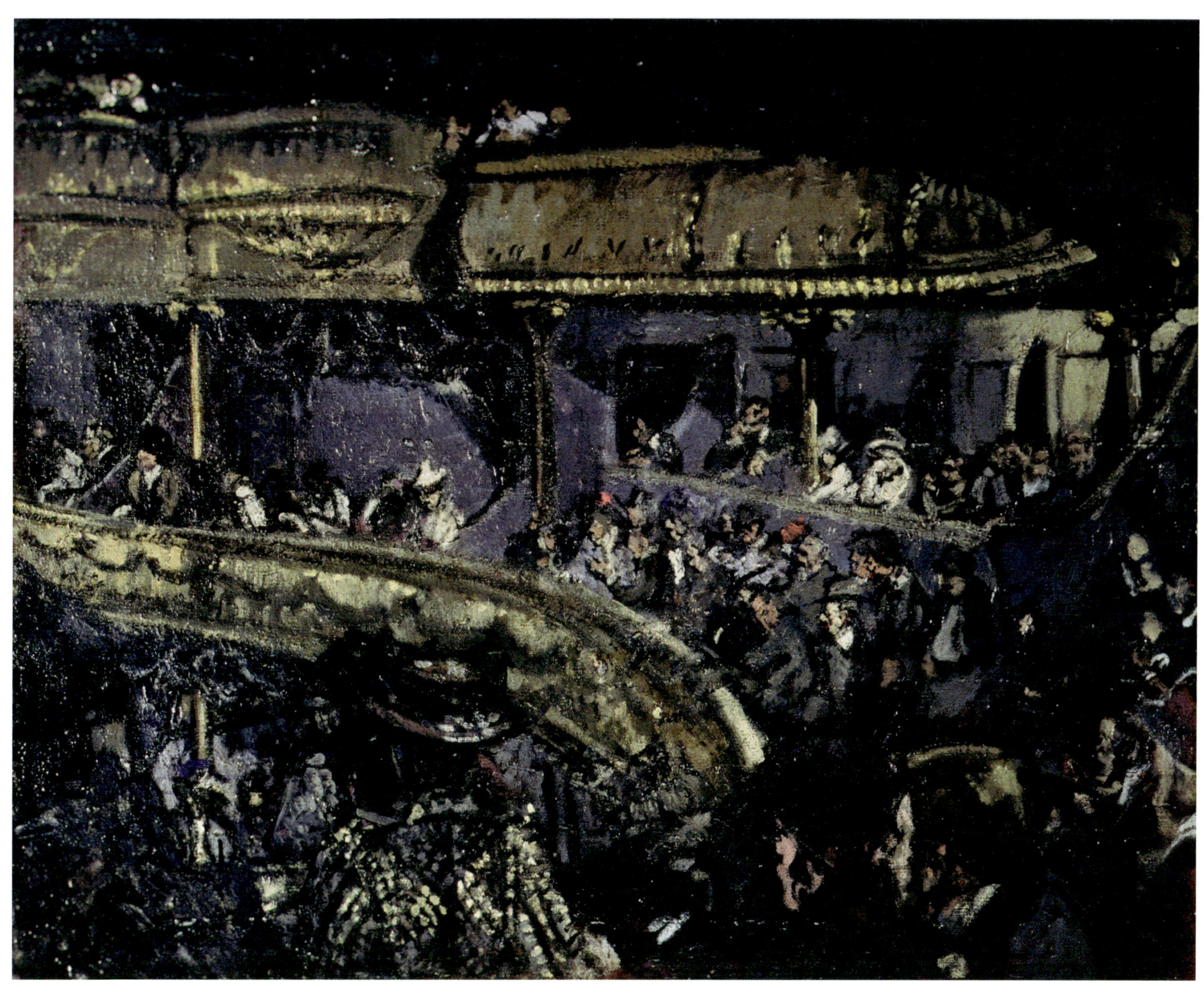

45
L'Eldorado c.1906
Oil paint on canvas
The Henry Barber Trust,
the Barber Institute of
Fine Arts, University of
Birmingham

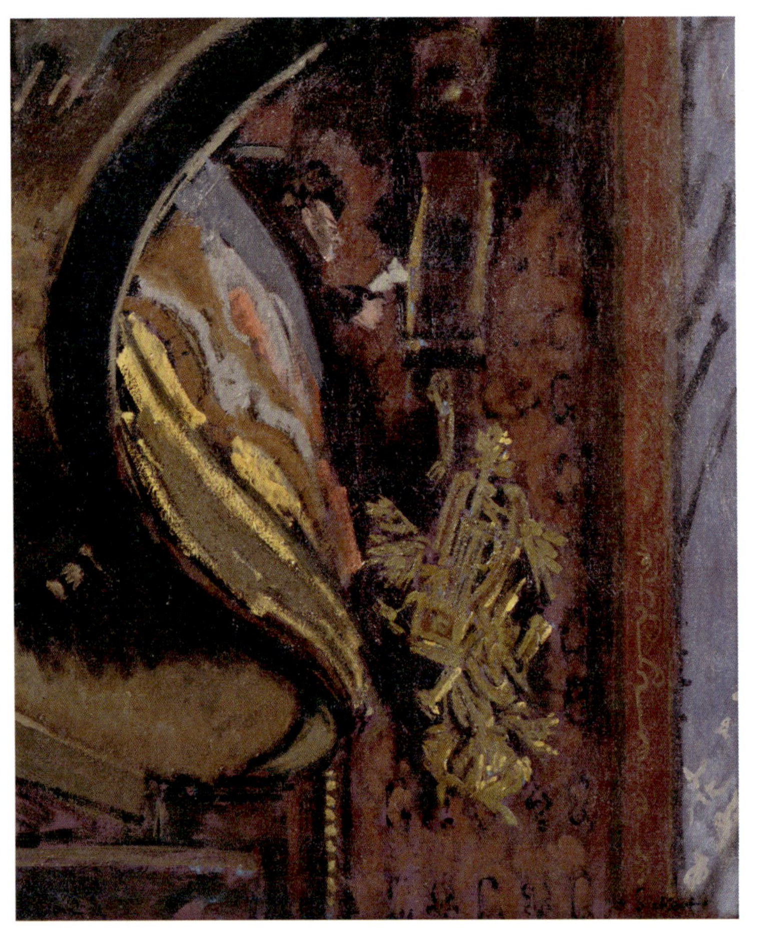

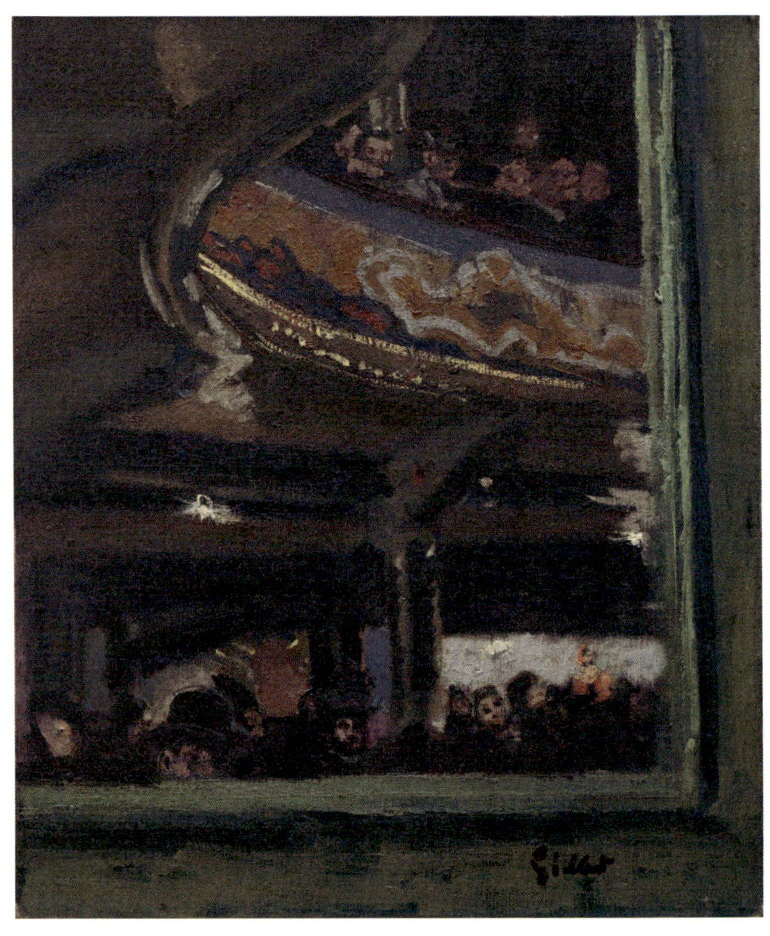

46
Gaîté Montparnasse,
dernière galerie de
gauche 1907
Oil paint on canvas
The Ashmolean Museum,
University of Oxford

47
Gaîté Montparnasse
c.1907
Oil paint on canvas
The Museum of Modern
Art, New York

48
Vernet's, Dieppe 1925
Oil paint on canvas
The Syndics of the
Fitzwilliam Museum,
University of Cambridge

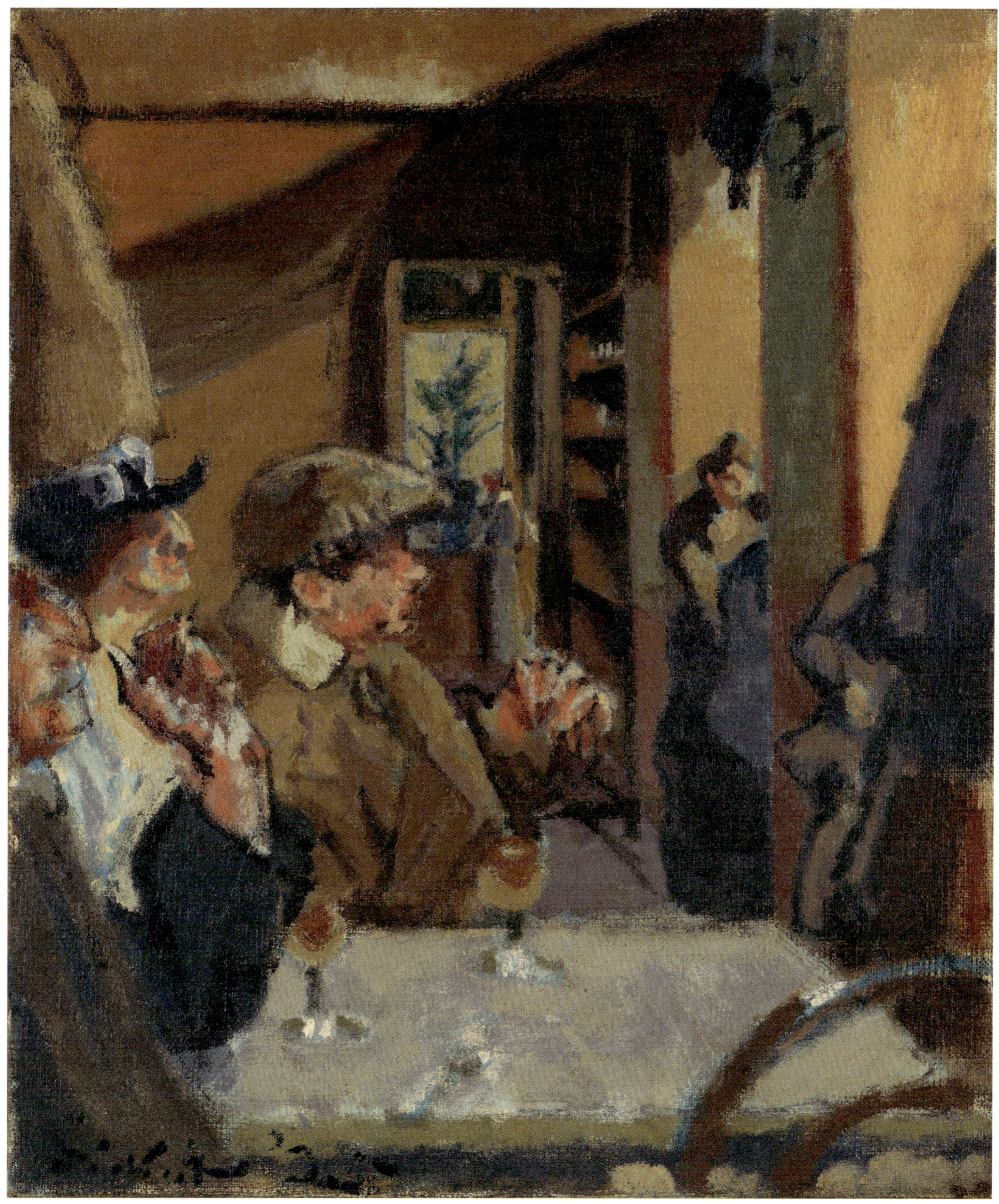

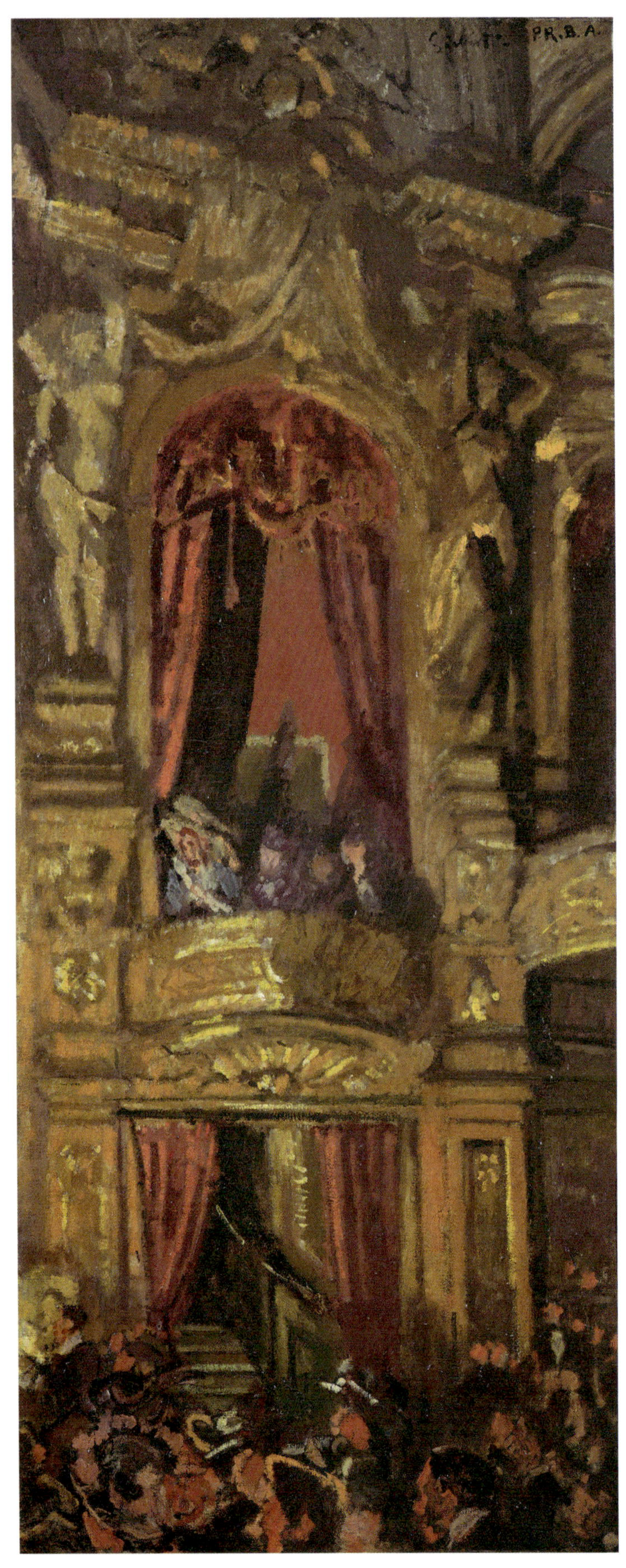

49
The New Bedford 1907–9
Oil with tempera on
canvas
Leeds Museums and
Galleries

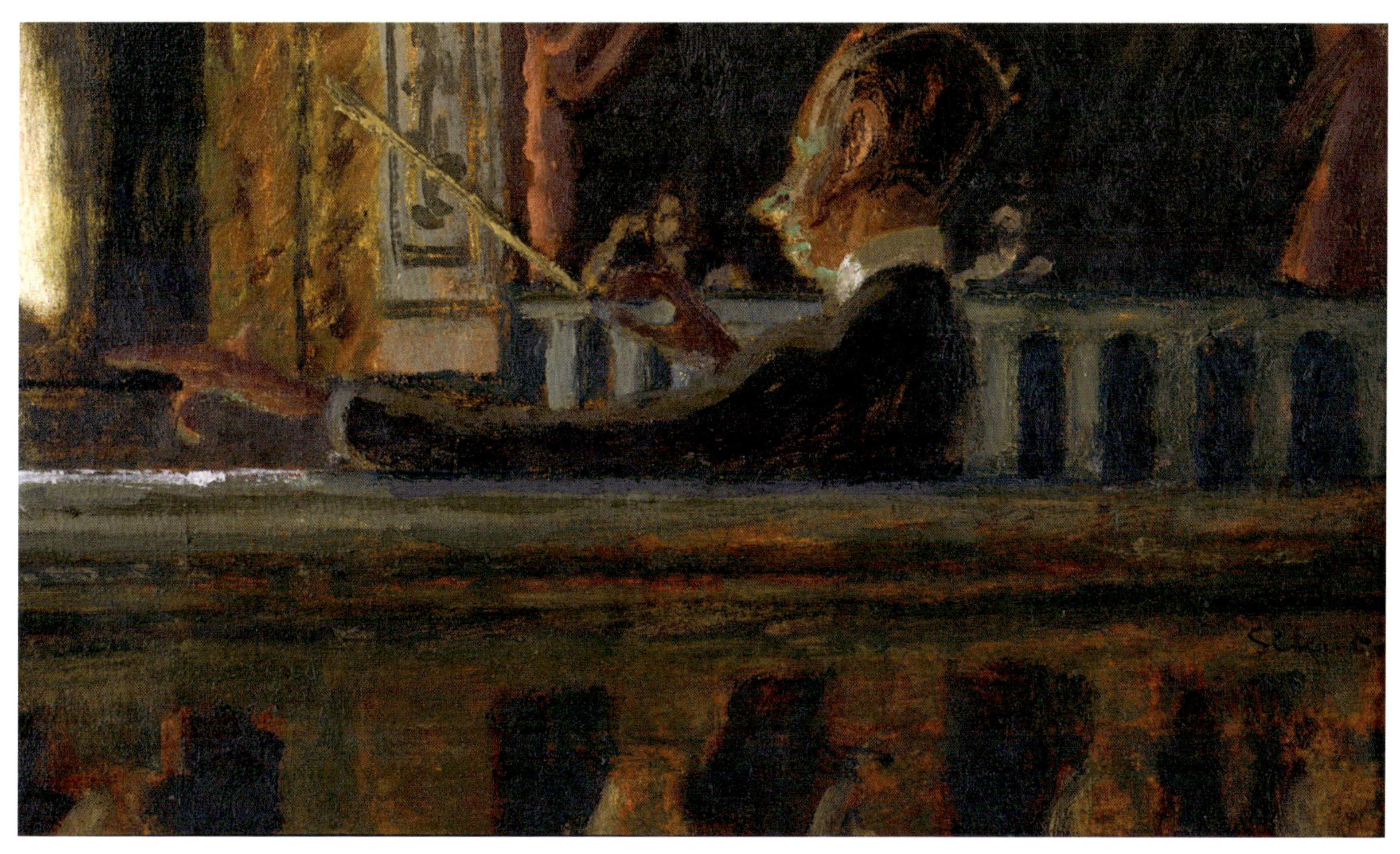

50
Eugene Goosens
Conducting c.1923–4
Oil paint on canvas
Daniel Katz Ltd, London

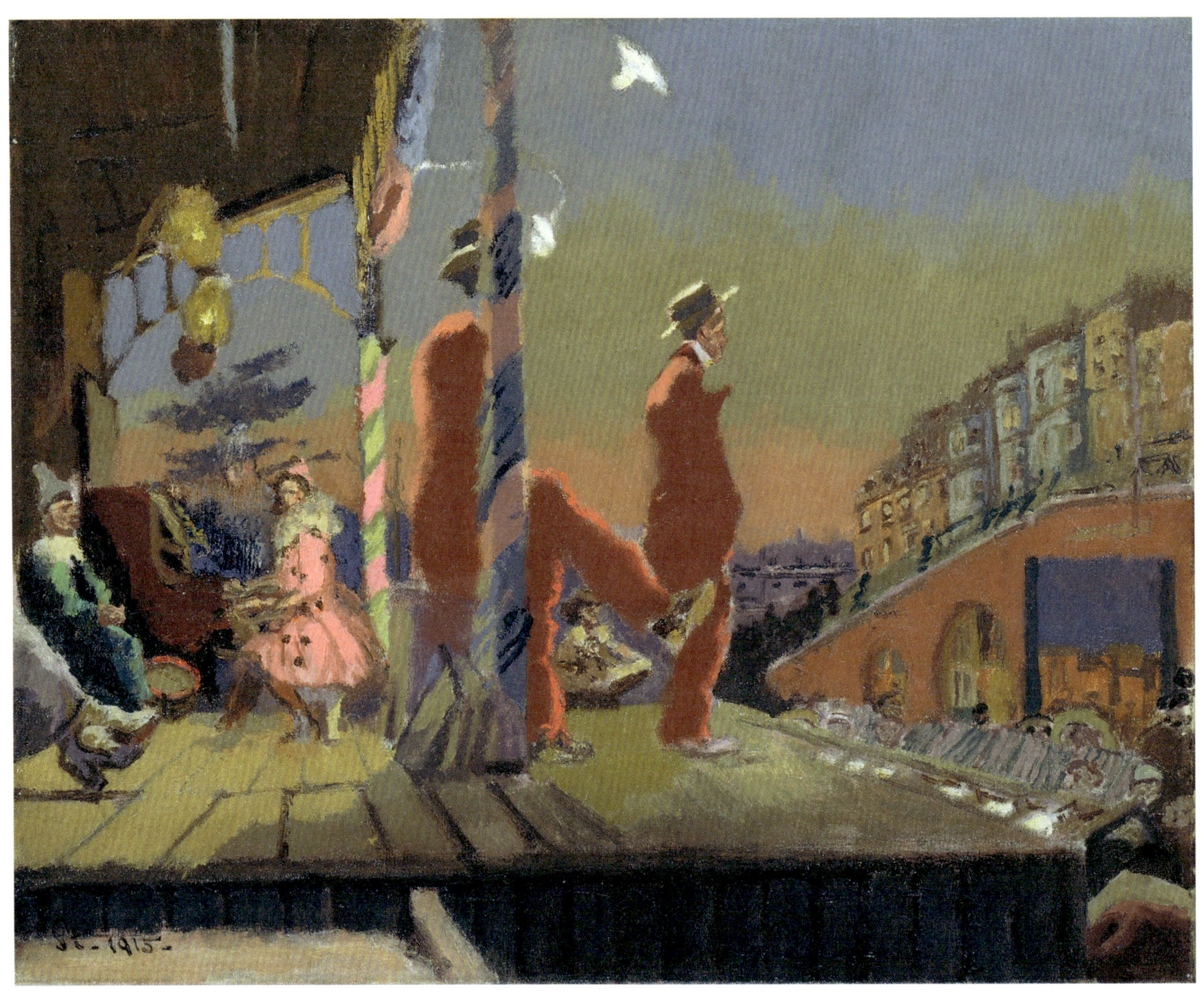

51
Brighton Pierrots 1915
Oil paint on canvas
Tate

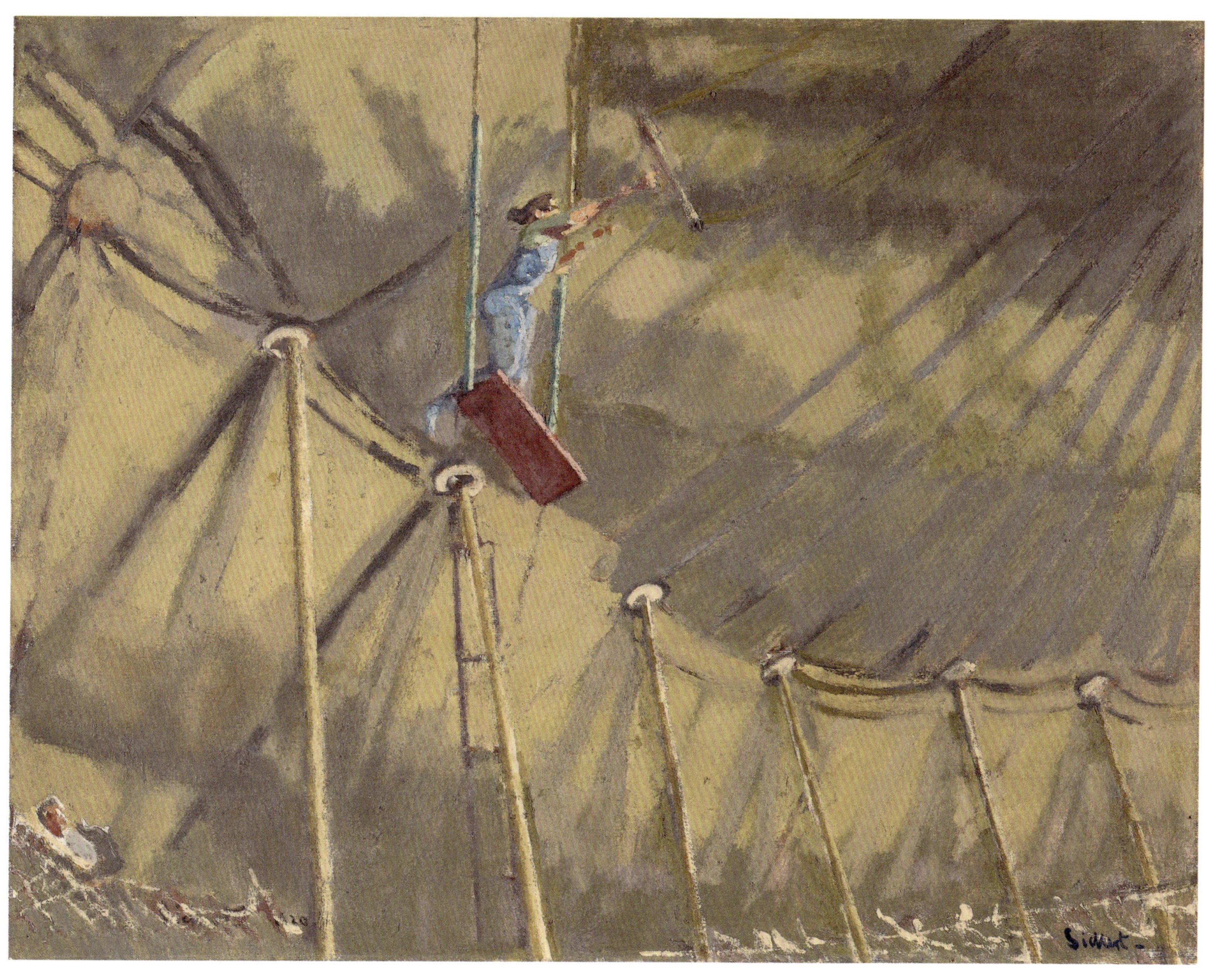

52
The Trapeze 1920
Oil paint on canvas
The Syndics of the
Fitzwilliam Museum,
University of Cambridge

BILLY ROUGH

THE MUCH-ABUSED APOSTLE OF MUSIC-HALL ART: SICKERT AND THE STAGE

In July 1890, Walter Sickert took part in an interview for the *Pall Mall Gazette*. Titled 'The Gospel of Impressionism', the article aimed to introduce readers to the artistic movement and its influence on modern British painting.[1] Characteristically it was a playful, yet informative piece, with a Baudelairean focus on the contemporary: 'We don't go back to other days,' said Sickert, 'our history is of to-day.'[2] He argued the case for casting an artistic eye over the modern metropolis, where one would find 'beauty somewhere in any surroundings', and predicted, while discussing Philip Wilson Steer's now lost music hall painting *Signorina Zozo in 'Dresdina'* 1890, that 'to posterity it will be an historic picture'.[3]

How true that prophecy was. Today London is home to only two original music halls: Wilton's (1859) and Hoxton Hall (1863). The Victoria Hall (1853) can be found in Settle, while in Glasgow stands the Britannia Panopticon (1857) and in Leeds the City Varieties (1865). The rest of the halls are now ghosts – long demolished or so heavily redesigned as to be unfamiliar to a visitor from the nineteenth century.

It is perhaps difficult today to appreciate the popularity of the halls in the late nineteenth century. The first purpose-built music hall, Charles Morton's Canterbury, opened in Lambeth in 1852. By the 1870s, London housed nearly four hundred.[4] Their heyday,

between the 1880s and early 1900s, coincided with Sickert's development as an artist. Consequently, as the exclusive champion of the music hall on canvas, Sickert offers the viewer unique insights into a now long-lost experience.

The music hall held a particular appeal for Sickert. It provided him with modern subject matter, and the opportunity to explore themes relating to gender, class and – significantly for a painter who had previously been employed as an actor – the ephemeral experience of performance. Sickert had a particular affinity with the stage, and no other artist would explore the domain of the halls with such passion and enthusiasm.

Gatti's Hungerford Palace of Varieties, Sam Collins's Islington Green and his Marylebone were just several of the halls that Sickert painted, but his particular favourite was the Bedford Music Hall, an inconspicuous venue located at the rear of the Bedford Arms Tavern in Camden Town. Opened in 1861, the Bedford was entered through a narrow alleyway between Arlington Street and Camden High Street. It was a small, popular venue, with large mirrors on its walls to create the illusion of space. Visitors crammed into every intimate nook: 'Sickert chose the smaller outlying Halls, where the relations between the audience and the stage were closer and less formal. Here was more vulgarity, but greater ease. The stars were at their best in the warmer emotional atmosphere.'[5]

The hall had hardly changed since the 1860s, which perhaps explains Sickert's fondness: 'The Bedford ... retains to the present day many of the features peculiar to the halls of a generation ago... [T]he hall has long maintained its popularity with the amusement-seeking public.'[6] It was this public that provided the focus for one of Sickert's early music hall paintings, *The P.S. Wings in the O.P. Mirror* c.1888–9 (see no.36).

First exhibiting the work at the 'London Impressionist' exhibition at the Goupil Gallery in December 1889, Sickert kept the name of the hall and performer anonymous, but preparatory drawings imply the Bedford as the location, with plans for the painting forming as early as 1888.[7] *The P.S. Wings in the O.P.*

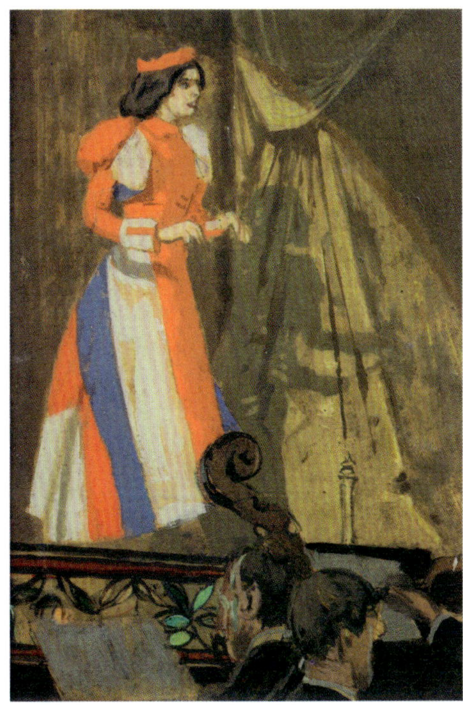

Mirror captures a young female performer reflected in one of the Bedford's mirrors, while the viewer sits snugly in the audience. It is a simple but effective juxtaposition. The spot-lit young performer, the vibrancy of her bright red dress repeated in the set design behind her, provides a glamorous contrast to the audience in shadow, an older trio in featureless browns and greys.

Robert Emmons, Sickert's biographer, noted the Bedford's patrons were generally 'the "lads" of the district, the local bookie and his clients... It was an enchanted palace, where they could forget their troubles in a warm world of magic and romance.'[8] Most halls, the Bedford included, were predominantly working class: 'the middle classes didn't go much to the Halls – unless they were male bohemians like Sickert ... since the Music Hall art was almost exclusively working and lower-working classes'.[9] Despite such a claim, the middle classes did attend, as did audiences both male and female. As Emmons noted, with regards to the Bedford: 'The audience was said to be the most democratic to be found in London.'[10] Interestingly, rather than the 'lads' of the hall, Sickert's painting is dominated by female figures. While men packed the halls, women did visit, and, as Sickert illustrates, they took to the stage too.

The 'magic and romance' that drew audiences to the Bedford certainly attracted Sickert, but it was the transformative power of performance – that ephemeral moment when the audience gives itself over to the performer and becomes lost in their song – that truly enthralled him. This transitory experience is perfectly witnessed in the open mouths of both performer and audience. Audience participation was a key attraction of the halls and here, in *The P.S. Wings in the O.P. Mirror*, the participants are bonded singing the same, familiar chorus.

In truth, during the 1880s and 1890s, the halls were under scrutiny. Critics accused them of being dens of vice, encouraging alcoholism and prostitution. By the mid-1890s, through the omnipresent inspectors of London County Council's Theatres and Music Halls Committee and the moral crusading of Mrs Ormiston Chant, a seismic shift towards respectability was being undertaken.

Recognising critics' aversion to paintings of the halls, in this case Steer's portrait of Signorina Zozo, Sickert explained: 'The distaste to it in your mind arises from the associations of a music-hall.'[11]

Sickert's own work was not without criticism: 'Mr Walter Sickert was always the most hopeless of the company. He is more than an Impressionist; he is an Incoherent. It is to be supposed that he knows what he is after; but it is certain that nobody else does.'[12] His familiarity with the art of Paris provided him with some reassurance in his aims but was not without its own problems. In April 1889, he exhibited *Collins's Music Hall, Islington Green* at The New English Art Club spring exhibition. 'What Mr Sickert's object is in choosing such a subject need not be inquired,' stated *The Scotsman*. 'Possibly he had no very clear motive at all, except that music-halls are often painted by some of the French impressionists.'[13]

Sickert's retaliation was considered, if laid a little thick: 'It is surely unnecessary to go so far afield as Paris', he wrote, 'to find an explanation of the fact that a Londoner should seek to render on canvas a familiar and striking scene in the midst of the town in which he lives.'[14] Despite such defence, there is undeniably a correlation between Sickert and the impressionists, in working practice as well as subject matter. *The Pit at the Old Bedford* c.1889 (see no.38) and *Red, White and Blue* c.1889 (fig.9) depict the Bedford's orchestra in similar poses, suggesting both paintings were constructed from the same series of sketches, and therefore they are, in most cases, not direct representations of particular performances, but rather an amalgamation of ideas and themes relating to the hall experience. The construction of a painting from several sketches was a practice which owed much to Degas, who, according to George Moore, stated 'no art was ever less spontaneous than mine. What I do is the result of reflection and study of the great masters.'[15] Sickert, who met Degas in the early 1880s and counted him as a friend, is clearly in his debt here.

Inspired by impressionism, the gaze of the *flâneur* is also present in *The Pit at the Old Bedford*, which sees Sickert shift the

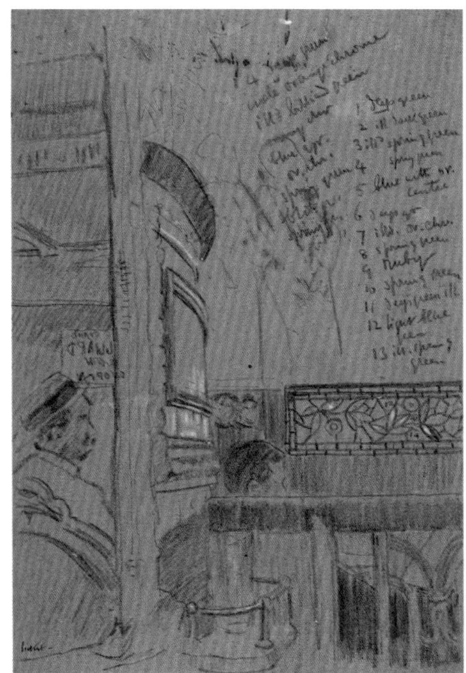

spotlight from the stage to the orchestra pit. The orchestra, comprising three figures including a violinist and cellist, sit below the stage, just in front of the Bedford's familiar colourful glass stage frieze. The performer is unseen but implied in the shadow cast on the stage curtain, while an audience member in straw hat watches from the right-hand side. The *flâneur*'s attention is drawn not to the performer, but to the audience and orchestra. Part of the halls' appeal, for the middle-class bohemians, such as Sickert's friends Arthur Symons and Max Beerbohm, was the observation of the audience as much as the performance. As Symons noted: 'In a music-hall the audience is a part of the performance...'[16]

By the early 1890s, Sickert's reputation as the 'apostle' of music hall painting was firmly established. He would return to his favourite hall for *Vesta Victoria at the Old Bedford* c.1890 (fig.10 and no.37), a painting which plays with several Sickertian motifs, and reveals much about the type of performance that was popular in the halls and the audiences who frequented them. A little-known name today, Vesta (1873–1951) was one of the most famous stars of the music hall stage, performing from the 1870s through to the late 1930s. Born Victoria Lawrence into a family of performers, her earliest appearance on the stage was at the very tender age of six weeks, taking part in one of her father's sketches. Originally billed as 'Baby Victoria', then 'Little Victoria', she had been performing under the stage name Vesta (see fig.11) from at least 1887.[17] In March 1890, *The Stage* noted an early appearance at the Bedford: '... a very pretty young lady, made an early appearance on the stage. Her dancing and singing are of an unusually high order, and elicited loud applause.'[18] The early 1890s were the founding years of Vesta's success. By 1892 she was even touring America with her most famous song, the Joseph Tabrar-penned 'Daddy Wouldn't Buy Me a Bow-Wow', written especially for her.[19]

Vesta's most famous song would also see her take to the stage with a particular prop, a kitten. Sickert's choice of prop for his performer, though, is telling. In her arms the performer plays a banjo, a popular instrument for young women in the 1880s and 1890s – the years of 'banjo mania'.[20] Not an instrument Vesta was known for playing, it is possible that she used one as part of her act, perhaps as a comment on its increasing popularity.

Preparatory sketches also tell us much about the class of visitor to the halls. On the bottom left of two, in particular, can be spotted a male figure wearing a straw boater (see fig.10).[21] Traditionally only worn in the country, the hat became popular city wear for the middle-class gent during the summer of 1893. 'It was only last summer that Londoners began to wear straw hats with any freedom,' noted the *Huddersfield Chronicle* in the August of 1894; 'before then, for as far back as the memory of man reaches, it would have been a social crime for a man pretending to fashionably dress to appear in London streets in any hat other that [*sic*] the silken tile.'[22] The figure's inclusion at the Bedford, a hall traditionally seen as an exclusively working-class venue, is therefore telling, reiterating Robert Emmons's claim on the democracy of the Bedford's audience.

There is another audience evident in *Vesta Victoria at the Old Bedford*. At the top left of the painting can be seen the boys of the gallery, traditionally the most rebellious and raucous section of the audience. Seated high in the cheapest seats, this is the same demographic depicted in Sickert's *Gallery of the Old Bedford* c.1894–5 (see no.41) and a similar group witnessing the performance of Ada Lundberg at the Marylebone in *Bonnet et Claque* c.1887 (no.34).

Like Vesta, Ada (1850–99) was one of the most popular female comediennes of the halls. Born in Bristol, Ada made a career out of performing character studies of Irish women, typically the worse for drink, but always performed with a considered pathos. She had 'truly admirable gifts as a comedienne', according to *The Era*. 'It is rare, indeed,' the paper noted, 'that an artist gets such a reception as that accorded to this clever low comedy lady.'[23]

Ada's serio-comic act often touched on the hardships experienced by her audience. In April 1889, for example, she appeared at the Bedford brandishing a poker and 'told the audience of the waywardness of her husband, and let us into the secret of how she intended to reckon with him'.[24]

A previous subtitle for Sickert's painting referenced one of Ada's most popular songs, the Harry Wincott-penned 'All Thro' Sticking to a Soldier', a 'gigantic success' for the performer.[25] Sickert depicts Ada mid-performance, capturing her at the Marylebone Music Hall, which was attached to the Rose of Normandy public house at 32–3 Marylebone High Street, where Ada performed regularly.

The performer was only one aspect of the hall's appeal for Sickert. Most performers had a group of enthusiastic supporters, the 'claque' of the title, who would follow them from hall to hall. Sickert, too, would follow his favourite female performers, such as Katie Lawrence and Bessie Bellwood, from hall to hall. Here, in the background of the painting, are Ada's 'claque'. Ada's audience, as that of *The P.S. Wings in the O.P. Mirror*, is enamoured, each figure lost in the escapism of the hall; their collective glare transfixed towards the stage, either silenced by the power of the performance or wholeheartedly engaging in song.

A final but important point, Sickert predominantly focuses on female performers; indeed, women were a formidable presence on the music hall stage. The 1878 edition of *The Era Almanack*, for example, lists an almost equal division of female to male performers of comic material. Of the 1,883 performers listed, '384 were described as "women serio-comics" and 357 as "male comic singers"'.[26]

In the patriarchal world of the Victorians, music hall offered women opportunity; crucially it provided them with a – very public – voice. It was on a music hall stage that women could explore issues prevalent in their own lives. They could sing of their hopes and disappointments, their fears and their joys, and in doing so share a world intimately familiar with their audience. The songs may have been spiked with humour, but the messages were nonetheless true.

The artist's decision to focus on female performers is significant. Not only do the paintings highlight the popularity of such performers, they also reveal Sickert's admiration of their talent. It is a necessity that performers have the ability to command an audience, especially so on a music hall stage. Perhaps Vesta and Ada demonstrated a stage presence that eluded Sickert during his own days as an actor on the boards of the Lyceum and Sadler's Wells.

Sickert's music hall paintings are palpably evocative. Throughout, he sought to capture the ephemeral moment between audience and performer; that elusive instant when the enchantment of the experience transports the audience. Idiosyncratic of modern city life, the halls were uninhibited, urban and captivatingly vibrant social spaces. For Sickert, they were a subject ripe for modern paint. As he noted in 1889, 'the most fruitful course of study lies in a persistent effort to render the magic and poetry which [artists] daily see around them'.[27] It was such 'magic and poetry' that greeted the artist as he stepped through the doors of his 'dear old oblong Bedford'.[28] The world of the music hall may be long gone, but through Sickert's paintings it can welcome us still.

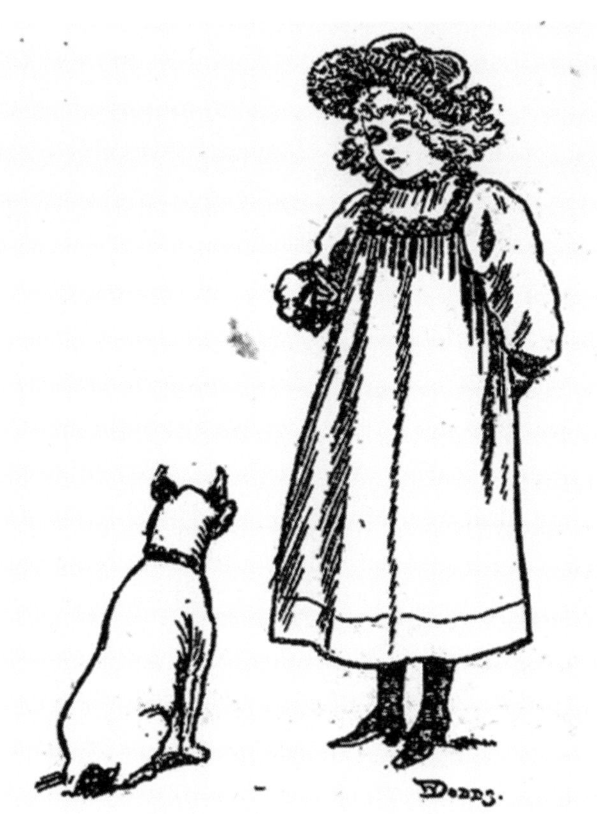

Fig.11
'Miss Vesta Victoria',
The Amusing Journal,
10 June 1893

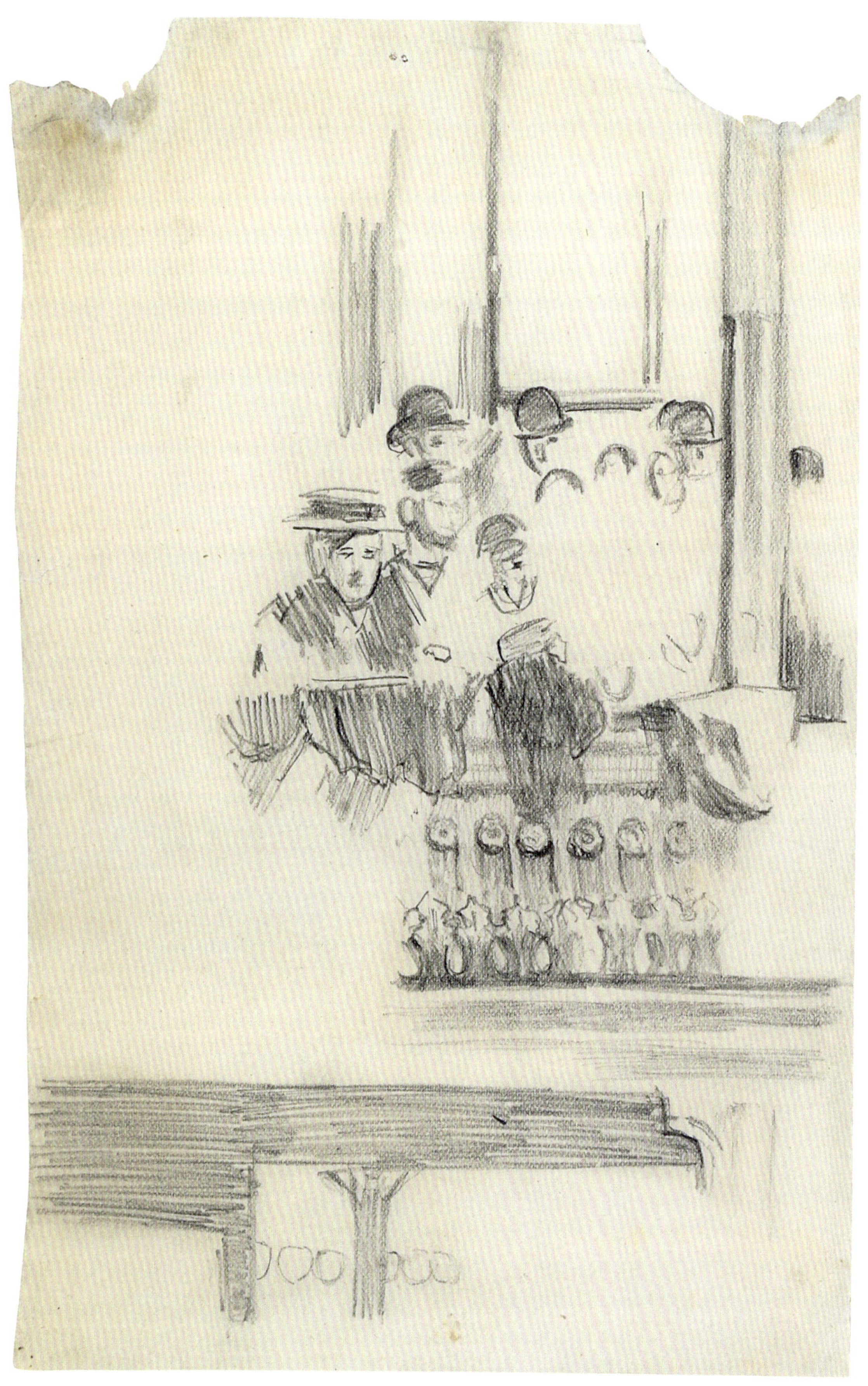

53
Music Hall Gallery with Figures
c.1888
Pencil on paper
National Museums Liverpool,
Walker Art Gallery

84

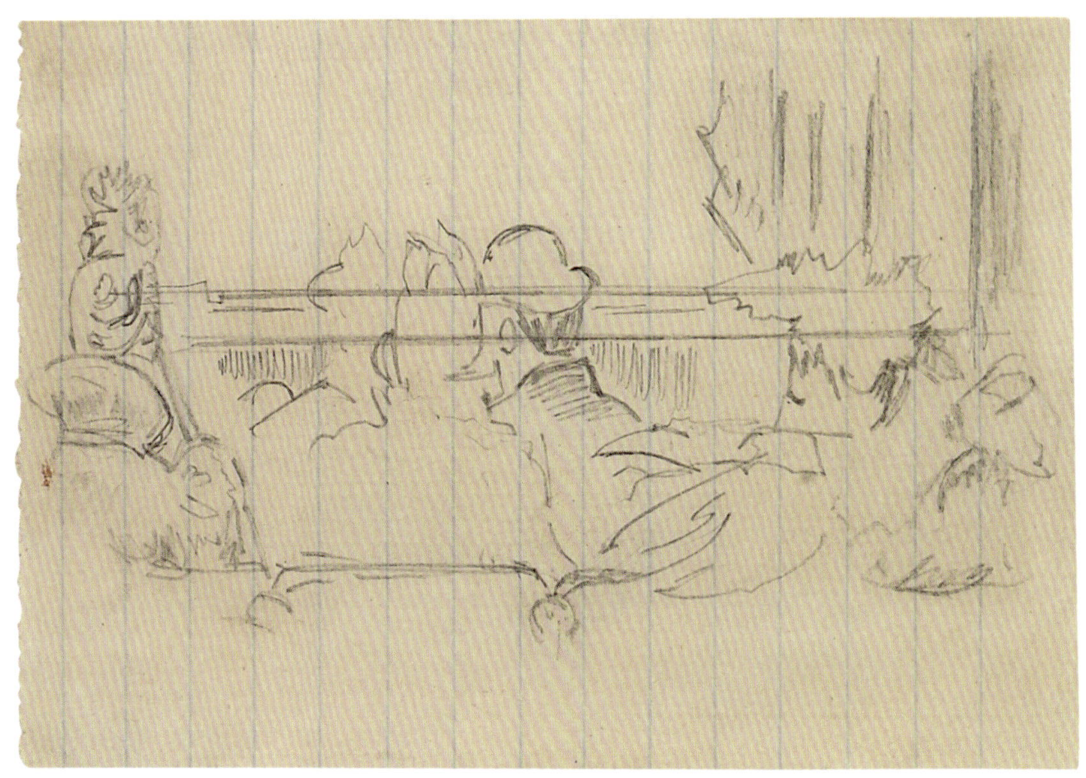

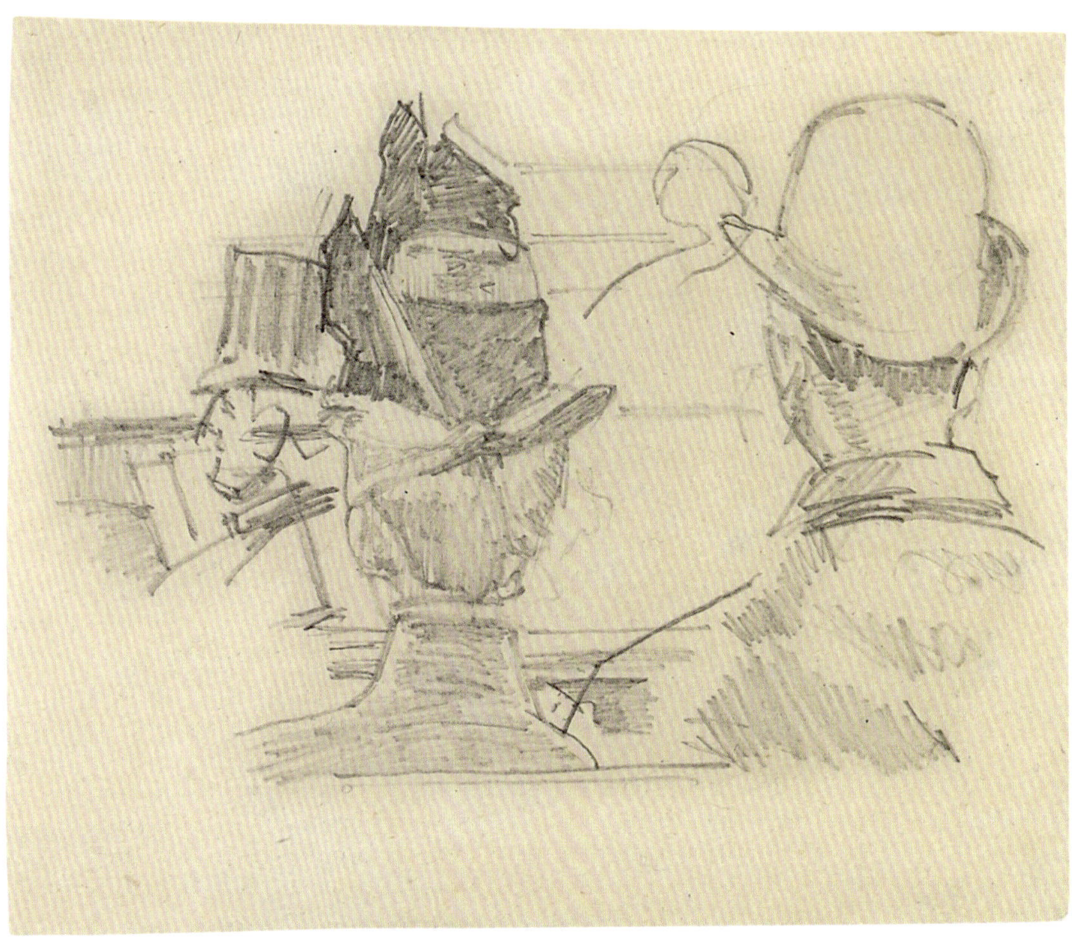

54
Figures in an Auditorium
c.1888
Pencil on lined paper
National Museums Liverpool,
Walker Art Gallery

55
*Audience with Woman in
Hat Seen from the Back*
c.1888
Pencil on paper
National Museums Liverpool,
Walker Art Gallery

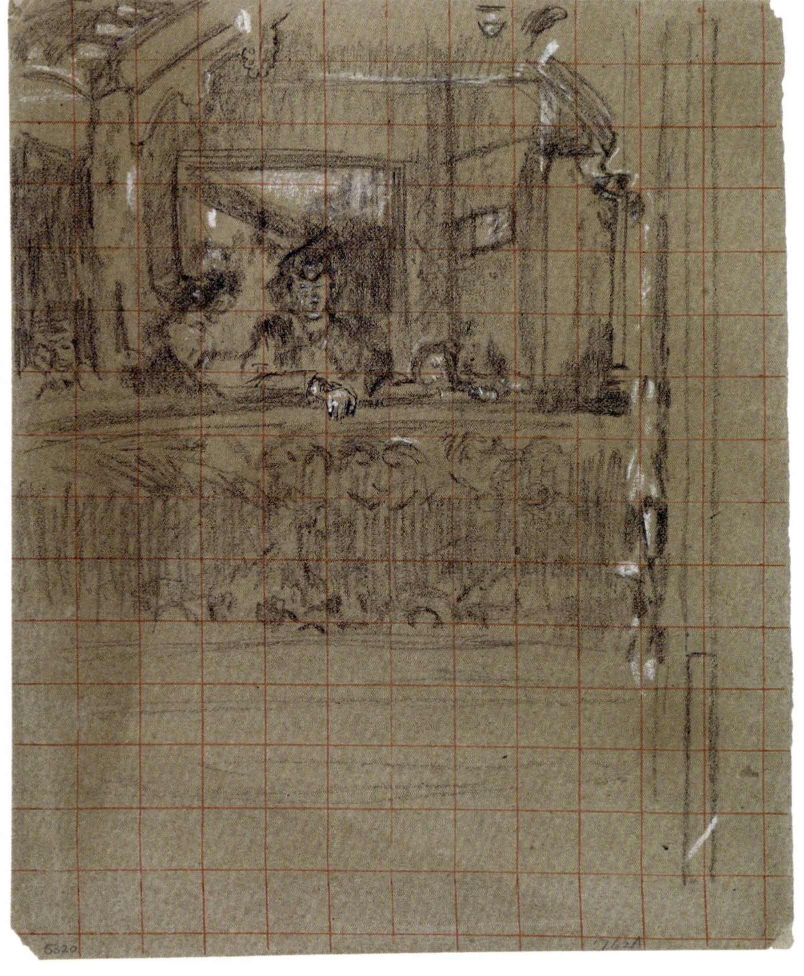

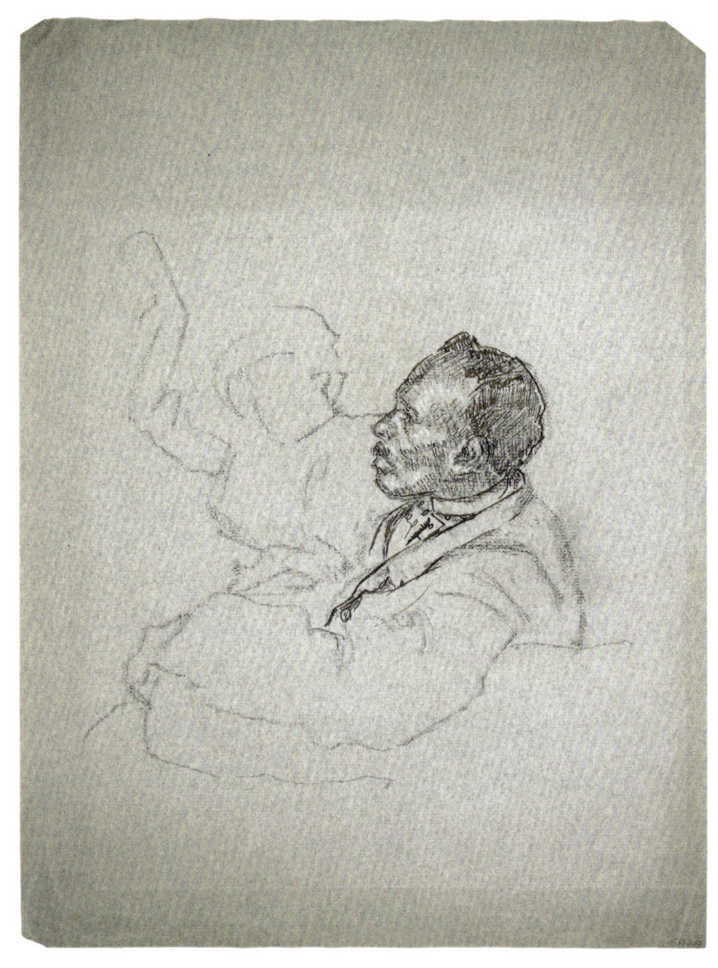

56
*Figures in a Box, Gaîté
Montparnasse* c.1907
Chalk, pen and ink, white
heightening on squared-
up paper
National Museums
Liverpool, Walker Art
Gallery

57
*Man Seated with a Woman
Alongside* c.1913–14
Chalk, pen and ink,
heightened with white,
on paper
National Museums
Liverpool, Walker Art
Gallery

58
*Drawing of a theatre/
music hall audience
[Vernet's café-concert,
Dieppe]* c.1919–20
Ink on paper
Tate

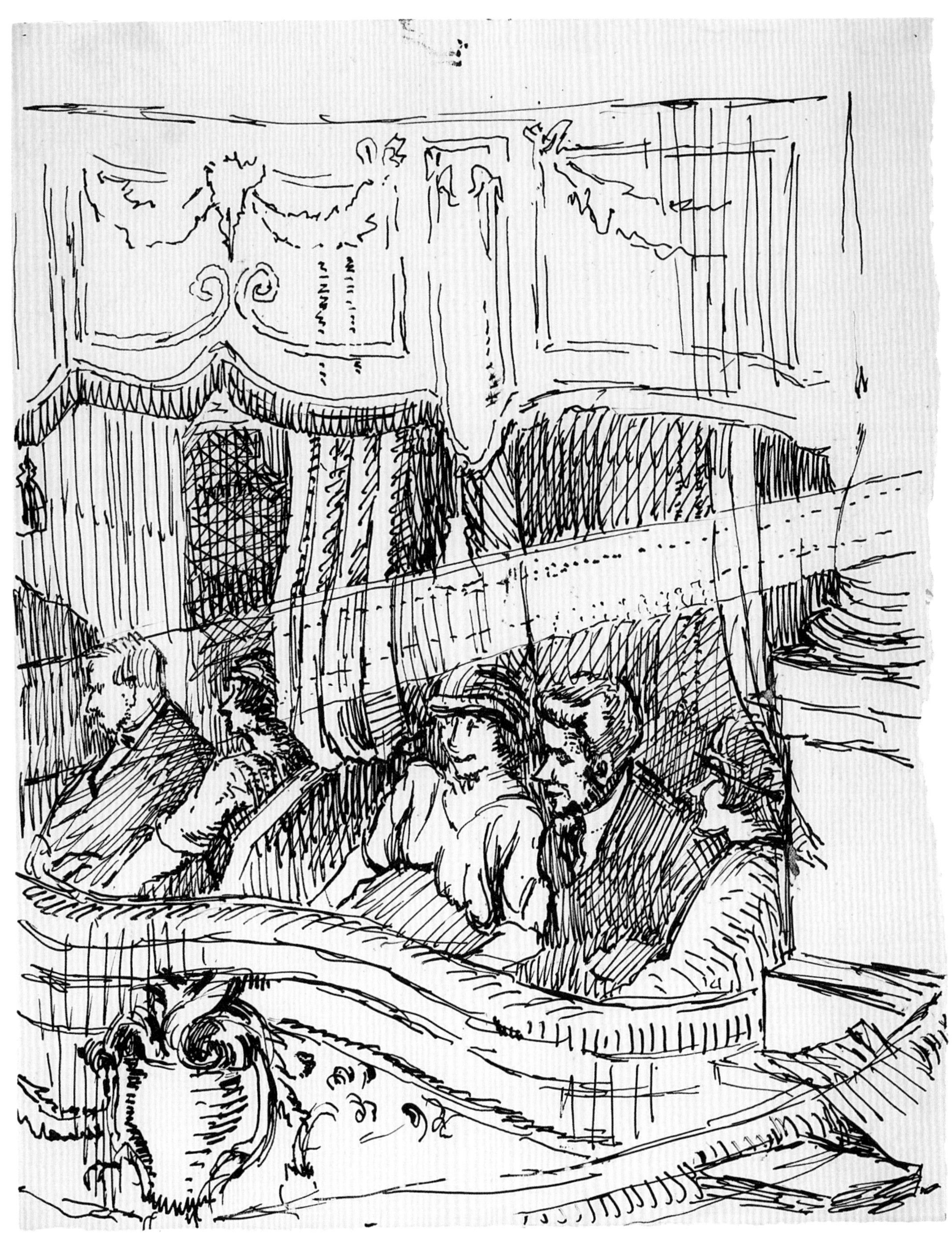

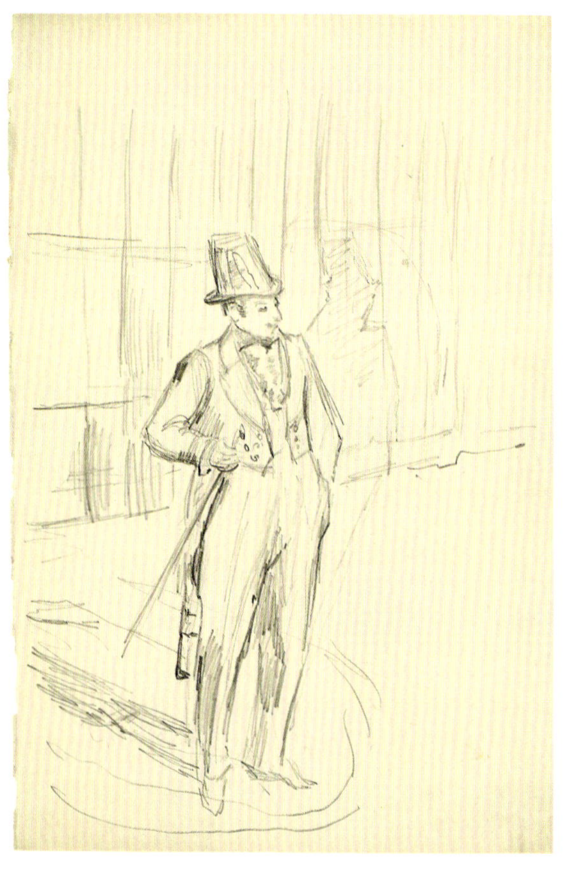

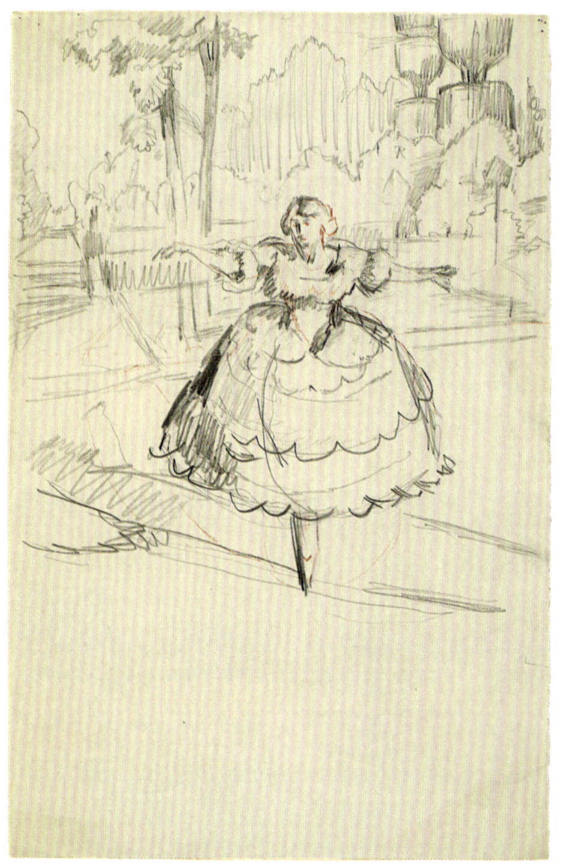

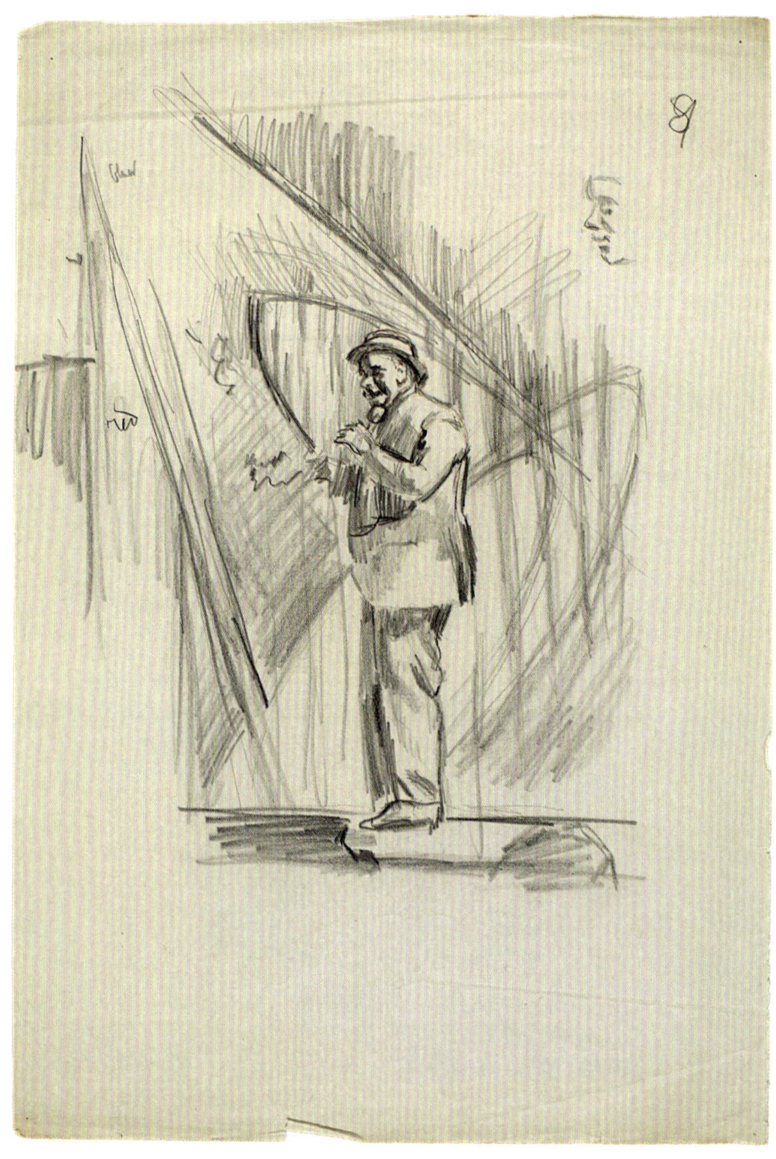

59
Drawing of a man in top hat and coat tails on stage [Vernet's café-concert, Dieppe] c.1919–20
Pencil on paper
Tate

60
Drawing of a ballerina pirouetting c.1919–20
Pencil on paper
Tate. Presented by Mrs Andrina Tritton, December 1981

61
Drawing of a man in hat and jacket on stage [Vernet's café-concert, Dieppe] c.1919–20
Pencil on paper
Tate

62
String Players in a Women's Orchestra c.1922–3
Pencil on paper
National Museums Liverpool, Walker Art Gallery

63
Studies of Dancing Couples n.d.
Pencil on paper
National Museums Liverpool, Walker Art Gallery

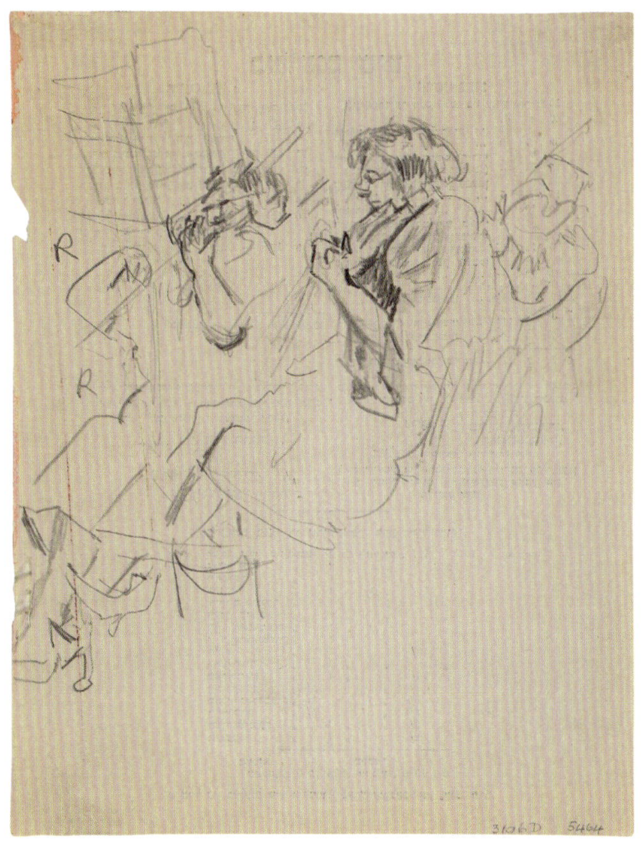

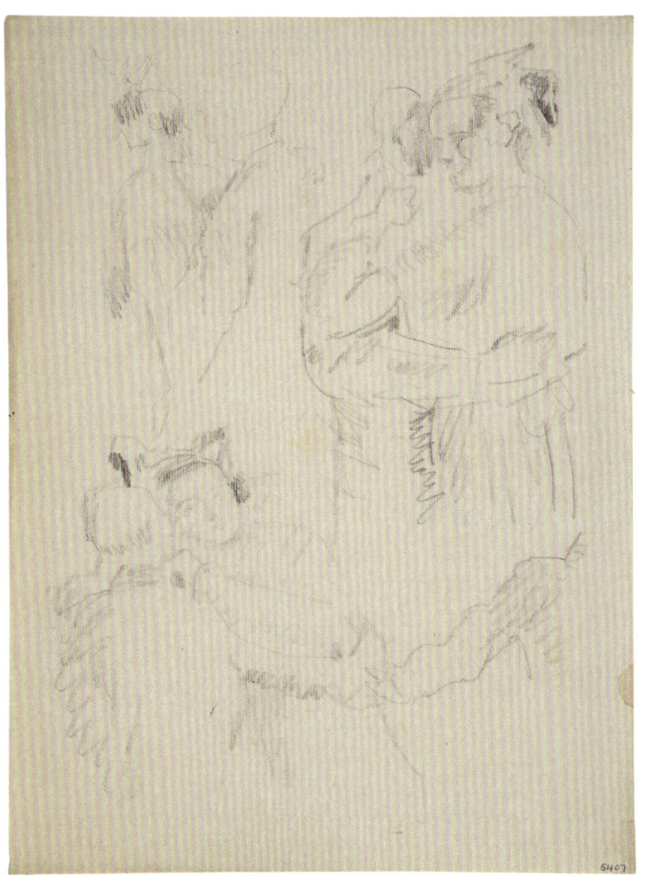

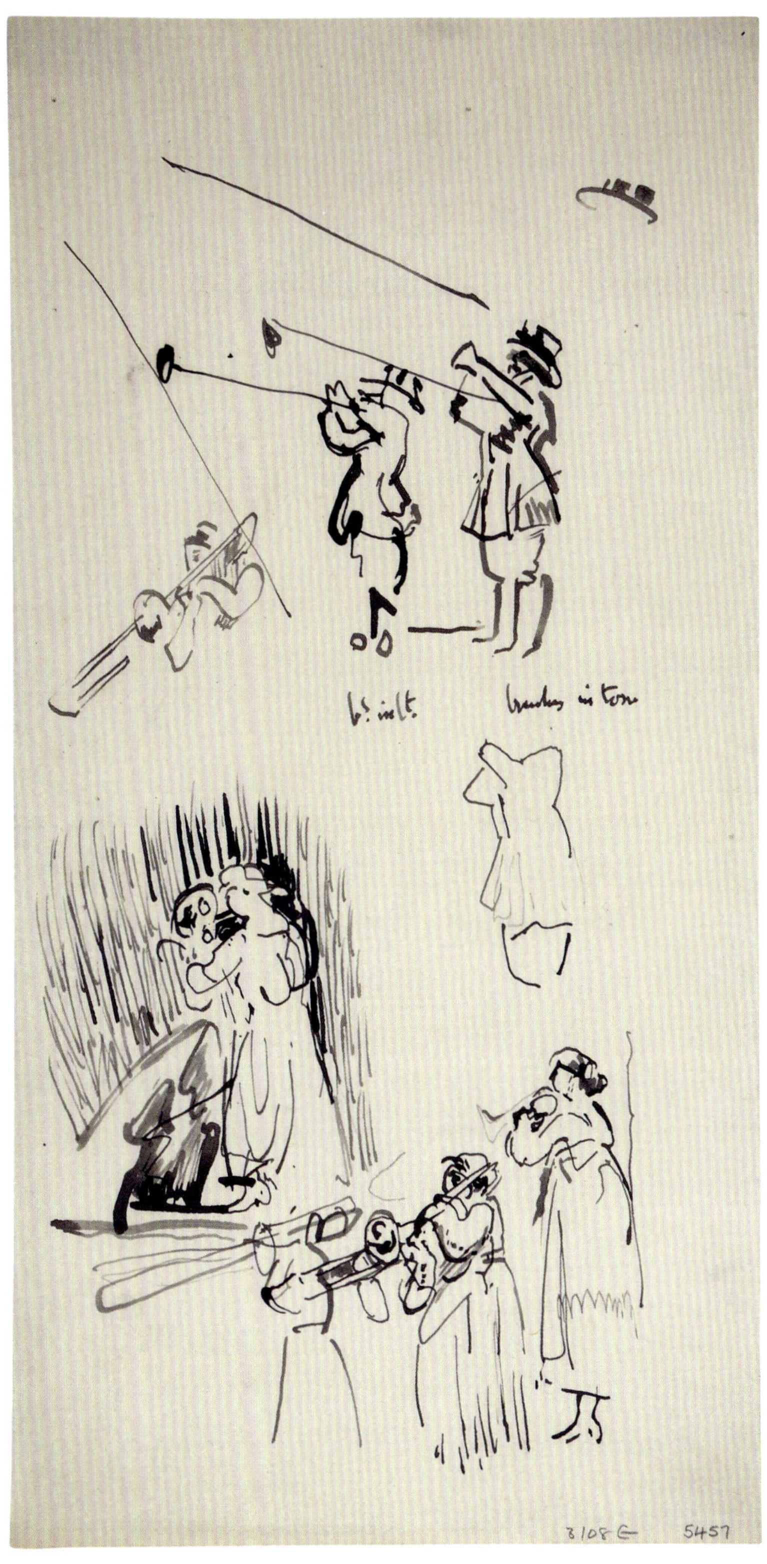

64
Brass and Wind Instrumentalists
c.1922–3
Pencil, pen and ink on paper
National Museums Liverpool,
Walker Art Gallery

BEYOND PORTRAITURE

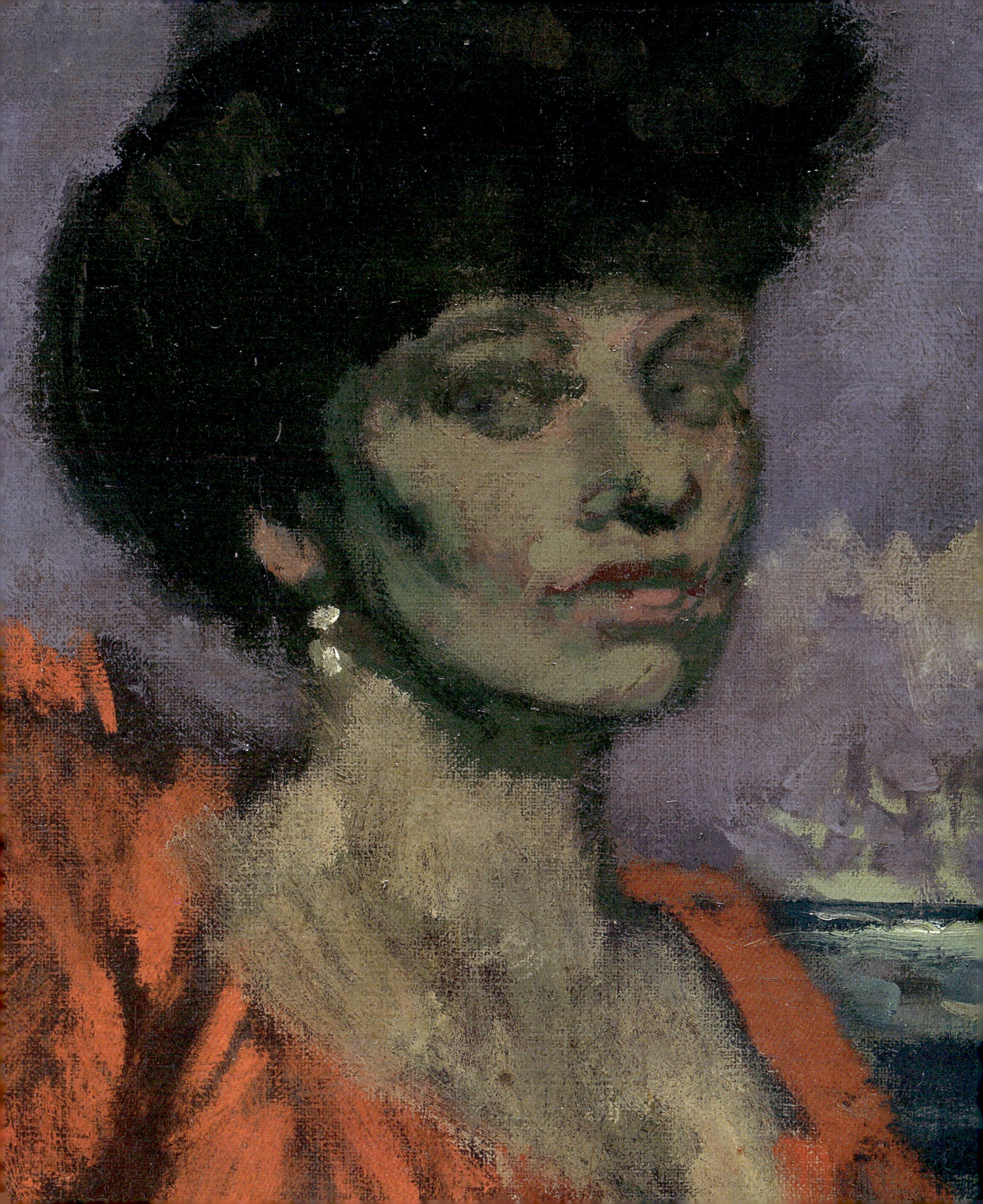

CAROLINE CORBEAU-PARSONS

BEYOND PORTRAITURE: SICKERT AND LIFELIKENESS

Sickert's relationship with portraiture was uneasy. In his writings as an art critic, he oscillated between an indictment of what he described as a commercial venture, and sheer pity for portraitists: 'the portrait-painter is not free – he fills a useful and honourable place in a world of supply and demand'.[1] Sickert did turn to portraiture in the 1890s, at a time when his marriage with Ellen Cobden was breaking down, and his footing was more uncertain. Significantly, more than half of the paintings that he exhibited at the New English Art Club (NEAC) between 1890 and 1895 were portraits. From a man who later described exhibitions as 'mainly useful … as advertisement',[2] this focus on a potentially money-spinning genre must have been a deliberate strategy. Sickert, however, was not highly successful in his endeavour to develop a portrait practice. At least, not on the shaky premise that he had serious ambitions of rivalling successful society portraitists.

Sickert painted a number of artistic personalities. While some of these portraits played a part in his exhibition strategy, they were no lucrative commissions. The sophisticated full-length painting of Philip Wilson Steer (see fig.12), seated nonchalantly in front of his own *Portrait of Miss Fancourt*, was among the works exhibited in 1890 at the NEAC. There,

visitors could see its pendant, a portrait of Sickert by Steer (now lost). Sickert also made a highly spontaneous, near-calligraphic portrait of his friend Aubrey Beardsley, the famous illustrator, emaciated by tuberculosis but always a dandy (see no.65). Later, in the 1900s, Sickert made an impressionistic portrait of the painter Jacques-Émile Blanche, a friend and patron, wearing a top hat (see no.67), opting to represent him as a socialite rather than an artist, as well as a dappled head of Harold Gilman (no.68), a fellow member of the Camden Town Group. The latter, although painted with a great economy of means, reflects the painting style of the group and captures Gilman's piercing, intense gaze. All these works, however, belong firmly in the category of the friendship portrait, and all were gifts to the sitters.

Sickert counted the celebrity writer Israel Zangwill among his sitters (see no.66), but this leading figure of Zionism was a friend of Ellen Cobden, and his portrait may also have been painted as a token of their friendship, or at a discounted fee, rather than as a profitable commission. The Sickerts and Zangwill spent time together in Venice. The Venetian architectural background against which Sickert represented him in profile may refer to this, as well as to Zangwill's *Children of the Ghetto*, set in Venice. Sickert did not paint many members of the elite, who traditionally were the main commissioners of portraits. *Mrs Swinton* 1906 (see no.69) is a notable exception and an enlightening example. John Singer Sargent, the chief portrait painter of the elite, had executed a full-length, dazzling, grand manner portrait of her ten years earlier (see fig.14). As would have been expected of Sargent, it projected of Mrs Swinton a poised, glamorous image that asserted her high status in society – by birth, by marriage, and as one of the most gifted singers in London. She was not just any sitter to Sickert, however. Richard Shone recorded that he met her at a party organised by Mrs Charles Hunter, a notable patron of the arts, to enable Rodin 'to meet the most beautiful women in London', and that Sickert 'obviously fell in love with her' then.[3] He painted three formal portraits of her, none commissions, and all departing from the canons of society portraiture.

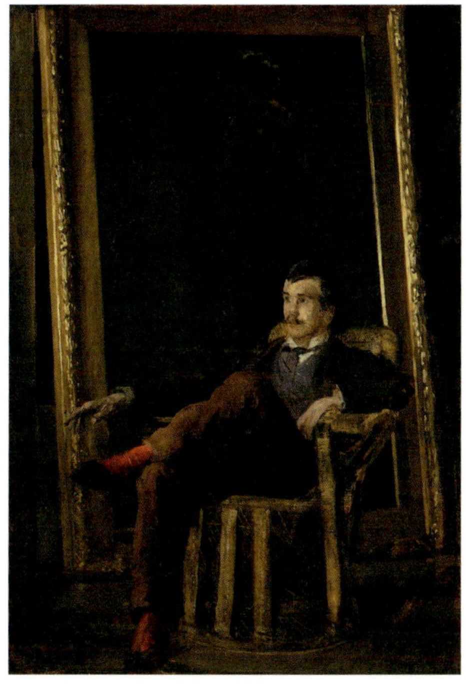

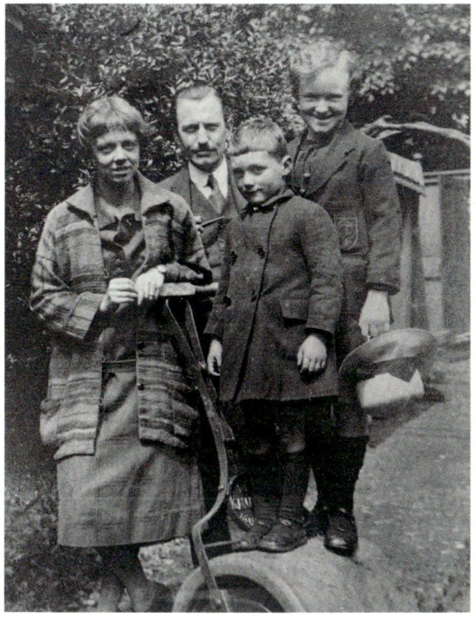

Far from depicting an English rose, like Sargent, *Mrs Swinton* is a half-length portrait of a mysterious, sensual woman with olive skin and generous lips and décolletage. In Virginia Woolf's words: 'She has seen every sort of sunrise and sunset whether dressed in diamonds or white night-gown; now all is ruin and shipwreck…'[4] The prominent background has traditionally been understood to represent Venice, where Mrs Swinton had actually never been.[5] Her portrait was painted from a photograph,[6] with the paint thinly applied, and the overall picture has an experimental quality to it. Her right hand is more indicated than clearly modelled, and from close-up her irises appear to be partially obscured by a veil of flesh-coloured paint, to uncanny effect. *Mrs Swinton* says little about the class, wealth and profession of the sitter, and more about Sickert's constant explorations in oil.

Revealingly, when describing the formal full-length portrait known as *Victor Lecour* (see no.79),[7] Sickert did not use the term 'portrait' to refer to the work. In a letter to his sister-in-law, Andrina Schweder, he explained that he was 'having sittings by electric light nearly every day' and was 'deep in figure subjects again… I am painting … Victor Lecour [*sic*], a superb creature, who used to run the Clos Normand at Martin Église.'[8] The resulting picture combines areas of bold, flat colour with rhythmic patterning, and reveals artificial lighting as one of Sickert's main preoccupations in this work. The back of Lecourt's suit and the outline of his beard are ablaze with light, which also bounces off the gold foil of the wallpaper motifs behind him, suffusing this evening scene with warmth. The rich, colourful interior in which Lecourt is posed is reminiscent of paintings by the Nabis, and Sickert's approach to Lecourt in this work recalls Édouard Vuillard's statement: 'I don't paint portraits, I paint people in their homes.'[9] Sickert's dramatic portrait of Cicely Hey 1923 (see no.78) focuses more on her face than on her surroundings, but its disquieting quality raises questions about his artistic goal with this picture. His fascination for the expressive power of light arguably climaxed in this work. A photograph in Sickert's archive of the artist and designer Hey (see fig.13) reveals the extent to which

he exaggerated the distorting effect of the light emitted by his studio's fireplace on her features. This striking monochrome painting underlines the fact that Sickert's primary interest as a portraitist lay not so much in psychology and characterisation as in the plastic powers of paint.

Sickert's ceaseless technical exploration of the medium, a driving principle in his art, blurs the categories of portraiture and figure painting in his oeuvre. Society portraiture aside, if one accepts Marcia Pointon's rigorous definition of a portrait – 'strictly speaking to mean an individual known to have lived depicted for his or her own sake. Some might add that a portrait, properly speaking, should aim to represent body and soul, or physical and mental presence'[10] – then Sickert did relatively few of them between the mid-1890s and mid-1920s, the time-span of this section. *Blackbird of Paradise* c.1892 (see no.73), with its vigorous, slashing brushstrokes, appears more like a *tête de caractère* for exuberance and energy than a portrait. Tellingly, it was first exhibited as 'A study of expression', and it was only later that Sickert adopted a title alluding to his favourite poem by W.H. Davies, 'The Bird of Paradise'. Similarly, *Jeanne. The Cigarette* 1906 (see no.74) appears more as the representation of a lively type than a portrait of the Belgian milliner Jeanne Daurmont, who, like her sister Hélène, modelled for Sickert. As Andrew Causey has argued, 'Sickert seems to have been more interested in generalising types of people than in actual portrait painting. This does not mean that he is distant or uncommitted in his attitude, as has sometimes been claimed… In many ways he is a genre or type painter rather than a portraitist.'[11] The same applies to the intimate paintings *The Mantelpiece* c.1906 (see no.75), *Girl at a Window, Little Rachel* 1907 (no.76) and *The New Home* 1908 (no.77), all single female figures in interiors inviting questions about their story.

Sickert the art critic denounced what he saw as the contrivance of the conventions of formal portraiture, their lack of truth and resulting inanity. Taking the fictitious Tilly Pullen as an example, he wrote: 'let us strip

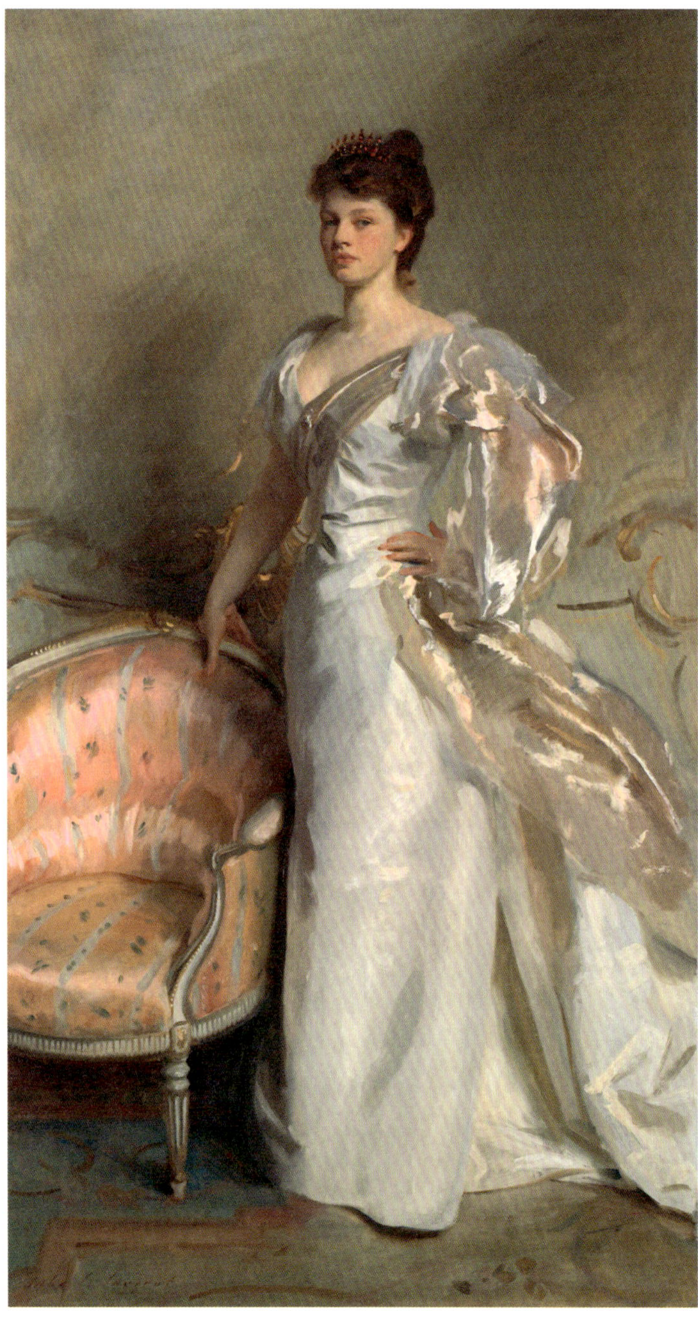

Tilly Pullen of her lendings and tell her to put her own things on again. Let her leave the studio and climb the first dirty little staircase in the first shabby little house. Tilly Pullen becomes interesting at once. She is in surroundings that mean something. She becomes stuff for a picture. Follow her into her kitchen, or, better still, for the artist has the divine privilege of omnipresence, into her bedroom; and now Tilly Pullen is become the stuff of which the Parthenon was made…'[12] Sickert took this aesthetic programme to the letter in Italy, when the sex workers he hired as models, most of all Carolina dell'Acqua and La Giuseppina, fuelled his artistic imagination. In *La Giuseppina against a Map of Venice* c.1903–4 (see no.72), the introspective young woman, posed against the floral motifs of an orange couch, her black hair up in a bun, evokes a geisha. In *Le Châle Vénitien* 1903–4 (see no.70), the model (in all likelihood Carolina) sits gracefully, full-length, at the end of the same couch, in a bare interior, looking amused and straight at the viewer, offering willingly a glimpse into her simple life. Sickert built her facial features through blotchy tonal brush marks, leaving them largely undefined, while still conveying her expression and mood. In *Two Women on a Sofa – Le Tose* (see no.71),[13] which belongs to the same period, Carolina and La Giuseppina's features are entirely blurred, and yet Sickert still successfully sketched out the emotional connection between the sitters and the narrative of lives. This picture marks a transition, equally blurred, between portraiture, figure studies and Sickert's renewal of the conversation piece (see p.166). Carolina and La Giuseppina were soon to pose to Sickert in a bedroom, much like Tilly Pullen, in the nude.

Fig.14
John Singer Sargent,
*Mrs. George Swinton
(Elizabeth Ebsworth)*
1897, oil paint on
canvas, 231×124,
Wirt D. Walker Collection

KAYE DONACHIE

ON SICKERT'S PORTRAITS THAT TELL A STORY

Virginia Woolf, in her essay 'Walter Sickert: A Conversation' (1934), recalls a fellow dinner guest's comment about Sickert's paintings: 'When he paints a portrait I read a life.' Woolf, thinking through the implications of this comment, had more sympathy for the idea that 'Sickert always seems more of a novelist than a biographer… He likes to set his characters in motion…'

This way of reading a painting – of allowing narrative impulses to emerge from inventive painterly descriptions – interests me. Sickert honed his vocabulary through preliminary sketches as structure, building the pace with tonal marks towards the final scene. The image emerges through expressive impasto daubs and strokes, evoking its subject and stories.

Mrs Swinton 1906 (see no.69) boldly depicts Mrs George Swinton (Elizabeth Ebsworth), a prominent Edwardian society figure. Mrs Swinton was a regular sitter for Sickert and other artists of the time. A brief career as a professional singer and performer was curtailed by family pressures, followed by charity work and investment in esoteric philosophies. The face is mask-like, the profile three-quarter, eyes fixed and partially glazed, perhaps preoccupied by people or events off set, elsewhere in the studio. The sitter, melodramatically, is both a projection and a reflection of affect, her sharp, glass-like expression a mirror to us all.

Curiously, Sickert places his subject against a Venetian setting, a city Mrs Swinton had never visited. This fictionalised composition is a particularly interesting fabrication. The landscape amplifies the artifice of the theatrical backdrop for the fictionalised performer. The muted green tones of the water peek through parts of her red dress and body, as if the scene were a film still caught midway in a cinematic dissolve. The figure and the background are painted with the same intensity, compressing the image into one moment of time.

The genre of portraiture fills museum and gallery walls, creating shadows of protagonists who weave time, history and power through a cast of the represented and the unrepresented. Sickert's portraits plot points of interest as he manages to go beyond the academic. For me, he is a painter who constructs ideas forged through his stylistic choices. I read Sickert's portraiture as a coat hanger on which he confers actors, framed through recollection and emotional connection, conjured in the act of painting. The gaps of unpainted canvas, created by scumbled brush marks dragged across a surface, articulate forms that seem to fade towards the edges of the frame and can be read as spaces or openings for subjective elucidation.

I enjoy the sense of theatricality in his portraits and the technical lens-like adjustments which pull into sharp focus the faces emerging from the grubby, blurred grounds. Sickert's experiments with painting show a changing visual world. He seeks to capture the electric atmosphere of early cinema; his paintings contend with the theatre of images, seemingly predicting the cultural significance of montage and assemblage.

Sickert's haptic melodramas attempt to move away from the literal descriptions of specific sitters 'setting his characters in motion'. Painting, instead, moves towards figuring a fiction, forming characters who are invented and evolve through painterly and compositional decisions.

If we consider Sickert a novelist, as Woolf did, then his fiction remains deliberately fragmented, leaving a narrative that is always present and continually reimagined. His portraits are stories constructed and captured within multiple time frames, making them as vital now as they were historically. He allows us to consider the portrait as a timely screen – an imaginative, playful stage onto which we have permission to continually re-enact our own emotive scripts.

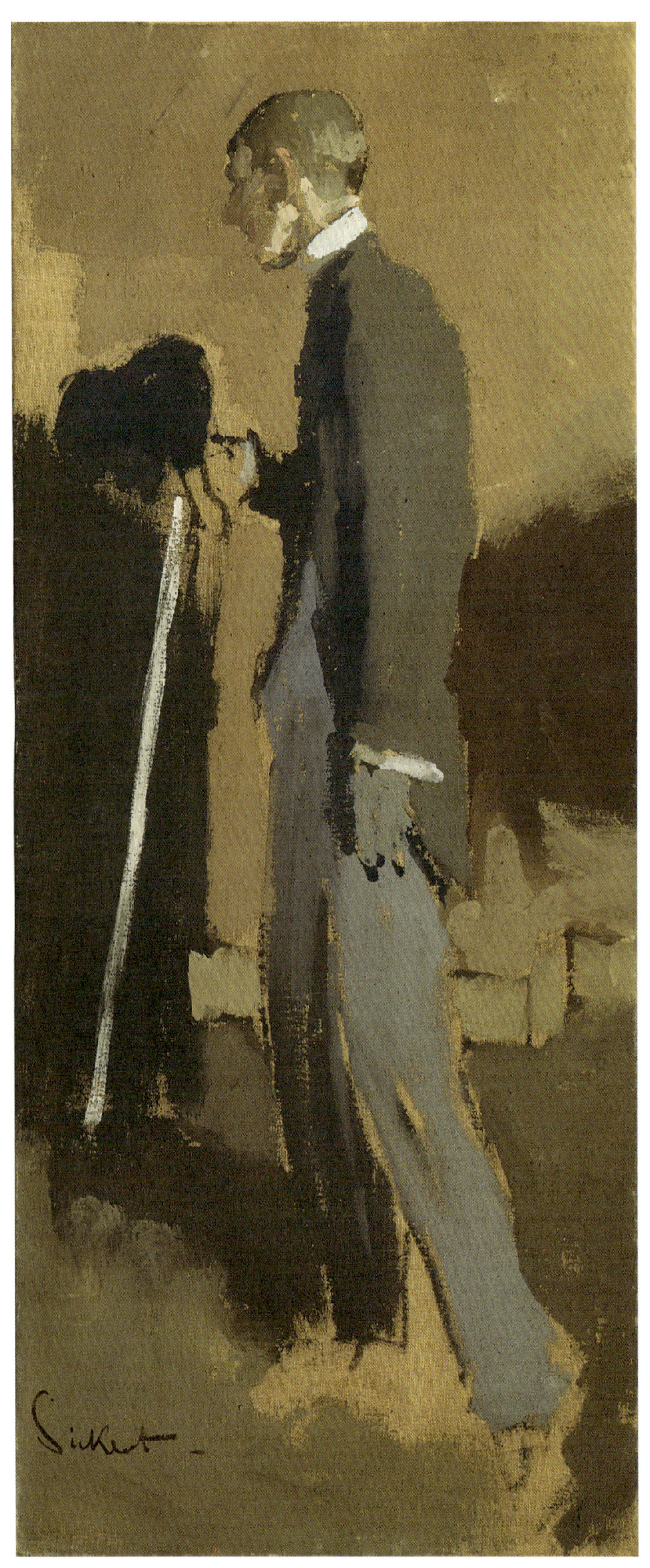

65
Aubrey Beardsley 1894
Tempera on canvas
Tate

66
Israel Zangwill c.1896–8
Oil paint on canvas laid
on board
National Galleries of
Scotland

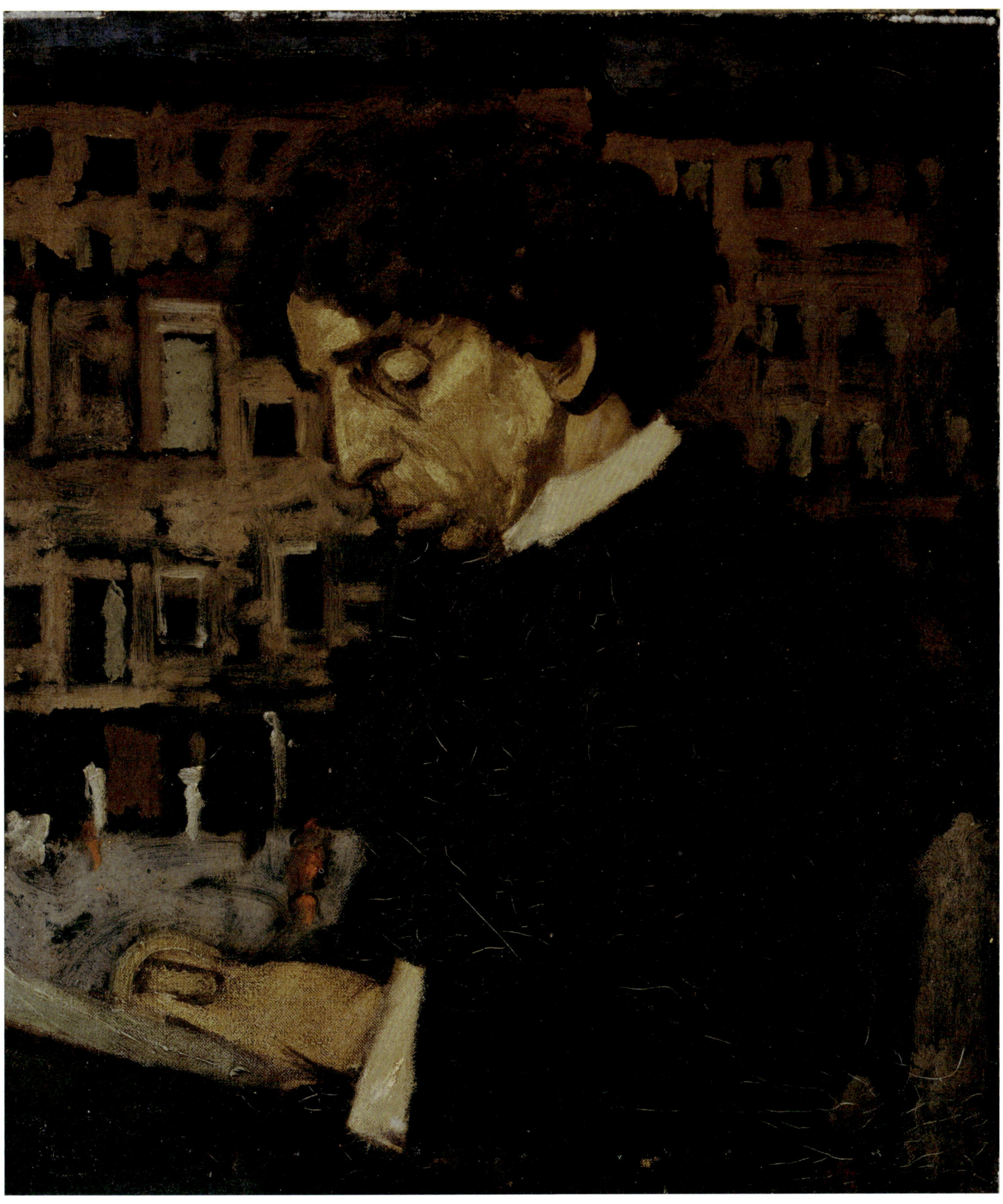

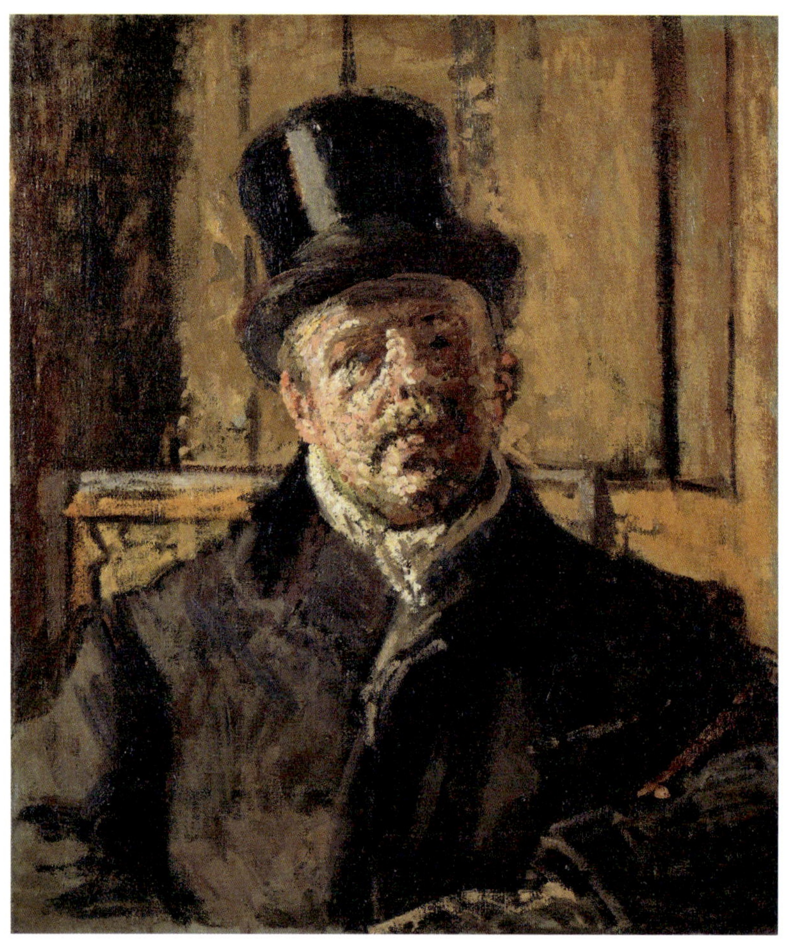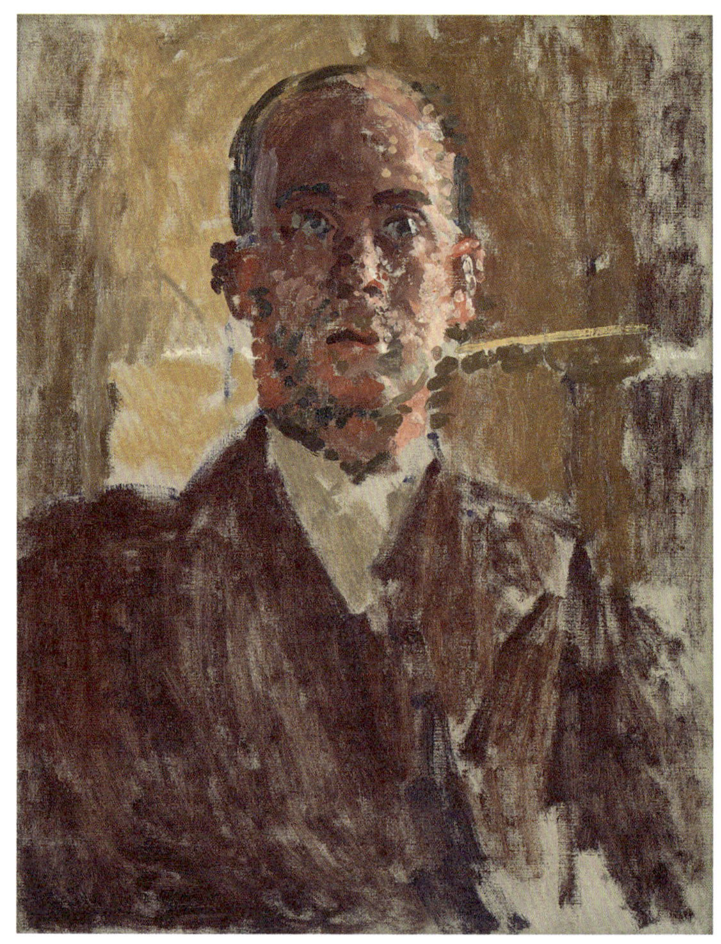

67
Jacques-Émile Blanche
c.1910
Oil paint on canvas
Tate

68
Harold Gilman c.1912
Oil paint on canvas
Tate

69
Mrs Swinton 1906
Oil paint on canvas
The Syndics of the
Fitzwilliam Museum,
University of Cambridge

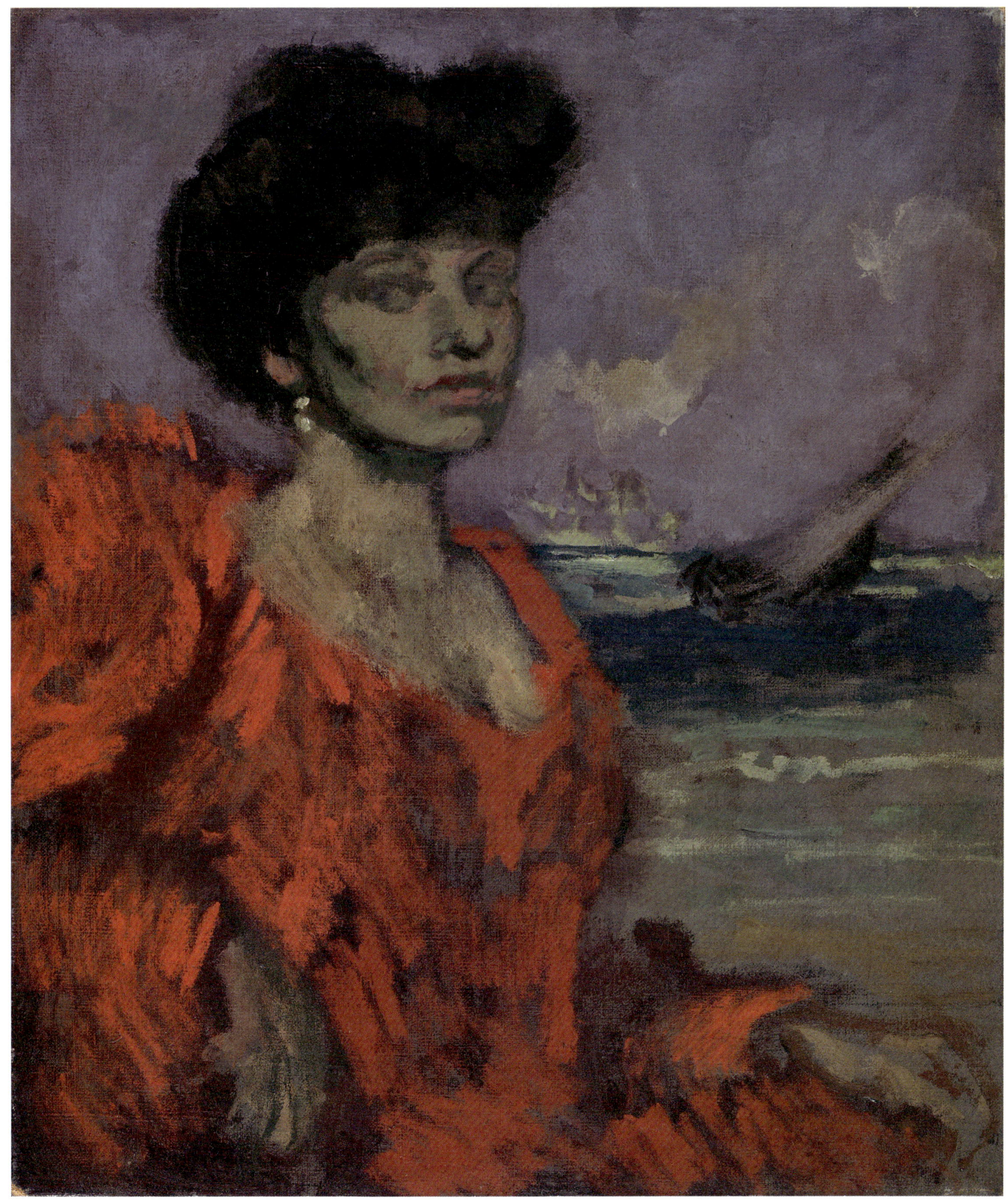

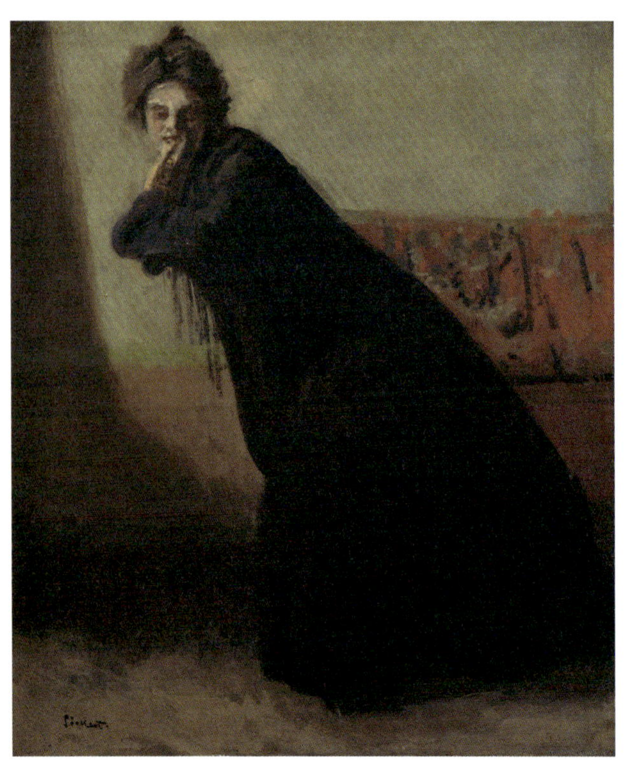

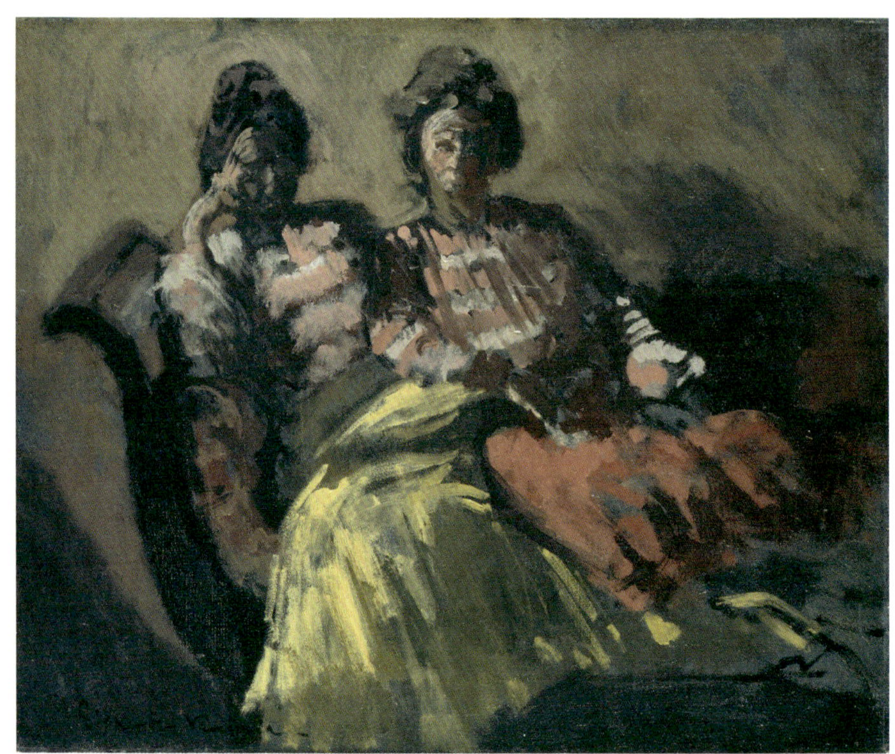

70
Le Châle Vénitien 1903–4
Oil paint on canvas
Ivor Braka

71
*Two Women on a Sofa –
Le Tose* c.1903–4
Oil paint on canvas
Tate

72
*La Giuseppina against a
Map of Venice* c.1903–4
Oil paint on canvas
Mr and Mrs Michael
Hughes

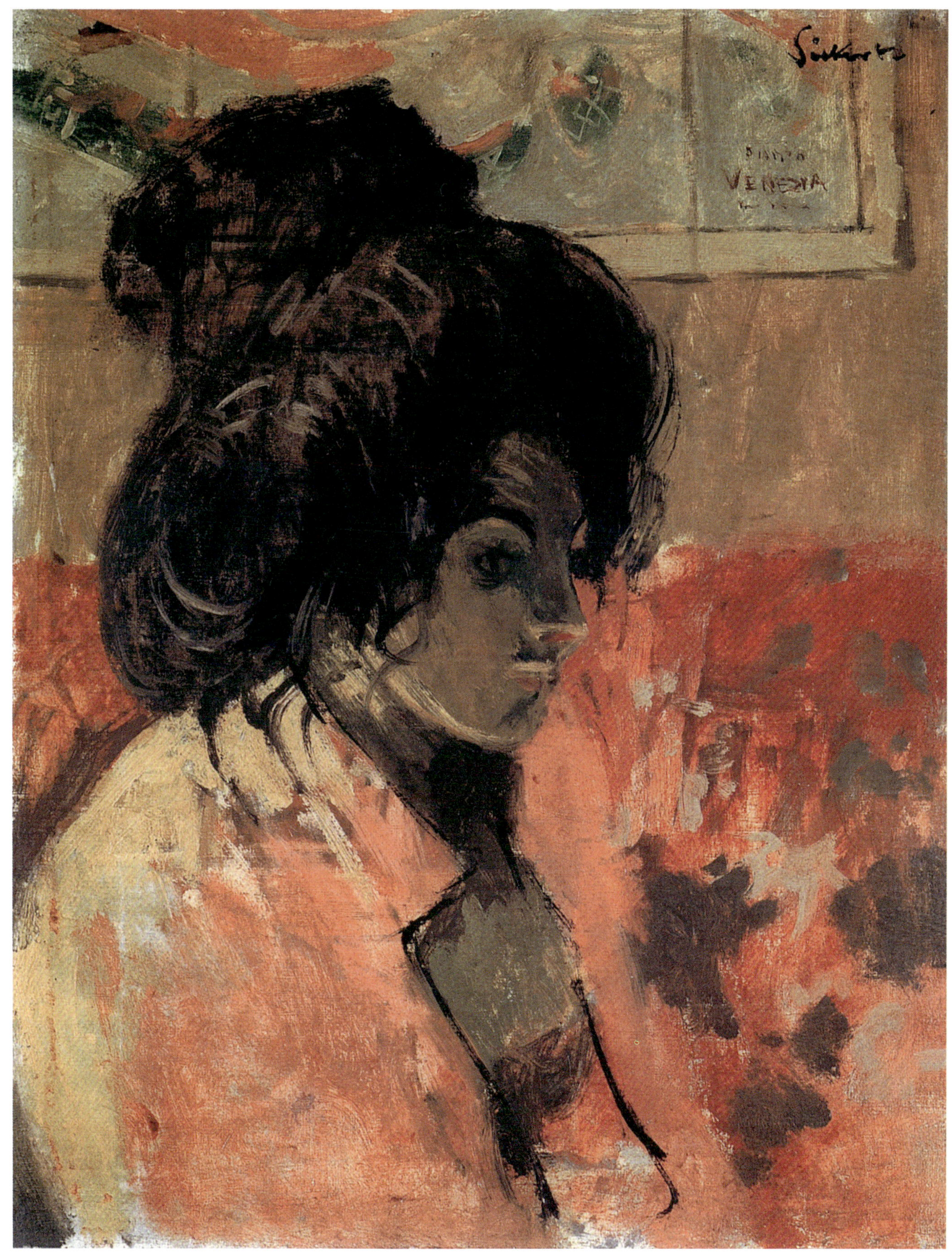

VENEZIA

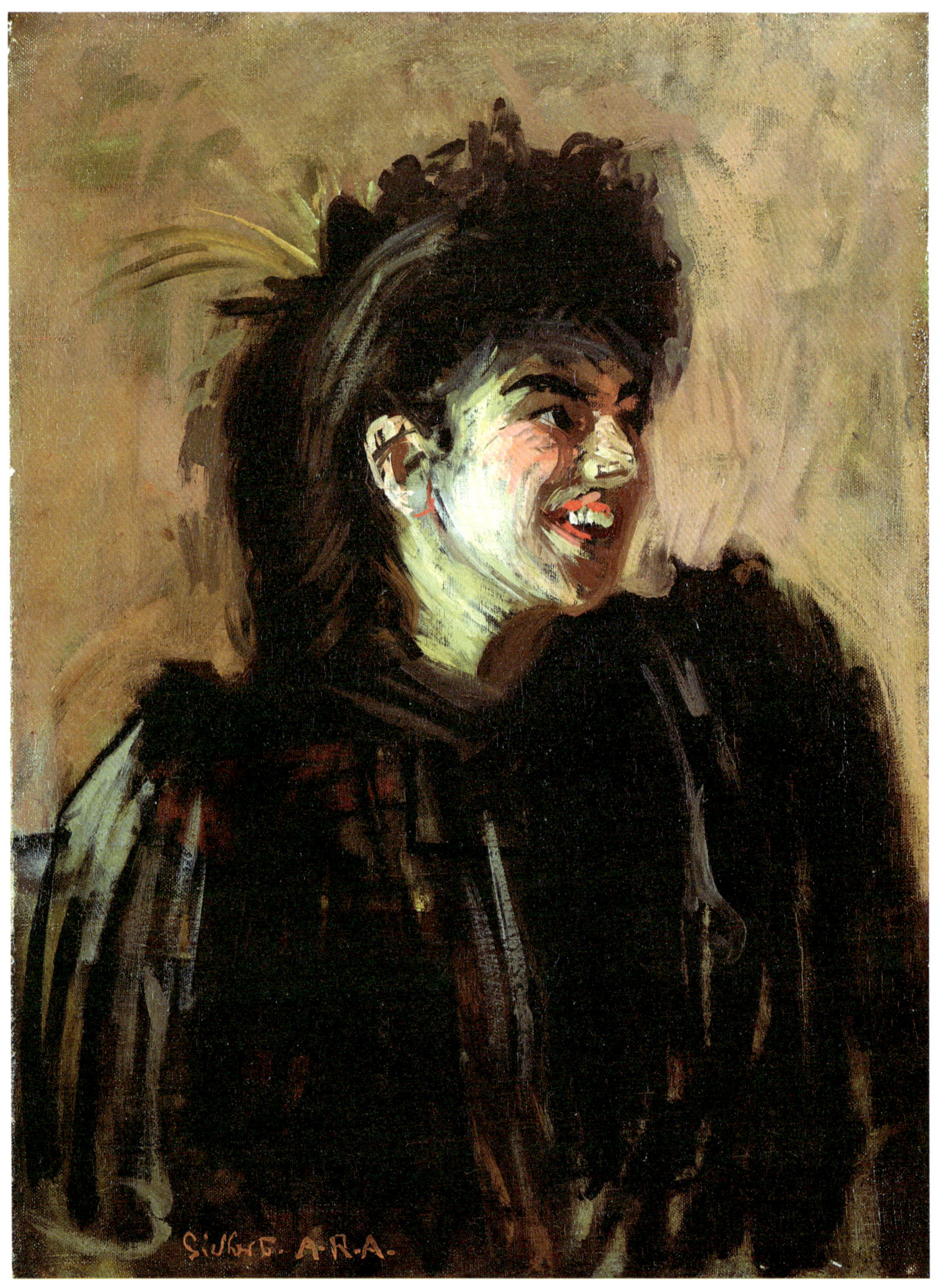

73
Blackbird of Paradise
c.1892
Oil paint on canvas
Leeds Museums and
Galleries

74
Jeanne. The Cigarette
1906
Oil paint on canvas
The Metropolitan
Museum of Art

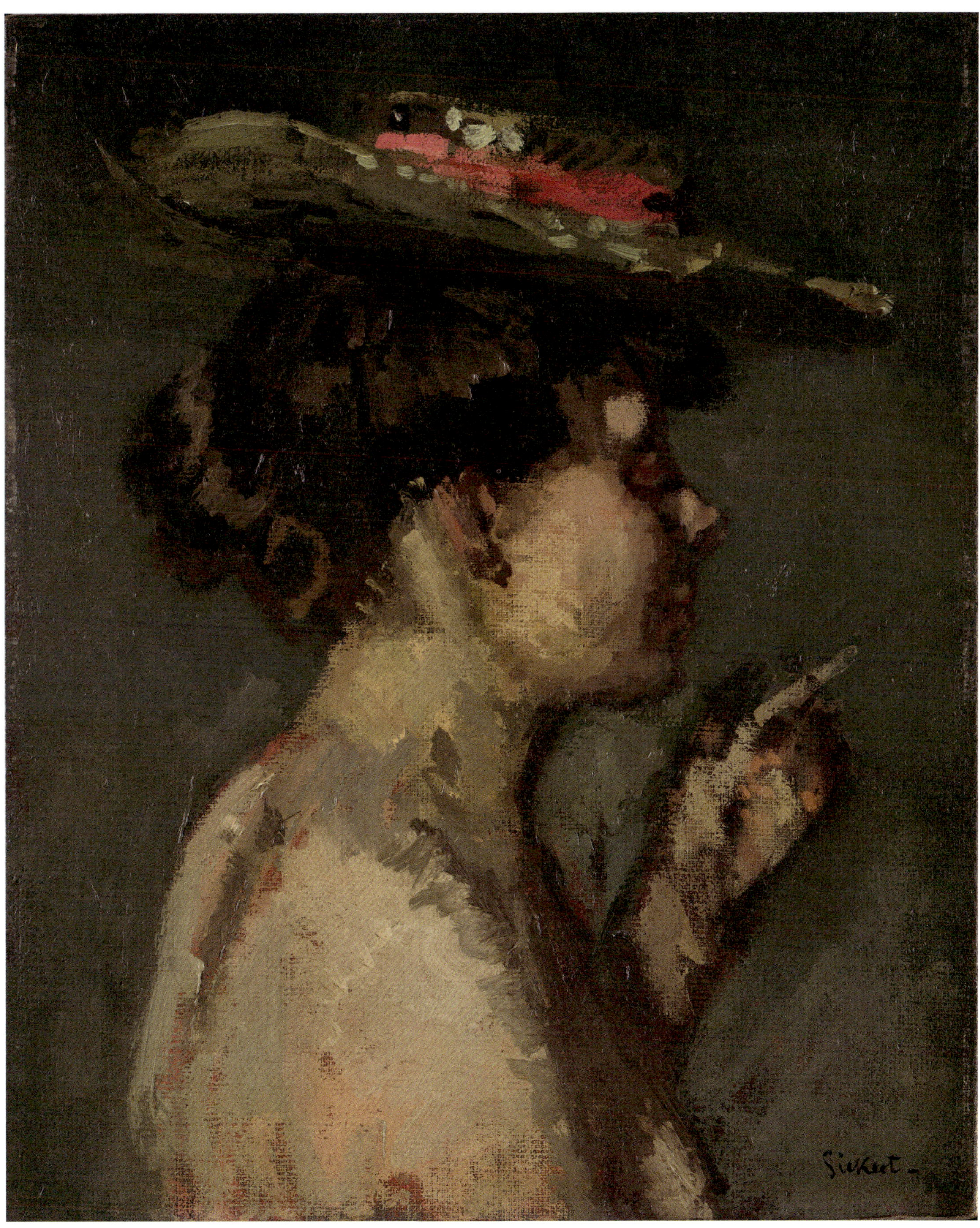

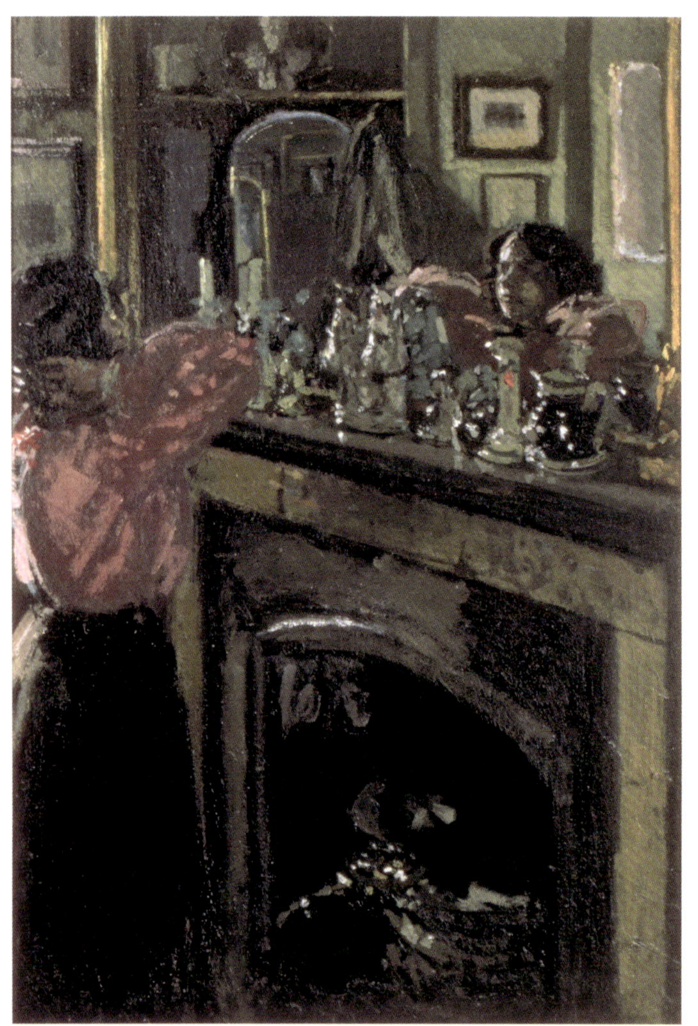

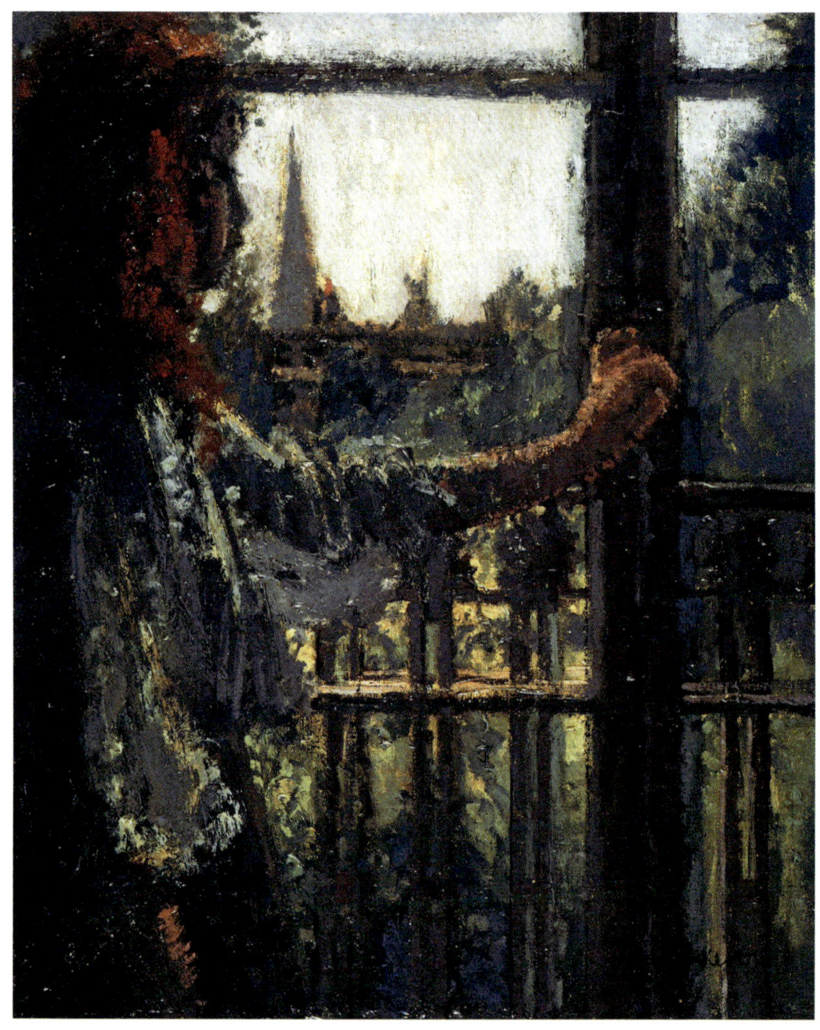

75
The Mantelpiece
c.1906
Oil paint on canvas
Southampton City
Art Gallery

76
Girl at a Window,
Little Rachel 1907
Oil paint on canvas
Tate

77
The New Home 1908
Oil paint on canvas
Ivor Braka

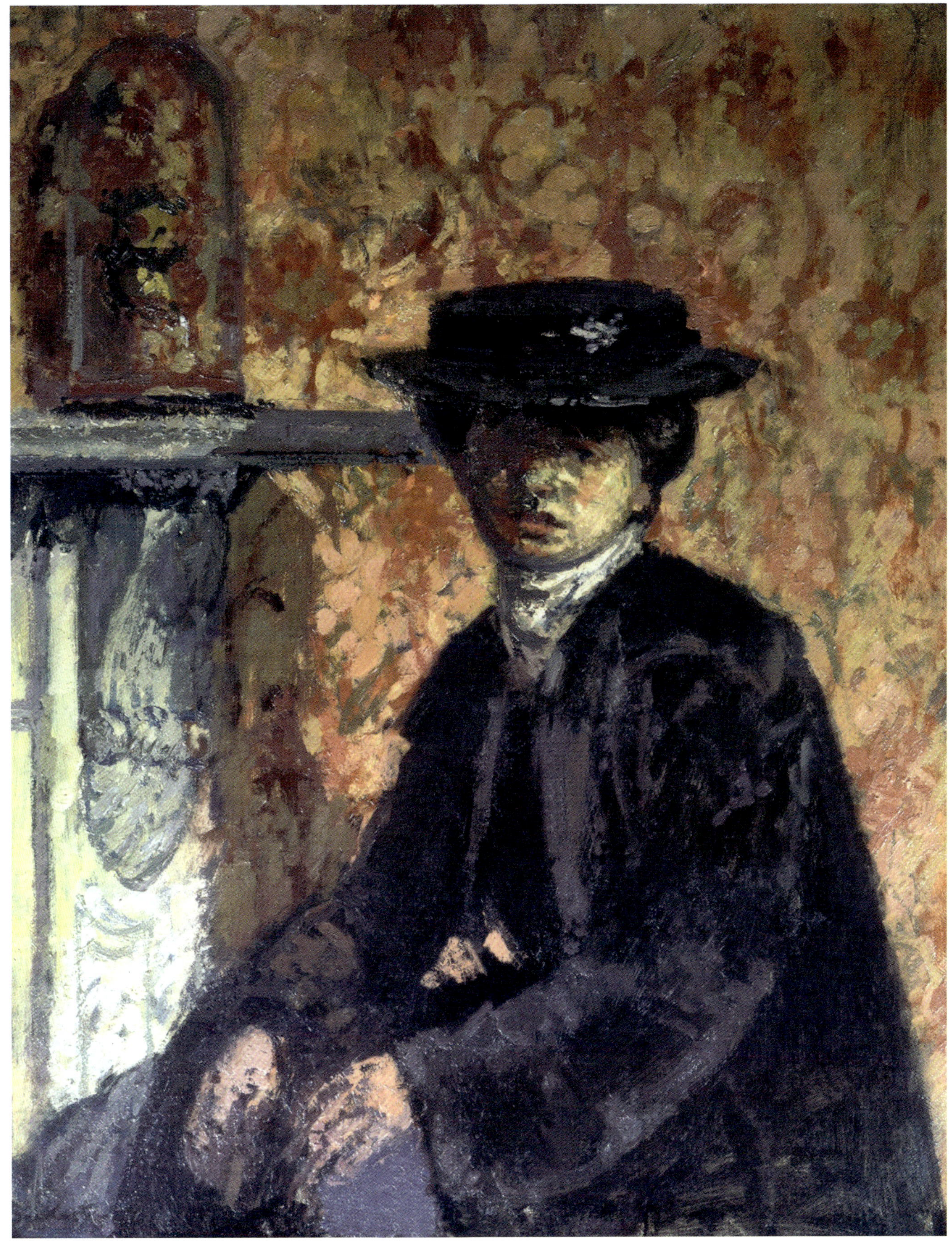

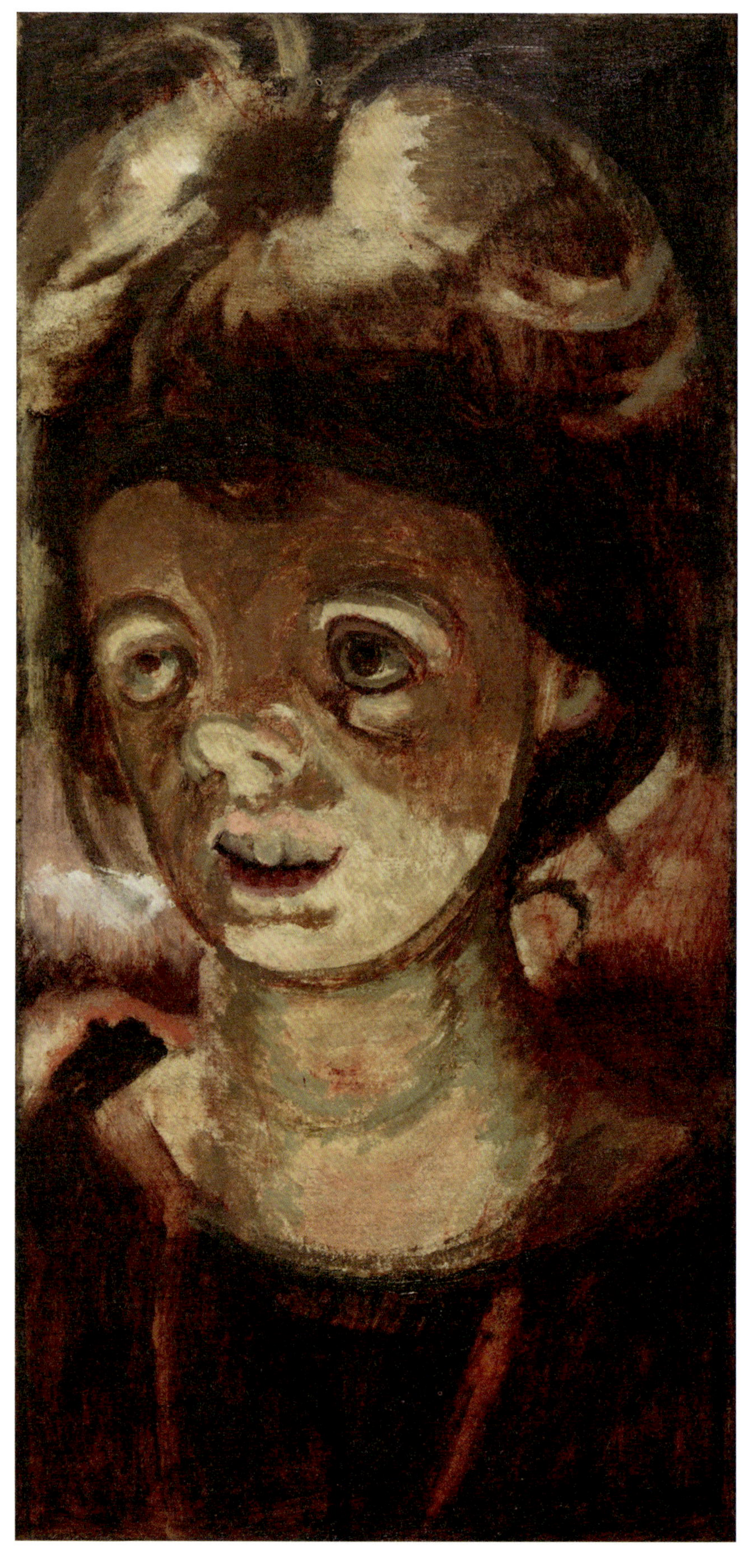

78
Cicely Hey 1923
Oil paint on canvas
The Whitworth, The
University of Manchester

79
Victor Lecourt 1921–4
Oil paint on canvas
Manchester Art Gallery

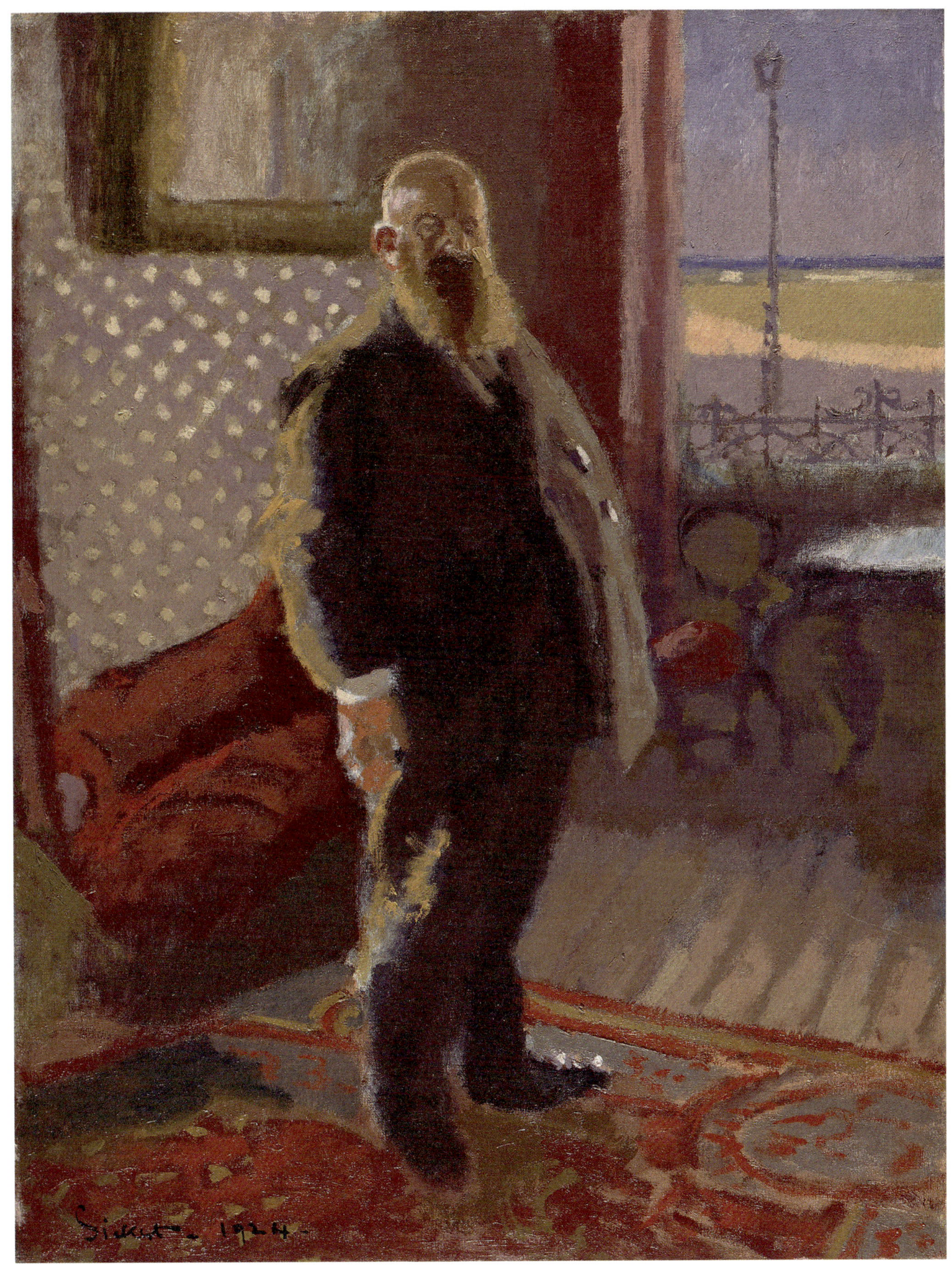

VENICE
AND DIEPPE

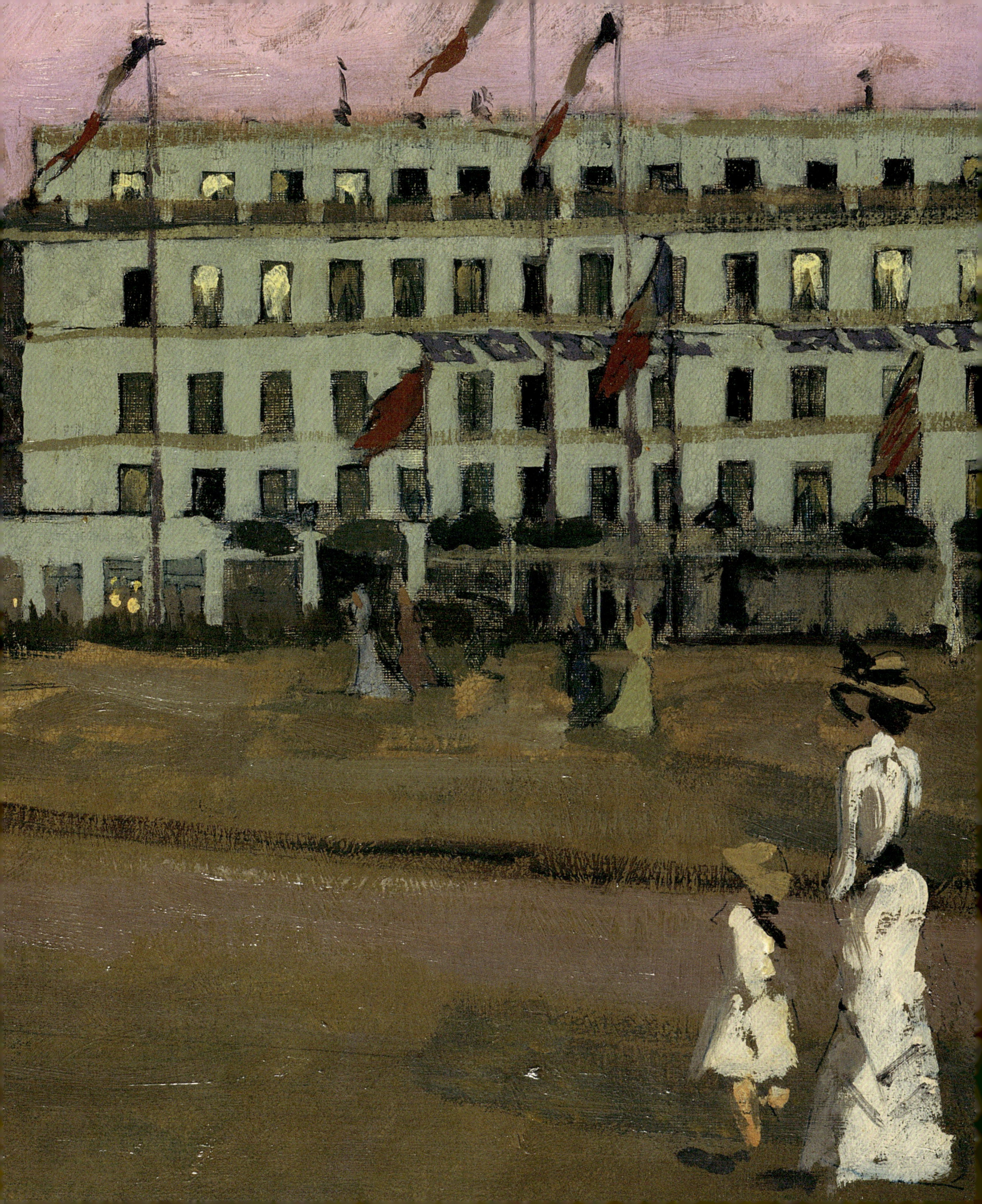

KATY NORRIS

'FULL OF APPEAL – SAD – WAN – TOUCHING': SICKERT'S 'PICTURESQUE' WORK

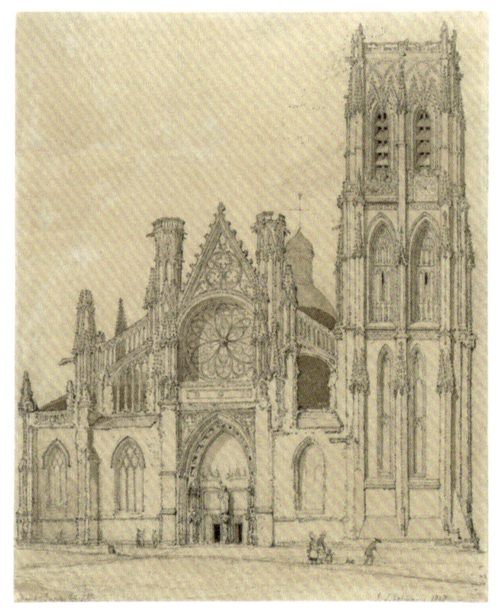

Fig.15
John Sell Cotman, *Saint Jacques Façade* 1818, pencil on wash and paper, 29.3×23.2, Birmingham Museums and Art Gallery

In 1898, Walter Sickert wrote to his friend Florence Humphrey that he could not stand another winter in London. 'It is too dark', he complained, 'and life is too short'.[1] Separated from his first wife Ellen Cobden and in financial if not artistic crisis, he was tired of the British capital, a city that was the centre of his social and professional activity. That summer he took a break in Dieppe on the Normandy coast.[2] By the following July, any plans to return were abandoned. He wrote again from his new home at the Maison Villain, instructing Humphrey to tie up any loose ends in London at his Robert Street studio. Sickert's future was, he asserted, in Dieppe, his livelihood dependent on a fresh avenue of landscape painting inspired by the town's eclectic mix of historic sites and newly erected entertainments. 'I see my line. Not portraits. Picturesque work', he declared; 'this place Dieppe, is my only up to now, goldmine, and I must work it a bit till I can get a little decent comfort'.[3]

By labelling the urban landscapes he created in Dieppe 'picturesque', Sickert was conscious that the word had vivid associations in the popular imagination back in Britain. The term had first appeared in aesthetic philosophy as far back as the eighteenth century, when it referred to an emotionally evocative, rustic ideal distinct from the rational construct of beauty emphasising harmony and symmetry. During the 1800s, artists and cultural theorists including John Sell Cotman (see fig.15), J.M.W. Turner and John Ruskin contributed to this discourse, extolling the virtues of a rugged visual attractiveness they identified in crumbling monuments and weathered architectural ruins. Their writings and imagery encouraged a new breed of leisured classes to travel throughout Britain and continental Europe to see these phenomena first-hand. Dieppe, with its abundance of decaying Gothic edifices, became part of a well-trodden trail for British sightseers, who recognised its medieval landmarks from antiquarian engravings and picture postcards.

For Sickert the reproducibility of this popular, readymade iconography was appealing. Between 1898 and his return to England in 1905 he made concerted efforts to maximise the financial viability of Dieppe's attractions, copying the structure and ornamentation of familiar sites in numerous prints, drawings and paintings, which he forwarded to galleries in London and Paris. Encouraged by the positive reception from his dealers, Sickert made several short excursions to Venice in search of picturesque motifs. Having first visited the city in 1895 he returned with restored motivation, each time developing new multi-layered compositions, primarily by making preparatory studies as he did in Dieppe, but also almost certainly using photography.[4]

By the early 1900s, he had established an extensive repertoire of source material that he developed into finished paintings in his studio. He returned repeatedly to the same motifs, rehearsing Venetian scenes featuring the Rialto bridge, the Salute church and St Mark's Basilica, alongside views of Dieppe's harbour, promenade and the church of St Jacques seen from different vantage points. The ubiquity of this architectural imagery in his practice amused him. Sickert explained to another correspondent that, since he nearly always painted his picturesque works away from the subject in his studio, he often found himself completing scenes of Venice in Dieppe and vice versa.[5] Such interchangeability was further hinted at by Jacques-Émile Blanche, Sickert's long-standing friend and patron in Dieppe, when he playfully described him as the town's Canaletto.[6]

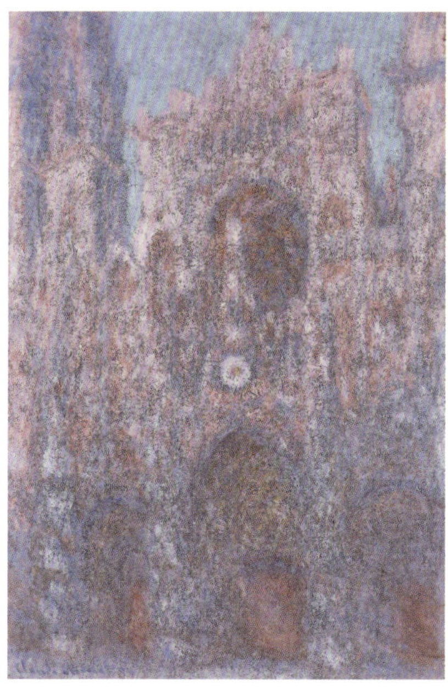

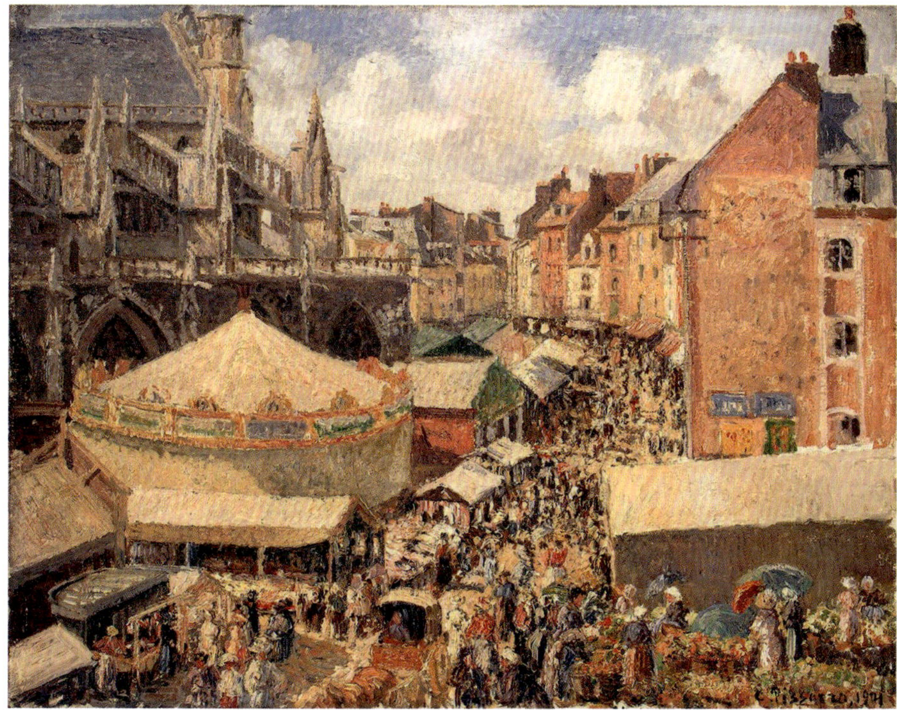

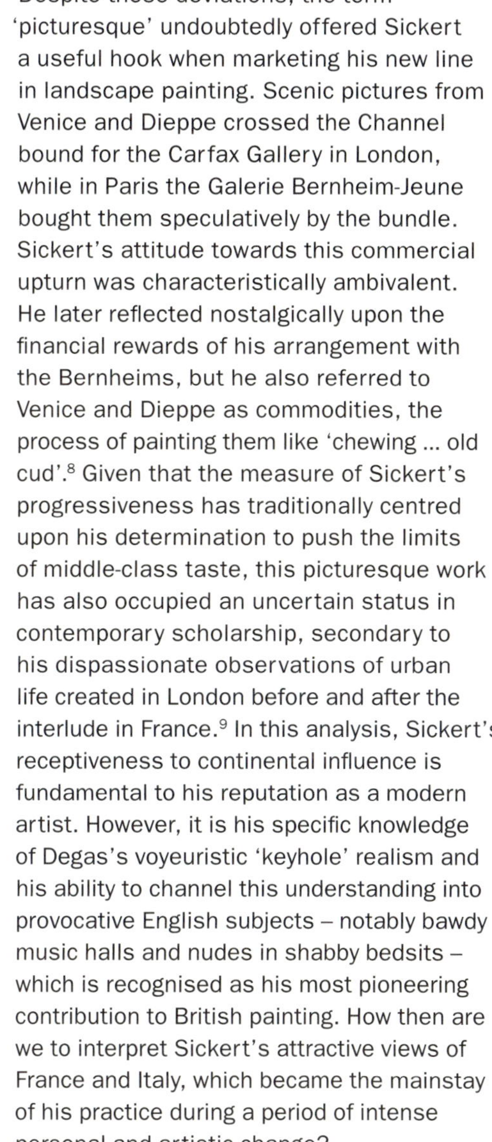

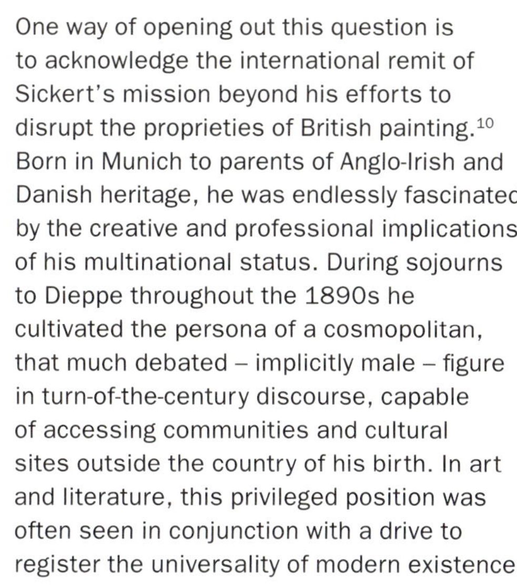

It is worth noting that Sickert's approach altered in the two locations. Whereas he was inclined to emphasise Venice's grandeur by focusing on its impressive vistas centring around the Grand Canal and Piazza San Marco, in Dieppe – with its old-town, domestic scale – he worked hard to draw out the understated charm of its architectural idiosyncrasies. It is also true that many of the scenes created in Venice and Dieppe demonstrated a style closer to naturalism than the romantic idiom usually associated with the picturesque. Sickert scrutinised St Jacques and St Mark's minutely, interrogating their façades at different times and under changing atmospheric conditions. Although he rarely painted *en plein air*, he undertook this activity in the spirit of impressionist naturalism, replaying the optical facts over separate compositions in a manner comparable to Monet's Rouen Cathedral series of 1892–4 (see fig.16). Drawing back to capture the clatter of Dieppe's streetlife, Sickert also invested his work with an everyday realism that he saw firsthand in Camille Pissarro's paintings of St Jacques completed in Dieppe in 1901 (see fig.17).[7]

Despite these deviations, the term 'picturesque' undoubtedly offered Sickert a useful hook when marketing his new line in landscape painting. Scenic pictures from Venice and Dieppe crossed the Channel bound for the Carfax Gallery in London, while in Paris the Galerie Bernheim-Jeune bought them speculatively by the bundle. Sickert's attitude towards this commercial upturn was characteristically ambivalent. He later reflected nostalgically upon the financial rewards of his arrangement with the Bernheims, but he also referred to Venice and Dieppe as commodities, the process of painting them like 'chewing … old cud'.[8] Given that the measure of Sickert's progressiveness has traditionally centred upon his determination to push the limits of middle-class taste, this picturesque work has also occupied an uncertain status in contemporary scholarship, secondary to his dispassionate observations of urban life created in London before and after the interlude in France.[9] In this analysis, Sickert's receptiveness to continental influence is fundamental to his reputation as a modern artist. However, it is his specific knowledge of Degas's voyeuristic 'keyhole' realism and his ability to channel this understanding into provocative English subjects – notably bawdy music halls and nudes in shabby bedsits – which is recognised as his most pioneering contribution to British painting. How then are we to interpret Sickert's attractive views of France and Italy, which became the mainstay of his practice during a period of intense personal and artistic change?

One way of opening out this question is to acknowledge the international remit of Sickert's mission beyond his efforts to disrupt the proprieties of British painting.[10] Born in Munich to parents of Anglo-Irish and Danish heritage, he was endlessly fascinated by the creative and professional implications of his multinational status. During sojourns to Dieppe throughout the 1890s he cultivated the persona of a cosmopolitan, that much debated – implicitly male – figure in turn-of-the-century discourse, capable of accessing communities and cultural sites outside the country of his birth. In art and literature, this privileged position was often seen in conjunction with a drive to register the universality of modern existence.

Definitions of the cosmopolitan and his ability to traverse national borders frequently overlapped with critical discussions of the pan-European symbolist movement, the proponents of which rejected naturalistic representation detailing local character and stereotypes in favour of more poetic expressions of shared human experience.

For Sickert, historic continental destinations were the perfect settings to explore his twin internationalist and symbolist leanings. Venice's crumbling Byzantine and Gothic edifices were a reminder of its legacy as a failed empire, providing a metaphor for man's frailty. Meanwhile, in Dieppe, the juxtaposition of dilapidated medieval structures and the glittering façade of its tourist industry presented a similarly useful analogy for the symbolist idea that essential truths lurked beneath the surface appearance of modern life. Sickert elicited this human drama through his representation of evening promenaders in front of Dieppe's modish Hôtel Royal set against a disconcerting purple-red sky (see no.93). In Venice he depicted St Mark's looming façade at dusk, completing two immense panoramas that were – much like musical 'variations on a theme' – compositionally indistinguishable apart from alterations in tonal key, colouration and painterly treatment (see nos.80 and 82).

This lyricism attached Sickert's work to an internationally expansive programme of aesthetic innovation, notably Whistler's atmospheric Nocturnes, as well as the poetry of French symbolist Charles Baudelaire, whose descriptions of Paris at twilight invoked feelings of alienation he considered inherent to the modern condition. The art historian and curator Robert Upstone has compared further examples of Sickert's Venetian nocturnes with a near-identical scene by Scottish watercolourist Arthur Melville (see fig.18), along with night-time depictions of Bruges by the Belgian painter Fernand Khnopff, noting how each artist captured their subjects under a veil of ambient darkness.[11] By focusing on a historic 'backwater', Khnopff – much like Sickert in Dieppe – shifted attention away from artistic centres like Paris or London, thus making a unique contribution to symbolist iconography and its representation of the urban environment as a universal object of beauty. Sickert's ability to move easily between different European destinations, meanwhile, served as an important marker for his own cosmopolitan credentials.

When Sickert started a new chapter in Dieppe in 1898, he enacted yet another turn in this kaleidoscopic international identity. The move was a deliberate severance not only from Ellen but also from Whistler, with whom he was embroiled in an acrimonious public wrangle. Shortly before Sickert left London, Whistler refused to invite him to join his society for likeminded cosmopolitans, the International Society of Sculptors, Painters and Gravers. Defiant, Sickert responded by declaring himself neither British nor cosmopolitan, but French. Settling in Normandy he entrenched himself in the Paris art market, submitting work to French sections of international exhibitions and mounting major shows with the Bernheims and the Durand-Ruel dynasty, who, along with Pissarro, encouraged him to develop a brighter, more saleable, impressionistic palette.[12]

Nevertheless, beneath this bravura lay the same hybrid identity rooted in Sickert's mixed ancestry. His art, too, was beset with inconsistencies. The art historian Richard Shone has argued that, even as Sickert began 'overhauling Whistlerian beginnings with the example of Monet and Pissarro', certain 'tics and echoes' carried through.[13] With the exception of some brighter Venetian scenes from 1901 and later paintings of St Jacques executed around 1907, Sickert's picturesque work was generally characterised by sharp tonal contrasts adapted from Whistler's teachings. The effects of this strategy are exemplified by large-scale canvases commissioned for a Dieppe restaurant in 1902, five of which represent standard scenic views, while another depicts bathers in striped costumes striding into the sea (see no.94). The tonality of these paintings gives greater definition to incidental figures and architectural pattern, yet it also imbues them with a sombre mood at odds with the fashionable environment for which they were intended. Although their strong scenic design is attractive, they are nonetheless tinged with an enigmatic scepticism present in many of Sickert's picturesque paintings, which one patron described as 'full of appeal – sad – wan – touching'.[14]

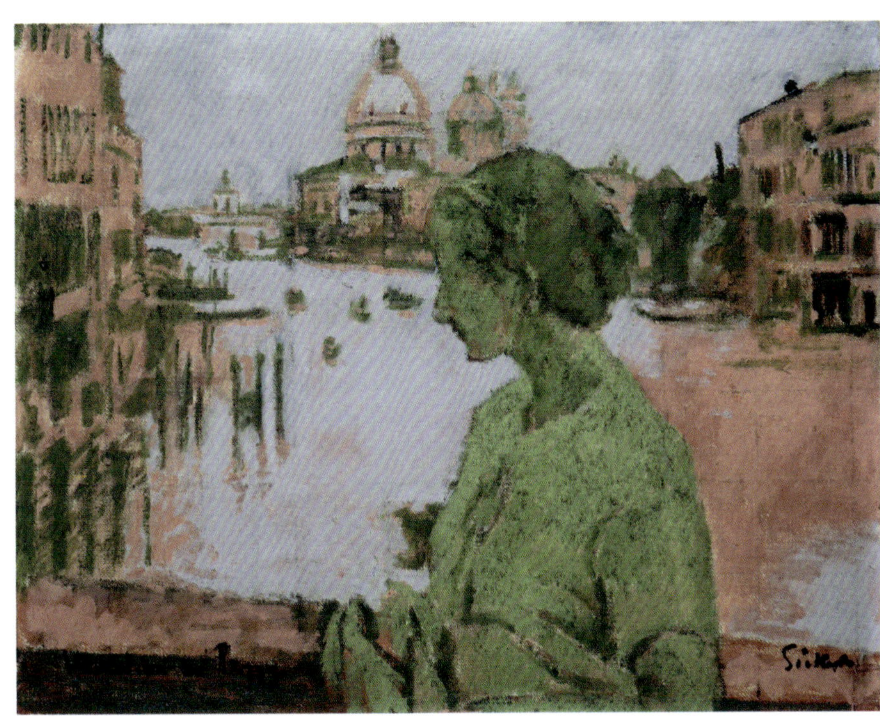

Fig.19
Variation on Peggy 1934–5,
oil paint on canvas,
57.8×71.8, Tate

Ultimately it was Sickert's tendency to skew mimetic truth through his rigorous studio work that held back any wholesale conversion to French impressionism. His methodology instead confirmed his commitment to the symbolist idea that aestheticism and artifice, as much as realism, were necessary tools for interrogating the essential character of the world around him. Crucially, Wendy Baron has recognised that Sickert signalled this interest in painting as artifice through his use of the term 'picturesque', which, interpreted using its original derivation from the Italian word *pittoresco*, means 'from a picture'.[15] Her analysis not only draws attention to the painterly techniques and pictorial devices that Sickert developed through his study of architectural subjects, but also shows how these basic components – much like the etymological roots of the word 'picturesque' – were transferable between different national contexts as a means to express 'mood, rhythm and tempo'.[16] Mimicking the structure of verbal or musical language, he deployed symbolic building blocks to summon emotion and create meaning across his creative sites, allowing him to pass, as Blanche described, like the prophetic Greek god Proteus 'through various stages in England, Dieppe and in Venice'.[17]

After five years dedicated to the picturesque, Sickert moved onto painting figures indoors. Nevertheless, he returned to architectural subjects intermittently. In 1934 at the age of 74 he began work on one of his final Venetian scenes, *Variation on Peggy* (see fig.19), which depicted his friend, the actress Peggy Ashcroft, standing before a view of the Grand Canal stretching across to the Salute church. Developing the work from a black and white photograph published in the *Radio Times*, Sickert heightened the emotional resonance of the image using a garish scheme of pink, green and blue. In many ways, this extreme level of artifice represents the logical consequence of his experiments in France and Italy completed three decades earlier. It helps us to consider our private relationship with popular media imagery as powerful signifiers of collective human emotion, while laying bare the mechanisms of the picturesque. Rooted in nostalgia, these devices have the capacity to move us, to elicit pleasure, but also, in equal measure, to provoke feelings of profound melancholy.

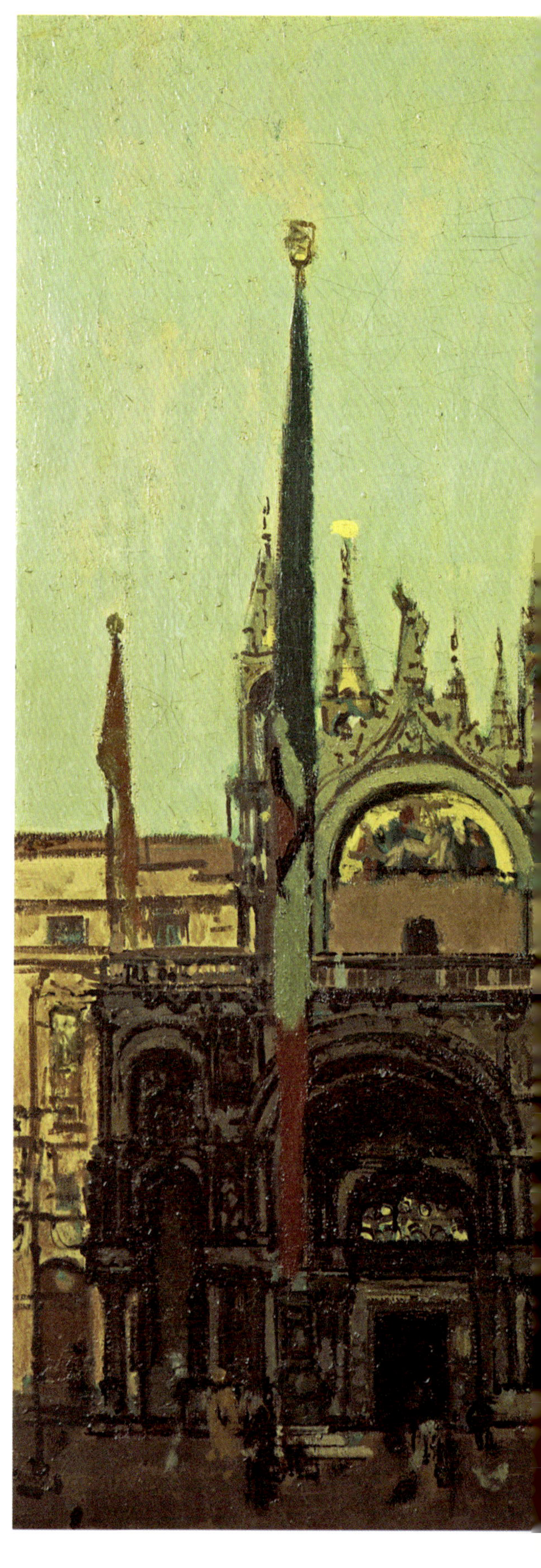

80
St Mark's, Venice (Pax Tibi Marce Evangelista Meus) 1896
Oil paint on canvas
Tate

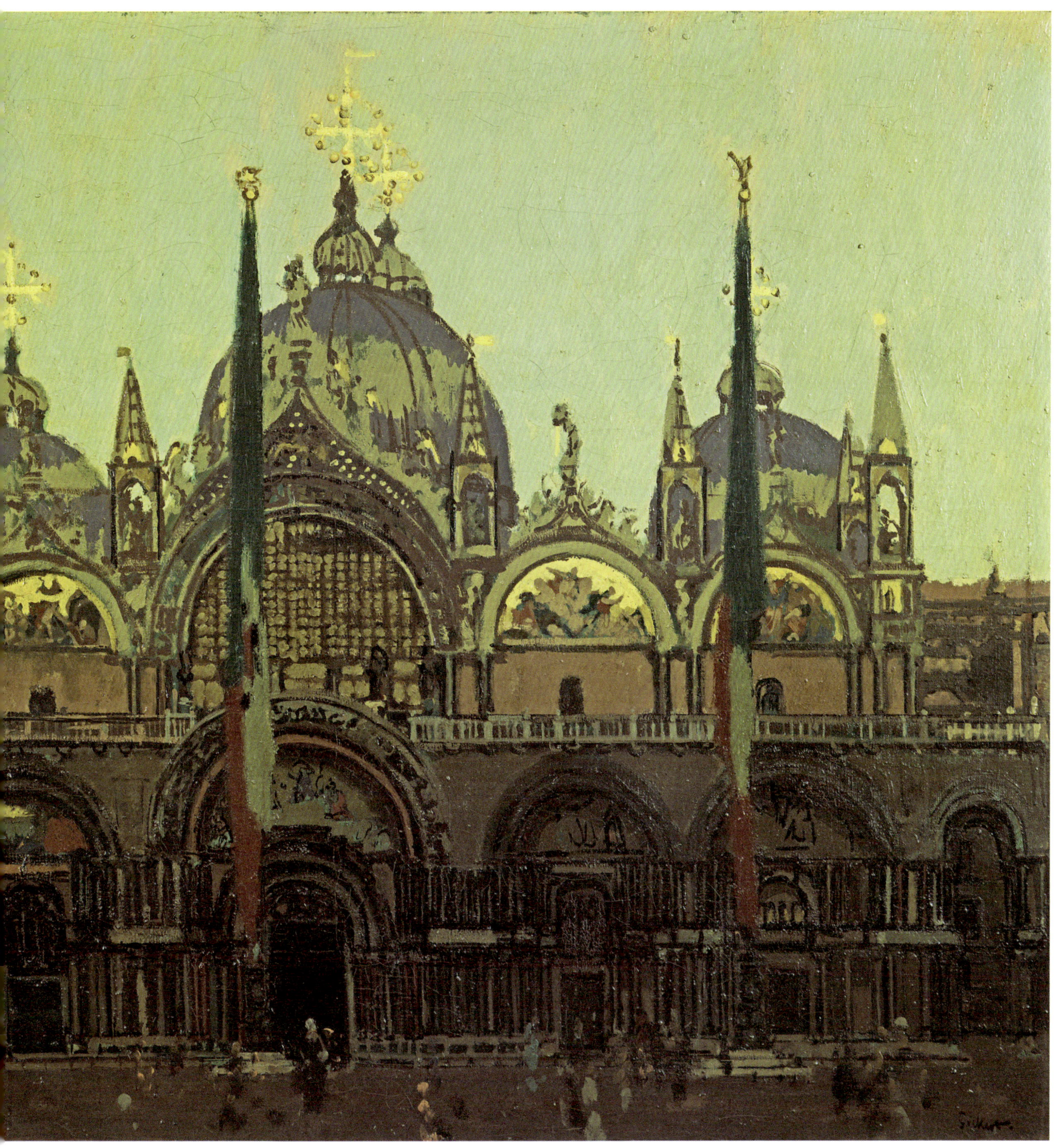

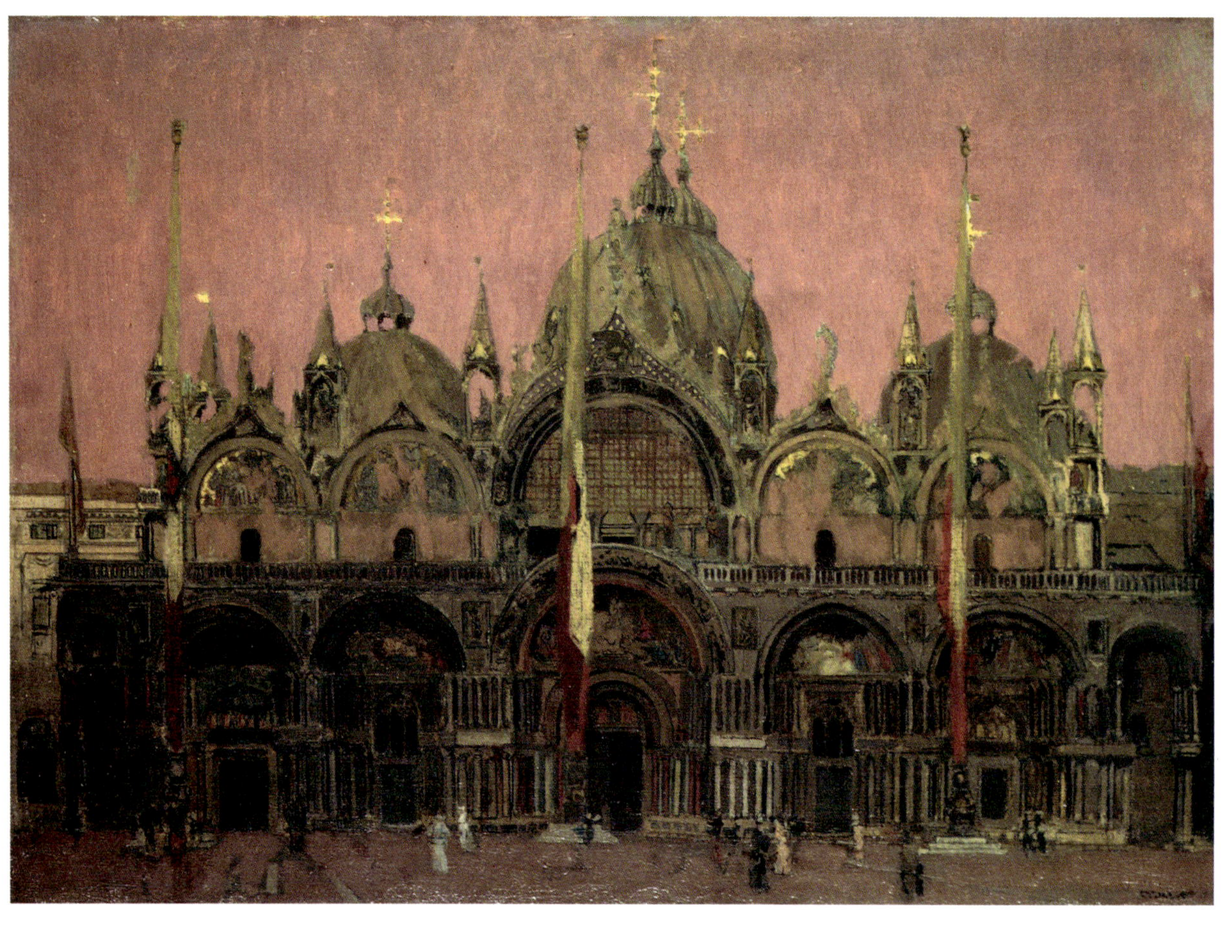

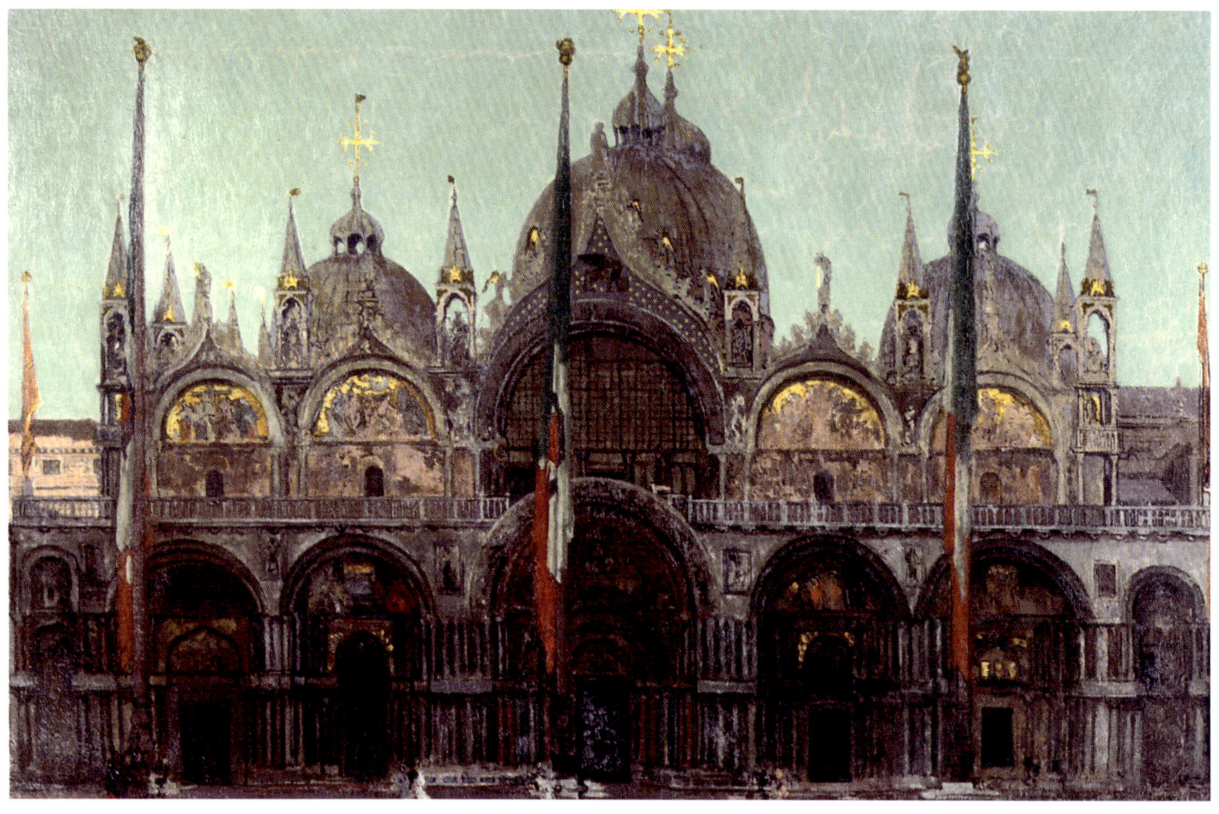

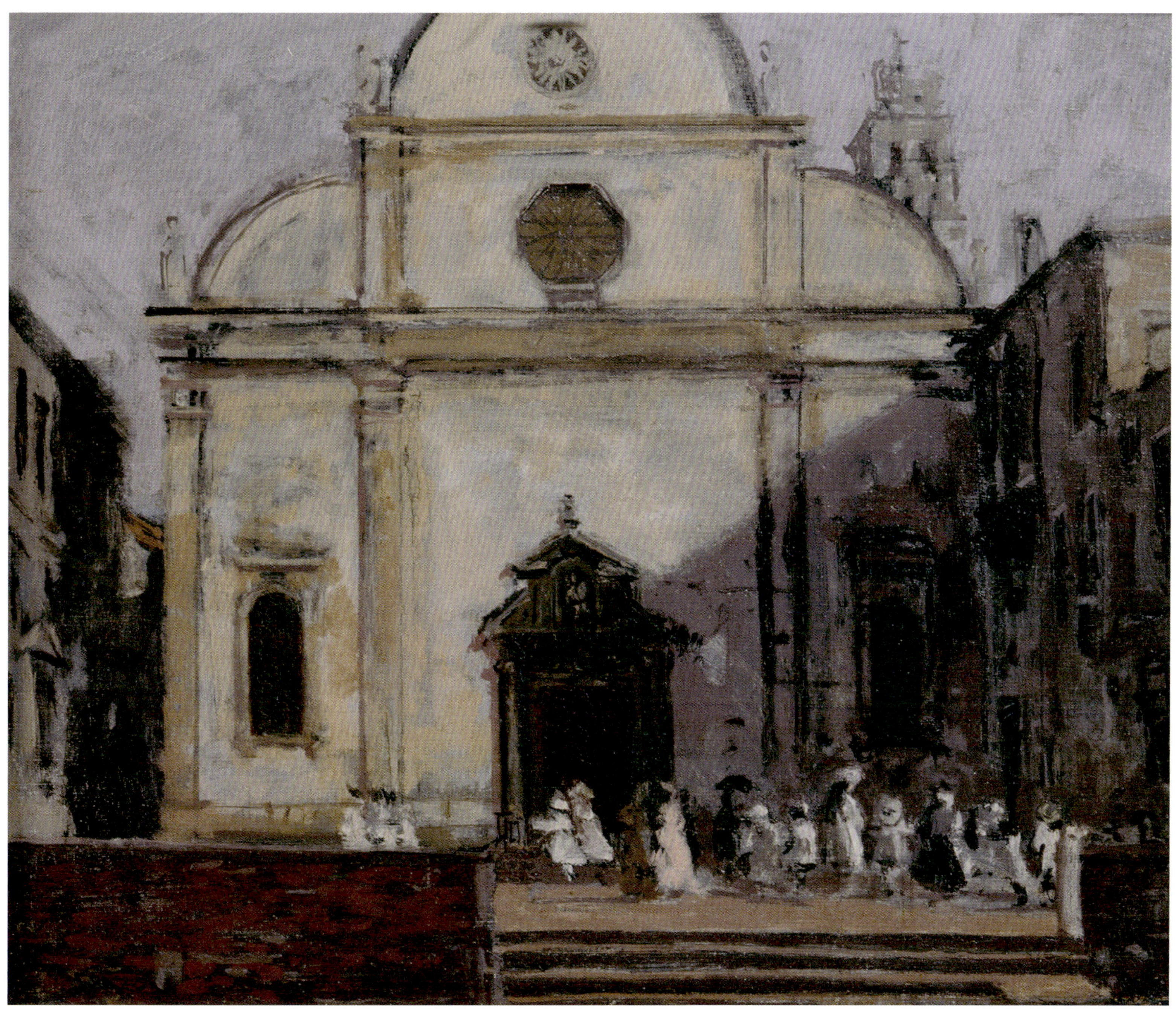

81
The Façade of St Mark's.
Red Sky at Night c.1895–6
Oil paint on canvas
Southampton City
Art Gallery

82
St Mark's, Venice 1896–7
Oil paint on canvas
Courtesy of the British
Council Collection

83
Santa Maria del Carmelo
c.1895–6
Oil paint on canvas
The Ashmolean Museum,
University of Oxford

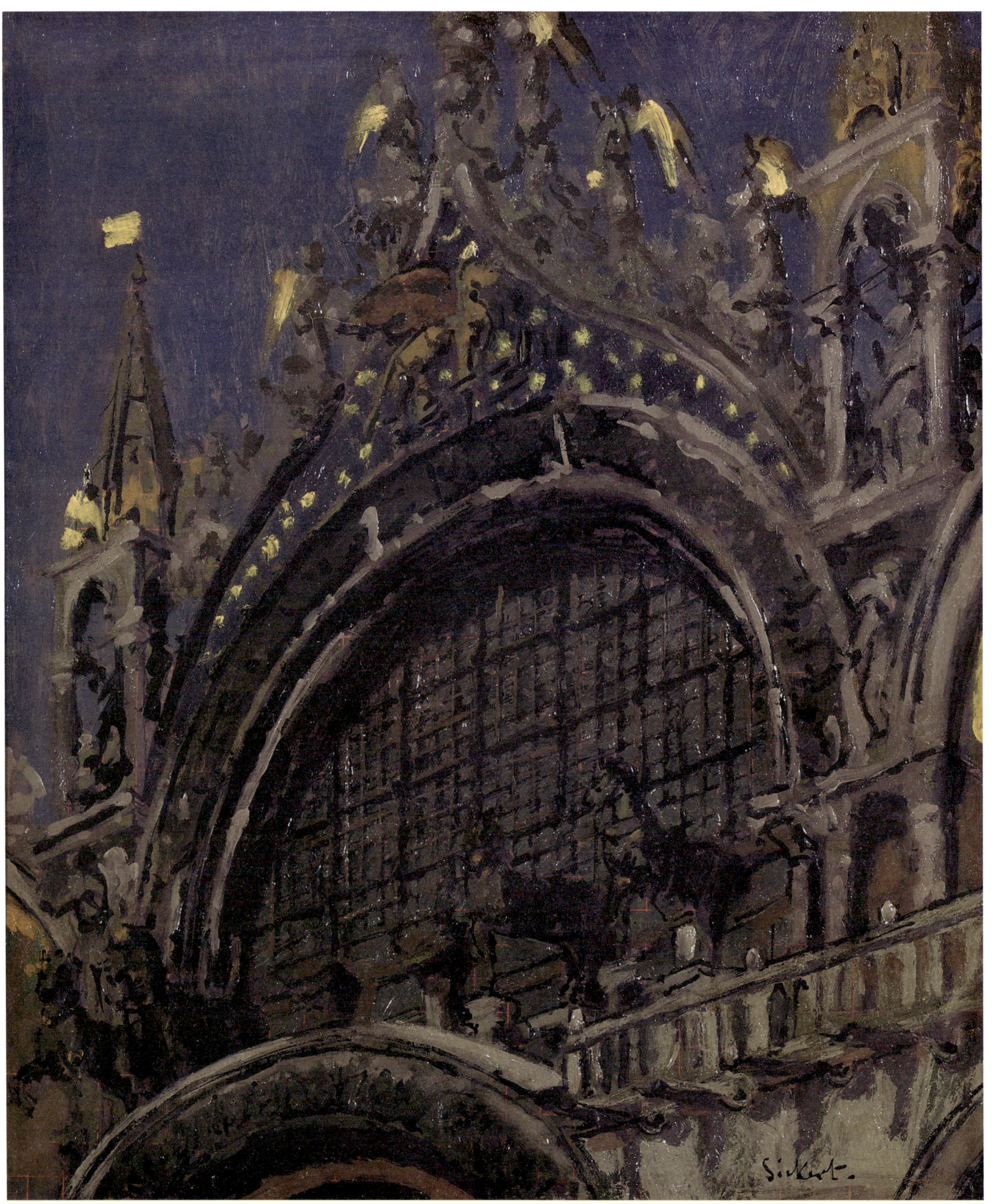

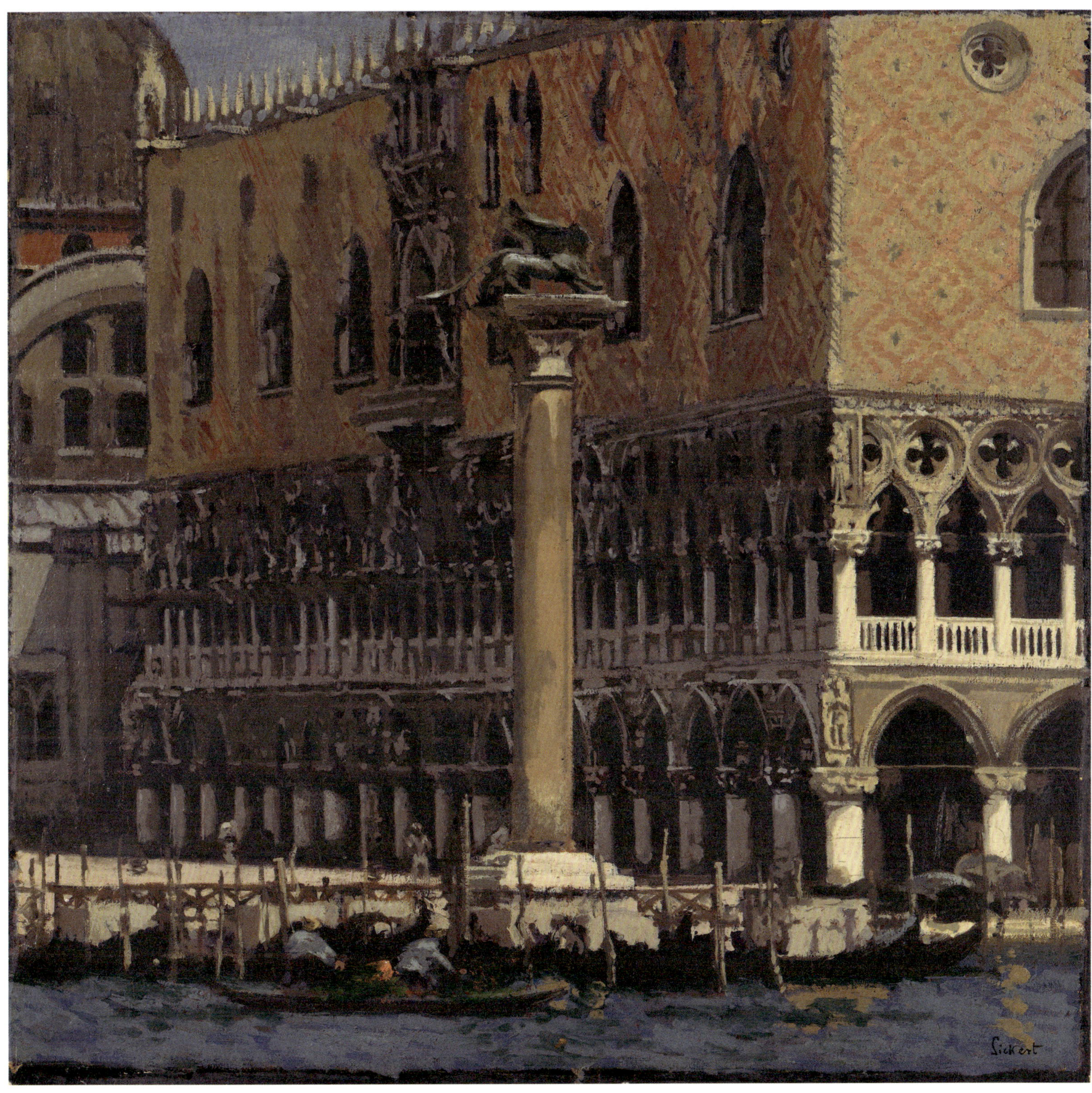

84
The Horses of St Mark's
1901–6
Oil paint on canvas
Bristol Culture: Bristol
Museums & Art Gallery

85
The Lion of St Mark c.1895–6
Oil paint on canvas
The Syndics of the Fitzwilliam
Museum, University of
Cambridge

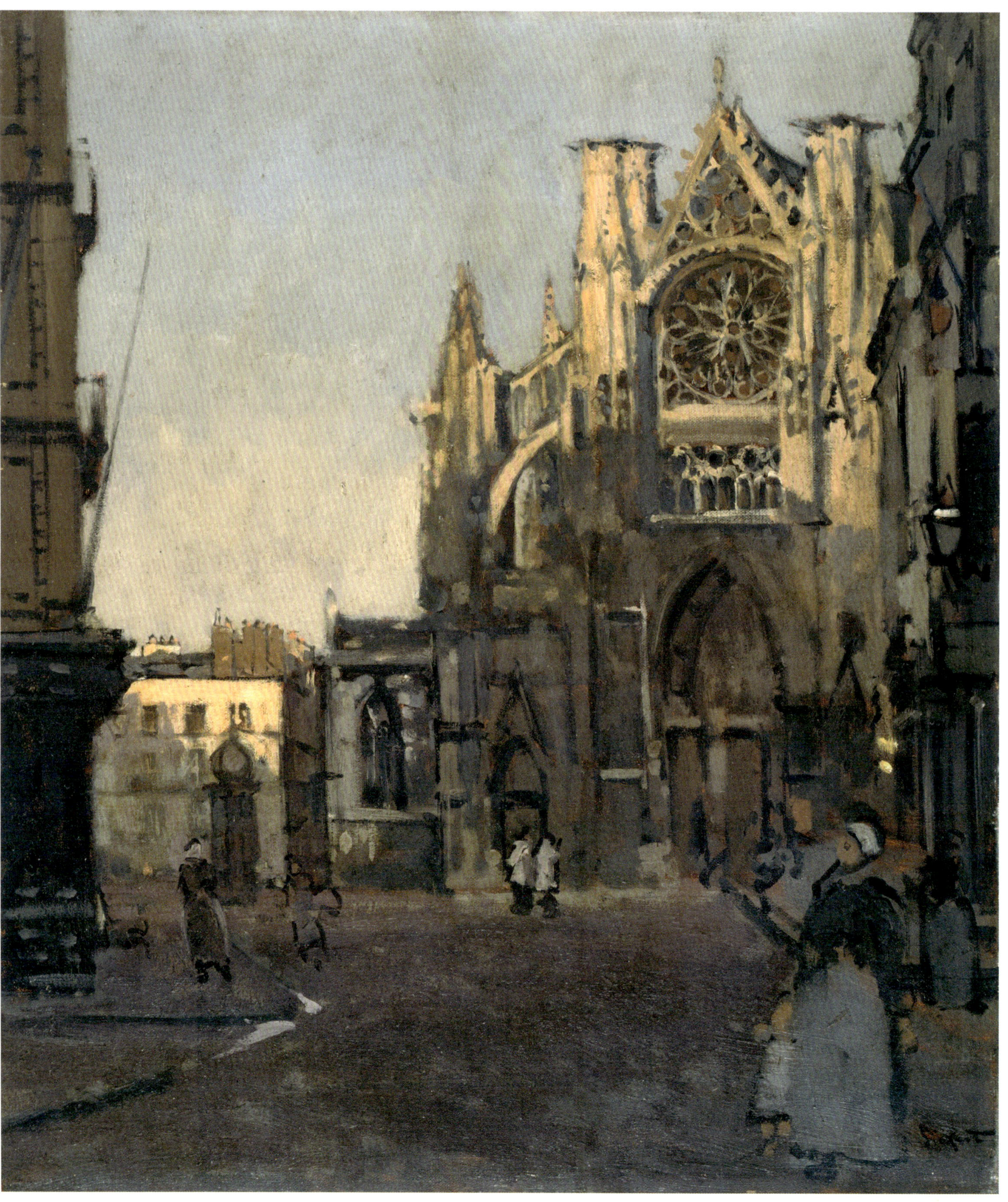

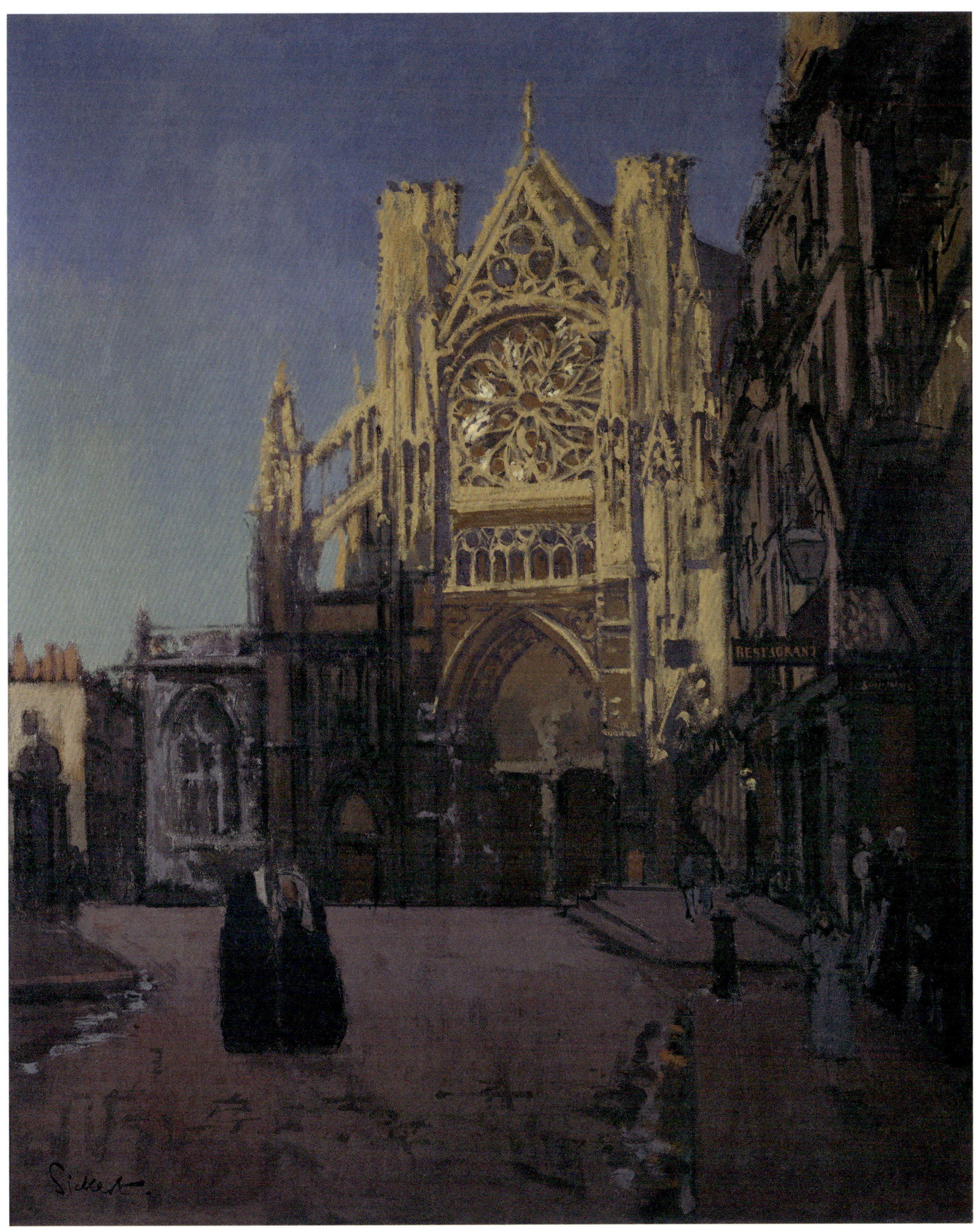

RESTAURANT

Previous page (left)
86
The Façade of St Jacques
1899–1900
Oil paint on canvas
The Whitworth, The
University of Manchester

Previous page (right)
87
The Façade of St Jacques
1902
Oil paint on canvas
Private collection

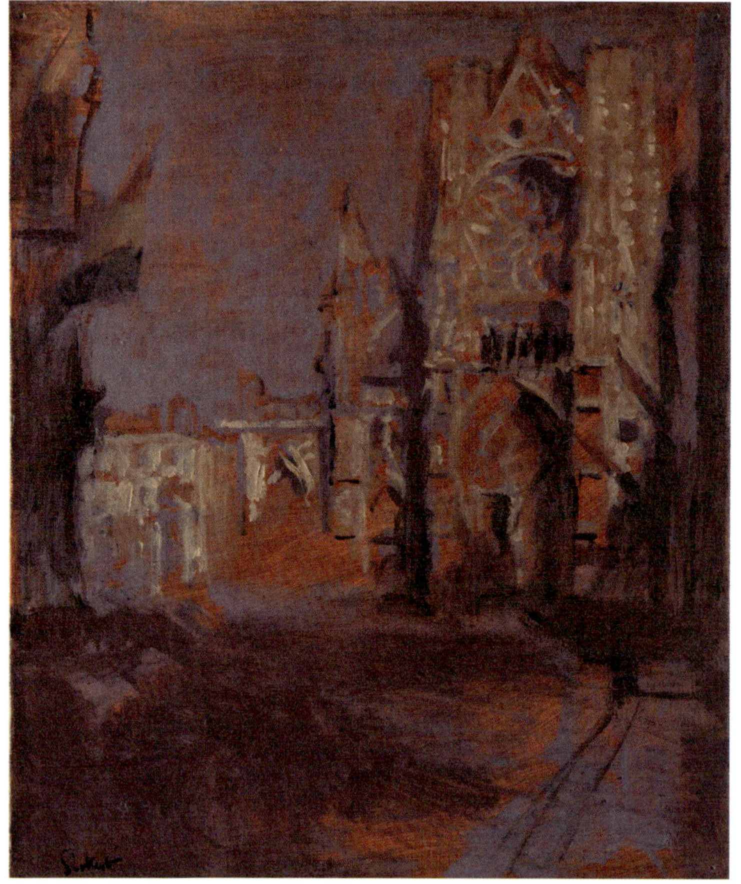

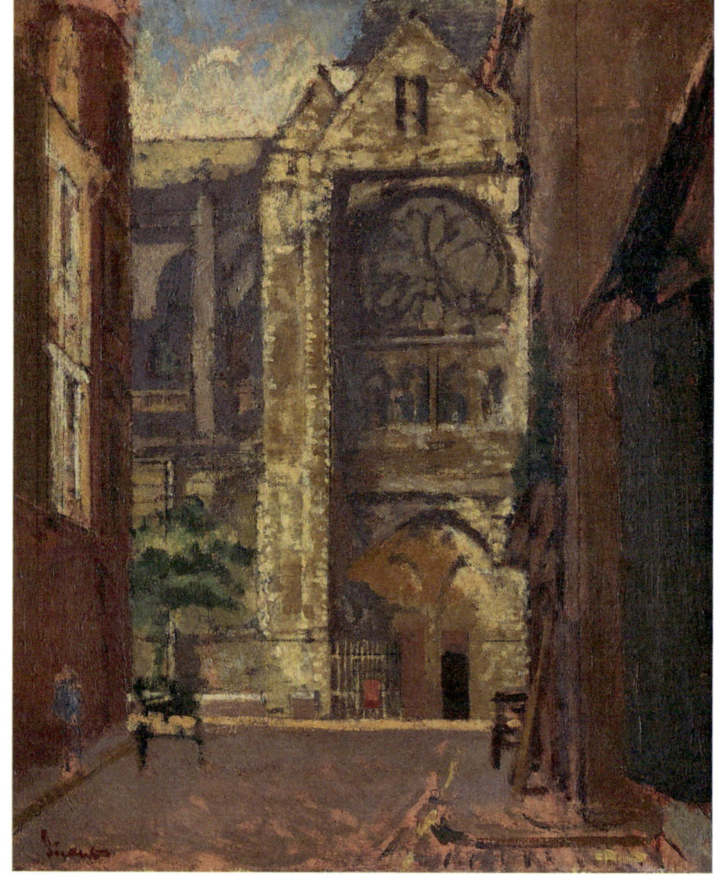

88
The Façade of St Jacques
1899–1900
Oil paint on canvas
Rouen, Musée des
Beaux-Arts

89
The Façade of St Jacques
1907
Oil paint on canvas
Pallant House Gallery,
Chichester

90
The Façade of St Jacques
1902–3
Pencil and oil paint on
canvas
Private collection

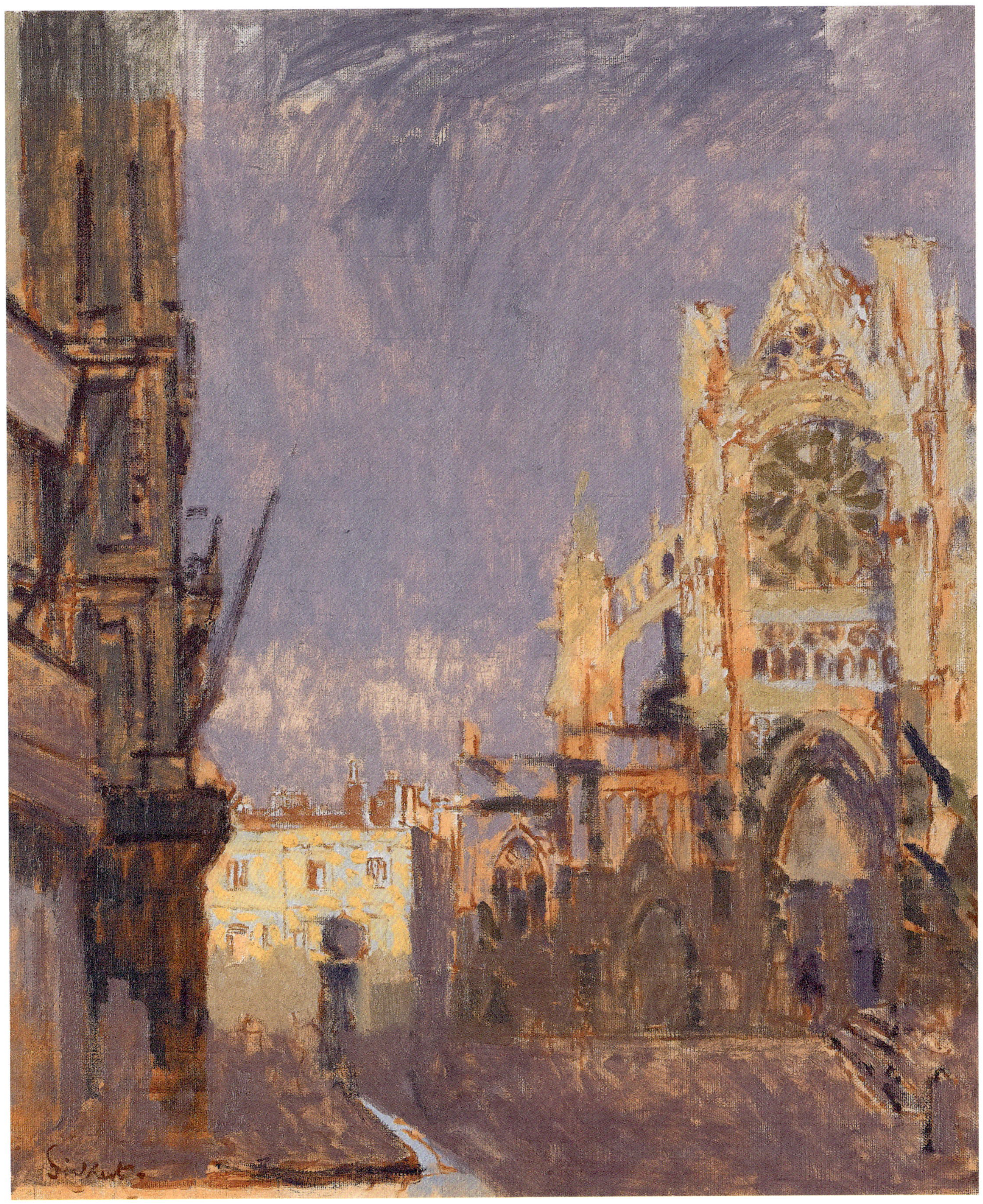

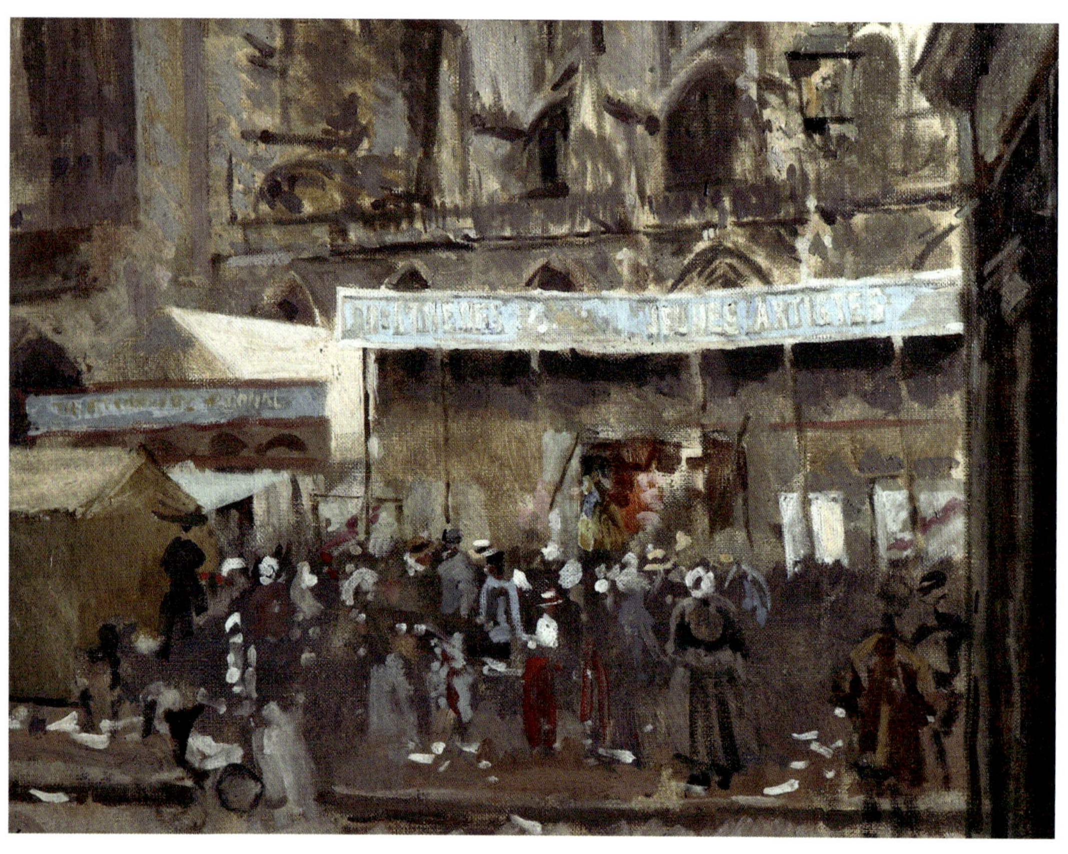

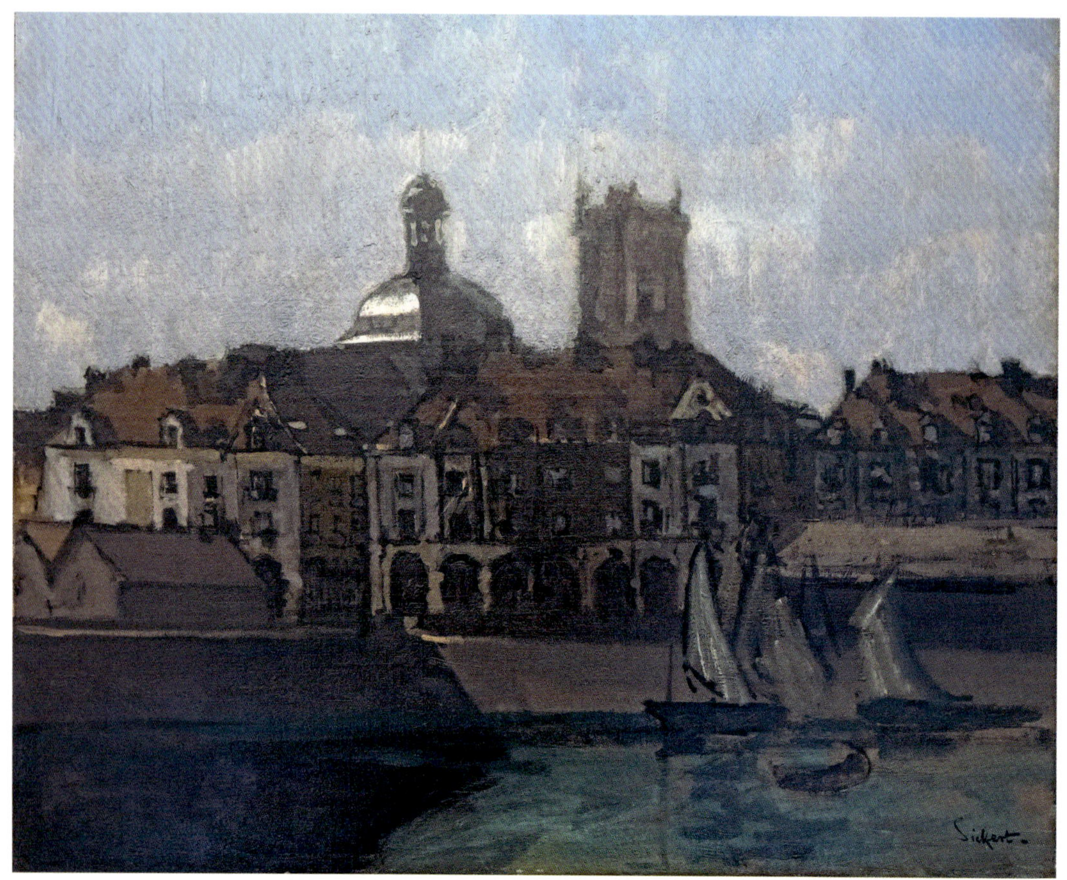

91
The Theatre of the Young Artists 1890
Oil paint on canvas
The Atkinson, Southport

92
Les Arcades et La Darse c.1898
Oil paint on canvas
Fondation Bemberg, Toulouse

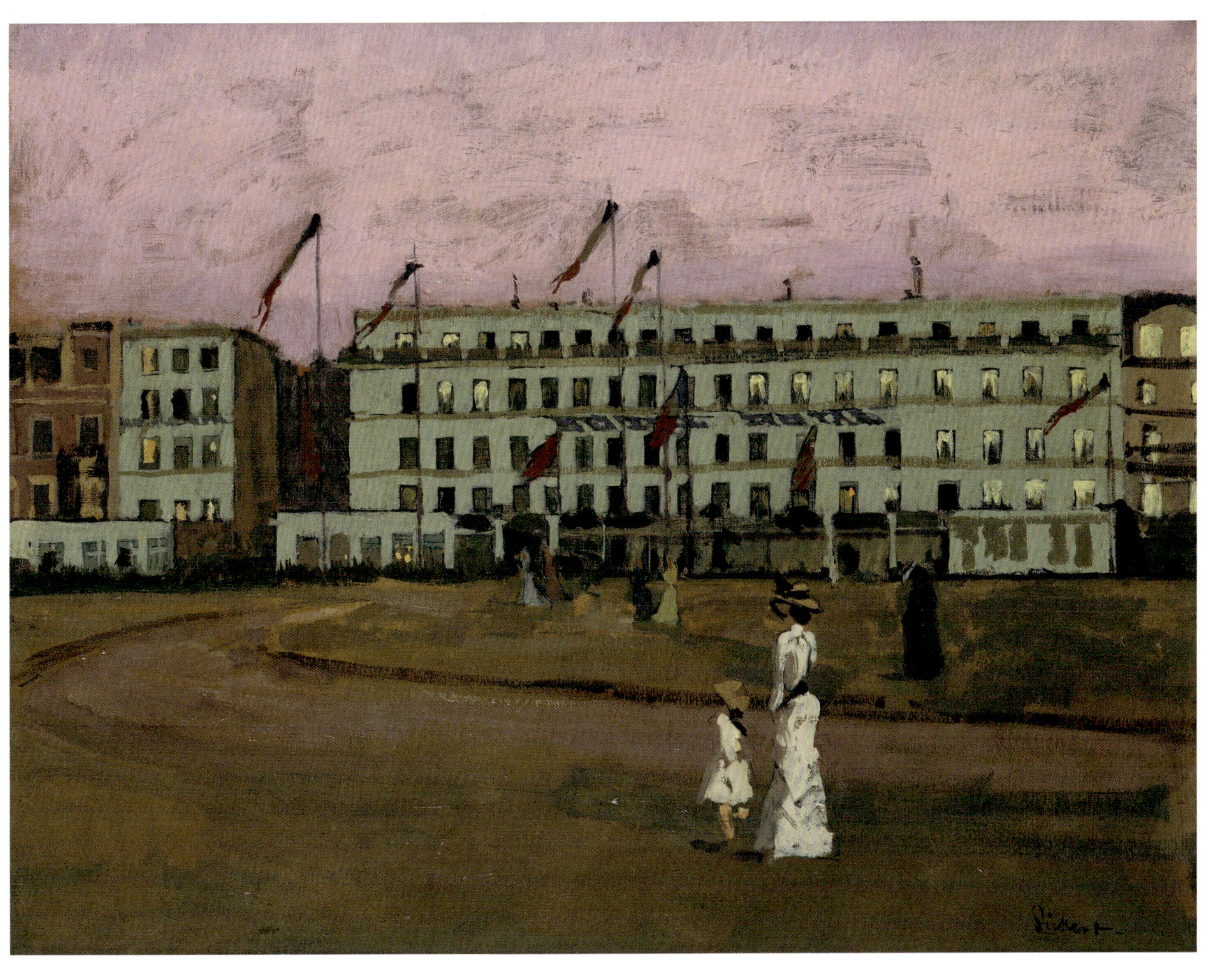

93
L'Hôtel Royal, Dieppe
c.1894
Oil paint on canvas
Sheffield Museums Trust

DELPHINE LÉVY, EDITED BY CLARA ROCA

SICKERT AND FRANCE

Walter Sickert maintained a deep and long-lasting relationship with France, but today this still appears to be largely forgotten by the French public. Yet French influences were part of the artist's very fabric – from the influence of Degas, his mentor after Whistler, to his close ties with contemporaries such as the impressionists, the post-impressionists, and indeed the Nabis, with whom he mixed. His work was well represented and received in France, where he was able to count on the support of the country's leading art dealers – the Galerie Durand-Ruel, then the Galerie Bernheim-Jeune – and, most importantly, on a large network, mainly of artist friends, who bought his works, including Jacques-Émile Blanche, Pierre Bonnard and Paul Signac. It was in France, where the way had been paved for him by a number of innovative painters working in this field, that Sickert first exhibited and sold his nudes and interior scenes. The critics there were supportive and recognised him to be an artist in a similar vein to his French contemporaries. However, after the First World War, Sickert distanced himself from the art market and, identifying increasingly with a new English school, distanced himself from France too. After his death, he sank into oblivion in France for over half a century.

French influences

It was through his father, who made a direct contribution to his training, that Sickert became very familiar with nineteenth-century French painting, and particularly the work of Ingres and Delacroix, the Barbizon School and the Batignolles Group. Oswald Sickert (1828–85) was an admirer of Courbet and, in his youth, had frequented the studio of Thomas Couture, where he met Manet. He also knew Alphonse Legros, who later tutored his son during his brief spell at the Slade School of Fine Art. Although Walter Sickert disliked Legros's teaching, he did write appreciatively of his work.[1] Another friend of his father, Otto Scholderer, who was living in London and was a close friend of Henri Fantin-Latour, also introduced Walter Sickert to contemporary French painting and taught him the method used by Horace Lecoq de Boisbaudran, based on cumulative observation and drawing from memory.

In addition to this theoretical knowledge, Sickert knew France well and was very familiar with the artistic movements that developed there, as he lived in the country for many years. Unlike many foreign artists who lived in France, he did not lead a bohemian life in Paris, but instead lived mainly in Dieppe, where he had connections through his mother, and produced numerous paintings of the town. He lived in Normandy for ten or more years altogether, between 1898 and 1905, then between 1919 and 1922, and also visited for short periods on other occasions. In Dieppe, he became a close friend of Jacques-Émile Blanche, and through spending time with him, and at his house and studio at Le Bas Fort Blanc, gained access to French artistic life and became part of the cultivated bourgeoisie who gravitated around his host, and which included the Halévy family. So, from the very start of his career, through Blanche, Sickert was acquainted with many well-known figures from the worlds of English and French culture, from Paris and from Dieppe, as well as gallerists such as Durand-Ruel and Bernheim-Jeune. The circle who frequented the place included Monet, Pissarro, Renoir, Helleu and Puvis de Chavannes, among others, and, most importantly, Degas.

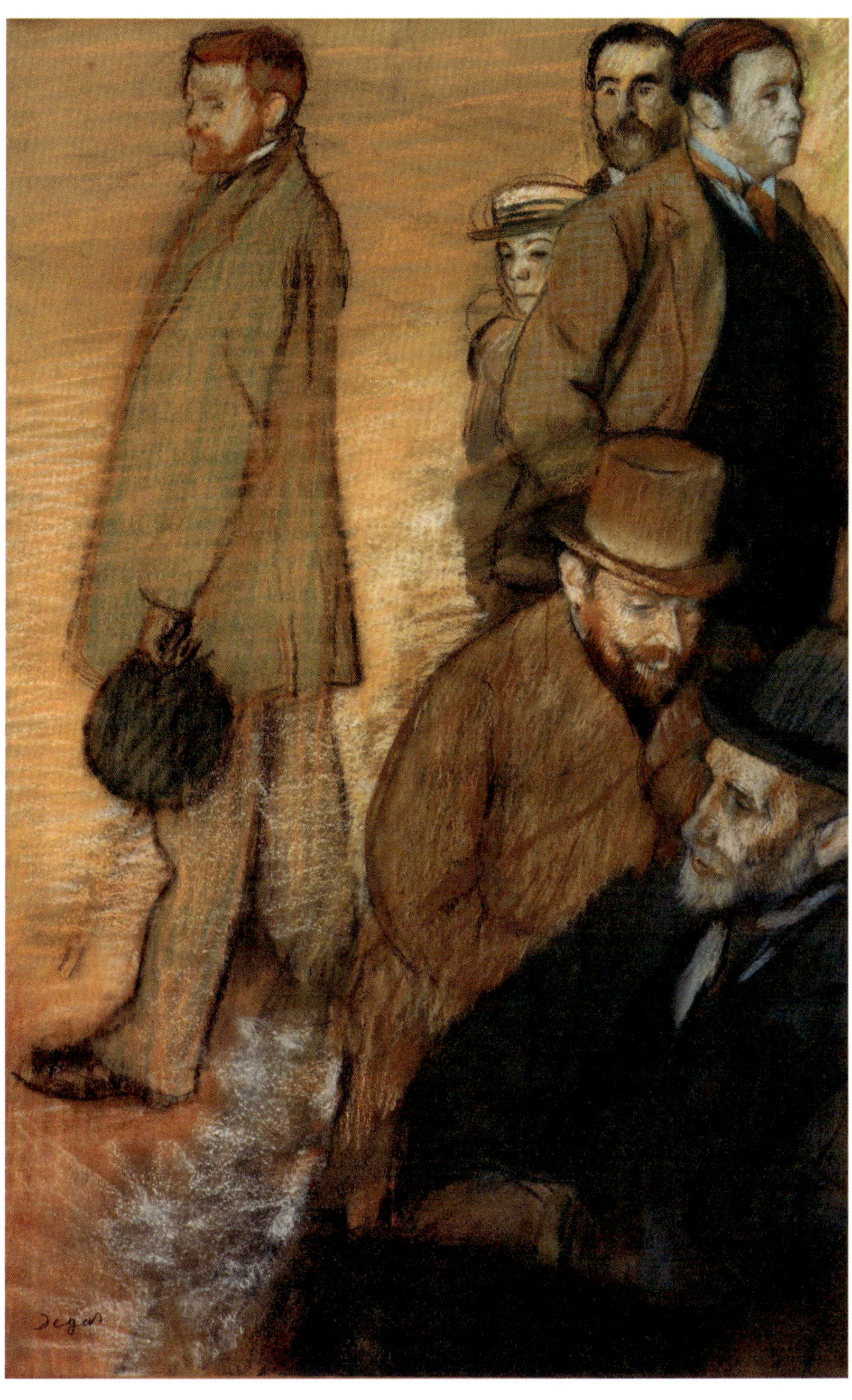

Fig.20
Edgar Degas, *Six Friends
at Dieppe* 1885, pastel
on paper on fabric,
114.9×71.1, Rhode
Island Museum

Sickert met Degas in Paris, where Whistler had asked him to take the portrait of his mother for the salon of April 1883. Degas became a true second mentor to him from the summer of 1885, when they both spent time in Dieppe. He encouraged Sickert to pursue a more constructed composition and to introduce figures. A large pastel by Degas entitled *Six Friends at Dieppe* (see fig.20) immortalises this summer and shows Ludovic Halévy and his son Daniel, as well as the painters Henri Gervex, Albert Boulanger-Cave and Jacques-Émile Blanche, with the young Walter Sickert, like a young lion, deliberately set apart. The rivalry between Whistler and Degas over Sickert in the summer of 1885 led the French artist to comment: 'It must be tiring to keep up the role of butterfly. Better to be an old bull like me.'[2]

Sickert was also interested in and frequented the Bande noire [Black Band], led by Lucien Simon and Charles Cottet. This group of painters, who were mainly from Brittany, like Sickert favoured the use of darker tones. But the artist also learned to handle more saturated tones, as shown in the Paris music hall series from around 1906–7. Through his contact with the many impressionists he spent time with in Dieppe, Sickert's painting evolved towards a more varied and brighter colour palette, with a thicker use of impasto. In an 'impressionist' spirit (he had also probably seen Monet's series of twenty Cathedrals at Durand-Ruel's gallery in May 1895 when he passed through Paris on his way to Venice), he began focusing on painting the same subject repeatedly, but with variations. He took a particular interest in the colouration of shade in the work of Monet, Sisley and Pissarro. In addition, he frequented and studied the neo-impressionists, from whom he adopted the juxtaposition of touches of pure colour. In an essay devoted to impressionism, Sickert notes with interest that each touch is applied knowingly, cleanly and separately, with a defined and planned function.[3] It was this approach that he then went on to explore in his painting after breaking away from the tonal harmonies of Whistler.

Sickert also took an interest in the Symbolists, in Puvis de Chavannes in particular, and in those artists who would become the Nabis.

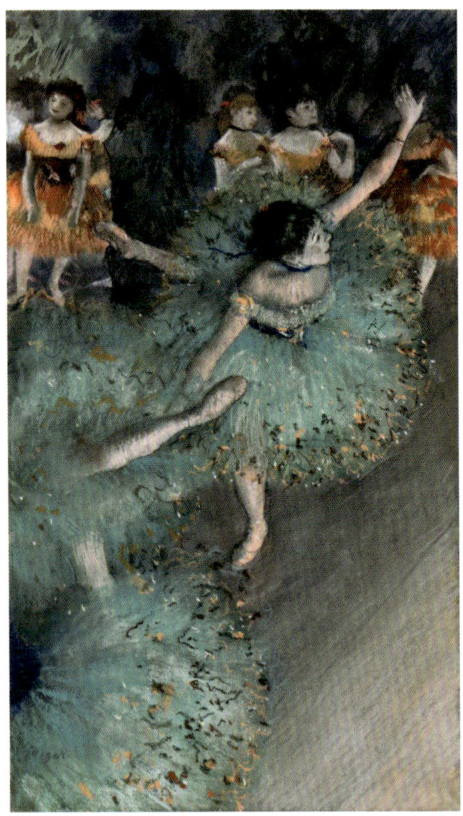

In England, he championed the painting of Vuillard in his critical writing.[4] From the mid-1910s, he developed a closeness to Bonnard in his treatment of colour. Writing in 1930, François Fosca considered that 'if there is a French painter with whom Sickert can be compared, it is Bonnard; both are at once free and naïve, knowing and free, colourist and refined. Dismissive of any kind of system and fundamentally independent, they never cease to be seduced by the perpetually changing spectacle of everyday life.'[5] Sickert and Bonnard were friends and shared the same art dealer, Bernheim-Jeune, with whom Sickert had a contract from 1903, and also had certain collectors in common, including André Gide. Sickert's admiration for Bonnard was in fact reciprocated, as Bonnard purchased several of Sickert's works. Two nudes – *Siesta* and *Femme assoupie sur un lit* – by Bonnard, painted in or around 1900, are particularly interesting to compare with Sickert's nudes: the latter (see no.106) is striking in the boldness of its pose, the framing and the setting of the bedroom, and Sickert would certainly have seen it when it was exhibited by Bernheim-Jeune. Another painting by Bonnard, *L'Homme et la Femme* 1900 (see fig.32), depicts, as does Sickert's work, the enclosed world of a bedroom, with a nude couple shown entirely through the reflection of a mirror. As Wendy Baron points out, at this period both artists shared the same muddy tones, olive green in particular, and the same way of outlining the figures with shadow.[6]

The impact of French models can also be seen in Sickert's choice of subject. His closeness to Degas played a clear role in his selection of music hall as a subject and in his painterly approach. Sickert and his wife had in fact purchased a number of works by Degas, including *Swaying Dancer (Dancer in Green)* (see fig.21) and *Mademoiselle Bécat at the Café des Ambassadeurs*. Sickert would later acquire another work by the artist, *Woman at a Window*, which he exchanged in 1902 for *Ballet Rehearsal on Stage*. Although his treatment of popular entertainment and music hall scenes may appear to link him to Toulouse-Lautrec – who was quite well known in London (notably with an exhibition at the Goupil Gallery in 1898) – Sickert never showed any enthusiasm for the artist in his critical writings. On the other hand, he experimented with the thick touch and bright colours of Rouault in certain of his late-period music hall pieces (Sickert saw Rouault's work at the Salon d'Automne of 1904 and himself exhibited at the 1906 Salon in the same room as Rouault). Music hall constituted a sort of English equivalent to the popular entertainments painted by French artists who represented the modernity that Sickert admired, and to whom he frequently referred in his writings; they included Daumier (*Aux Champs-Élysées*), Manet (*The Street Singer, A Bar at the Folies-Bergère, The Waitress*) and Degas (*Café-Concert at Les Ambassadeurs*). Sickert, who was well acquainted with French literature, adopted the position of the Baudelairean *flâneur* in his descriptions of urban modernity,[7] as Anna Gruetzner Robins points out.[8] Even though he does not refer to this text in his writings, he was interested by Baudelaire's vision of art as expressed in reference to Constantin Guys, whereby modernity is 'the ephemeral, the fugitive, the contingent, the half of art whose other half is the eternal and immutable'.[9]

The same French influence continued in his new approach to the treatment of the nude. Sickert disparaged the idealised nudes that proliferated in the salons, but was interested in those which expressed the modernity of nineteenth-century French painting. Having lived in France and having mainly exhibited his nudes in Paris, Sickert was perfectly aware of the transformation in the representation of the nude that took place at the turn of the century among the impressionists, the symbolists, the Fauves and the Nabis. He took part notably in the 1905 Salon d'Automne, at a time when the Fauves were together in one room. These artists took a provocative interest in the nude, showing a desire to move away from the realism of form and colour that marked a major genre in the history of art. Sickert was also in contact with Europe's avant-garde who were well represented in Paris. The artist was clearly inspired by the modernity of French and European painting in his treatment of the nude, although subsequently, after the First World War, this influence became less noticeable in his later oeuvre.

From influence to identity

Sickert openly expressed his debt to French artists in a letter of 1901 written to Sir William Eden, a collector of Degas and an amateur painter: 'Stick to the French school. *Il n'y a que cela* in modern art. We are good only in as much as we derive from them. I certainly would rather live in England if I were well off, but I have learnt here what I couldn't have learnt in a lifetime at home.'[10] He explains to him the reasons for his exile in France: 'So I suppose an all-wise Providence is interested in my technique, & exiles me from beef, beer & music-halls, most of my friends, & all my mistresses so that I may leave behind an oeuvre.'[11]

In the late 1870s and early 1880s, French modernity – quite present in London, largely thanks to George Moore and Paul Durand-Ruel – was curiously well accepted despite the relatively academic culture of British art and a Victorian puritanism that was at odds with the state of mind of the young French Republic. It was not until a little later that the innovations of French art began to arouse hostile reactions in the United Kingdom, when, in 1893, the intense polemic that ensued regarding Degas's *L'Absinthe*, exhibited at the Grafton Gallery, triggered an outburst of francophobia. French art was judged to be morally decadent, and critics expressed their wish that British artists return to subjects and approaches more in line with British tradition. The fact was that the most innovative groups of artists in London at that time were usually foreign in origin (notably, the Americans Whistler and John Singer Sargent). Sickert himself was both very grateful for what the French school had brought him and, at the same time, keen to play his part in the affirmation of the British school.

He was ambiguous about the national question, since he had a genuinely cosmopolitan dimension to his own history, but also an awareness of the issues surrounding patriotism. He wished to fight against the conformity of British art of the period, taking inspiration from French modernity, but was also determined to consolidate and extend a British school of painting. In this avowed affiliation to British painting one can detect the desire to establish a new national art capable of rivalling that of Europe, and of France in particular – French painting being very present in London with exhibitions of contemporary French art arranged by Durand-Ruel as early as the 1870s and the later 'post-impressionist' exhibitions organised by Roger Fry in 1910 and 1912.

Sickert and the French art market: dealers, exhibitions and art lovers

By the early 1880s, Sickert was well known to his French contemporaries and had become part of the cultural and artistic world of Paris, thanks to Whistler, Degas and Jacques-Émile Blanche. As we have seen, his art dealers in the capital were Durand-Ruel in the early years of the twentieth century, followed by Bernheim-Jeune. In December 1900, he presented his first major monographic exhibition at Durand-Ruel's gallery. In total, Sickert exhibited in Paris on fifteen occasions between 1900 and 1909, and also showed his work at the three alternative salons: the Salon de la Société Nationale, the Salon des Indépendants and the Salon d'Automne. It was as part of the French section that he exhibited at various international exhibitions, including the Venice Biennale of 1903. Even after his return to England, Sickert maintained his links with the French art world, continuing, for example, to exhibit at all the Salons d'Automne between 1905 and 1909 – and he was made a member of this salon in 1908. He mainly exhibited nudes. He exhibited again at the Galerie Bernheim-Jeune in 1907 and 1909. Here he was able to count on the support of Félix Fénéon, who had been directing the gallery's activities since November 1906. Fénéon also included Sickert in various exhibition projects at rue Richepanse (where the Bernheim-Jeune gallery was located), even after the artist's collaboration with Bernheim-Jeune had come to an end. Sickert took part, too, in an exhibition of nudes in May 1910, the 'La Faune' exhibition in December 1910, the 'L'Eau' exhibition in June 1911 and 'Soixante nus' in April 1921.[12]

By this stage of his career, in the early twentieth century, Sickert had already gained some prominence through his music hall paintings, and he went on to acquire a certain rating in the art market thanks to his portraits in England and his landscapes in France – Durand-Ruel and Bernheim-Jeune had no difficulty in selling his views of Dieppe and Venice in France. His paintings of nudes and interior scenes were also much more rapidly and widely exhibited and more favourably received in Paris. In the early twentieth century, France was better placed than England to show and appreciate these aesthetically and morally subversive scenes. At the major monographic exhibition that Bernheim-Jeune mounted for Sickert in June 1904, numbers 10 to 19 were figures in interiors (including *Devant la Glace*, *Jeune Femme* and *Le Déshabillé*). *Cocotte de Soho* (see no.111) and *Le Lit de Fer* (no.113) were exhibited at the Salon d'Automne of 1905; *La Coiffure*, *Early Morning*, *Réveil*, *Woman Washing her Hair* (see no.116), *Femme nue couchée*, *Jeanne*, and probably *Blanche* and *Femme nue rousse*, *La belle rousse*, *Nu au miroir*, *Le grand miroir* and *Nude at a Mirror* were shown at Sickert's exhibitions at the Galerie Bernheim-Jeune in 1907; and some were shown again in 1909. Paul Jamot purchased, as did Étienne Moreau-Nélaton and Adolphe Tavernier who wrote the preface for the 1909 exhibition. Tavernier was associated with a sale at the Drouot auction house (see fig.22) that achieved only moderate success (*Le grand miroir* did not find a new owner despite the quality of its execution).

Sickert's paintings were therefore acquired for modest sums but, as was his wish, by enlightened collectors – intellectuals such as André Gide, Daniel Halévy, Félix Fénéon, Romain Coolus, Paul Jamot and Adolphe Tavernier, as well as his painter friends including Bonnard, Blanche, Pissarro, Signac and Maximilien Luce. At the 1904 exhibition, seventy-two of the ninety-six pieces shown were loaned by an impressive list of well-known figures from the world of culture, and only twenty-one works were for sale.

Critical reception in France
Generally speaking, France's critics were favourable to Sickert. Arsène Alexandre, writing in *Le Figaro* about the 1904 exhibition, had this to say: 'Walter Sickert. Take note of this name as that of one of the most exquisite, most edgily personal artists, whose works before long will be sought after by art lovers as the precious ornaments they are. His exhibition at the Bernheim gallery of some hundred paintings, principally views of Venice, combines an oddly modern flavour with the most impeccable eighteenth-century traditions. This somewhat sad, somewhat painfully dream-like temperament takes pleasure in revelling in a sombre and sober richness. One view of San Marco appears as if painted with faded roses, while a view of the Piazzetta is like a jewel of jet.'[13] Several critics underline his affiliation with French painting, while others, like Robert de Tanlis, also point to the singular atmosphere of 'spleen' found in his work: 'All these scenes, all this nudity lying prostrate on fabrics in poison-engorged tones, are spread forth here, these landscapes and these views of Paris, Italy or London are set out in a fuliginous atmosphere which shivers with anguish and appears heavy with a fateful *spleen*.'[14] Paul Jamot, in *La Chronique des arts et de la curiosité*, is equally glowing in his appreciation of the exhibition that followed in 1907: 'It does not surprise the visitor to find that this highly gallicised English painter should take pleasure, like Baudelaire, in reading the Latin poets. Whether nude or clothed, whether seen in the feathered plumes of the midnight reveller or in the black shawl of a Venetian woman, he observes in his customary, professional poses of lassitude, ennui or wariness, a foolish, oblivious or pitiful girl, a contemptible plaything attractive to male caprice. He paints her with a humour the pungency of which is far from bland; and he demonstrates a talent which, though it may spring from a Whistlerian dilettantism, appears to have become humanised on contact with our own young school.'[15]

Louis Vauxcelles took a particular interest in Sickert. Writing about the pastels he exhibited at the 1905 Salon d'Automne, he observes: 'Sickert is the man of vinous and blackish harmonies, of nudes flung on a bed, of evening when the curtains intercept all light; seeing with these leaden complexions, these degradations of cadaverous tonalities, one thinks of Edgar Allan Poe.'[16] The critic Gustave Geffroy writes: 'Monsieur Sickert observes figures dying in obscure rooms in London.'[17] On the subject of *Mornington Crescent Nude* (see no.119), exhibited at the 1908 Salon d'Automne, Louis Vauxcelles notes: 'The weight of the sleeping girl is rendered with an extraordinary sense of volume. Monsieur Sickert knows better than anyone at the present time that on a dark and transparent sketch, and most notably on black, light tones take on a violent radiance, and that light impasto in ambiguous tones (winey mauves, grey-greenish-blues, dull shades of orange, whites broken, warmed up or made cold, sing out with finesse.'[18] Sickert's highly individual palette was therefore well perceived in France. Sickert was keen to explore the treatment of colour and had the courage to use colours some considered glaucous, in keeping with the subjects he was painting. In 1907, Raymond Bouyer writes that 'this worshipper of Whistler cultivates with talent the monotone sketch, the philosophical bitterness of grisaille and the preciosity of sullied tones'.[19] And the critic Félix Monod notes in 1909: 'His palette is a poor wretch in faded rags. Exquisite in its sullied tones, a mix of greens and blacks, of muddish green, of caviar grey, decaying, smothered blues and pinks, reddish-brown, greyish-brown and dead lilac, it has been steeped in the winters of London and in the rotten waters of the Thames.'[20] Some years later, in 1930, François Fosca, writing with the hindsight of Sickert's postwar artistic evolution, also draws attention to the singularity of his palette: 'And once again, what an extraordinary grasp of colour! Sickert is as much at ease balancing faded greys as he is when braving strident harmonies, colour accords the sweetened acidity of which is like a visual transposition of *chutney* and of sweet and sour. As with Bonnard, it is because he began by combining tones which others judged "dirty" that he is now able to play with the purest of tones.'[21]

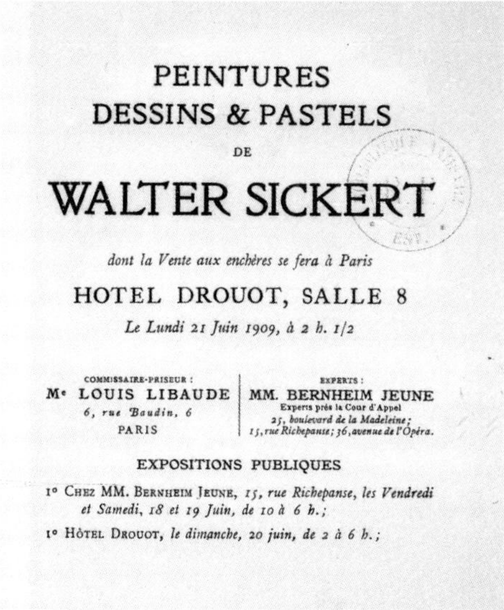

However, after Sickert's death, appreciation of the artist switched to the other side of the Channel, while in France he sank into oblivion. Although his paintings had been extensively exhibited in France for almost half a century, between 1903 and 1954, essentially they only became part of the country's public collections thanks to donations made by Jacques-Émile Blanche, and even then they remained in museum reserves for many years. Wendy Baron recounts that when, preparing her thesis, she visited the Musée des Beaux-Arts in Rouen, hoping to see *Vénitienne allongée à la jupe rouge*, she was told that the subject was too indecent for the painting to be shown in public. Since then the situation has changed and Sickert's paintings have been put on display as part of the museum's permanent collection.[22]

This essay was edited by Clara Roca. It includes extracts from texts written by the late Delphine Lévy, a French specialist on Walter Sickert, and takes the place of the essay she would have written as curator of the exhibition for its Paris stage at the Petit Palais. These extracts focus on Sickert's relationship with France. They have been selected mainly from Lévy's first and second Master's dissertations, both of which were devoted to Sickert, with some additions from her book Walter Sickert (1860–1942): L'Art de l'énigme *(Paris 2016), published in association with the Dieppe exhibition and updated in reference to her monograph published by Cohen & Cohen, which appeared posthumously in 2021. Further additional sources and publications have been called upon to enrich this source material in keeping with the theme chosen for this catalogue essay.*

Fig.22
Peintures, Dessins & Pastels de Walter Sickert, sale at Drouot auction house, 21 June 1909

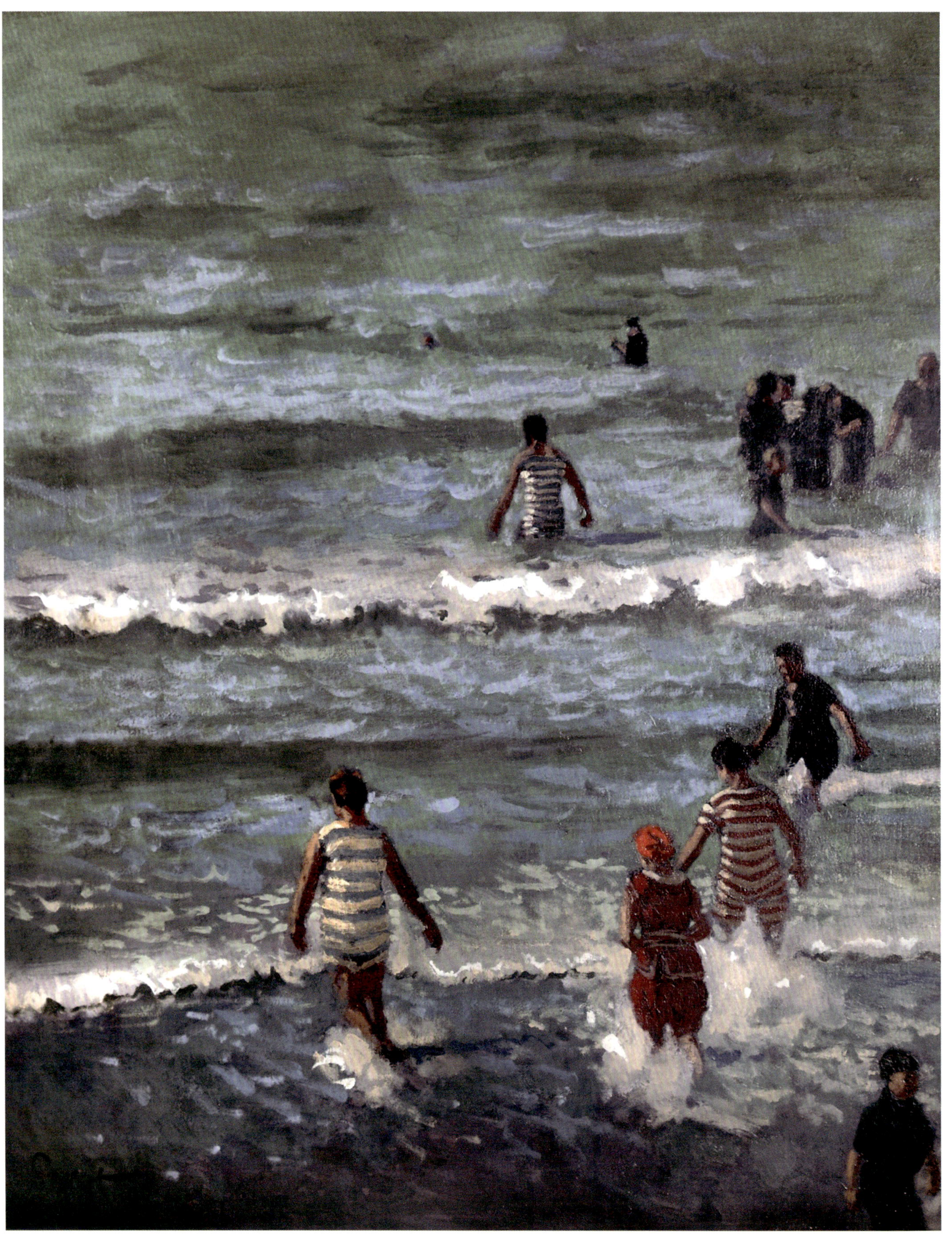

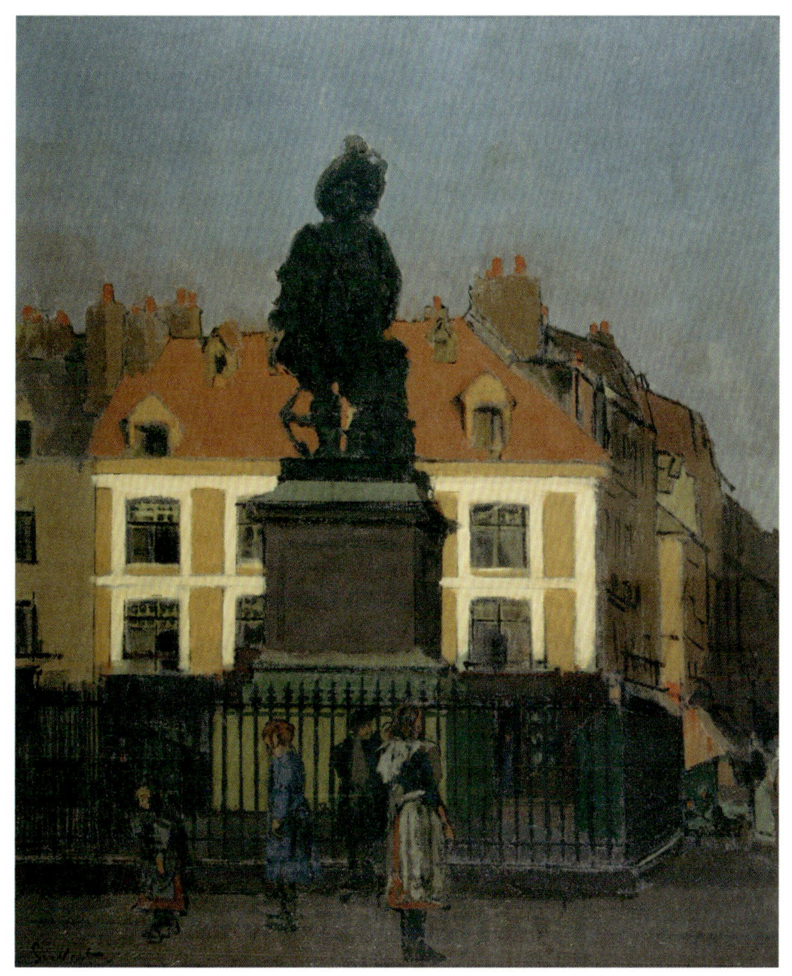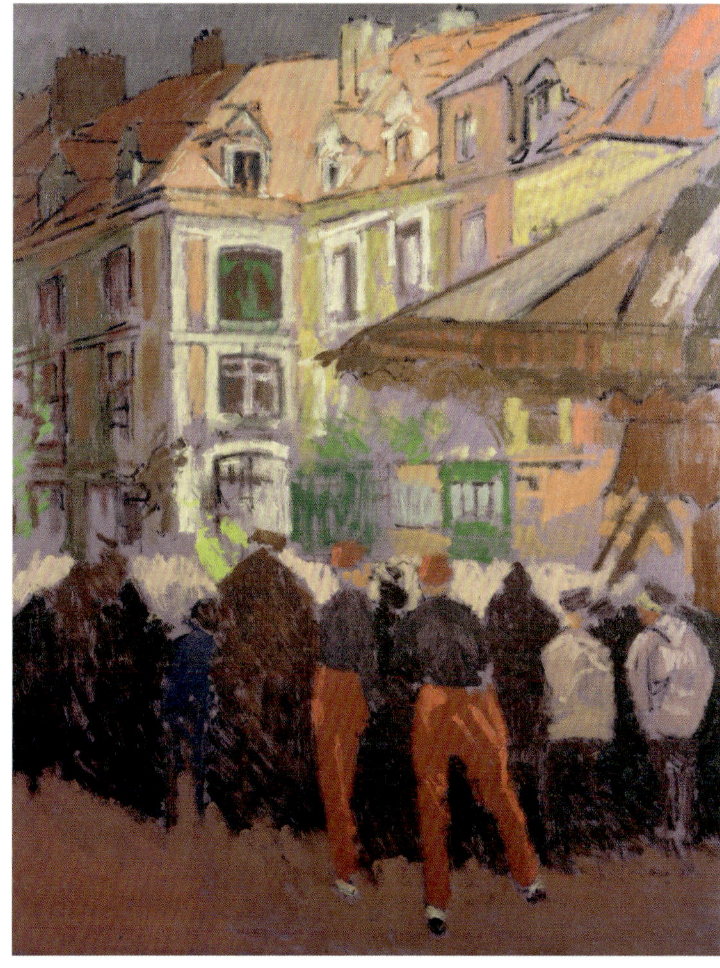

94
Bathers, Dieppe c.1902
Oil paint on canvas
National Museums
Liverpool, Walker Art
Gallery

95
Le Grand Duquesne
1902
Oil paint on canvas
Manchester Art Gallery

96
The Fair at Night
c.1902–3
Oil paint on canvas
Touchstones Rochdale
Art Gallery, Link4Life

133

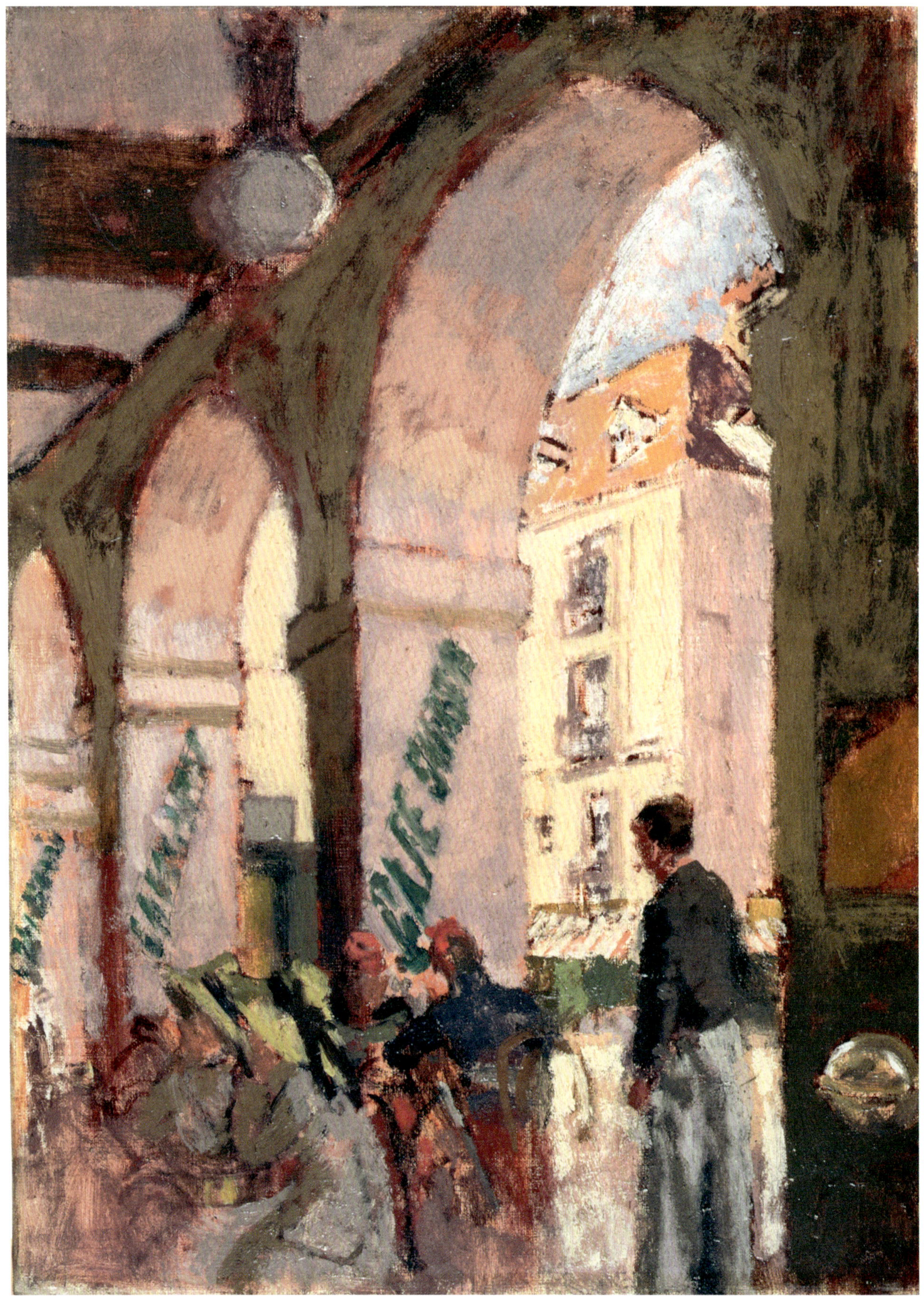

97
Café des Arcades
(*or Café Suisse*) c.1914
Oil paint on canvas
Leeds Museums and
Galleries

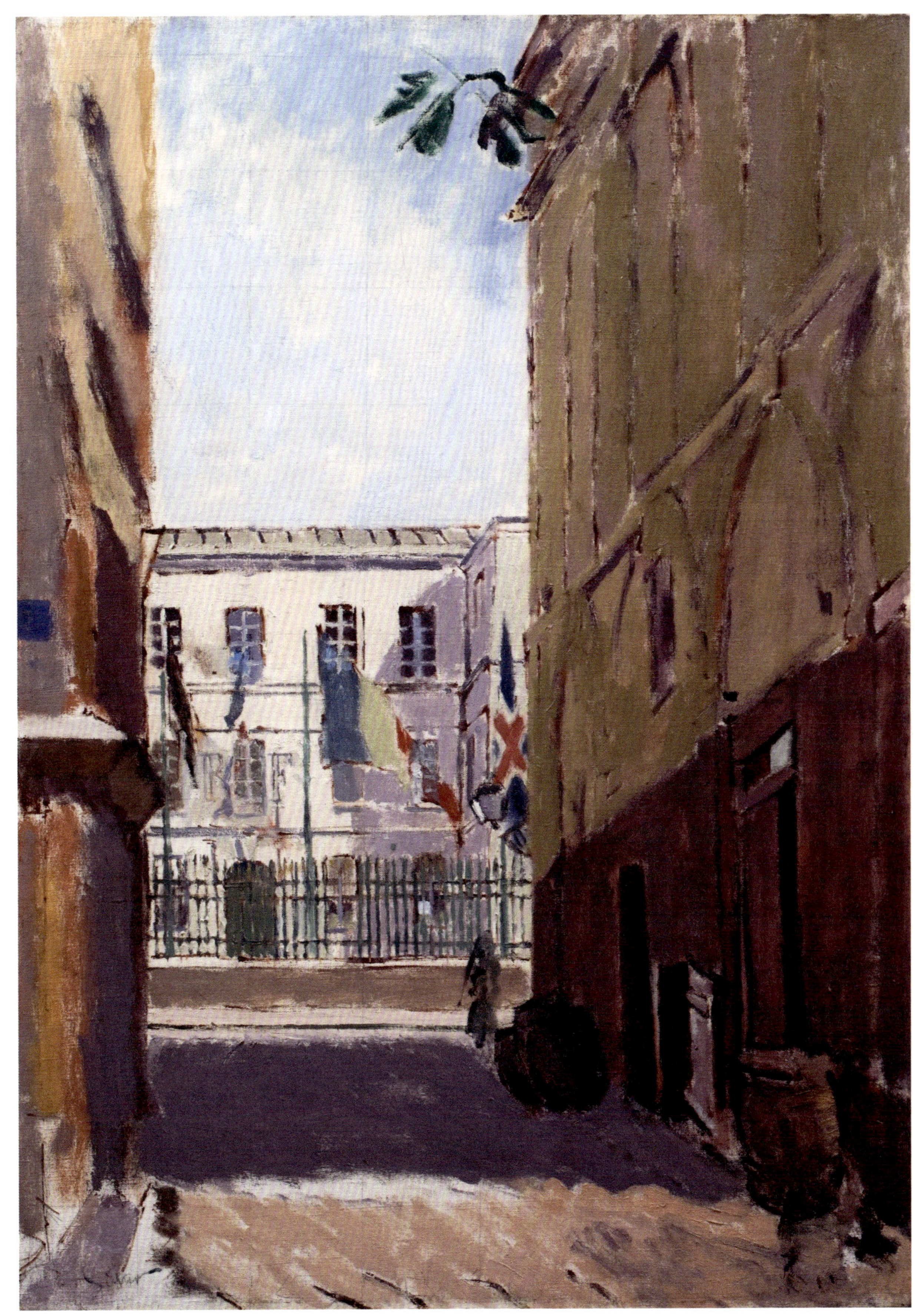

98
Celebrations, Dieppe 1914
Oil paint on canvas
Private collection.
Courtesy of PIANO
NOBILE, London

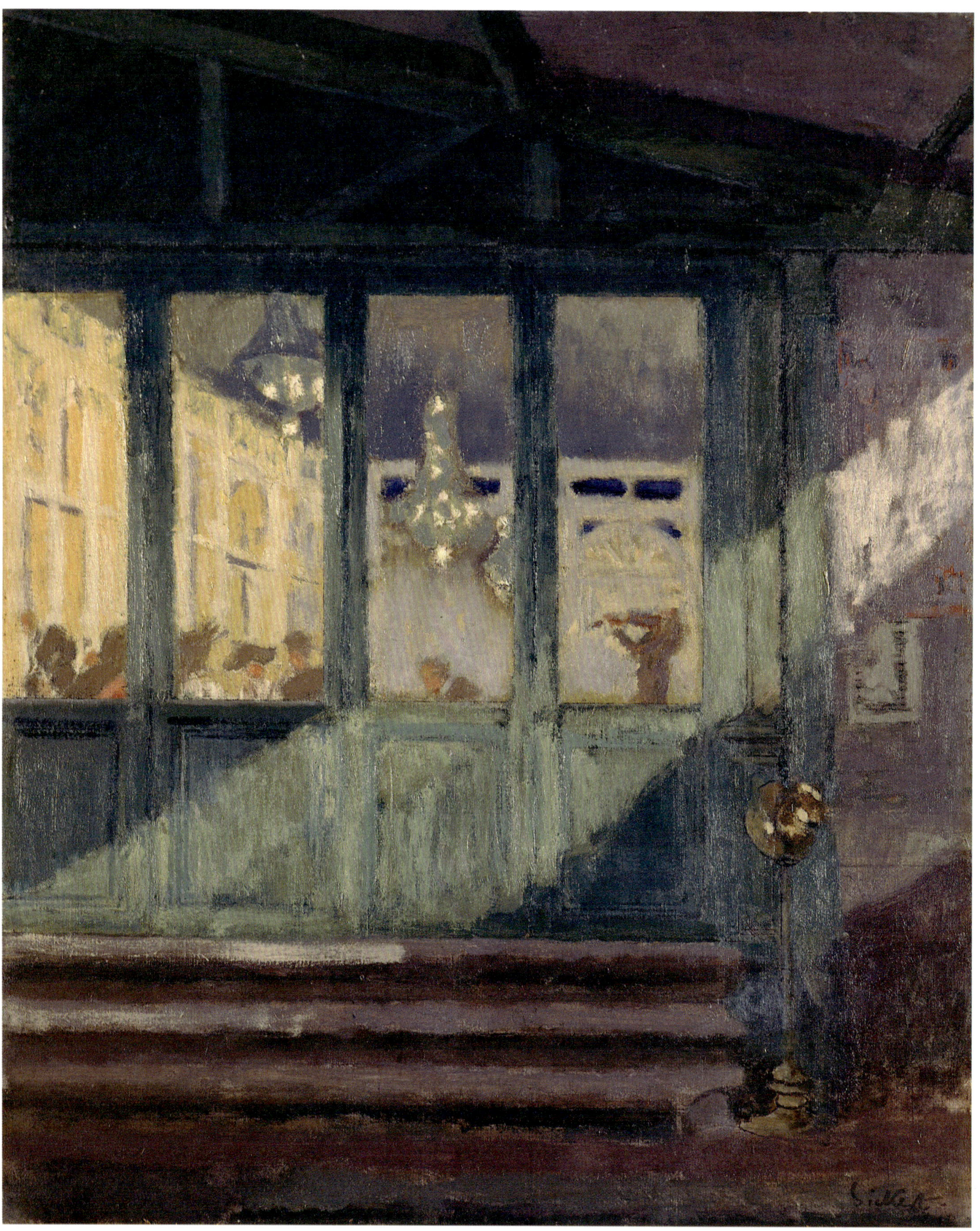

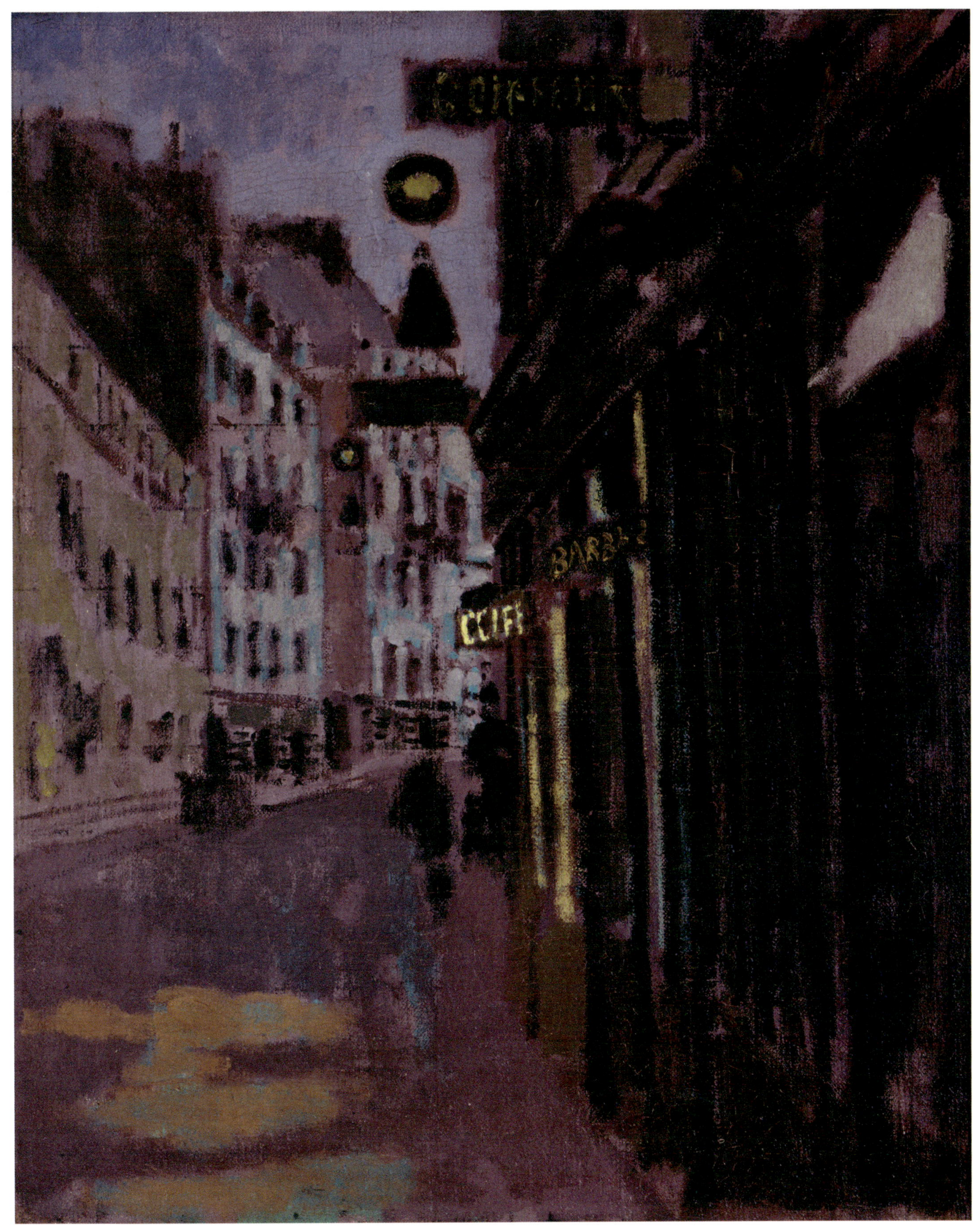

Coiffeur
BARBI
COIFF

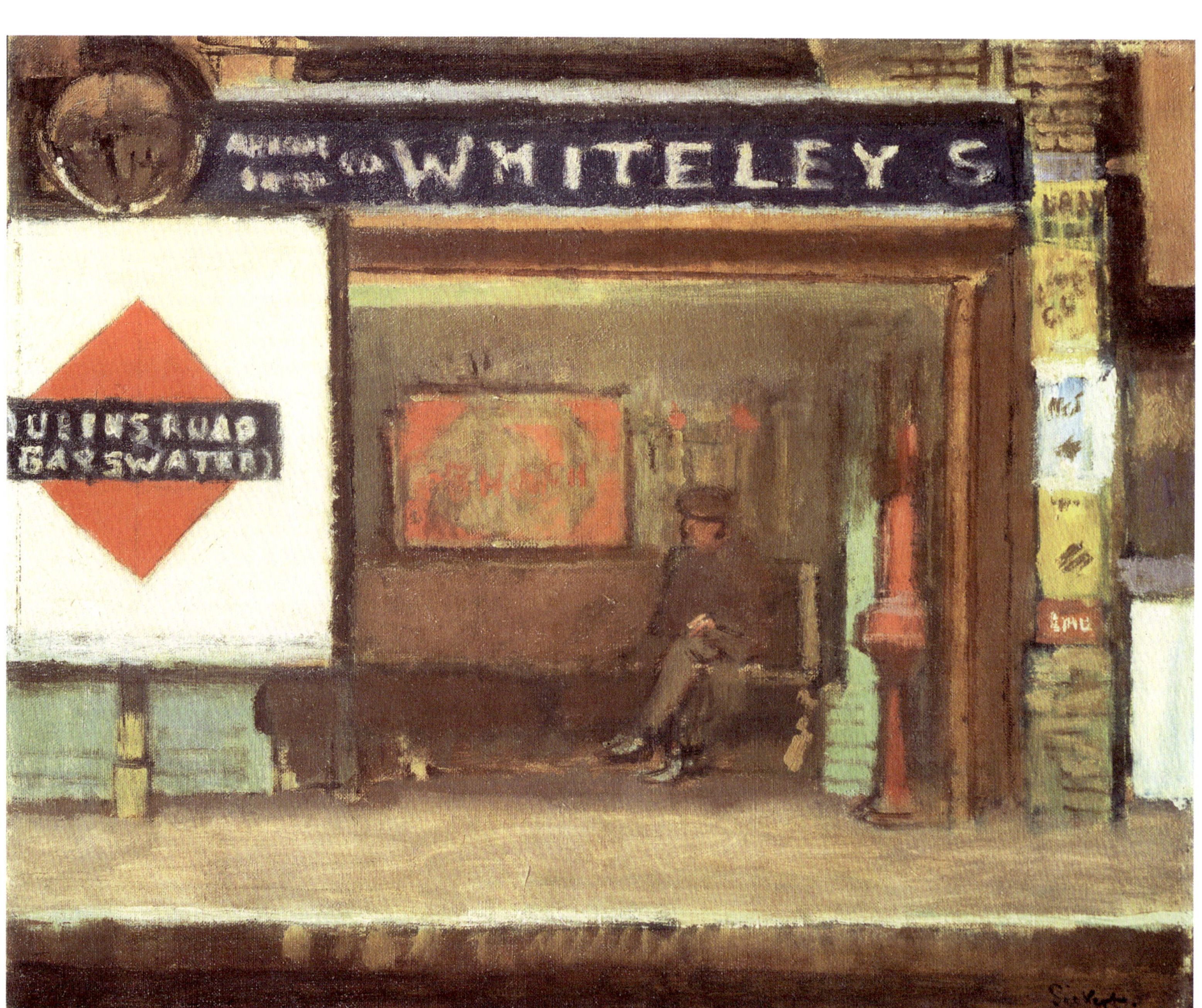

101
*Queens Road Station,
Bayswater* 1915–16
Oil paint on canvas
The Courtauld, London
(Samuel Courtauld Trust)

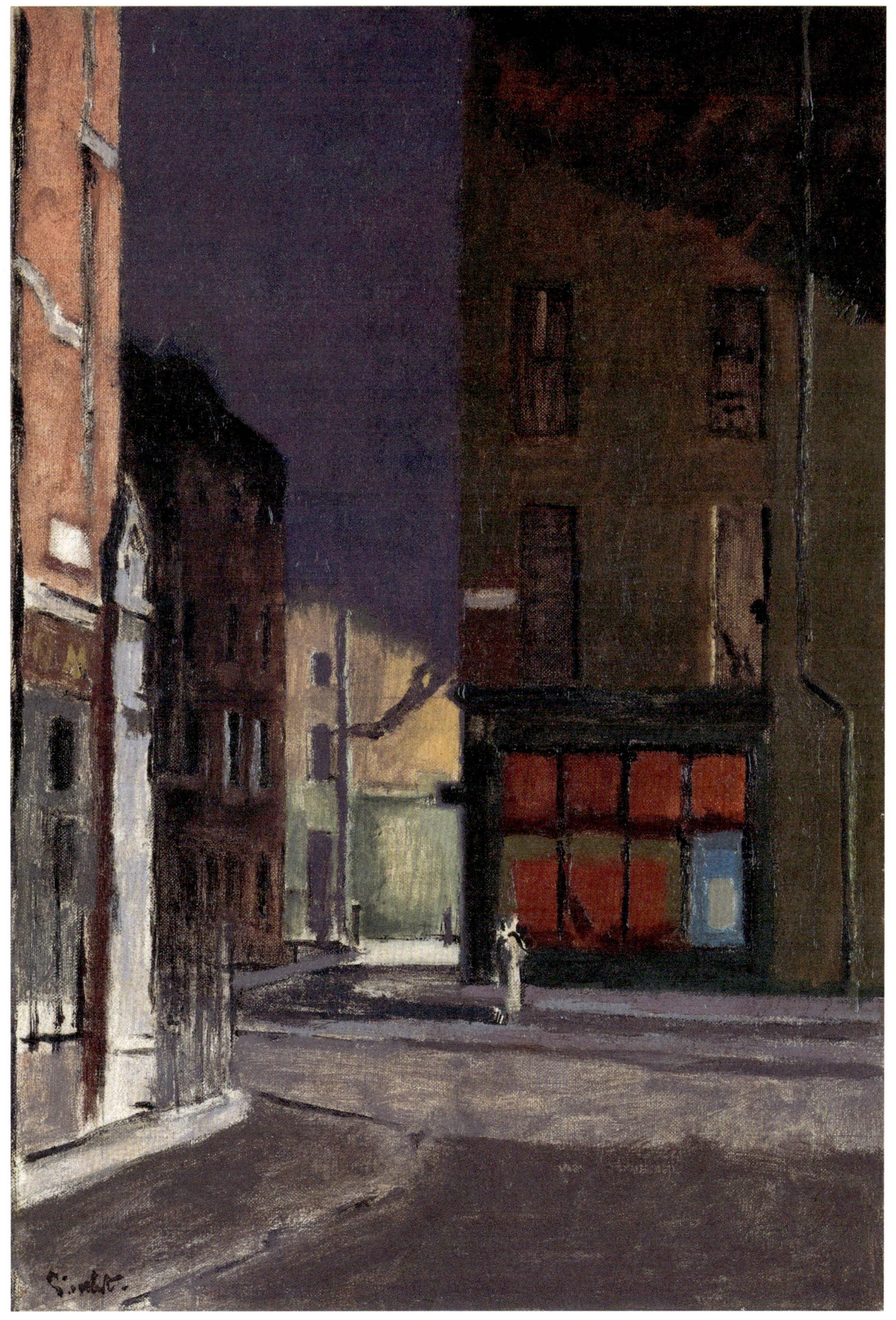

102
Maple Street
1916
Oil paint on canvas
The Metropolitan
Museum of Art

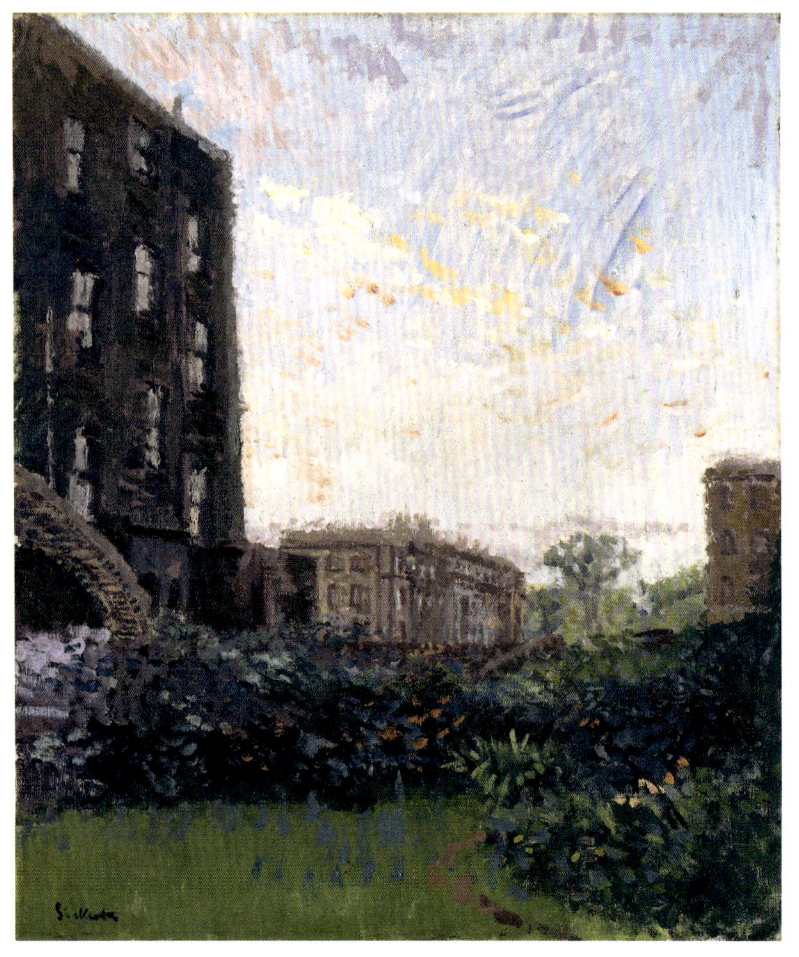

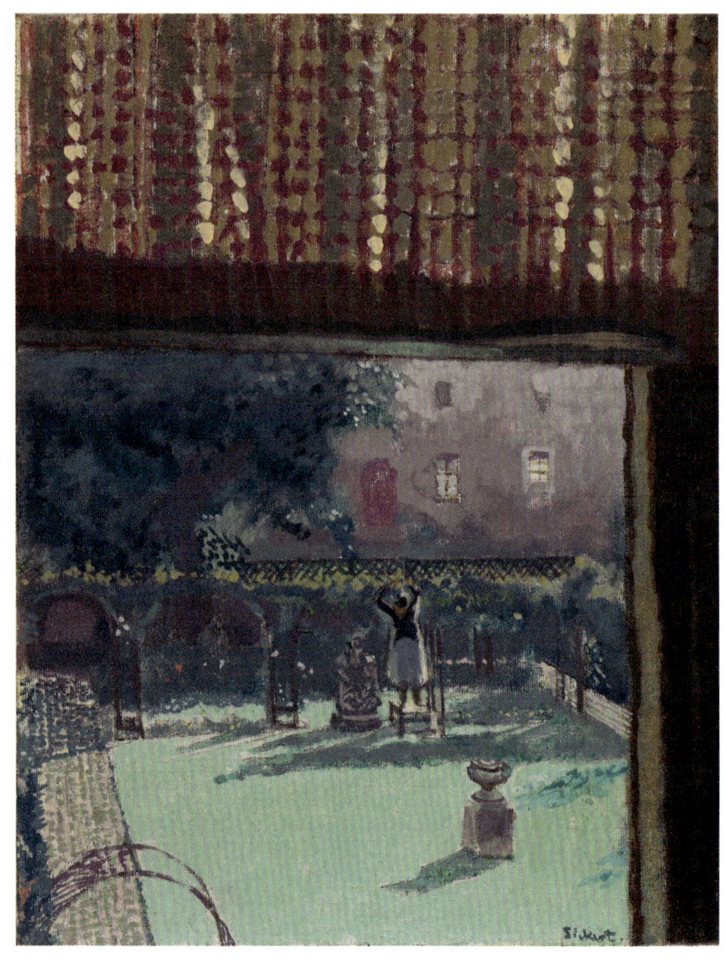

103
*Rowlandson House –
Sunset* 1910–11
Oil paint on canvas
Tate

104
*The Garden of Love
or Lainey's Garden*
c.1927–8
Oil paint on canvas
The Syndics of the
Fitzwilliam Museum,
University of Cambridge

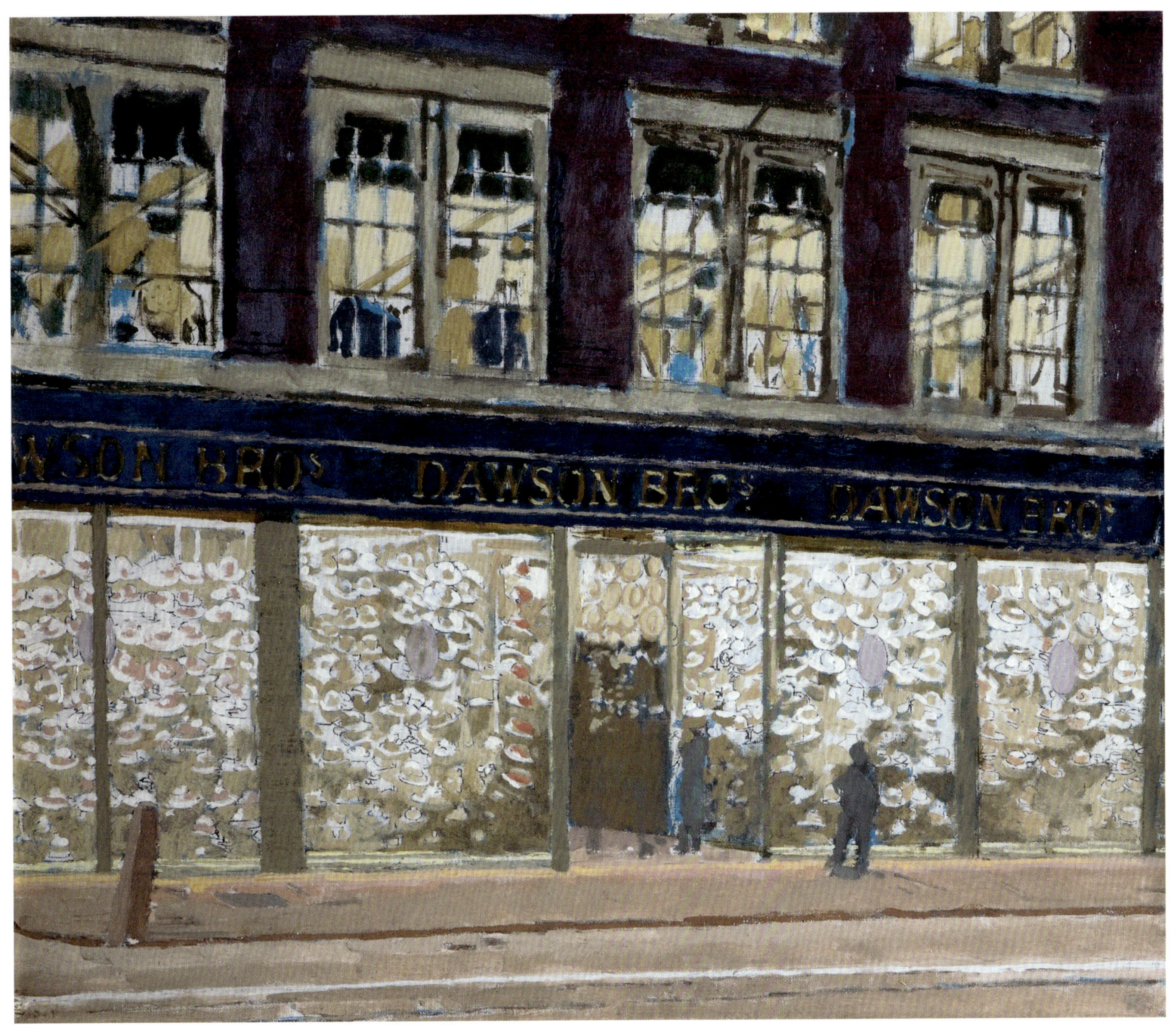

105
Easter c.1928
Oil paint on canvas
Courtesy of Board of
Trustees of National
Museums NI

THE NUDE

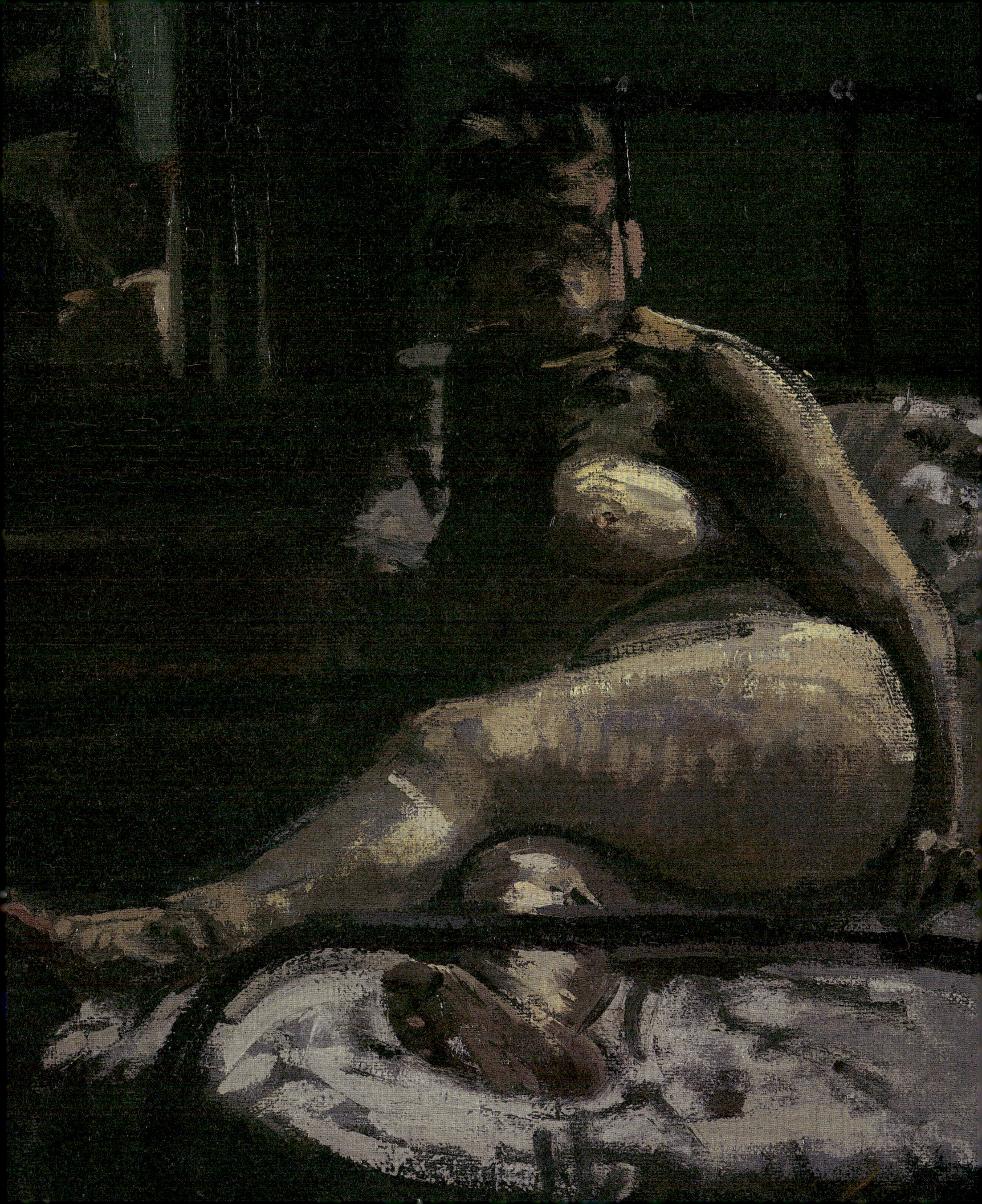

LISA TICKNER

SICKERT AND THE NUDE

across the mattress from the left. Figure, bed and setting merge in a restrained tonality, the brightest accent a single rose-lined black shoe at centre stage, 'voluptuous', 'flamboyant', 'flashy and coquettish'.[6] This is what the eye first registers: a distinctive colour and shape in the organisation of the picture, but at the same time an invitation to narrative (kicked off in passion, exhaustion or despair?) and to metaphor (hinting at pinkly enfolding interiors).[7]

While based in Dieppe from 1898 to 1905, Sickert made three extended visits to Venice. On the last of these, between autumn 1903 and the summer of 1904, he turned from landscapes to 'figure pictures'.[8] Among his models were the local prostitutes La Giuseppina and her friend Carolina dell'Acqua, who posed separately and together, clothed and unclothed, in Sickert's rooms at 940 Calle dei Frati. The combination of a naked with a clothed figure in an intimate setting, and the adoption of brusquely foreshortened, sexually explicit poses, were new developments anticipating the Camden Town nudes and 'conversation pieces' that followed Sickert's return to London in 1905. He aimed for 'the sensation of a page torn from the book of life', rather than the idealised bodies and smooth finish of an academic nude, which meant casual poses, intimate settings, abandoned clothing – and pubic hair. [9]

Nudes

Sickert was well known – even notorious – in the Edwardian art world as a painter of nudes. (Sir William Blake Richmond, a Royal Academician, described what he called his 'disgusting Bordello exhibition' of drawings at the Carfax Gallery in 1911 as 'worse than Slum Art, worse far than Prostitution, because it is done by a man who should know better'.[1]) Sickert had strong views on the feebleness of Royal Academy and Salon nudes lightly veiled in allegory or myth (see figs.24 and 25). He urged the modernising and 'real-ising' of the nude – in composition, setting and handling – as a plausible representation of a contemporary '*someone, somewhere*'.[2] The intensity of his engagement with the nude in paintings, drawings, prints and published criticism has, however, somewhat obscured the fact that nudes were only a small fraction of his extensive output, confined to little more than a decade in a sixty-year career.[3]

Sickert was an established artist in his early forties living in Neuville, near Dieppe, when he painted *The Shoe with a Rose* c.1902–4 (see no.108), which seems to have been his first nude subject.[4] The model was probably his lover Augustine Villain, 'la belle rousse', doyenne of the Dieppe fish market.[5] *The Shoe with a Rose* is an intimate bedroom scene, relaxed but with a subtle tension in the composition: the bed at a slight diagonal rising on the right, the naked woman sprawling

Sickert set out his position with characteristic verve in 'The naked and the Nude', an article for *The New Age* published in 1910.[10] Part-provocation, part-manifesto, this mocked the 'prurient puritanism' that had evolved 'an ideal which it seeks to dignify by calling it the Nude, with a capital "n", and placing it in opposition to the naked'. Here Sickert anticipates, but in reverse, a well-known distinction in Kenneth Clark's *The Nude: A Study of Ideal Art* (1956).[11] For Clark, the lumpen and imperfect human body requires transfiguring into the harmonious proportions of the ideal Nude. For Sickert, this had led to a 'modern flood' of 'vacuous images' in official exhibitions: products of 'an intellectual and artistic bankruptcy' that had spawned volumes of reproductions such as *Le Nu au Salon* and photographs of naked models trading as 'artists' studies'. The Salon nude was no better and in his view more pretentious than *tableaux vivants* (see fig.28) in the contemporary music hall.[12] How many years had artists wasted, painting Tilly Pullen in borrowed finery on a life-sized canvas?

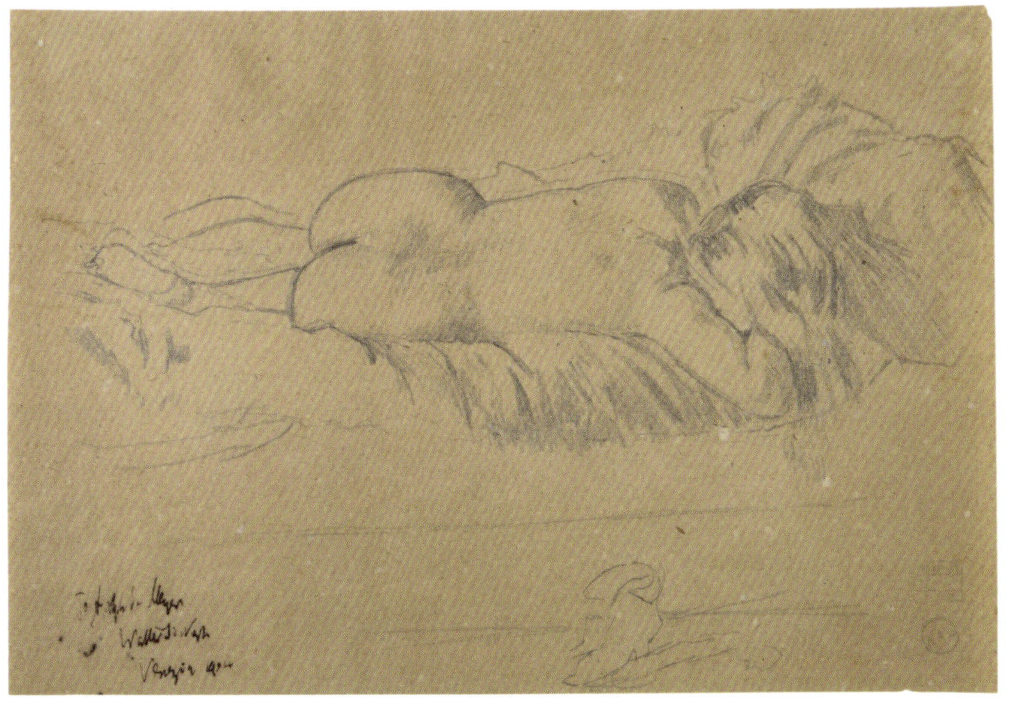

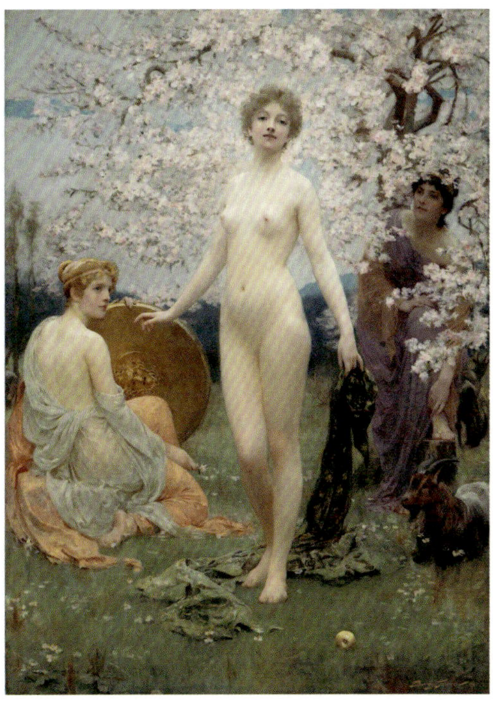

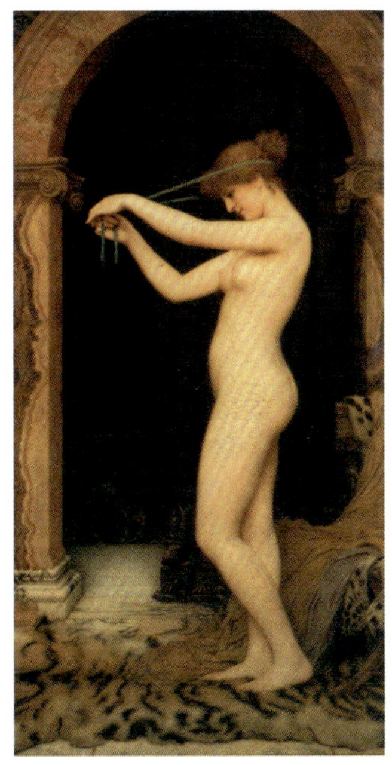

Fig.23
Nude on a Couch 1914,
graphite on paper,
22.3×31.6, Princeton
University Art Museum

Fig.24
John William Godward,
Venus Binding her Hair
1897, oil paint on
canvas, 227.7×113.4,
Private collection

Fig.25
Joseph Solomon,
Judgement of Paris
1891, oil paint on
canvas, 236.2×165.7,
Private collection

[S]trip Tilly Pullen of her lendings and tell her to put her own things on again. Let her leave the studio and climb the first dirty little staircase in the first shabby little house. Tilly Pullen becomes interesting at once… She becomes stuff for a picture. Follow her into her kitchen, or, better still … into her bedroom; and now Tilly Pullen is become the stuff of which the Parthenon was made, or Dürer, or any Rembrandt.[13]

The 'abler moderns' – Sickert had artists such as Degas and Bonnard in mind – painted the modern nude not as Venus or Primavera but as a body emerging from bathtubs and crumpled sheets. It was necessary to 'keep out of the old ruts of expression'. Degas had 'incessantly chosen to draw figures from unaccustomed points of view' and, following his example, the artist 'must try so to pose, so to light, and so to "cut" the nude' as to 'forget the lifeless formulas of generations'.[14]

Sickert had seen Degas's *Bathers* in his studio on their first meeting in 1883, and again at the last Impressionist Exhibition in 1886 (comparable Degas pastels were not shown in London until 1905).[15] In Paris, where Sickert exhibited regularly at the Salon d'Automne and with the dealers Durand-Ruel and then Bernheim-Jeune, he was established as a painter of 'modern' nudes, influenced by Degas and familiar with the work of Bonnard and Vuillard.[16] In 1910 he had yet to exhibit nudes in London. 'The naked and the Nude', his blast against 'Idealism' and his evocation of Tilly Pullen in 'The Study of Drawing', were perhaps intended to prepare the ground for his drawings at the Carfax Gallery in January 1911 (which so offended Sir William Blake Richmond) and his contribution to the first Camden Town Group exhibition the following June.[17]

Sickert's return to London in 1905 marked the beginning of a sustained engagement with the female nude in an overlapping series of rented rooms. In 1905 he took lodgings at 6 Mornington Crescent in Camden Town, expanding in 1907 onto the first floor, and renting 247 Hampstead Road in 1908. Camden Town, developed as a middle-class suburb in the early nineteenth century, had been blighted with the coming of the railways. Property values slumped and family villas were subdivided into multiple lodgings for a shifting population of working-class tenants.[18] Sickert had started out as an actor and in these rented rooms he dressed his sets, posed his models and arranged the furniture (some of which was his). The basic hoop-backed iron bedstead, a regular feature, was used in lodging houses, servants' rooms,

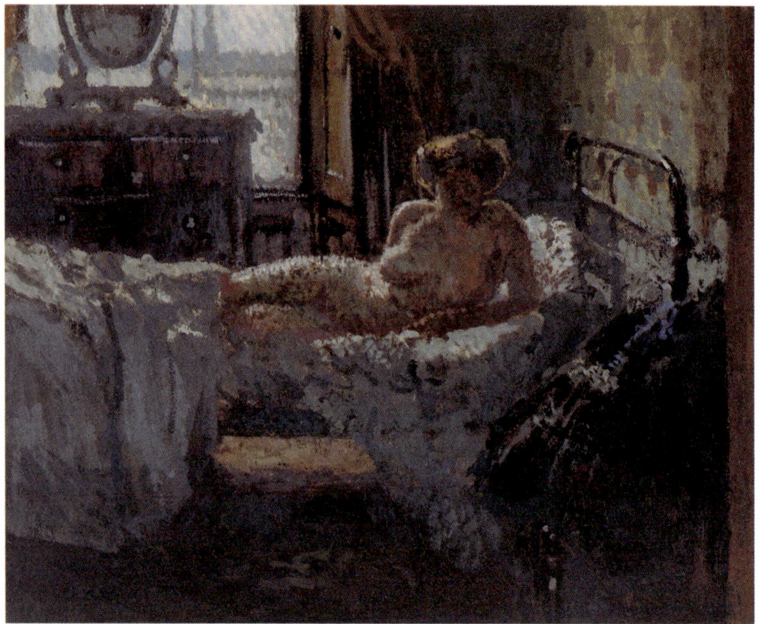

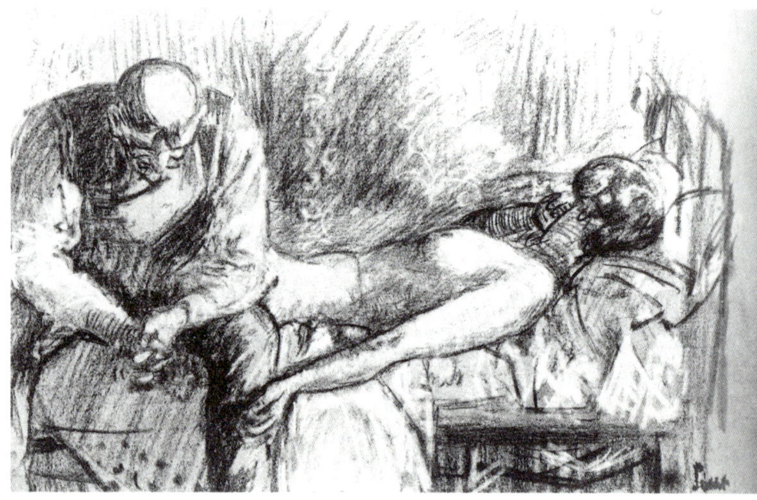

Fig.26
Mornington Crescent nude, contre-jour 1907, oil paint on canvas, 50.8×61.1, Art Gallery of South Australia

Fig.27
What shall we do about the rent? 1909, black and white chalk drawing, 23.5×37.5, Private collection, USA

barracks and hospitals because it was cheap, 'hygienic' and convenient to move around.[19] There is an intimacy between these rooms and their inhabitants, as Virginia Woolf noted, and 'of course Sickert composes his picture down to the very castors on the chairs and the fire-irons in the grate'.[20]

Le Lit de Fer, *Nuit d'Été*, *La Hollandaise*, all dating from c.1906 (see nos.113, 117 and 120), and other Camden Town nudes, were exhibited first in Paris, where they confirmed Sickert's reputation as an artist exploring the seedier corners of London life. Reviewing his exhibition at Bernheim-Jeune in 1907,

the critic Louis Vauxcelles described 'a series of nudes, painted at twilight, amongst the impoverished disorder of cluttered hotel rooms … whores collapsed on the unmade bed, whores with withered bodies, weary from the harsh work of prostitution'.[21]

In the Parisian context, Sickert's nudes were assumed to be prostitutes and, as such, to belong to a recent tradition of modern nudes by Manet, Degas, Toulouse-Lautrec, Bonnard or, by 1907, Picasso and Matisse. Unlike Degas in his monotypes of the 1870s, or Toulouse-Lautrec in the 1890s, Sickert did not produce scenes of brothel life; but he sometimes used prostitutes as models, his titles could be explicit (*Putana Veneziana* 1903, *Cocotte de Soho* 1905), and the brusquely genital focus of works such as *Nuit d'Été* and *L'Affaire de Camden Town* 1909 (see no.128) signalled prostitution to contemporary viewers. In *La Hollandaise*, the upward push of the model's torso against the twist of her hips can suggest that the gaze she meets is that of a client, rather than a lover or friend.[22]

The Studio: The Painting of a Nude c.1906 (see no.121) is strikingly different. Here, a naked woman and a clothed man are pictured in workmanlike collusion. The model is upright, active and less exposed. The light, falling full on her back, shimmers in dabs of paint along the outlines of her torso, catches the top of her hip in a brusque chevron, scrapes a bright sweep along the edges of her arm, and models the volumes of breast, belly, haunches and thigh.[23] Only gradually does the scene make sense as a mirror reflection (*The Studio* may have been first exhibited as *Le grand miroir*).[24] The artist has his back to the model and paints her reflection, along with the further reflection of her back in a mirrored wardrobe to the rear of the room. It is presumably his jacket, hanging to one side, which with the lower edge of the mirror cuts her reflected body into something like the truncated back of an antique cast. The surface of the painting as a physical object is at the same time, within the notional space of the picture, the surface of the mirror. Where a conventional nude offers untrammelled access to the naked body, here the painter's arm, turned towards us, bars entry to the room and the model behind. The pleasures of looking – at art, at the nude, at the private space of the studio – are acknowledged and challenged, turned back on us as it were.

In October 1906, Sickert went to Paris for the Salon d'Automne and stayed on through the autumn, working on a series of nudes in his rooms at the Hôtel du Quai Voltaire, including *Woman Washing her Hair* (see no.116), one of several intimate scenes of women at their toilette in the tradition of Degas or Bonnard.[25] He returned to London in January 1907, and in May expanded onto the first floor of his Mornington Crescent lodgings. He moved some of his furniture upstairs, and in the better light embarked on a series of 'Studies of illumination': portraits of a young Jewish girl (Rachel Siderman) and nudes on alternate days.[26]

There is in Wendy Baron's phrase a 'flickering luminosity' to the surface of these paintings, countered in *Mornington Crescent Nude* c.1907 (see no.119) by the compact and sculptural quality of the body pressing into the mattress.[27] With her legs covered mid-thigh by a sheet and her features in shadow, the torso echoes that of the Hellenistic nude, presumably a cast, in the foreground of Sickert's *Self-Portrait. The Painter in his Studio* 1907 (see no.3).[28] We can imagine it laid flat as the *Mornington Crescent Nude*, although the colouring, the indication of pubic hair and the discarded clothes suggest living flesh: an actual naked body.

The nude was a constant theme in Sickert's work from 1902 until around 1912, while he was also painting music halls, townscapes, portraits and interiors. In modernising and radicalising the nude, he settled for the everyday, for Tilly Pullen rather than Venus, for iron bedsteads rather than marble halls. His models convey neither 'that dreamy offering of self' nor the coyly averted gaze that T.J. Clark defines as 'the nude's most characteristic form of address'.[29] There is already a hint of narrative where the model pushes up to engage the viewer, as in *La Hollandaise* or *Mornington Crescent nude, contre jour* (see fig.26), interpreted by French critics in terms of a 'nocturnal poem of London destitution and prostitution'.[30] The suggestion of narrative heightens, first with the introduction of a clothed male figure in the Camden Town Murder series 1908–9, and

then in conversation pieces where 'the nude' reverts to 'the naked' in an atmosphere of domestic boredom, resentment or fatigue.[31] From around 1912 Sickert was moving away from the nude and on to other subjects. In 1914, Wyndham Lewis teased that after twenty or thirty years in which Sickert's 'bedroom realism' had been 'the scandal of the neighbourhood' he had 'sunk into the bandit's mellow and peaceful maturity'.[32] The iron bedstead appears for almost the last time in *Wounded* 1915, a picture Sickert described as 'a Red Cross nurse tucking up a soldier with his head tied up'.[33]

Bodies
Reviewers often objected to Sickert's bodies and their surroundings as interchangeably 'musty', 'flabby' and 'sordid'. In 1911, the *Daily Telegraph* deplored body-types reminiscent of 'serio-comic and grotesque fantasies' and a general 'state of dust, untidiness, and don't-careishness' in their vicinity.[34] In 1912 P.G. Konody, reviewing Sickert's exhibition at the Carfax Gallery in the *Observer*, regretted 'the perverse delight he takes in unsavoury and sordid phases of town life' and his attention to 'debased types of humanity'.[35] *The Star* described *Summer in Naples* (now known as *Dawn, Camden Town*; see no.129), exhibited in December 1912, as 'a hideous middle-aged woman in a state of nature seated on a bed' (with 'an ordinary street-corner loafer').[36] Claude Phillips, in the *Daily Telegraph*, praised the bravura and subtlety of its execution while asking if Sickert was 'really content with these musty, flabby realities?'[37] Similar adjectives, not unreasonably, are still in use. David Peters Corbett, in an essay on Sickert, sexuality and identity in the modern city, claims that: 'Seediness, dirt and squalor, pendulous breasts and middle-aged bodies stand for the reality that Sickert argued had been denied in art…'[38]

How far is this lexicon of 'sordid', 'flabby', 'gross', 'dirty', 'shabby', 'musty' and 'unsavoury' justified? How do we know from the paintings that the rooms are 'squalid' rather than sparsely furnished; or that the bodies are 'seedy' and 'hideous', rather than shocking to viewers attuned to the ethereal creaminess of the – capital N – Nude? The reader of Wendy Baron's monumental *Sickert: Paintings and Drawings* encounters a normal

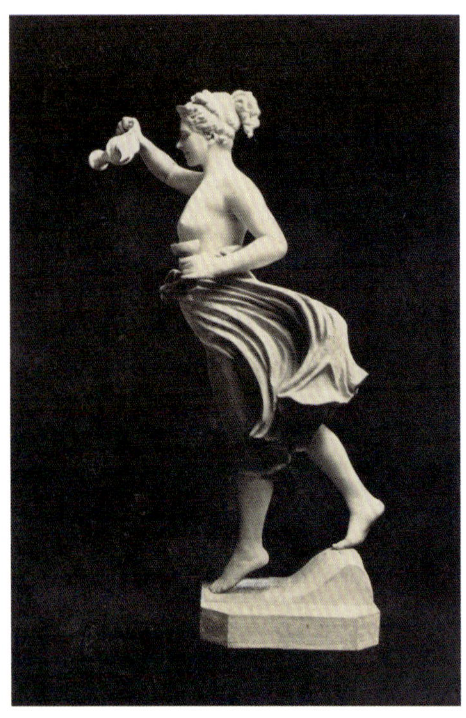

Fig.28
Pansy Montague,
Australian chorus girl
and leading exponent
of 'poses plastiques'

Fig.29
Alice Neel, *Cindy Nemser
and Chuck* 1975,
oil paint on canvas,
105.4×151.8, Lillian and
Bill Mauer collection

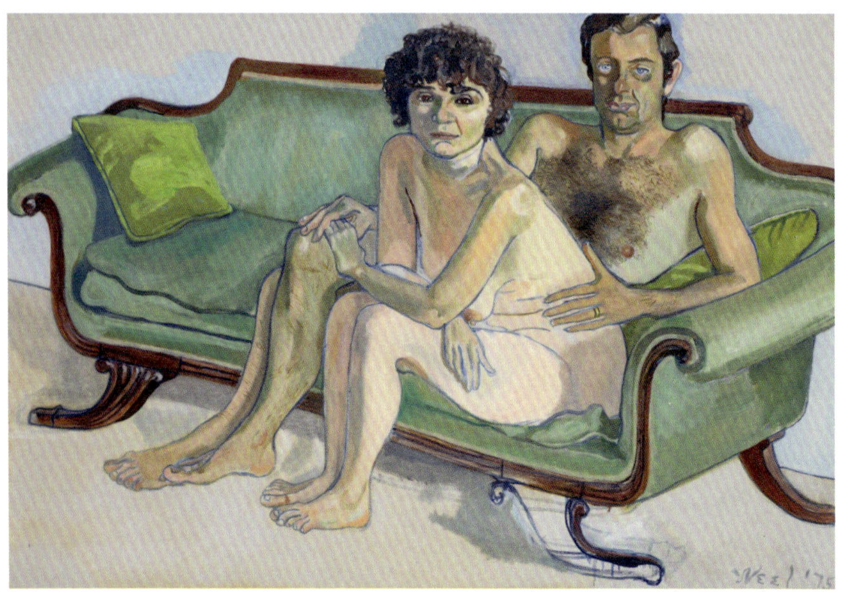

range of female bodies: Mme Villain, 'la belle rousse' (probably) in *The Shoe with a Rose*; Carolina and Giuseppina, the young prostitutes in Venice; more substantial bodies in provocative poses in *Nuit d'Été* and *La Hollandaise*; Blanche 'like a little eel' in Paris in 1906; the full-breasted model in *Mornington Crescent Nude*; the solid volumes and explicit pose of the woman in *L'Affaire de Camden Town*, who also modelled for *Dawn, Camden Town*; arriving finally at one of the last nudes and the closest to a description of 'pendulous breasts and middle-aged bodies' – *Jack Ashore* 1912–13 (see no.132).[39]

A rough-and-ready survey suggests that Sickert selected models – 'my own particular brand of frump' – and exaggerated their physical characteristics as part of his move from the drama of the Camden Town Murder to the domestic tensions of *Dawn, Camden Town* or *Jack Ashore*.[40] Reviewers already challenged by the unidealised, everyday character of his nudes thought frankly depicted middle-aged bodies 'hideous'. They would have found common cause with Kenneth Clark, who wrote that:

> there are more women whose bodies look like a potato than like the Cnidian Venus. The shape to which the female body tends to return is one which emphasizes its biological functions; Venus is always ready to relapse into her first vegetable condition.[41]

Sickert is often quoted from his article on 'Idealism' in *Art News*, 12 May 1910: 'The plastic arts are gross arts, dealing joyously with gross material facts … and while they will flourish in the scullery, or on the dunghill, they fade at a breath from the drawing-room.' Less familiar are his preceding lines on the painting of Juno in Raphael's *Council of the Gods* at the Villa Farnesina in Rome:

> Raphael conveys her to us by a most material form, with a fleshy lustrous face, like one of Rowlandson's wenches. Her hands are gross, material hands, the hands, let us say, of a milkmaid. They hang from the wrists much more like a sailor's hands do than like the almond-tipped fingers that clutch the satin of Mr Sargent's portraits.[42]

Also on 12 May Sickert published 'Goosocracy' in *The New Age* (and a week later 'Sargentolotry'). What he sometimes called 'the supergoose' was the antithesis of Juno and his 'own particular brand of frump'. The required ideal, promoted on 'every other page of our daily and weekly papers' and leaching into fashionable portraiture, comprised an amusing little face, a ravishing hat, and in place of 'the obscenity called the body' a 'perpendicular cascade of chiffon'. A long, thin chain was obligatory, twisted around 'delicate fingers without nails' to suggest 'a soul slightly misunderstood'.[43]

Woolf reminds us that Sickert's bodies are 'bodies that work, hands that work, faces that have been lined and suppled and seamed by work', and that his paint 'has a tangible quality; it is made not of air and stardust but of oil and earth'.[44] The 'gross material facts', in other words, extend from bodies (someone, somewhere, physically and in social life) to pigment (lumps of matter resolving into contours splintered and spattered with light). For Sickert, art was 'a robust and racy wench' and the refined 'perhaps further from art … than any class'.[45] His work is often linked to the School of London, to Francis Bacon and Lucian Freud, but he would, I think, enjoy a change of scene – perhaps in the company of Alice Neel (see fig.29), Maria Lassnig, Marlene Dumas, Jenny Saville, or the other robust and racy women with an interest in the naked over the Nude.

SOMAYA CRITCHLOW

ON SICKERT'S REFRAMING OF THE NUDE

Walter Sickert's painting *The Studio: The Painting of a Nude* c.1906 (see no.121), part of his Camden Town nudes series, has a nude figure as its central focus. She has become a staged duplicate of multiples, sandwiched between the reflections of a mirror on either side. It is a scene in which we, the viewer, bear witness to the artifice and staging of image-making. But we are not alone as viewers: in the foreground, cutting across the woman's body, is the arm of a man – that of the painter and observer, Sickert himself. He is controlling the viewpoint of the audience, just as he is controlling the positioning and portrayal of his model.

While Sickert's intentions initially seem clear – to reframe and reposition the nude – the paintings themselves plague the viewer with their unnerving psychological tension; a tension that plays with viewership, the history of the nude, and the acceptable subjects of painting.

In Sickert's 1910 essay 'The naked and the Nude', he wrote that modern representations of nudity had become so vacuous that they could not be considered anything but degrading. The nude in the 1900s had become synonymous with the female figure in art, as a vision of perfection idealised to the highest aesthetic. In contrast, Sickert's

Camden Town nudes allow nakedness to operate outside the confines of the nude. They are paintings that depict women and sex workers in run-down apartments, among cheap furnishings, and leaning against or lying on iron bedsteads.

The subject matter is controversial, perhaps like my own depictions of the Black female body. Sickert's paintings of women explore anti-academic poses and the composition of woman as subject/object. They are at times bleak and contain traces of violence, particularly in the group of four Camden Town Murder paintings, in which a clothed male figure is introduced. These paintings are challenging and innovative, appealing to a darker, more carnal human intrigue and curiosity. The sombre images take their place among those such as Édouard Manet's *Le Suicidé* (*The Suicide*) c.1877, or the grim depiction of rape in *Intérieur* (*Interior*) 1868–9 (see fig.30), also known as *Le Viol* (*The Rape*), by Sickert's predecessor, Edgar Degas.

At a dinner hosted by Virginia Woolf, she and her guests discussed Sickert's 'silent land', a capacity for 'seeing things that we cannot see, just as a dog bristles and whines in a dark lane when nothing is visible to the human eyes'. It is true that there is something poetic and moody in Sickert's

work which you can't put your finger on, an abstraction of life that investigates its darker side. The 'silent land' is the creation of things that can be felt without being seen, an experience that seems familiar while being intangible. Sickert's *The Studio* reminds us of the familiarity inherent in nakedness by dispelling the idealisation of the nude, but it further unsettles us by situating this in an explicit façade – the act of painting, a construction of art.

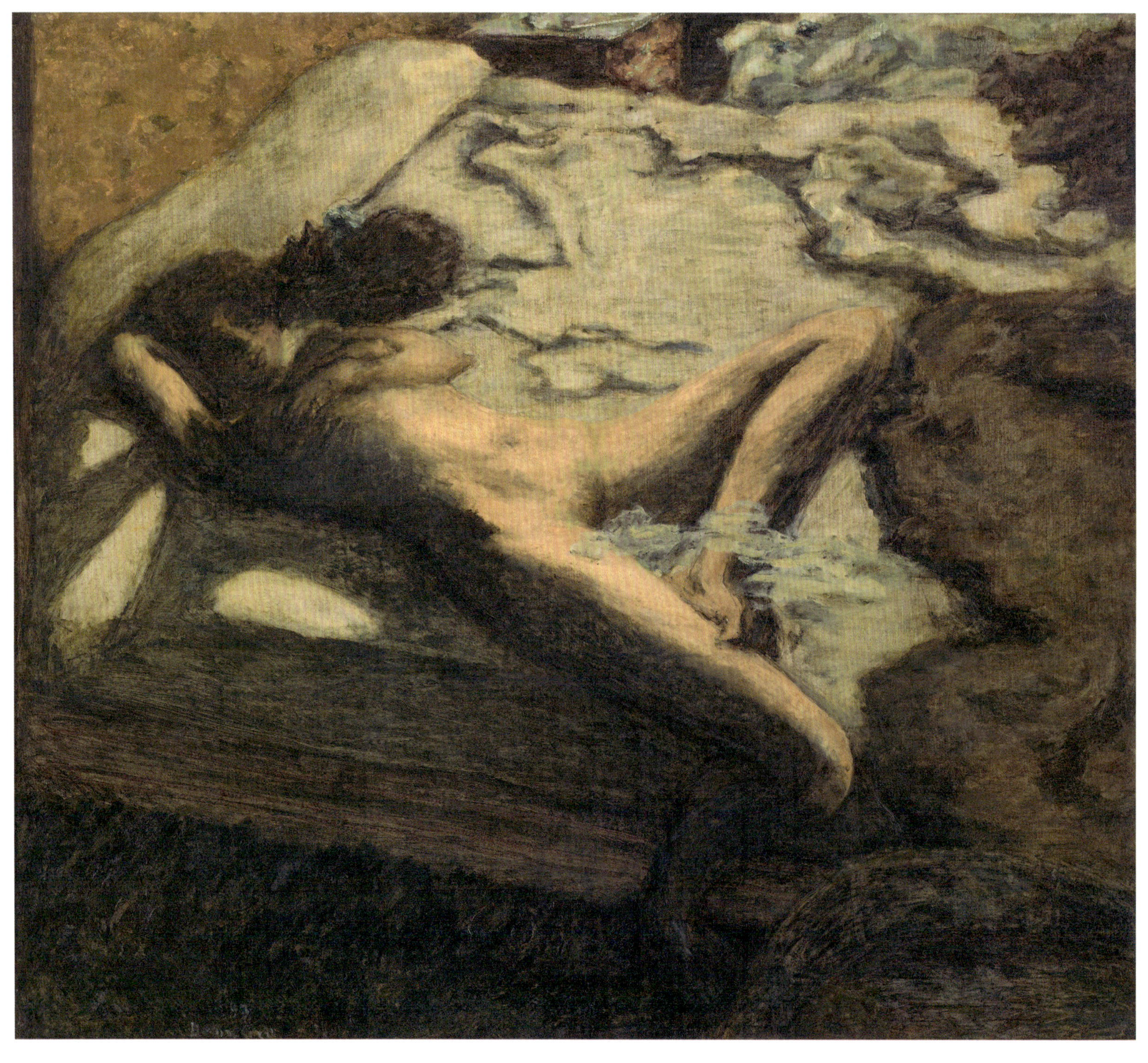

106
Pierre Bonnard
*Femme assoupie
sur un lit* 1899
Oil paint on canvas
Paris, Musée d'Orsay

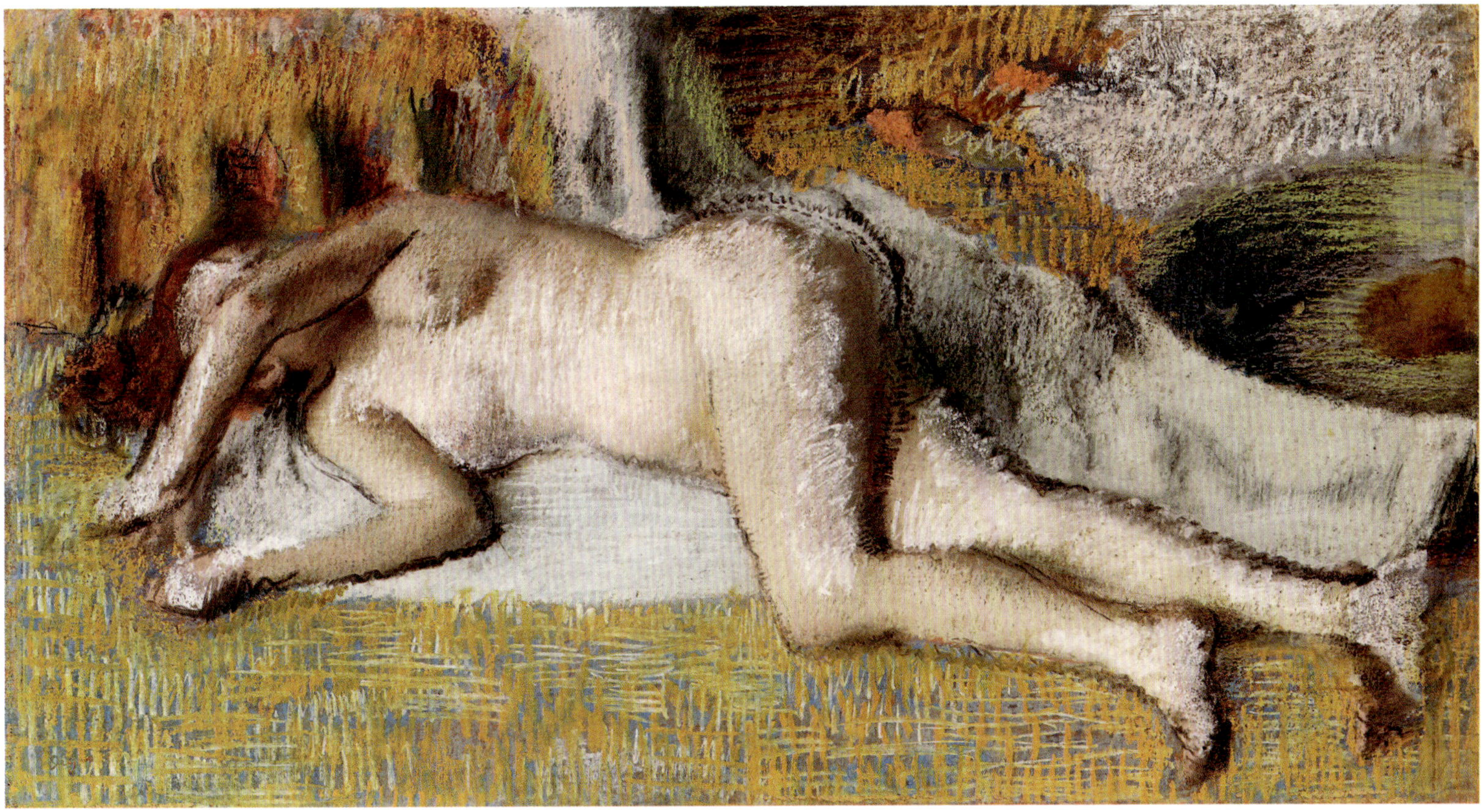

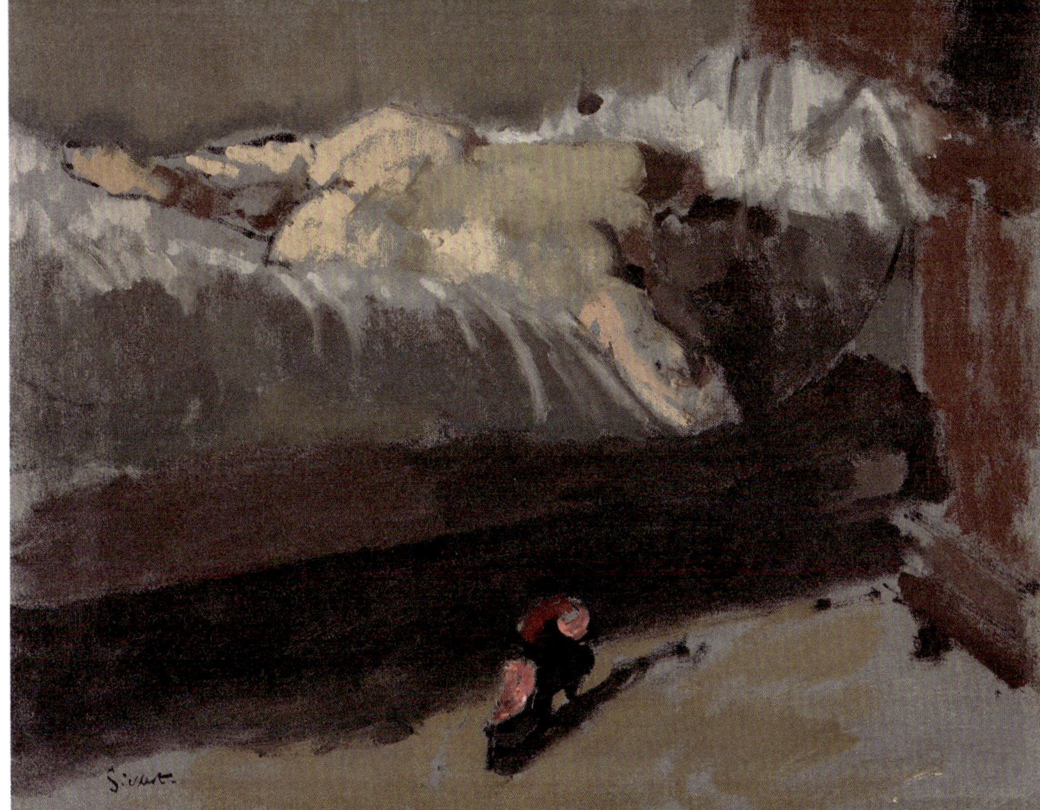

107
Edgar Degas
*Après le bain, femme nue
couchée* 1885–90
Pastel on paper mounted at the
edges by the artist on board
David and Ezra Nahmad
Collection

108
The Shoe with a Rose
c.1902–4, oil paint on canvas,
36.9×44.5, Daxer and
Marschall

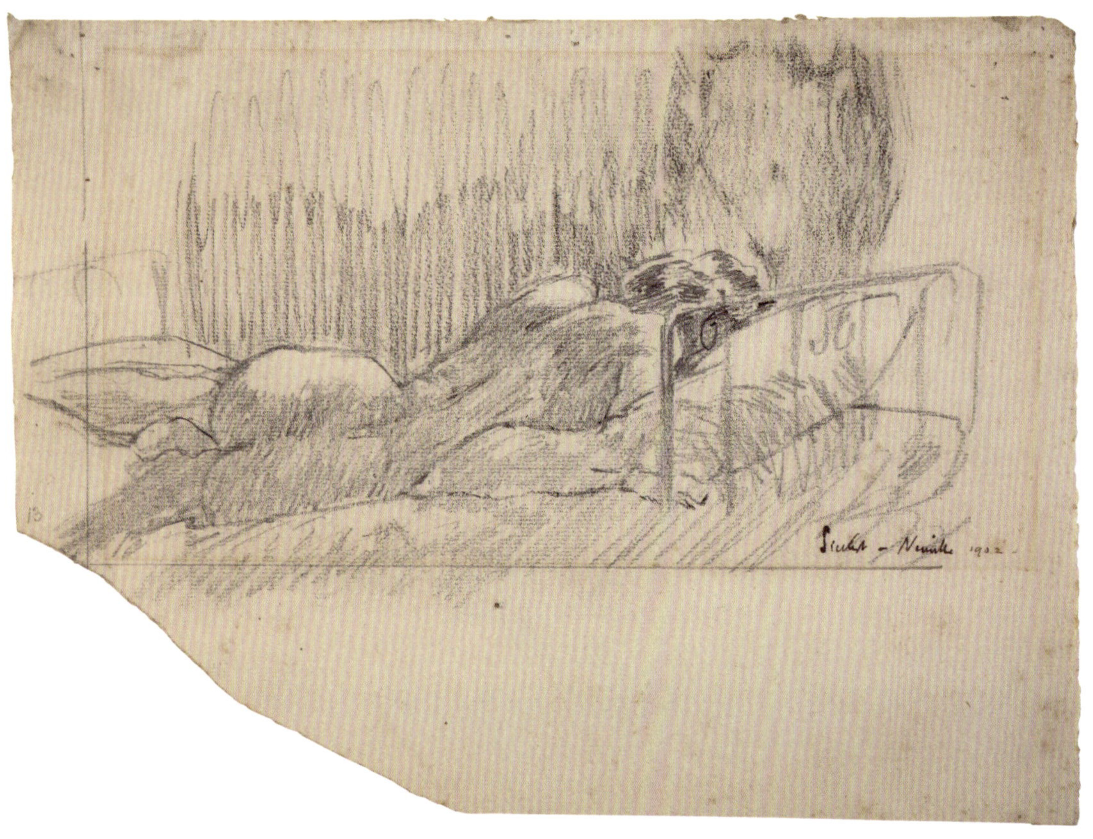

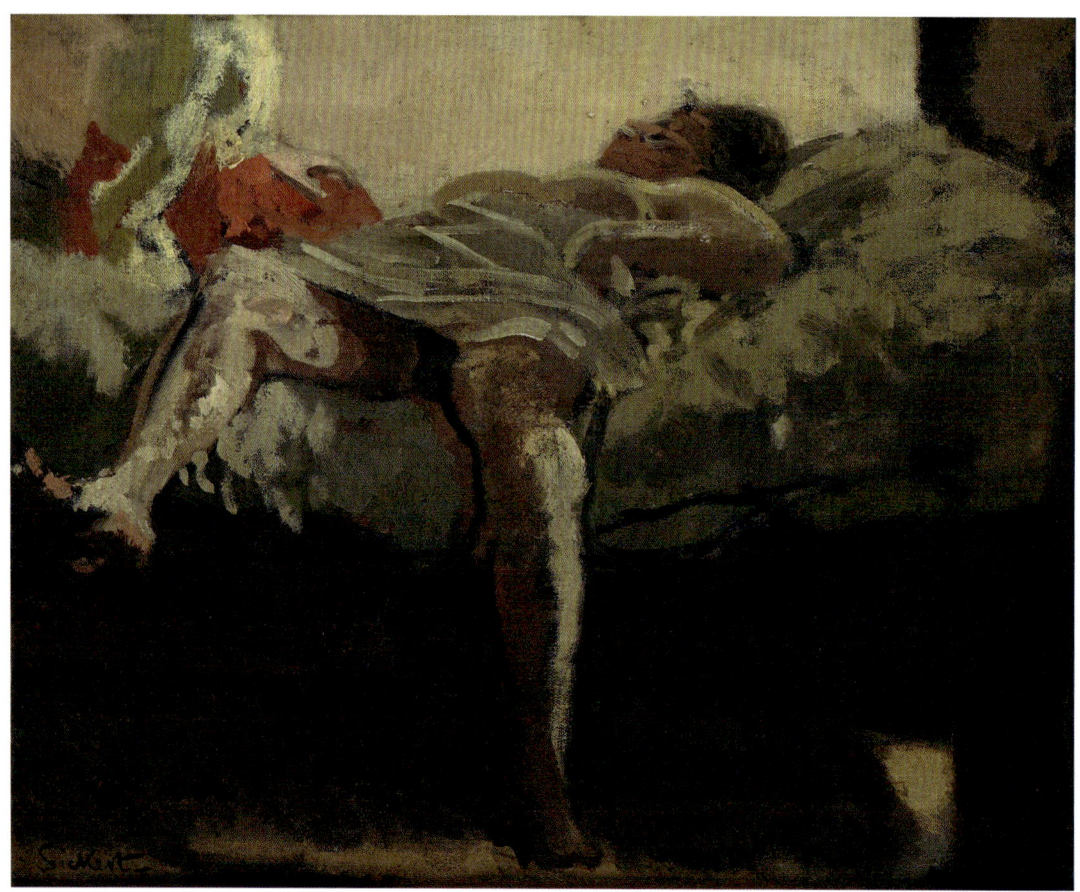

109
The Little Bed 1902
Pencil and chalk on
paper
University of Reading
Art Collection

110
*Fille Vénitienne
Allongée* 1903–4
Oil paint on canvas
Rouen, Musée des
Beaux-Arts

111
Cocotte de Soho
1905
Pastel on millboard
Private collection

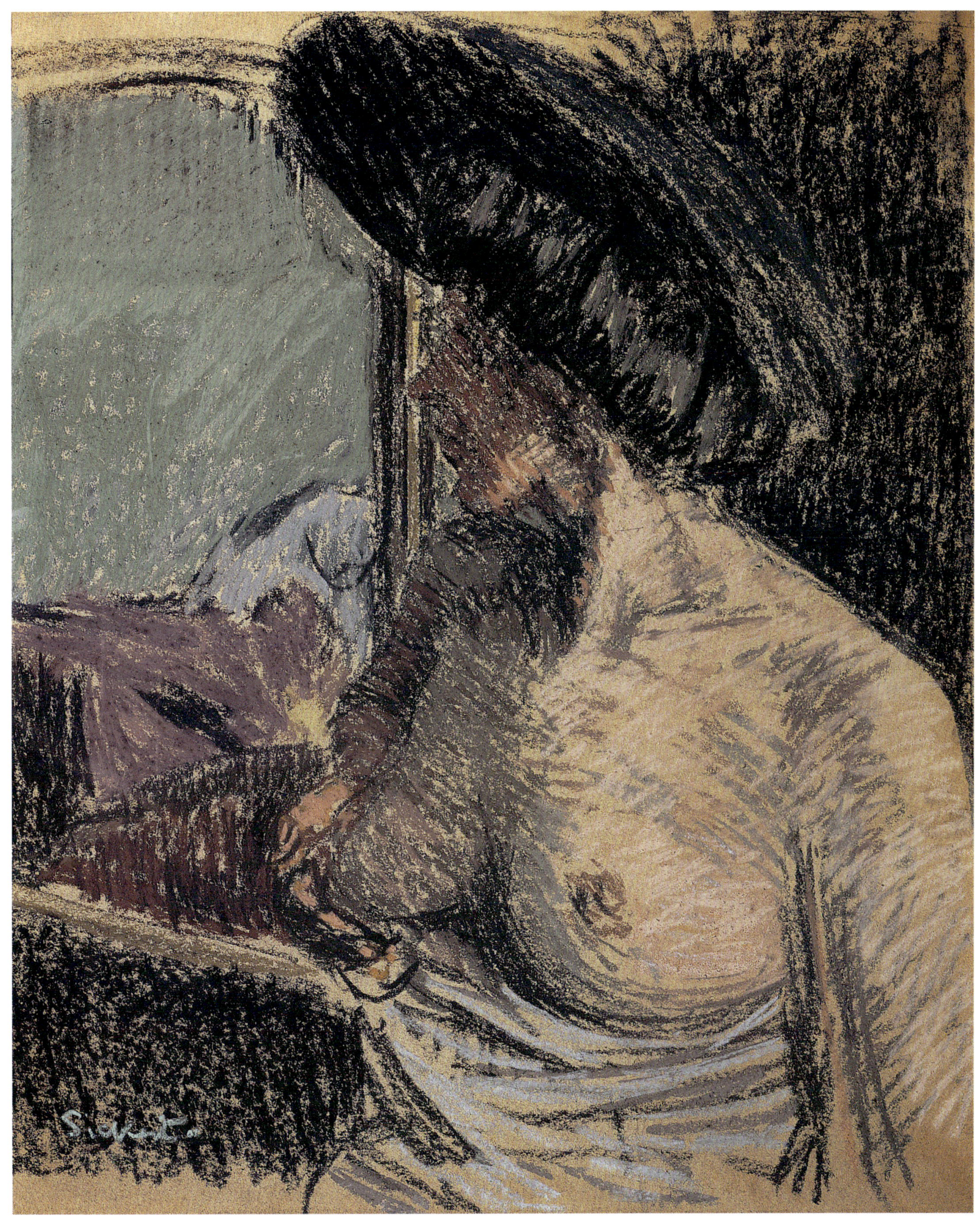

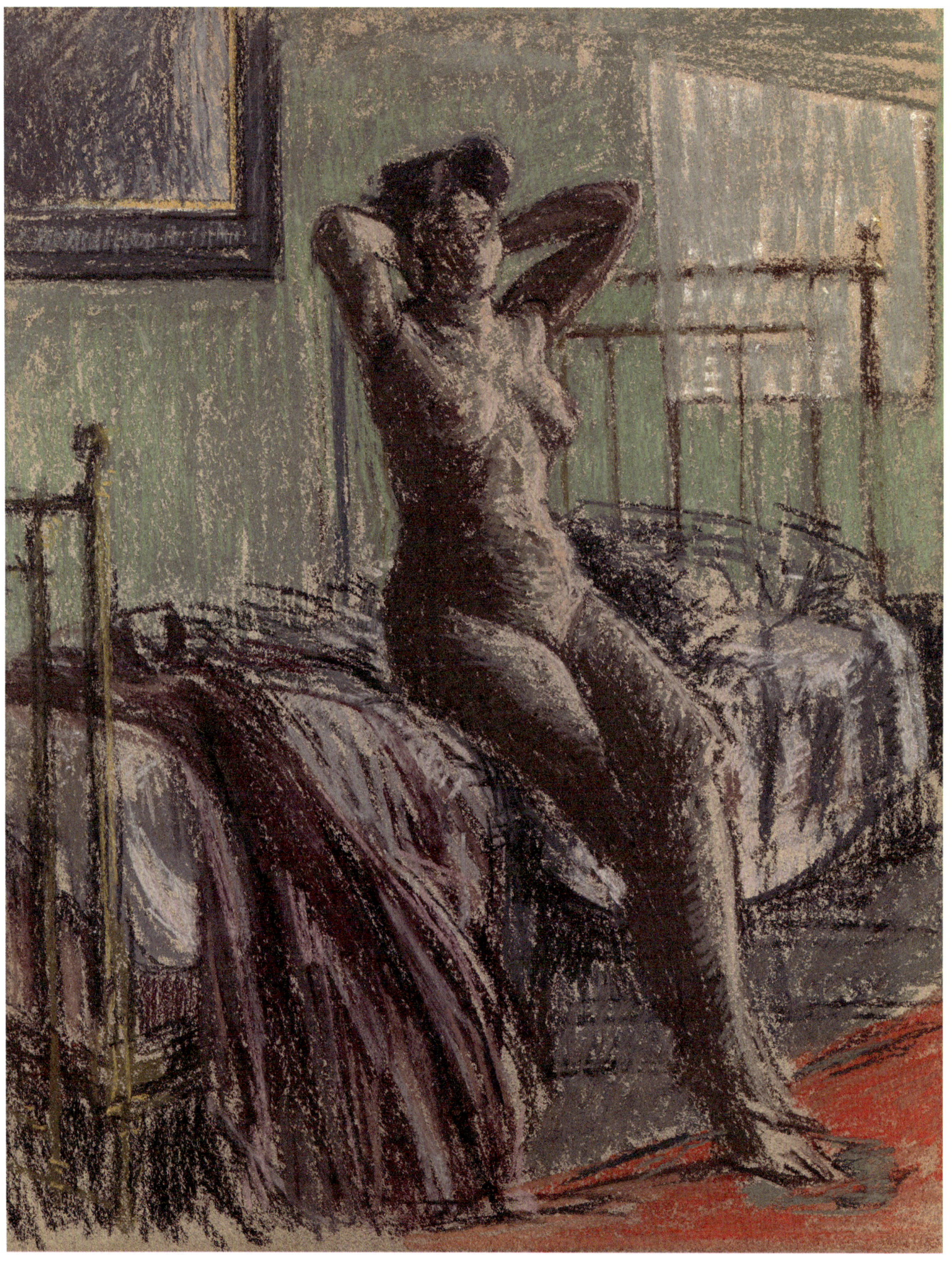

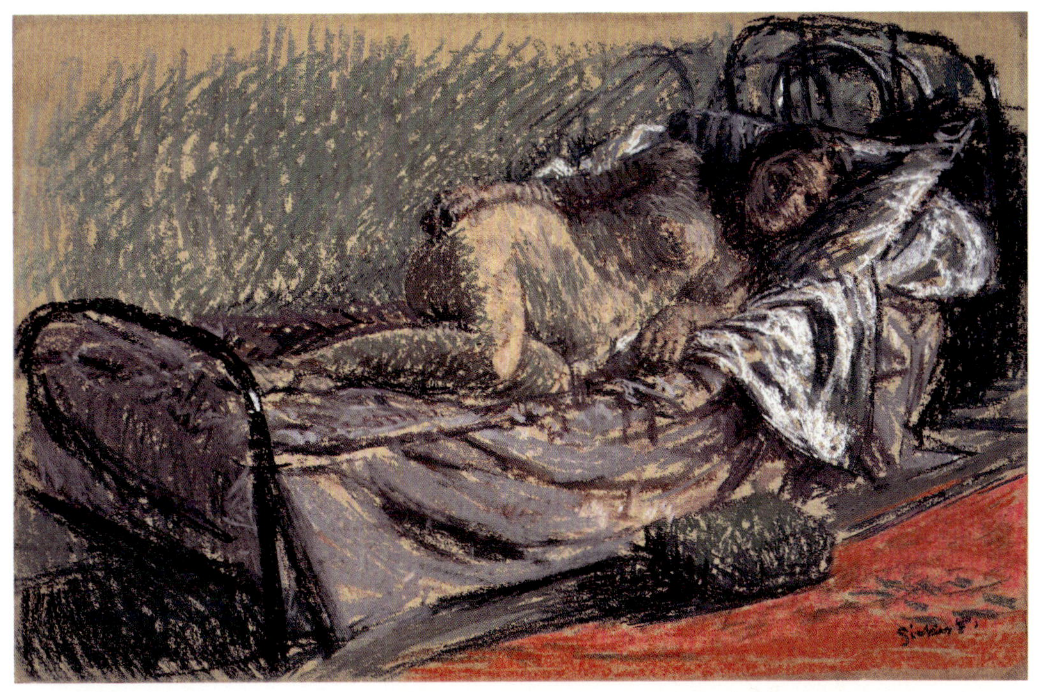

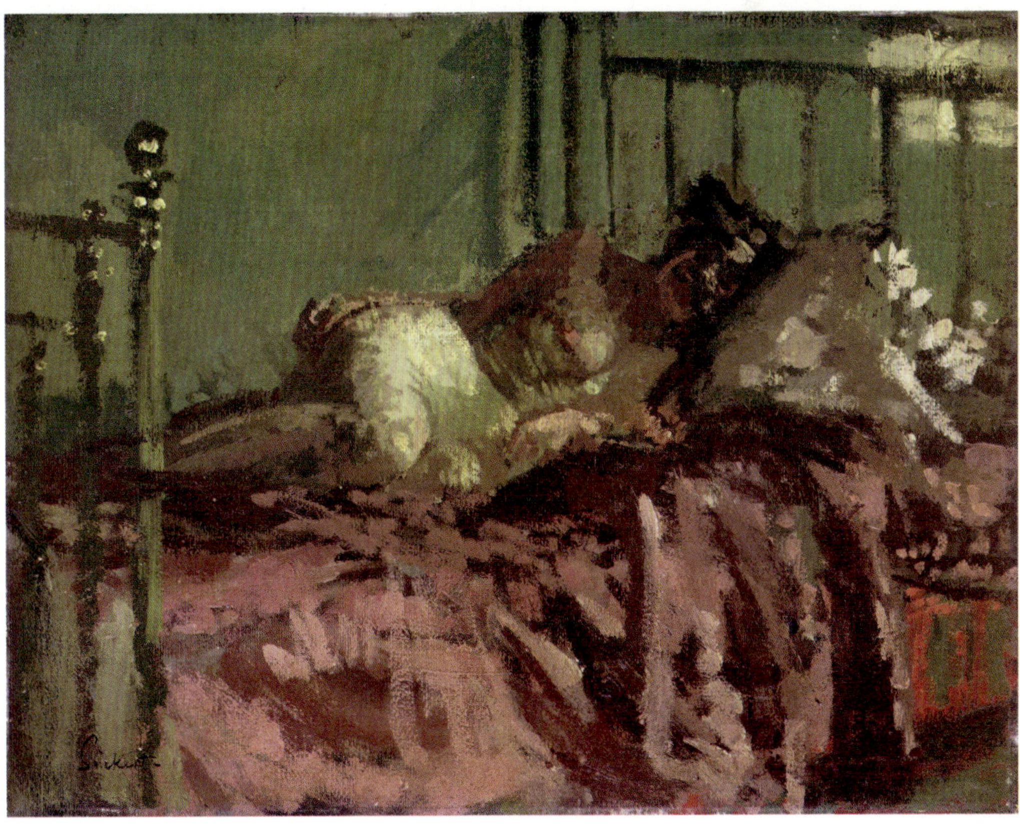

113
Le Lit de Fer 1905
Pastel on buff paper
Private collection

114
Le Lit de Cuivre c.1906
Oil paint on canvas
The Royal Albert
Memorial Museum &
Art Gallery, Exeter City
Council

112
Nude Stretching:
La Coiffure 1905–6
Pastel on paper
Private collection

Overleaf (left)
115
La Maigre Adeline 1906
Oil paint on canvas
The Metropolitan
Museum of Art

Overleaf (right)
116
Woman Washing her Hair
1906
Oil paint on canvas
Tate

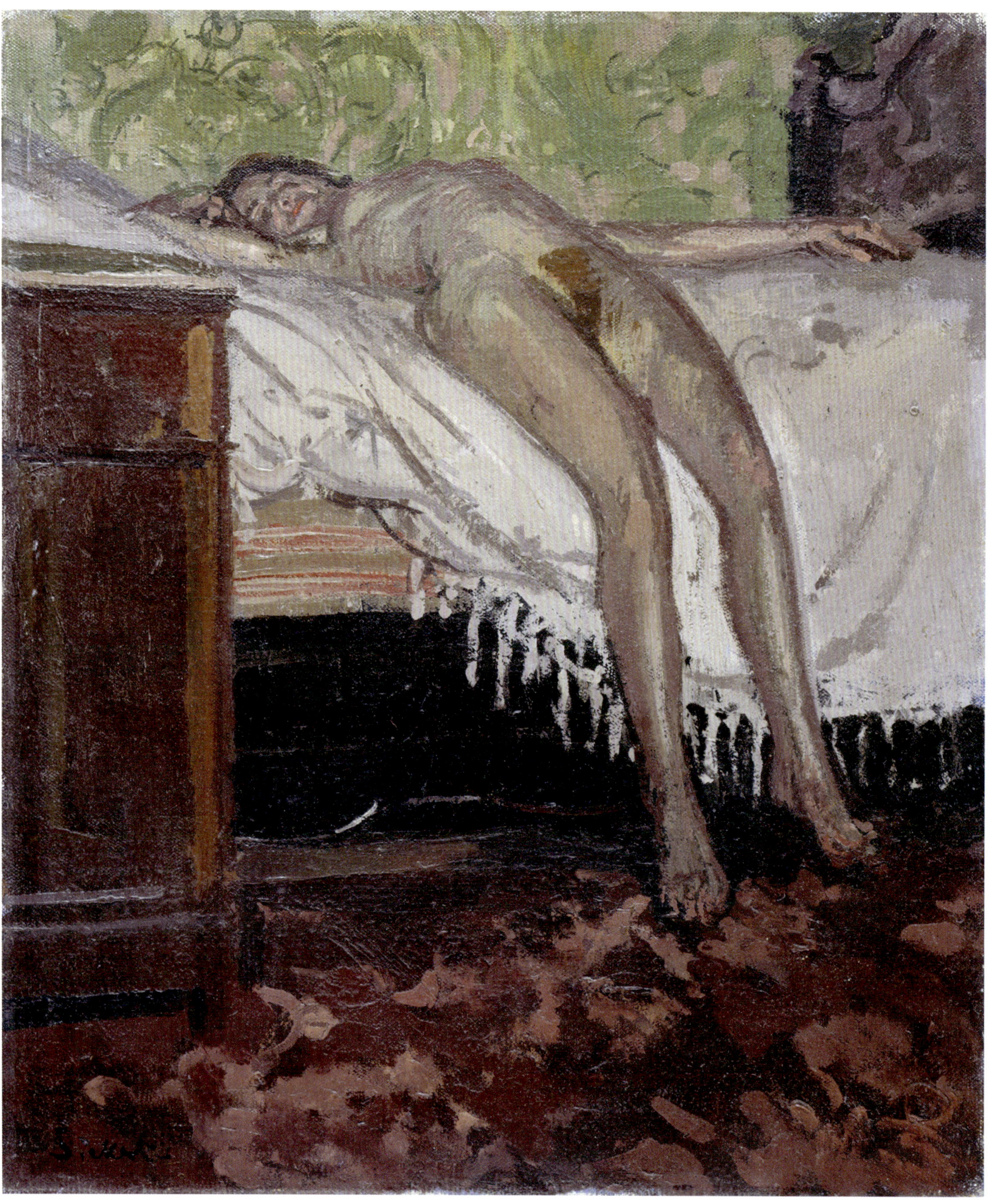

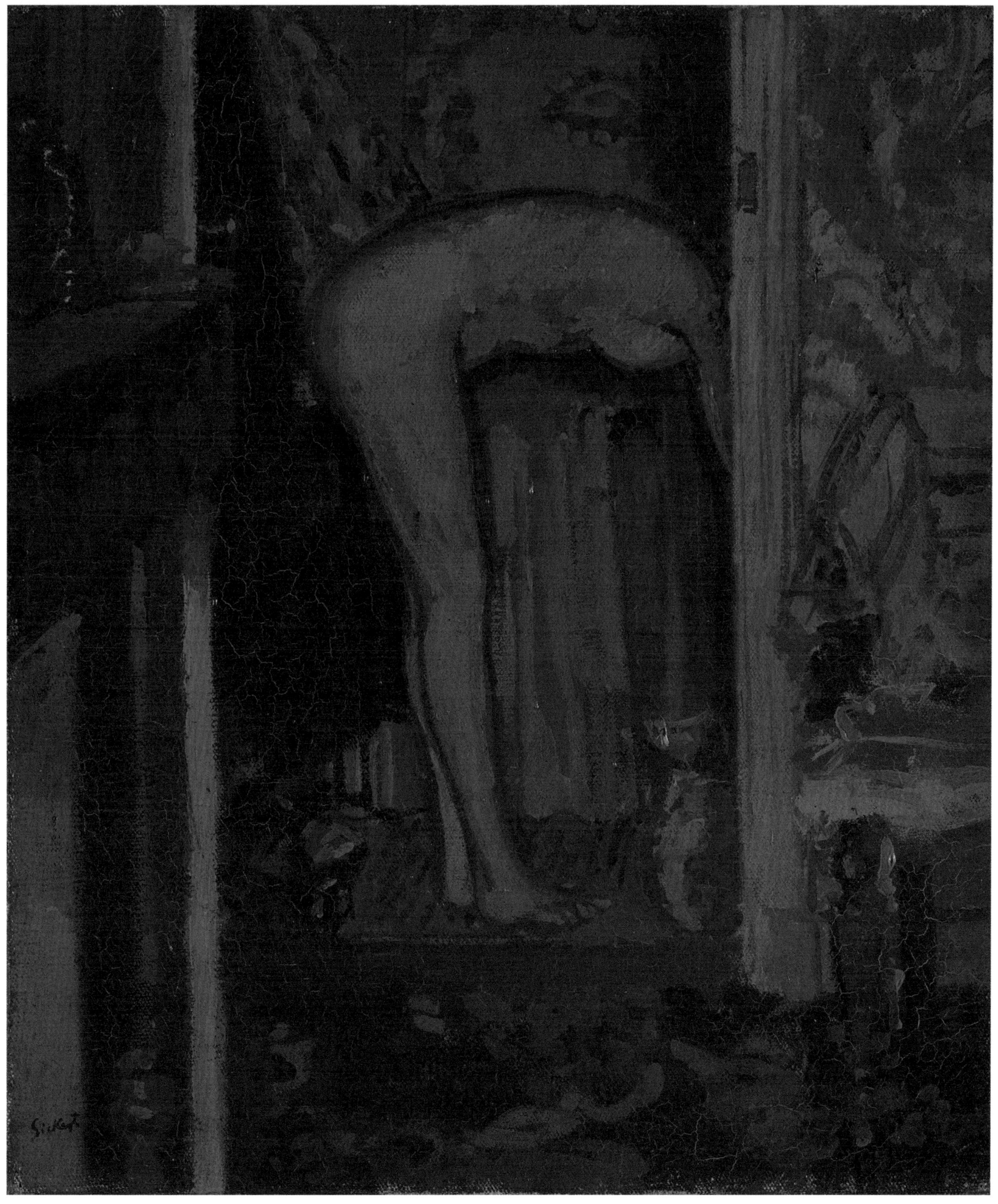

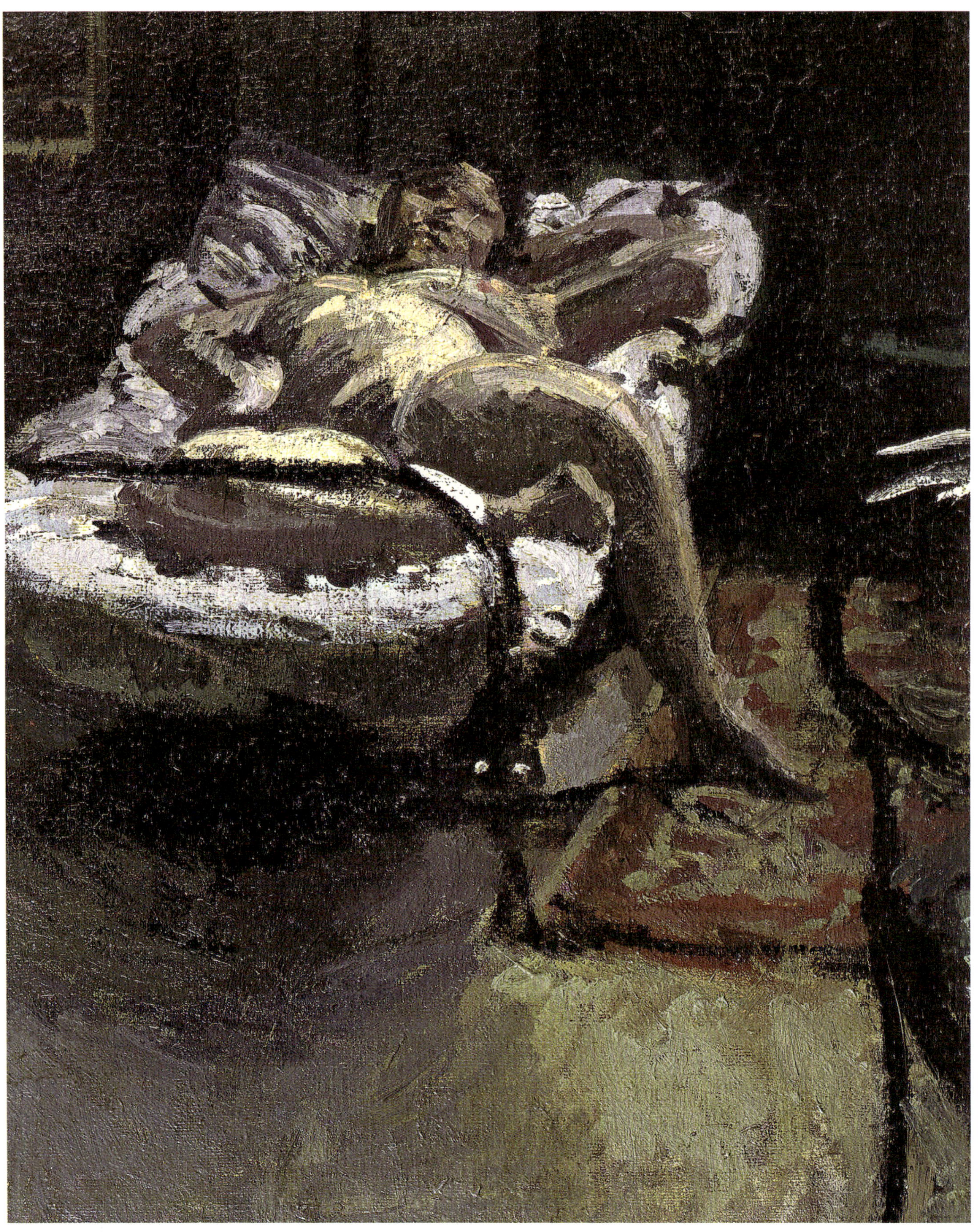

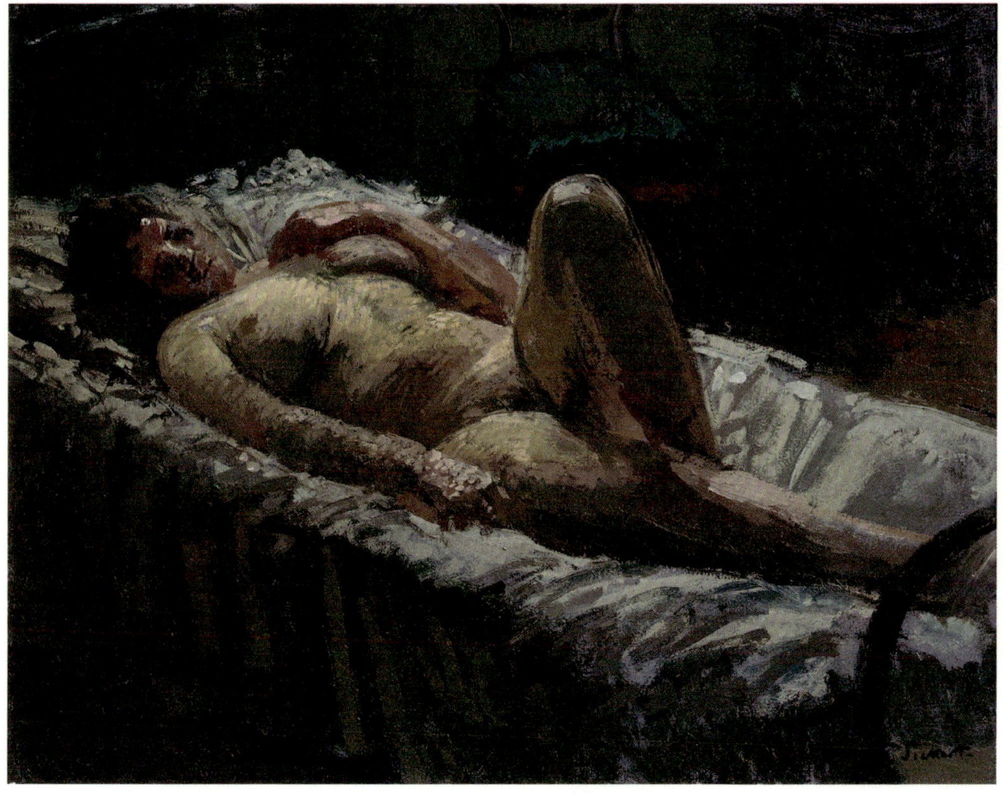

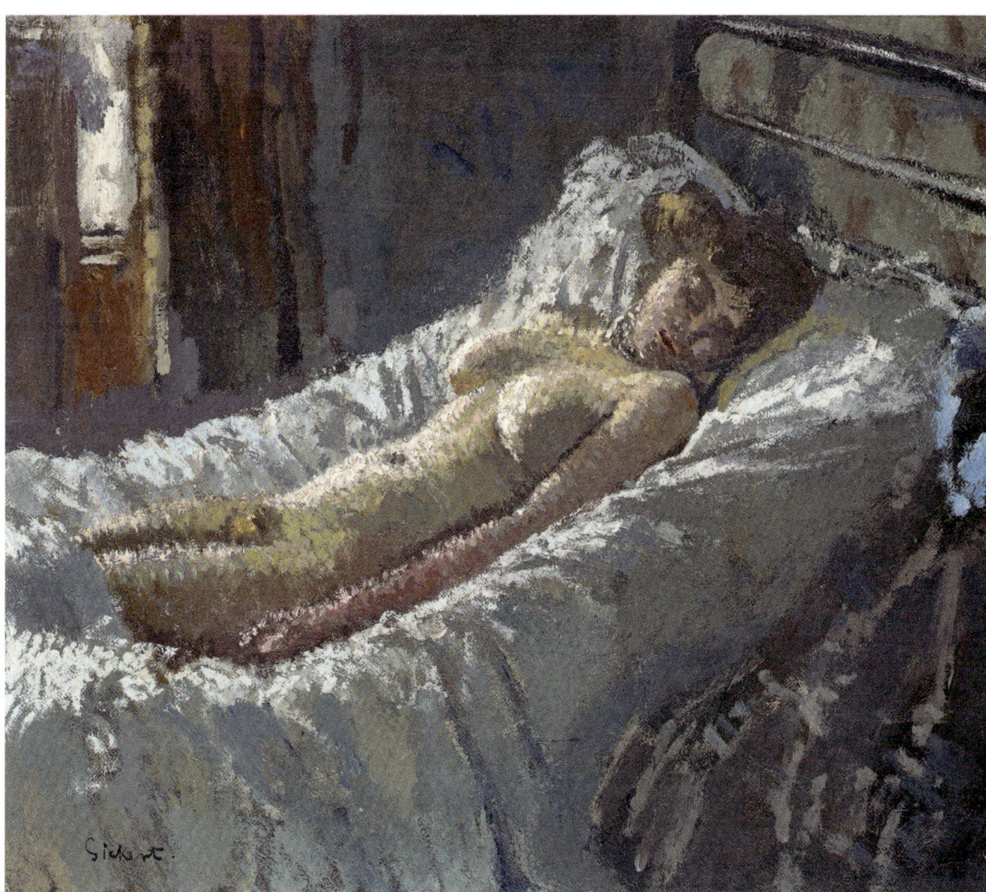

117
Nuit d'Été c.1906
Oil paint on canvas
Private collection,
courtesy of Offer
Waterman, London

118
The Iron Bedstead c.1906
Oil paint on canvas
Private collection,
courtesy Hazlitt
Holland-Hibbert

119
*Mornington Crescent
Nude* c.1907
Oil paint on canvas
The Syndics of the
Fitzwilliam Museum,
University of Cambridge

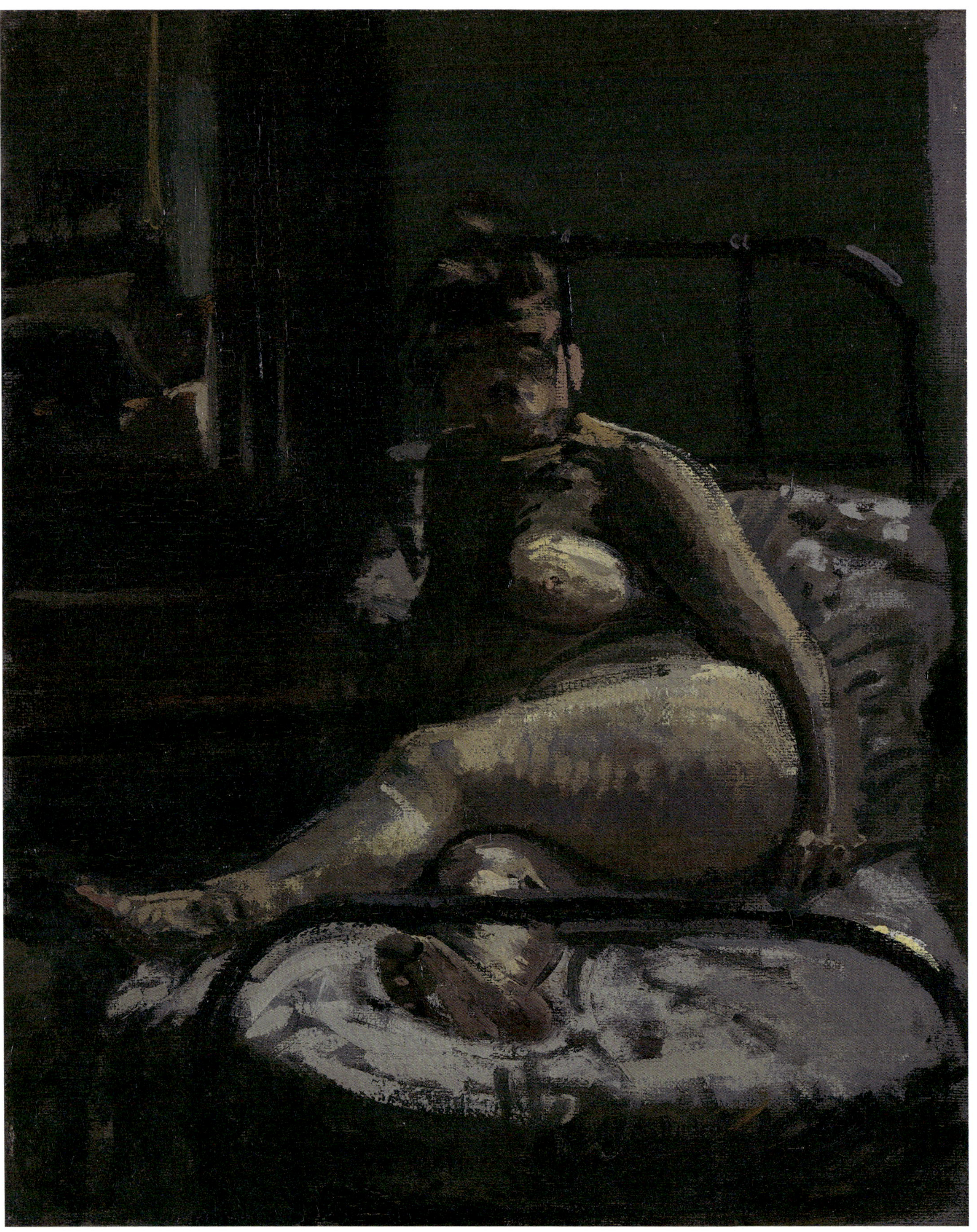

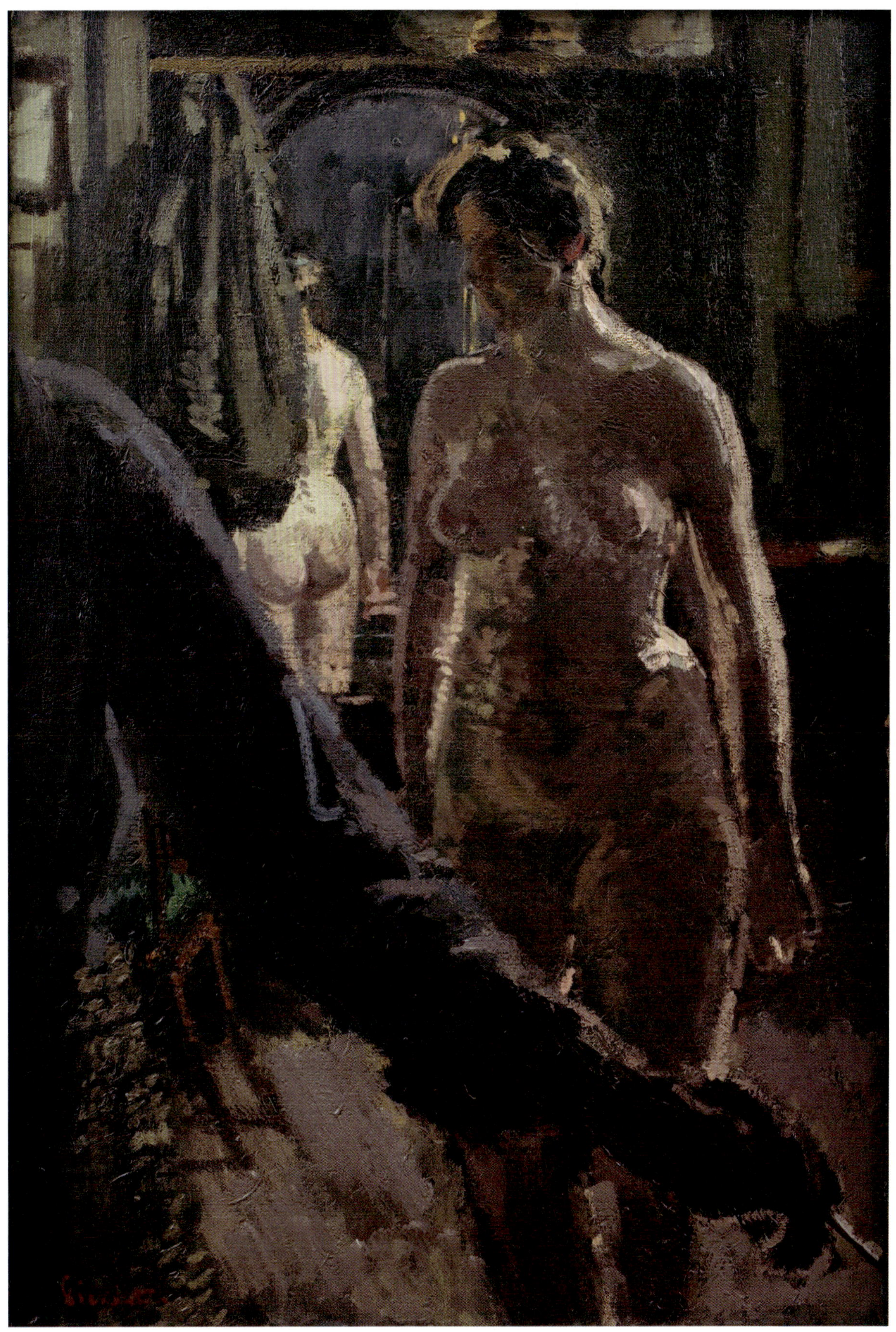

120
La Hollandaise c.1906
Oil paint on canvas
Tate

121
The Studio: The Painting of a Nude c.1906
Oil paint on canvas
Property of a European Collector. Courtesy of PIANO NOBILE, London

122
Lucian Freud
Naked Portrait 1972–3
Oil paint on canvas
Tate

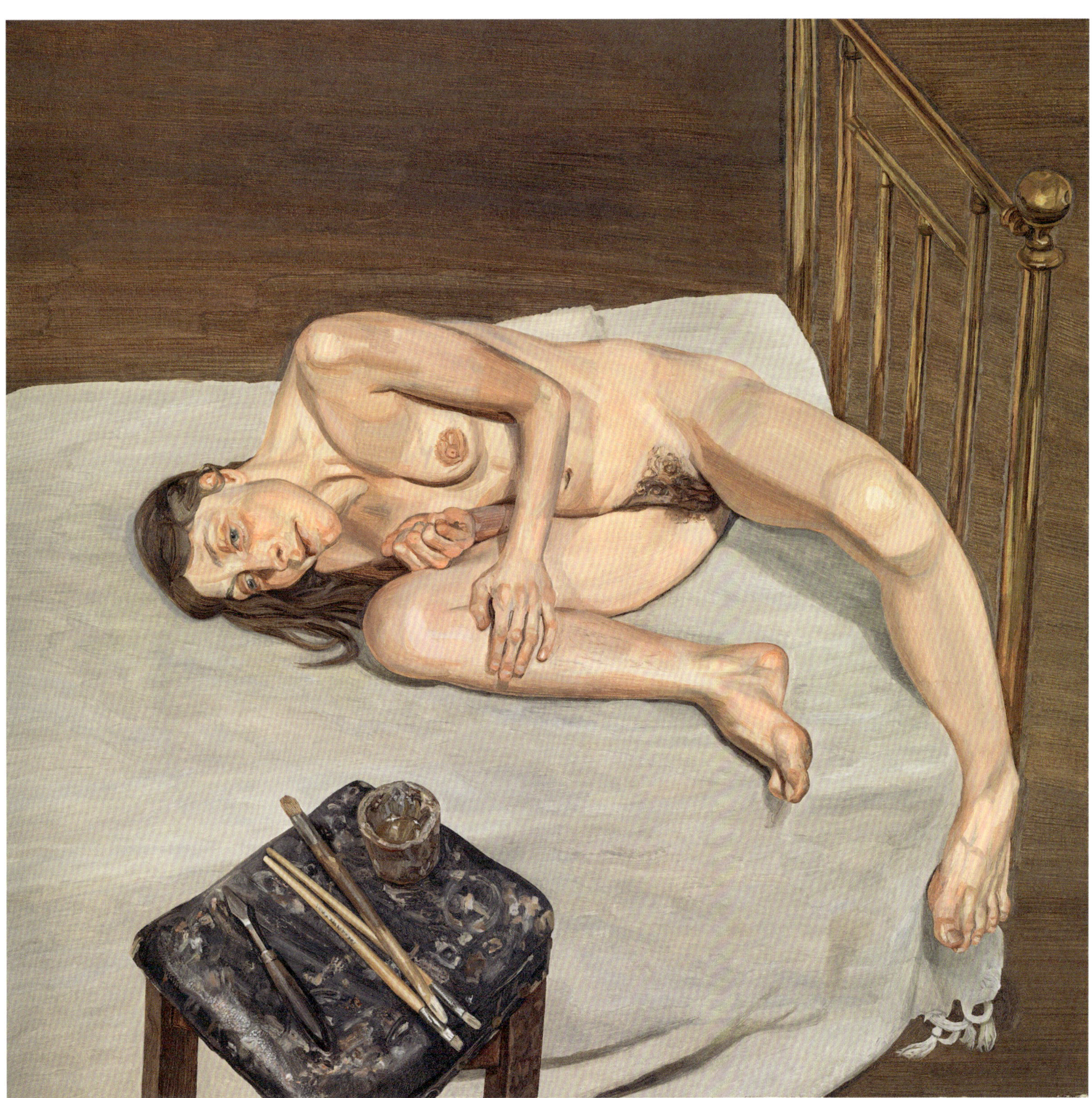

THE MODERN
CONVERSATION PIECES

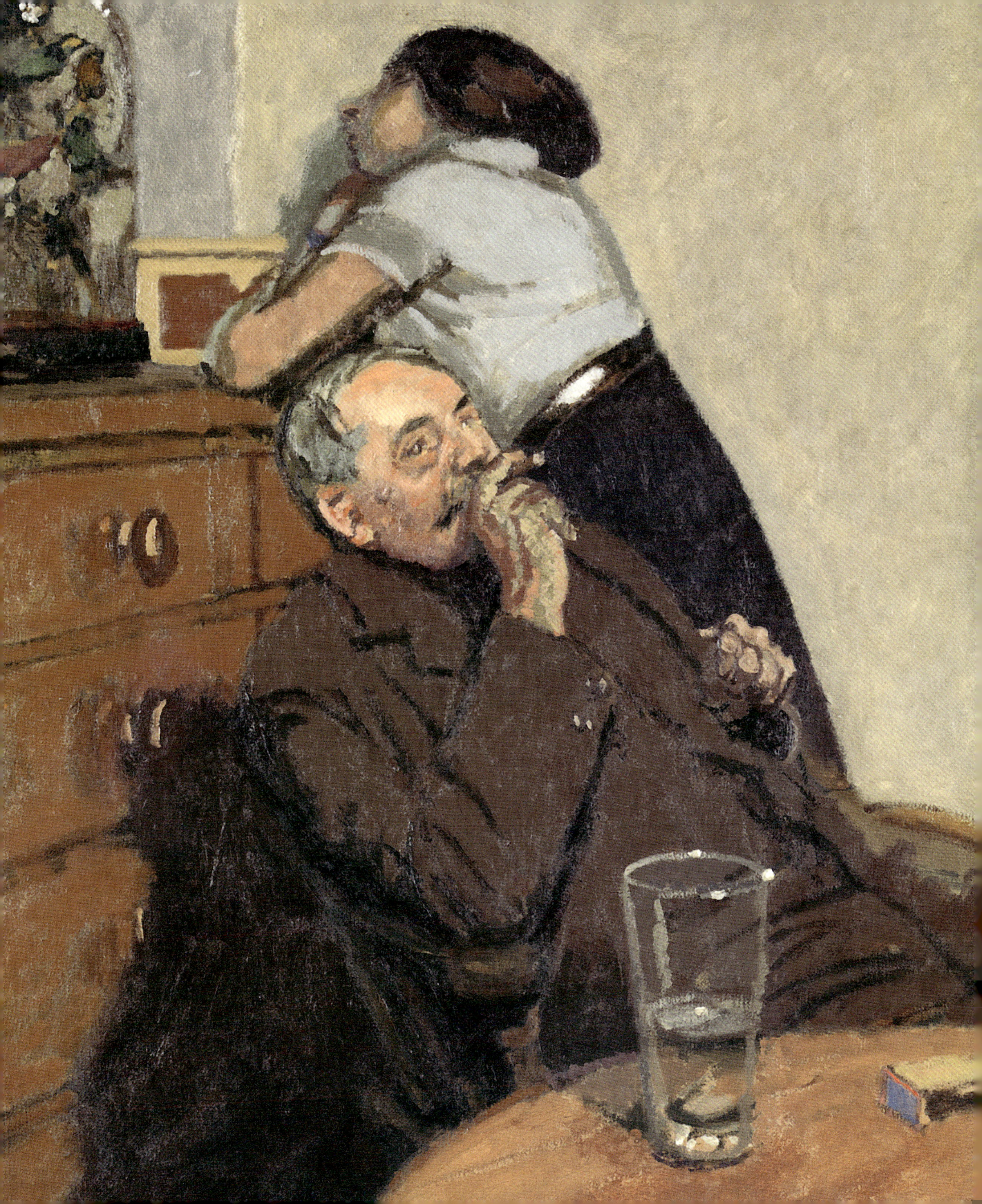

WENDY BARON

THE MODERN CONVERSATION PIECES

In December 1915, reviewing an exhibition of work by Maurice Asselin,[1] Sickert stated: 'One of the things in which it seems to me that we have a right to speak of progress is the intensity of dramatic truth in the modern conversation-piece or *genre* picture.' The terms 'conversation-piece' and 'genre picture' are not interchangeable. The former, predictably, requires more than a single figure. The latter can have any number, or none. However, both entail a degree of informality and intimacy; and both shun the academic and stylistic conventions of their time and place. They do not preach. They tend to represent modest, everyday subjects.

Sickert illustrated his contention by comparing two paintings wildly incompatible in style, content and intention: an eighteenth-century group portrait by William Hogarth of an upper-class family and their dogs in a fine drawing room[2] and a single-figure study by Maurice Asselin of a little girl, cutting her nails 'with the intensity and concentration of a monkey'.[3] Hogarth's self-conscious figures, assembled to demonstrate their status and wealth, are posed with the stiffness of a nineteenth-century wedding photograph. Nearly 180 years later, the genre painting by Asselin offered a chance glimpse of a private grooming ritual. Was Sickert's choice deliberate, or lazy, or careless? The Hogarth is a traditional 'conversation piece',

defined as an informal, often small-scale, arrangement of figures, whether families or groups of friends, in domestic indoor or garden landscape settings. Sickert could have used a more objective comparison, for example either of two conversation groups of figures gathered indoors to celebrate Manet: Fantin-Latour's *A Studio at Les Batignolles* 1870 (Musée d'Orsay, Paris) or William Orpen's retrospective British counterpart of 1909, *Homage to Manet* (Manchester Art Gallery), in which Sickert himself appears. These paintings supported a relatively dramatic and truthful narrative. However, Sickert did not intend his argument to be analysed too closely. He wanted to express his admiration for the urgent realism of Asselin's painting and take the opportunity to make a general point about modern figure paintings.

For Sickert and some of his French contemporaries, the kind of subject matter implied by the term 'modern conversation-piece' drew inspiration from an enigmatic two-figure *Interior* by Degas (Philadelphia Museum of Art; see fig.30). Painted around 1869, it was not seen in public until 1905.[4] Degas kept it in his studio where it was known only to his intimates, Sickert among them. Interpretation of the painting has preoccupied art historians and critics for well over a hundred years. The apparent confrontation between the clothed man and the partially undressed young woman prompted the painting's usual subtitle, *Le Viol* (*The Rape*). Did it illustrate a lurid scene from a contemporary novel?[5] Was it a narrative invented by the artist, or (as Sickert claimed Degas had told him) an innocuous family scene?[6]

Resident in France during the early years of the twentieth century, Sickert was wholly integrated into the French art world. He knew Degas's monotype brothel scenes of the 1870s (see fig.31) and Toulouse-Lautrec's brothel pictures of the 1890s. His dealers were Parisian, Durand-Ruel and Bernheim-Jeune, who also supported Pierre Bonnard and Édouard Vuillard. From 1902, although based in Dieppe, Sickert taught and had a studio in Paris. He matured as a painter of figure groups within a milieu that nurtured Bonnard's frank nudes, including his ambiguous two-figure group *L'Homme et*

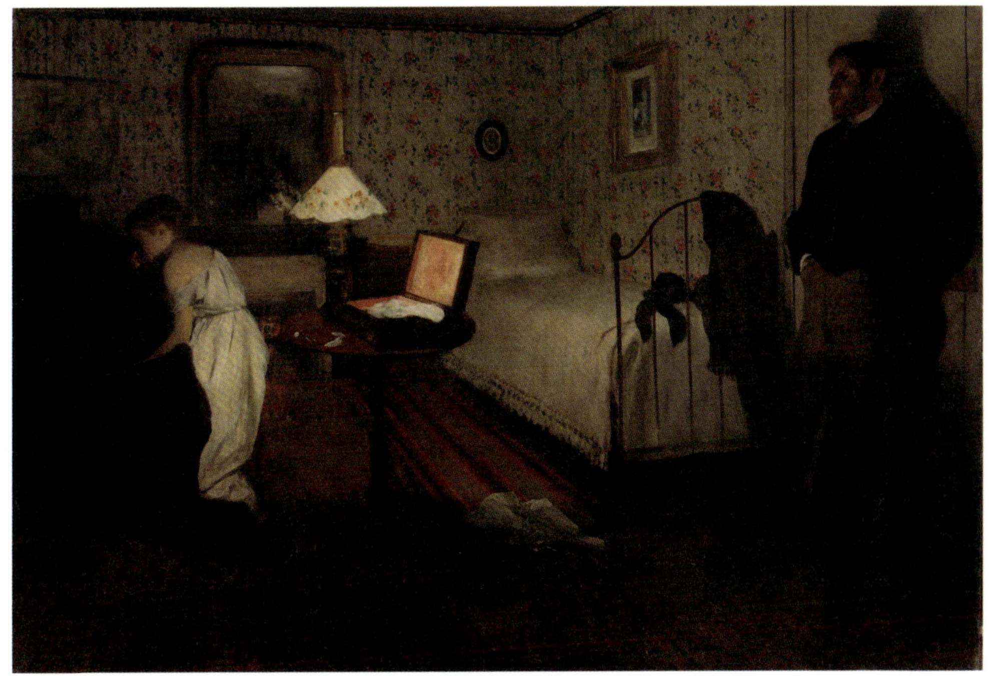

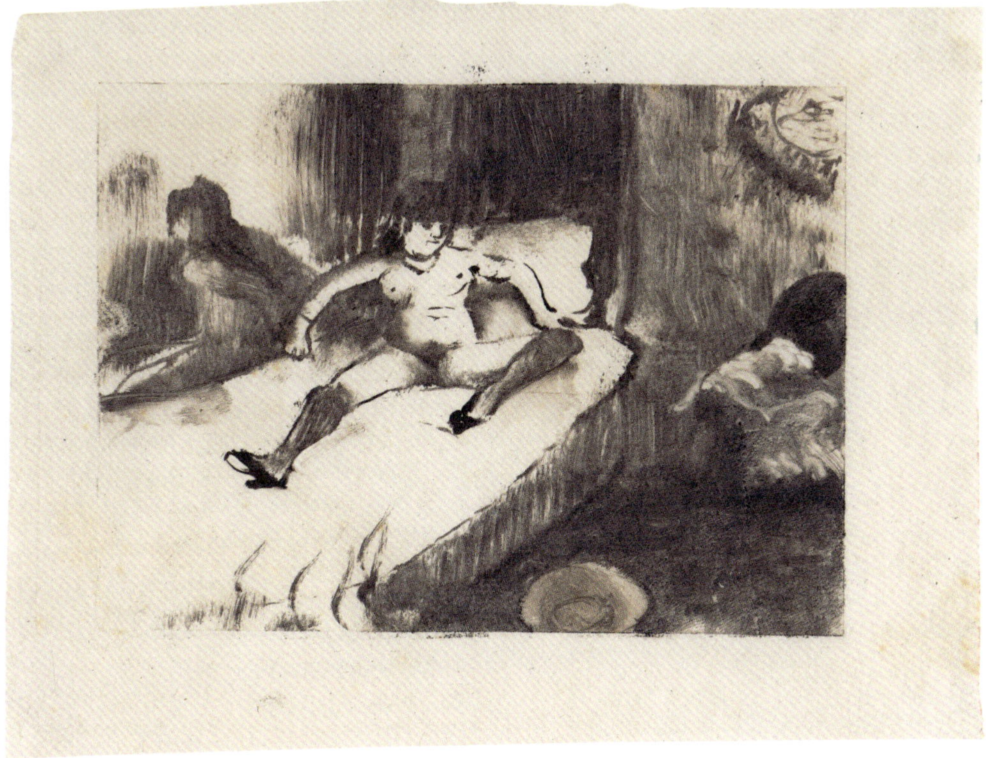

la Femme of 1900 (Musée d'Orsay, Paris; see fig.32).[7] This intimate bedroom interior shows a naked man (the artist) and a naked woman (his model Marthe, later to become his wife) in a family scene which contrives to be both perplexing and dramatic. Bonnard achieved this result through multiple pictorial devices, above all the contrasts of light and dark areas, and the deliberate confusion of the spatial ground plan by splitting the picture surface with the edge of a triple folding screen, and by painting the entire scene as reflected in a mirror. Despite incompatible interpretations of the painting as representing the couple before or after sexual congress, it is clear that Bonnard's real focus was to convey their psychological and emotional connection.

Sickert's earliest intimate interiors, featuring one or two female figures, were created during his visit to Venice of 1903–4 when he was already 43 years old. Most of his models were prostitutes, happy to earn money by posing in the relative comfort of Sickert's studio at 940 Calle dei Frati. He wrote to tell his friend and patron, the painter Jacques-Émile Blanche,[8] that his working day was bliss from 9 to 4, with his little models laughing, relaxed and telling him dirty stories, while posing like angels. A couch or bed became the stage for two-figure paintings featuring his favourite models, Carolina dell'Acqua and La Giuseppina, together. Within his tightly focused group, Sickert juggled with the precise relationships of the figures. On the couch, both were clothed (see no.71); on the bed, one lies nude or exposed while the seated clothed figure talks to her (see no.110). We imagine confidences as the two interact, their gaze locked. The titles give nothing away: *Conversation*, *Caquetoeres* (Venetian dialect for *chiacatores*, or chatterboxes).

Having warned Blanche of his new subject matter, Sickert submitted some ten Venetian interiors with figures to the Bernheim-Jeune show in June 1904. None can be identified from their title. It would be fascinating to know the original title of the painting now called *The Shoe with a Rose* (see no.108), the most romantic and immediately alluring image of the nude ever created by Sickert. It was

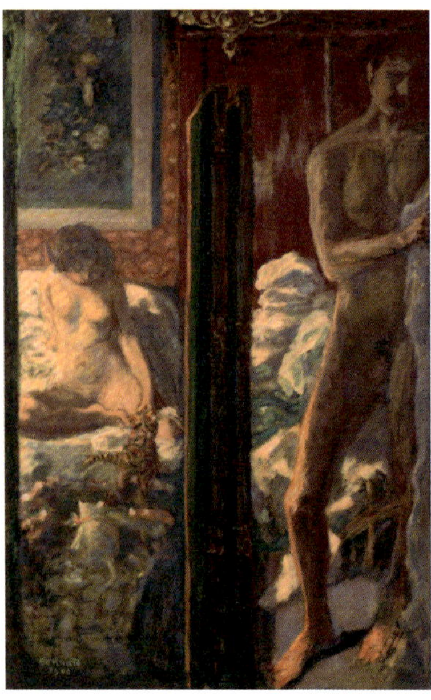

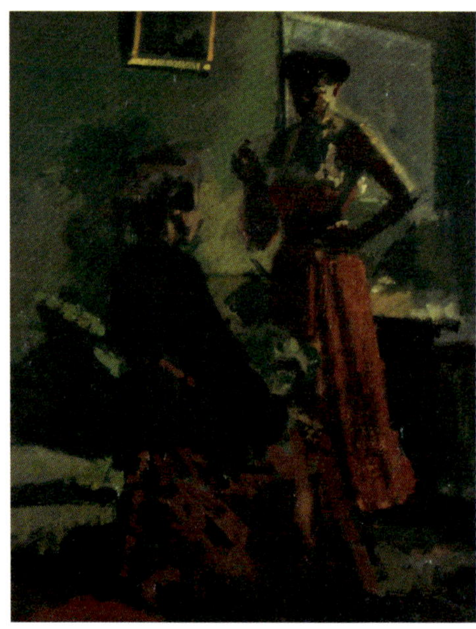

Fig.32
Pierre Bonnard,
L'Homme et La Femme
1900, oil paint on
canvas, 115×72.3,
Musée d'Orsay, Paris

Fig.34
*The Poet and his Muse
(or Collaboration)* 1907,
oil paint on canvas,
45.5×23, Private
collection

Fig.33
*The Belgian Cocottes
(Jeanne et Hélène
Daurmont)* 1906,
oil paint on canvas,
51×41, Portsmouth
City Museums

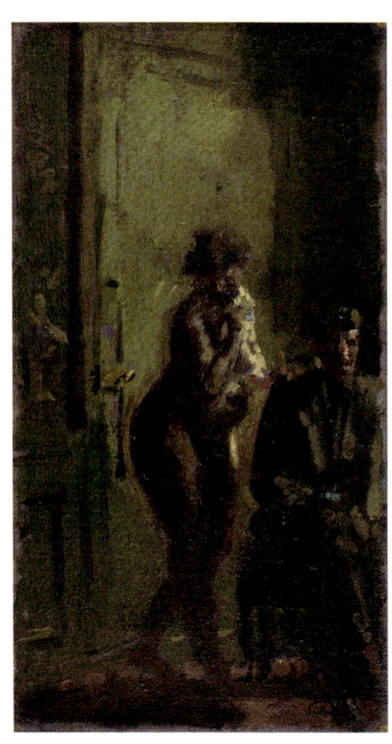

a work of precisely this period. Could
it have been *Lassitude* in the 1904
exhibition? Blanche wrote the preface to
the catalogue, in which seventy-two of the
ninety-six paintings on show were loans
from distinguished French collectors,
including thirty-two from Blanche himself,
six from André Gide[9] and ten from Adolphe
Tavernier,[10] who, two to three years later,
became a talent scout for Bernheim-Jeune.

Tavernier probably influenced the selection
for Sickert's next exhibition at Bernheim's
in January 1907. None of the eighty-one
oil paintings and four pastels was on loan.
Judging by the titles, around a dozen were
landscapes of Venice or Dieppe, and eight
were music halls. The remaining works were
figure subjects: some Venetian interiors
of 1903–4, but most subjects painted in
London within the last two years, or in Paris
during the autumn of 1906.

Sickert had returned to London in 1905
where over the next decade, in his art, his
writings and teaching, he conducted a
fierce polemic against the timid puritanism
of British art. His French contemporaries
treated the nude without recourse to
mythological window-dressing. They found
the bedroom or kitchen as valid a setting
for a painting with figures as a fashionable
salon or drawing room. Sickert determined
to foster similarly relaxed attitudes on

the British side of the Channel. Yet the
domestic interiors Sickert produced over
the next twenty years were not imitations
of French precedents. They form a distinct
and uniquely British strand within the
vocabulary of European art during the early
twentieth century, encompassing subjects
as diverse as the life of a brutalised
underclass in *L'Affaire de Camden Town*
(see no.128) and the mundane tedium
of *Ennui* (no.133).

Sickert found perfect models in Soho when
he overheard two young women ask an
uncomprehending policeman, in French,
where they could buy coffee.[11] Sickert
directed them before asking them to model
in his Fitzroy Street studio. Over the Easter
week of 1906, Belgian sisters Jeanne and
Hélène Daurmont posed for six paintings.
Jeanne. The Cigarette (see no.74) was in
the 1907 exhibition, as were two paintings
showing Jeanne and Hélène together. One
of these, now known as *The Belgian Cocottes*
(Portsmouth City Museums; see fig.33), is a
case history in Sickert's use of wayward titles.
Its first title, *The Map of London*,[12] is explained
by the inscription in a pen and ink sketch of
the painting,[13] over the framed picture behind
the standing figure. This may well have been
an ingenious reference to Sickert's first
meeting with the sisters when they were lost
in Soho. His titles often embodied a private
code, which, however opaque, was seldom
meaningless. However, when the painting
was included in a major retrospective Sickert
exhibition at Agnews in 1933, it was renamed
Rose and Marie, a random choice of names.
Virginia Woolf read the painting as an episode
in a novel:[14]

> Marie on the chair has been sobbing out
> some piteous plaint of vows betrayed
> and hearts broken to the woman in the
> crimson petticoat. 'Don't be a damned
> fool, my dear,' says Rose, standing before
> her with arms akimbo … in the intimacy
> of undress, experienced, seasoned,
> a woman of the world. And Marie looks
> up at her with all her illusions tearfully
> exposed … takes heart again.[15]

The figure paintings at Bernheim's in 1907
also included *The Poet and his Muse (or
Collaboration)*, one of three works on the

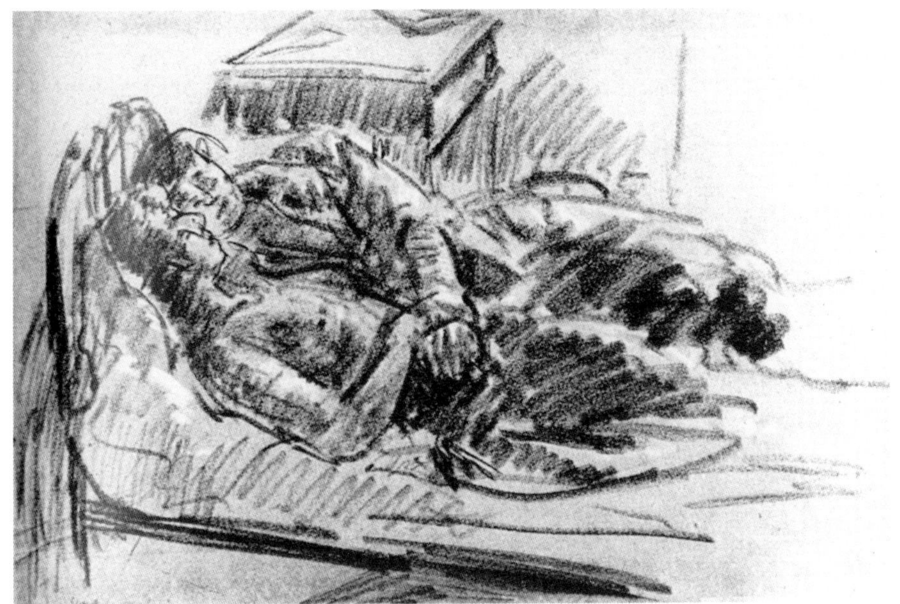

theme in which Sickert first juxtaposed a naked woman and a clothed man (see fig.34). By presenting the figures in the quasi-mythological roles of poet and muse, or painter and model, Sickert toned down his radicalism. Instead, he wreaked havoc on the mise-en-scène by painting what he saw in reflection, or possibly at two removes as a reflected reflection. Sickert had been fascinated by the use of mirror images since 1883, when he had visited Manet's studio and viewed *A Bar at the Folies-Bergère* (Courtauld Gallery, London). Thereafter, especially in his music hall subjects, he had used mirror images both to challenge the analytical powers of his viewers[16] and to create a pleasing counterpoint of colours and shapes across the surface of his paintings.[17] With the possible exception of *The Studio: The Painting of a Nude* (see no.121), where the painter is represented by the powerful diagonal of his arm across the canvas, none of these painter and model pictures hints at a lucid narrative. They are graded pictorial experiments designed to achieve the disintegration of form. Their incoherence anticipates developments in British postwar painting by some seventy years.

Sickert's studios, the books he read, the people he met, contemporary gossip, news reports: all were capable of triggering his imagination towards the creation of a 'conversation piece'. The murder in September 1907 of Emily Dimmock, a prostitute, was the catalyst for his imaginative elaboration of pictures which have shaped the perception of his oeuvre ever since. Dimmock's body was found by Bertram Shaw, with whom she lived, when he returned to their Camden Town lodgings after his night-shift as a cook on the London to Sheffield run of a Midland Railway restaurant car. She was lying naked, face downwards, in bed, her blonde hair in curling pins, her throat cut. Robert Wood, a commercial artist accused of her murder, defended by the brilliant advocate Marshall Hall, was acquitted a week before Christmas. The evidence against him had been circumstantial and contradictory. However, a vivid portrait of low life in Camden Town emerged in the exhaustive press reports of the trial. The case has never been solved.

Prostitutes often modelled for artists during the day, so the murder of Dimmock in his own neighbourhood would have resonated powerfully with Sickert. He was fascinated by the habits and dramas of their daily lives:

> Extraordinary lives. Men, who live on them, now & again hitting them with 'ammers, putting poisonous powders on cakes, trying to cut their throats, drugging their whisky &c.[18]

Early in 1908, with his keen instinct for topicality and publicity, Sickert appropriated the title 'Camden Town Murder' for his several independent series of paintings, drawings and etchings featuring a naked woman, a clothed man and a bed, within his first-floor front room at 6 Mornington Crescent. Rex Nan Kivell, managing director of the Redfern Gallery,[19] told me that for added authenticity Sickert hired Robert Wood to model for the 'Murder' paintings.[20] The earliest of the series are two closely related, enigmatic canvases, exhibited at the Salon d'Automne in Paris in 1909 and at the first exhibition of the Camden Town Group in June 1911 under the 'Murder' title. Like Bonnard, Sickert used light to heighten the drama of the emotional relationship of his figures, stripping the woman naked and, bypassing the man, transforming him into a brooding silhouette. The title encouraged viewers to read the paintings as prostitute

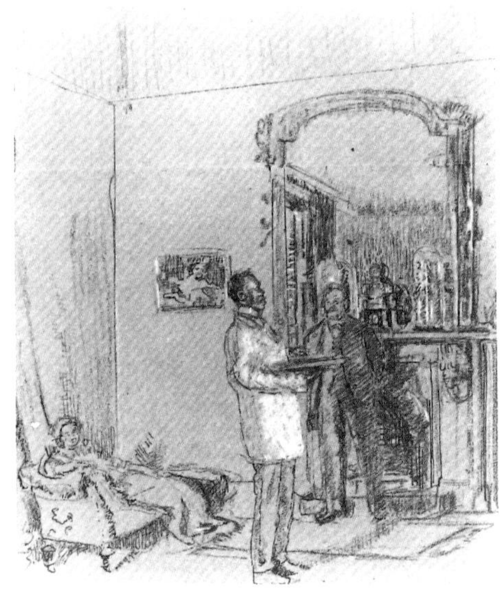

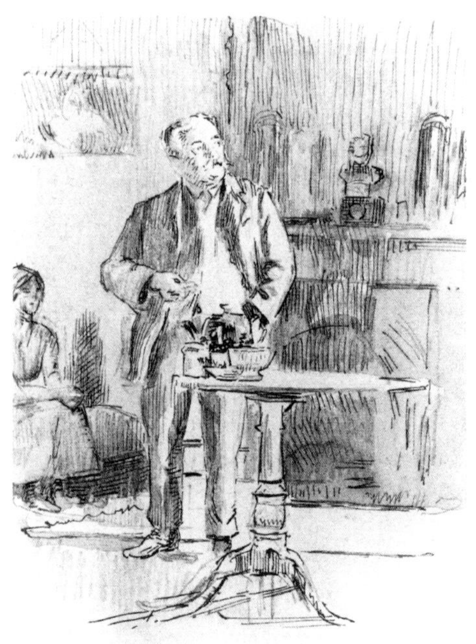

Fig.36
The Artist's Home in New Orleans c.1913–14, chalk, pen and ink, heightened with white, 38.7 × 32.4, Private collection

Fig.37
Interior with Figures c.1913–14, pen and ink, wash, 29.2 × 20.3, New Grafton Gallery

and client, victim and murderer, endorsing the notion that Sickert's pictures dealt with 'the utter depravity of a particularly unsavoury phase of life'.[21] In due course, the lack of any illustrative relationship to the circumstances of Emily Dimmock's death led to alternative titles attaching themselves to these two paintings: *What Shall We Do for the Rent?* and *Summer Afternoon*.

While the murder scene itself was ignored by Sickert, his habit of immersing himself imaginatively in the mental as well as the physical settings of intimate life in Camden Town led to more subtle narratives. As he argued in 1912:

> All the greater draughtsmen tell a story. When people … criticise the anecdotic 'Picture of the Year', the essence of our criticism is that the story is a poor one, poor in structure or poor as drama, poor as psychology… A painter may tell his story like Balzac, or like Mr. Hichens.[22]

In the 'Murder' context, the tragedy of Bertram Shaw was largely overlooked as a prurient public concentrated on the more lurid aspects of the story. One painting in the series (see no.123) has an authentic alternative title, *What Shall We Do for the Rent?*, which captures the resigned intimacy of the painting: the figures alone with their thoughts, the man with head bowed and hands clasped in despair as he knows his earnings won't cover the rent; his common-law wife facing the wall as she realises all they possess to sell is her body. She reassures the man by lightly touching his knee. A squared-up composition study, inscribed with the rent title, was exhibited in 1911 as *Consolation*,[23] while a drawing of the two figures in the same setting, lying side by side on the narrow bed, his arm gently resting on her body, has the title *Stemmo Insieme* (see fig.35).[24]

Nonetheless, it is unwise to attach much significance to the title as an indication of the story Sickert was telling in his conversation pieces. *Summer in Naples* and *Dawn, Camden Town* are alternative titles for a single painting of a fat nude and a clothed working man seated back to back on a bed in a dingy attic (see no.129).[25]

L'Affaire de Camden Town, the latest painting in the 'Murder' series, is the only one with no alternative title.[26] Sickert discarded the planar parallel geometry of earlier paintings in favour of a narrow space with the active elements viewed in emphatic foreshortening. This allowed him to make the focal point of his composition the sex of the woman on the bed. The painting was the climax of an interrelated sequence of drawings which began with a conversation between two women, one naked and supine on a bed, the other standing to one side in her shift and corset (see no.125). Sickert then transformed this intimate scene into one of imminent brutality. The standing woman became a man in his shirtsleeves; the relaxed interaction between the two figures became a hostile confrontation; the posture of the supine woman became more awkward and twisted, her arm ready to fend off an attack. The handling of the painting supports the dramatic implication of the narrative: it is deep-toned, with a palette dominated by sombre grey-blues; the contrasts of light and shade are strong, the cast shadows adding a sense of menace; the patterned surface is agitated; the brushwork is alive with aggressively hatched areas and broken jabs and dashes of paint. Rather than attempt to document the facts of the murder, Sickert used his imagination to conjure an atmosphere of fear and sexual violence, and his skills as a painter to convey that atmosphere.

Although Sickert's paintings seem to have a realistic, documentary character unprecedented in British art, his use of the term 'dramatic truth' hints at their dependence on his lifelong engagement with theatre. His predilection for simultaneously renting rooms in different lodging houses is at once explained if we accept that each room, with its quota of iron bedsteads, bedside cabinets, chamber pots, washbowls, chests of drawers, dressing mirrors and pianos, was an individual stage set. The vivid cameos he produced were fictitious – products of a subtle imagination nourished by his enduring passion for British and European nineteenth-century literature.

Sickert's unusually spacious studio on the corner of 247 Hampstead Road and Granby Street (Wellington House Academy, to Sickert)[27] offered multiple settings for multiple dramas, most featuring his general factotum 'Hubby' and his cleaner Marie Hayes. *Ennui*, created within a corner of this studio, furnished with a round table and a chest of drawers, shares its setting with drawings that imply inhabitants of greater social pretensions. By replacing the chest of drawers with a couch, by revealing the entire fireplace and its overmantel glass, and by placing a sculpted bust on the mantelshelf,[28] the interior is transformed into a grand salon (see fig.36). A diminutive Marie reclines on the couch, while Hubby stands in proprietorial fashion in front of the fireplace, hands behind his back, addressing his order for drinks to a Black butler wearing a white jacket and holding a tray. This Black model, by helping to evoke gracious living in the Deep South of the United States, inspired the titular reference to Degas's maternal origins: *The Artist's Home in New Orleans*.[29] In a related drawing, the small circular table from *Ennui*, set with a large tea pot and a few other dishes, occupies the centre foreground with Hubby standing immediately behind it (see fig.37). The subject is now afternoon tea in England.

Another area of Sickert's studio furnished with an iron bedstead and a dressing table, in front of a square-paned window with diaphanous curtains, is the setting for an interrelated series of drawings, usually in pen and ink, featuring Hubby in his shirtsleeves and a female model (often, but not always, Marie) in semi-undress. Sickert's chosen titles – *The Tiff* (see fig.38), *Home Truths*, *Curtain Lecture*, *The Argument* and *Amantium Irae*[30] – stress their common theme, identified by Sickert as 'Scenes of intimate life'.[31]

In most examples, the process of suggesting various narratives travelled from drawings to paintings and back again, sometimes incorporating prints en route. A characteristic sequence begins with *Sunday Afternoon*, in which Hubby is seated on the near edge of the bed, square to the surface, while Marie behind him holds the bedrail. She retains that pose in *Granby Street* (see no.134), but Hubby has moved to a chair in the background by the window. Two drawings and a print play with slight alterations to this design: *Vacerra*, the print version of one of the drawings, is embellished with the text of

a scurrilous epigram by Martial; in *My Awful Dad*, Marie is replaced by a sulky young girl with plaited hair. In both cases, Sickert used his design, with its zooming recession, to emphasise the theme of alienation. The viewer is influenced by the titles to interpret the relationship of the figures: between a petty criminal and his partner; and between an adolescent child and her embarrassing father.

Titles are helpful pointers when reading Sickert's conversation pieces, but they are seldom exclusive. A telling illustration of this point is Sickert's addition, three years later, of a topical title to a mundane bedroom encounter painted around 1912 in Wellington House Academy. When he exhibited the painting in 1915 as *The Prussians in Belgium* (see no.130), the *Daily Telegraph* accepted the bait: 'Mr. Walter Sickert presents in a sordid interior a half-nude, weary-eyed girl seated on a bed, and with her a bald-headed elderly German of more or less Bismarckian type, sitting at ease as he smokes a cigarette.'[32]

Sickert's mischievous habit of changing the titles of his paintings had a serious purpose, namely to demonstrate that:

> Pictures, like streets and persons, have to have names to distinguish them. But their names are not definitions of them, or, indeed, anything but the loosest kind of labels that make it possible for us to handle them, that prevent us from mislaying them, or sending them to the wrong address… The real subject of a picture or a drawing is the plastic facts it succeeds in expressing, and all the world of pathos, of poetry, of sentiment that it succeeds in conveying, is conveyed … by the suggestion of the three dimensions of space, the suggestion of weight, the prelude or the refrain of movement, the promise of movement to come, or the echo of movement past. If the subject of a picture could be stated in words there had been no need to paint it.[33]

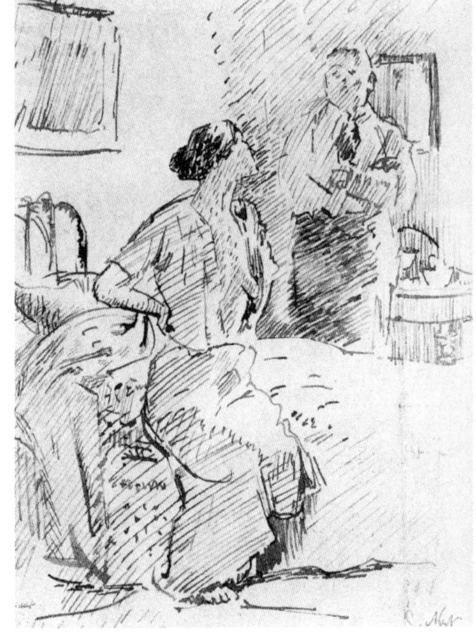

Fig.38
The Tiff c.1912, pen and ink, 28.5×22.9, Private collection

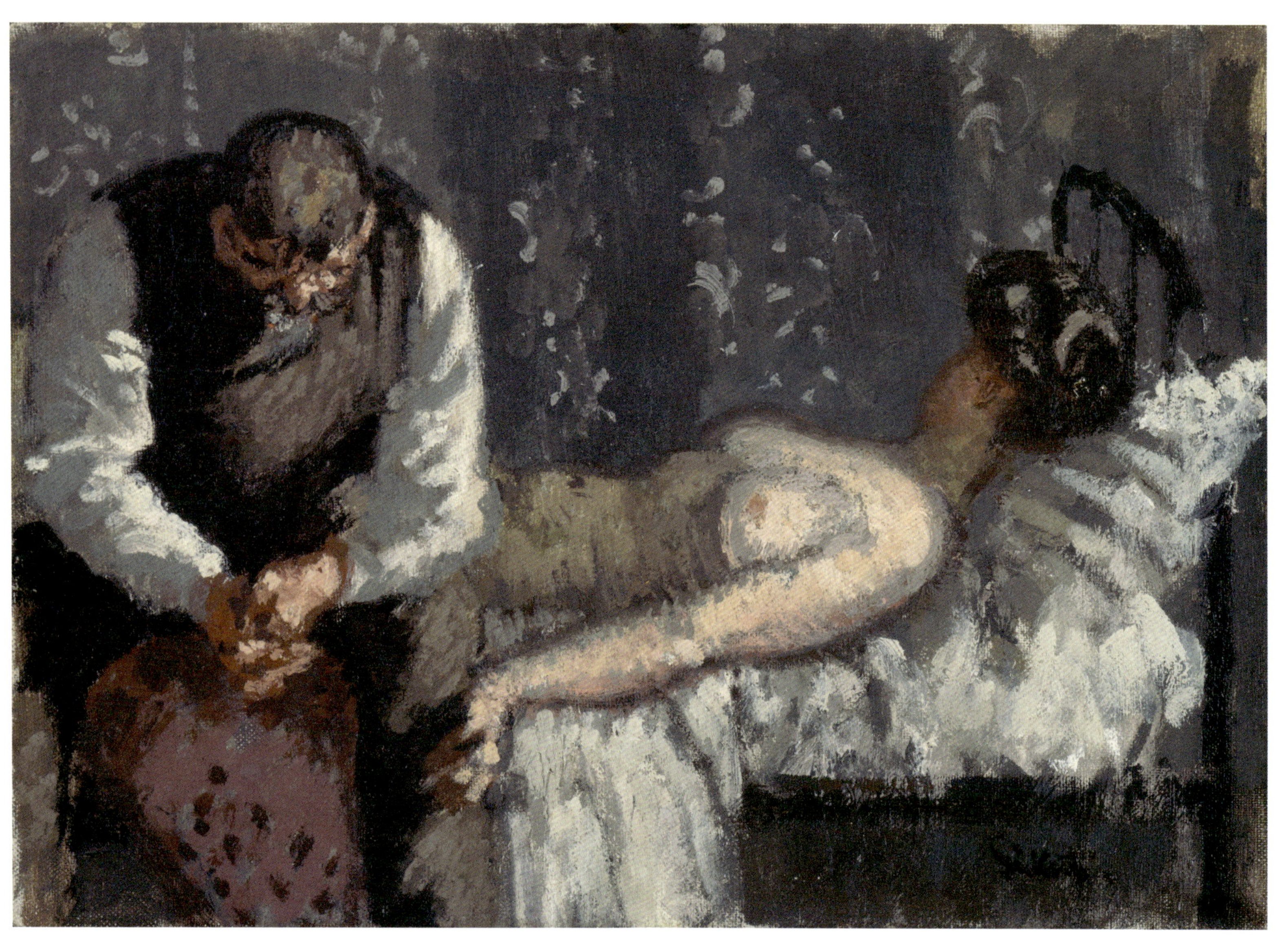

123
*The Camden Town
Murder*, or *What Shall We
Do for the Rent?* c.1908
Oil paint on canvas
Yale Center for British
Art, Paul Mellon Fund

124
The Camden Town Murder
c.1907–8
Oil paint on canvas
Daniel Katz Family Trust

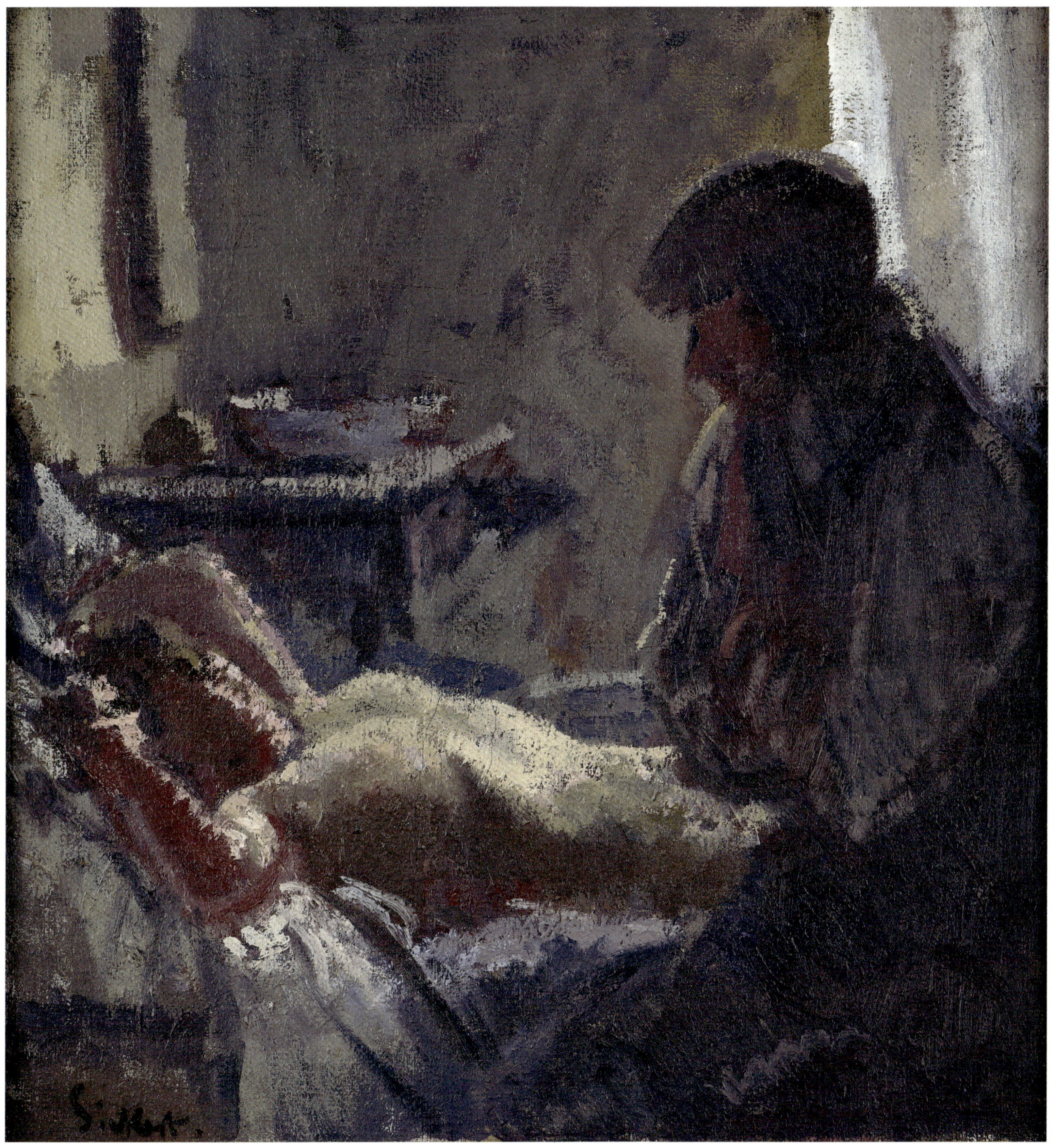

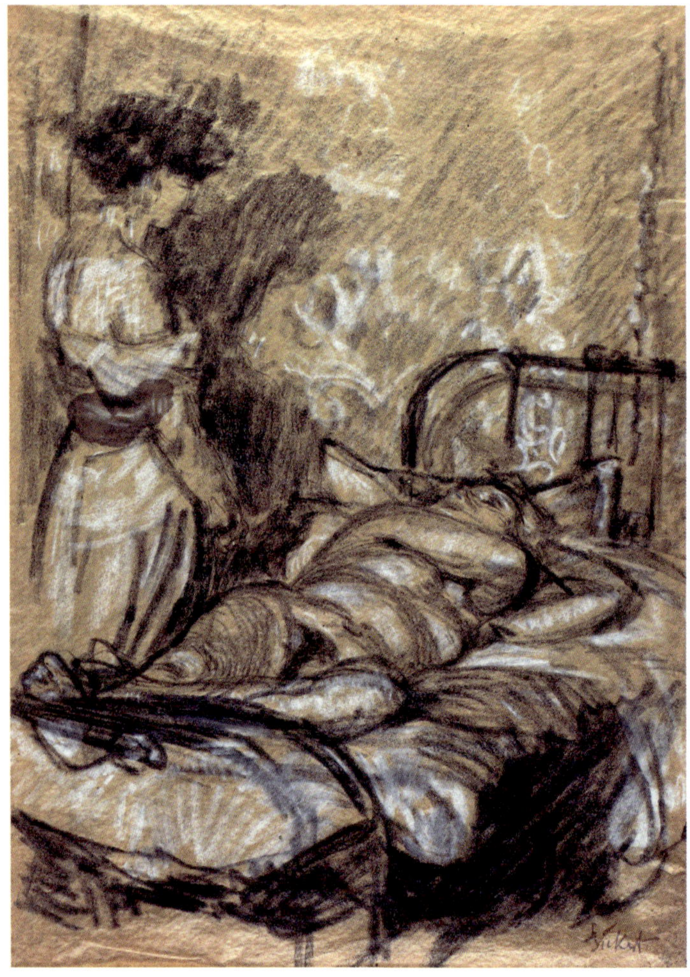

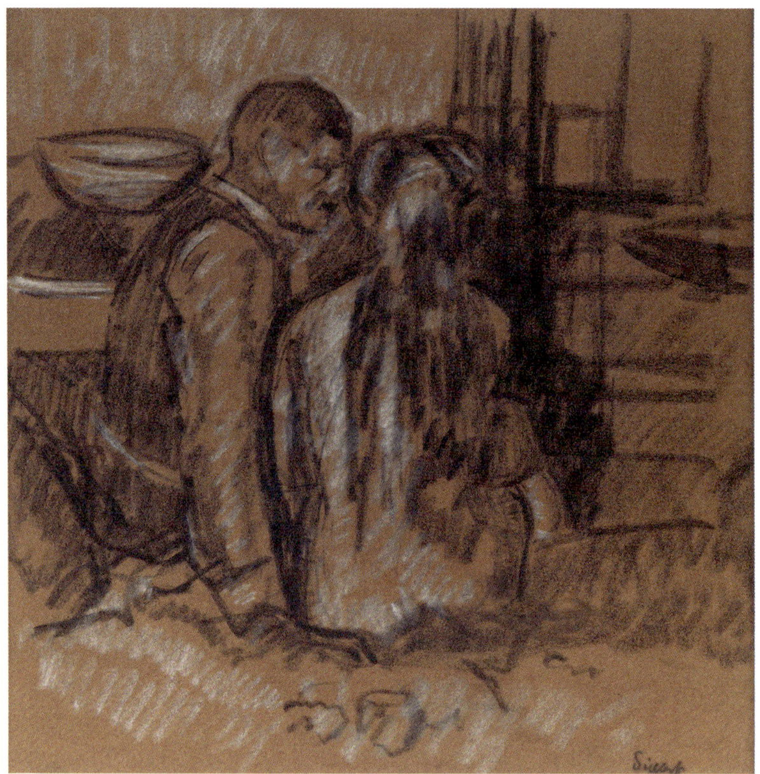

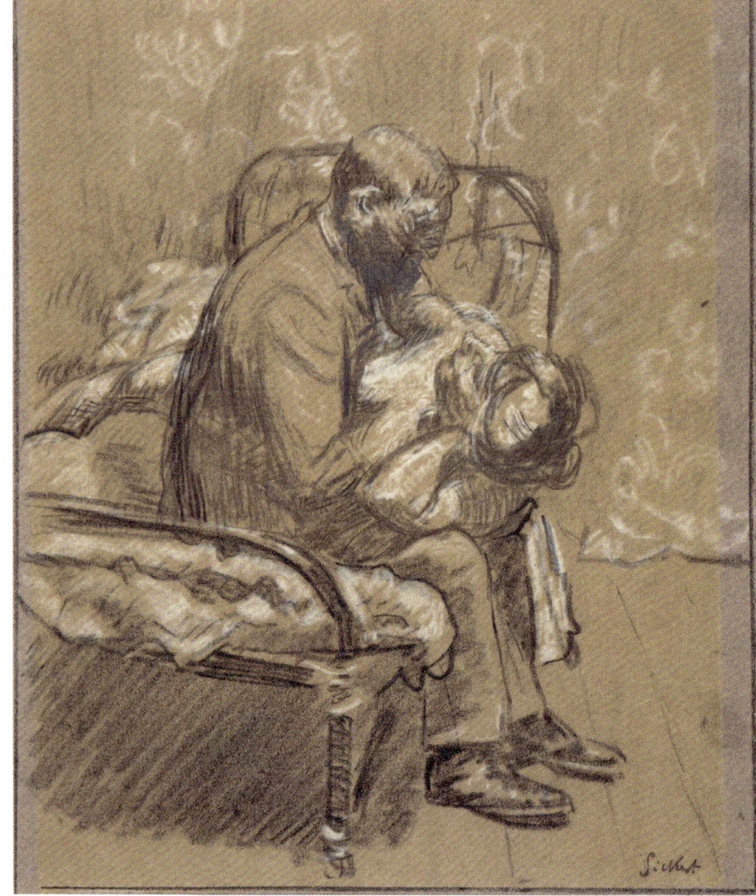

125
Conversation 1909
Black chalk, heightened
with white, pen and ink
on buff paper
Royal College of Art
Collection

126
A Consultation 1907–8
Chalk, heightened with white
on faded green paper
Lord and Lady Irvine of Lairg

127
Persuasion. La Belle Gâtée
c.1908
Black chalk, heightened
with white on violet – faded
to buff – paper
Bristol Culture: Bristol
Museums & Art Gallery

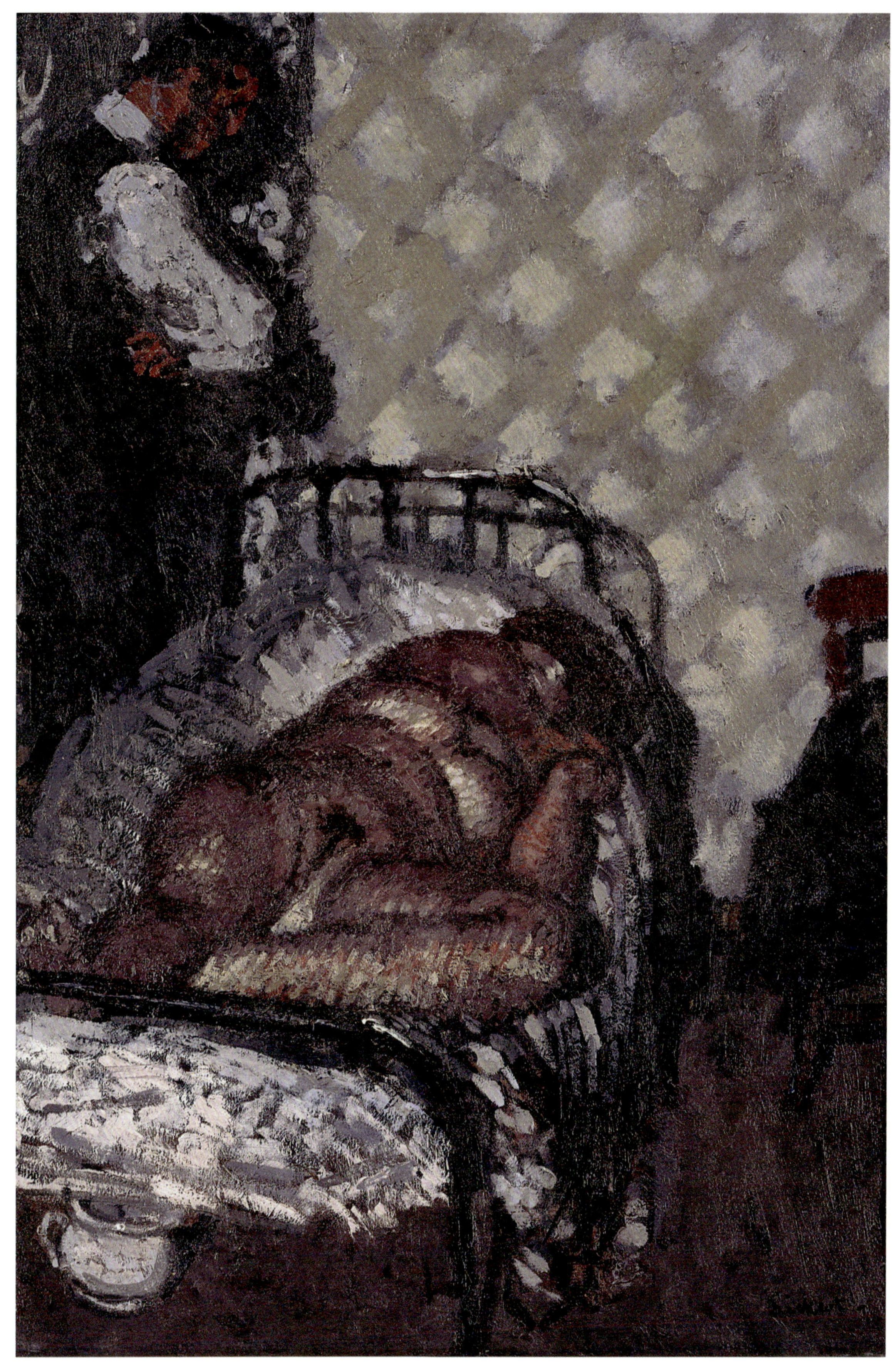

128
L'Affaire de Camden Town
1909
Oil paint on canvas
Private collection

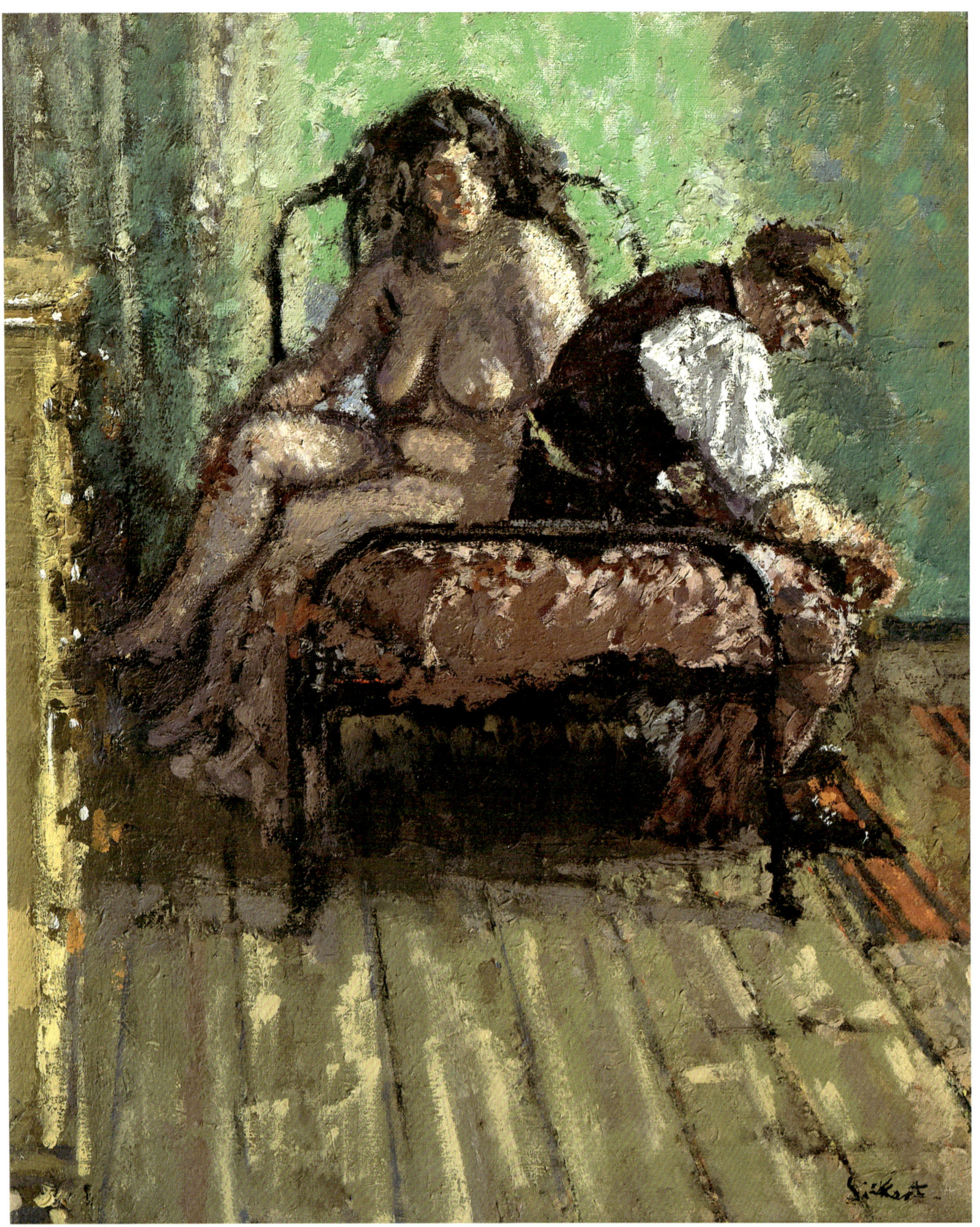

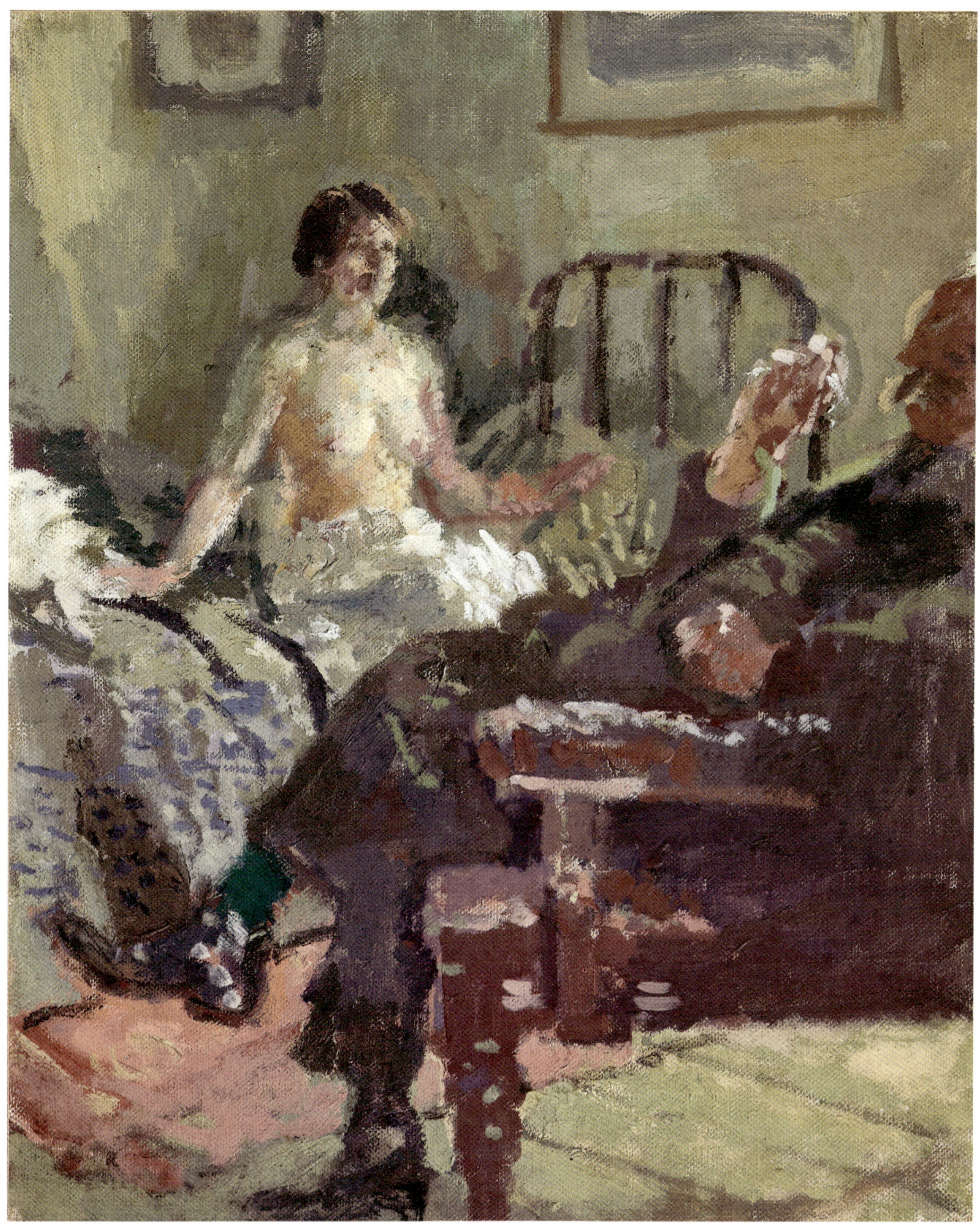

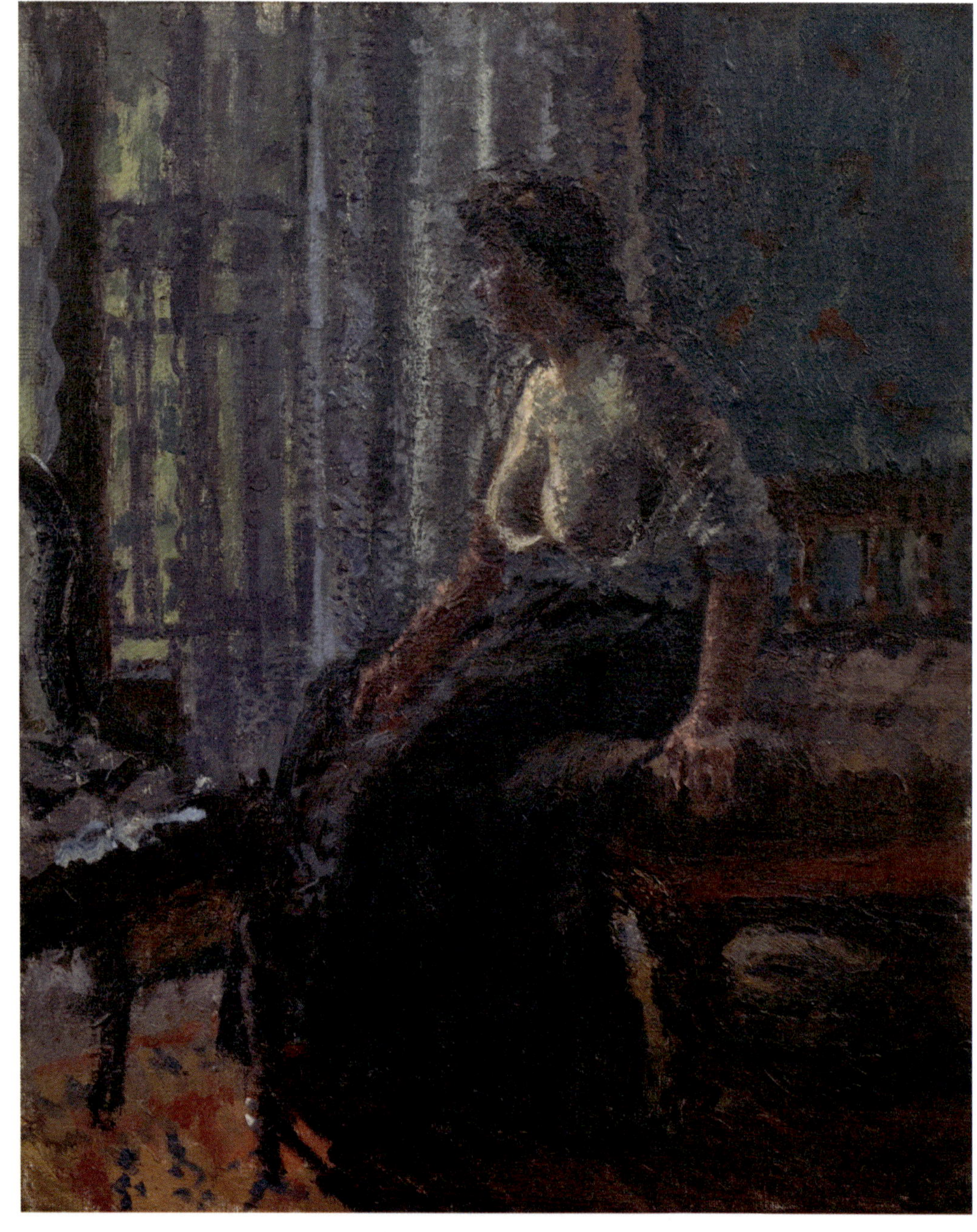

131
*Woman Seated at
a Window* c.1908–9
Oil paint on canvas
Private collection

132
Jack Ashore 1912–13
Oil paint on canvas
Pallant House Gallery,
Chichester

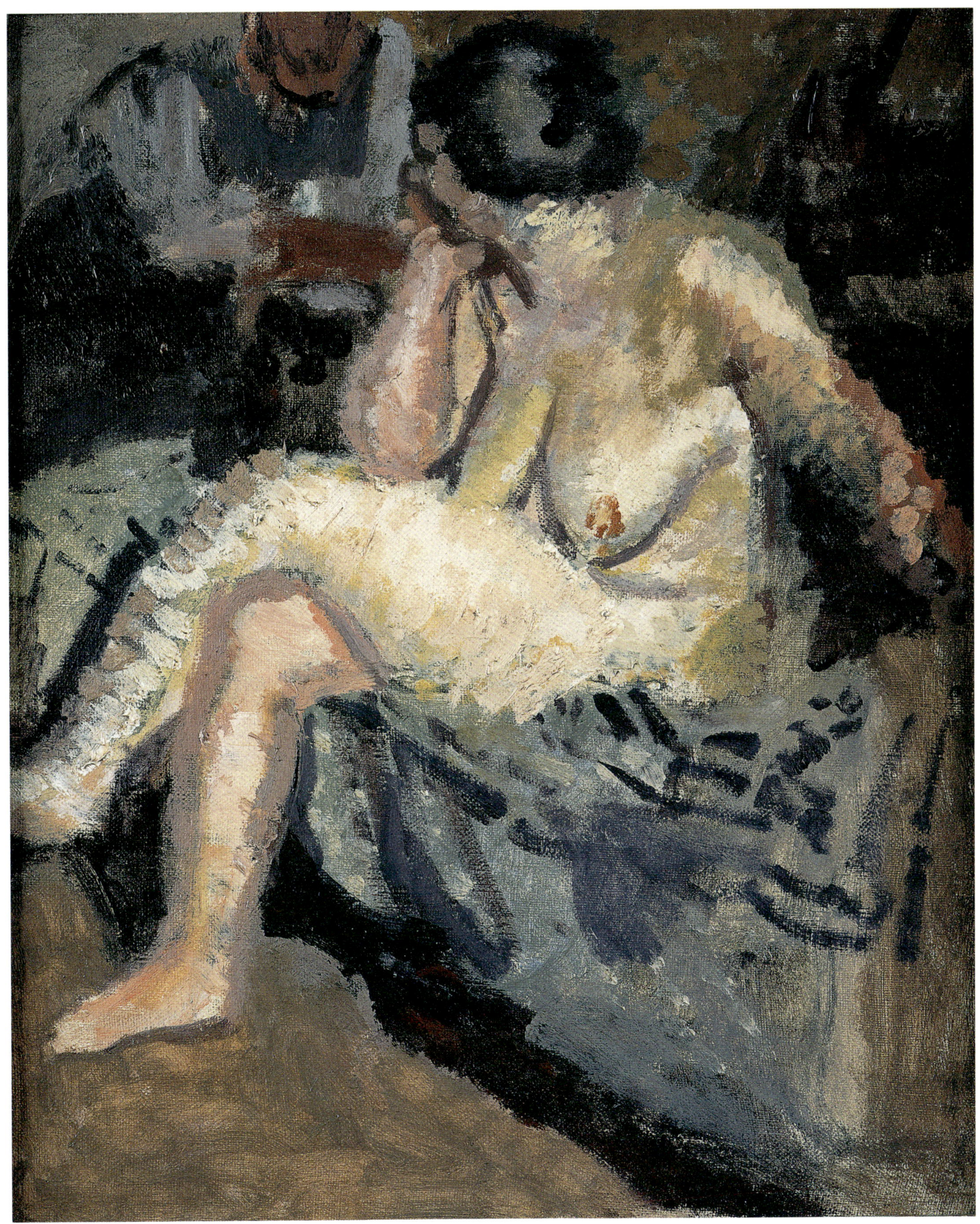

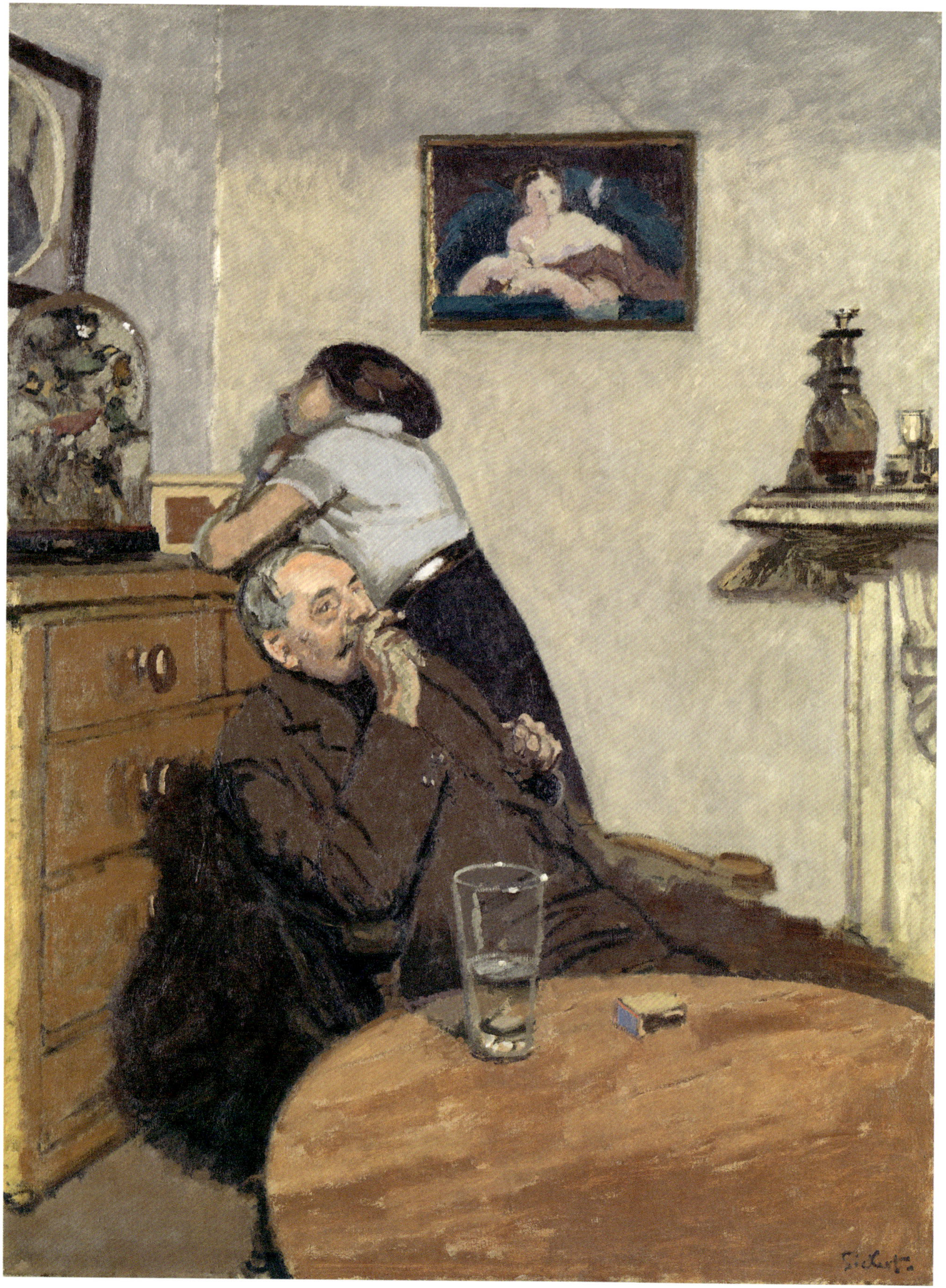

133
Ennui c.1914
Oil paint on canvas
Tate

134
Granby Street
c.1912–13
Oil paint on canvas
Private collection

180

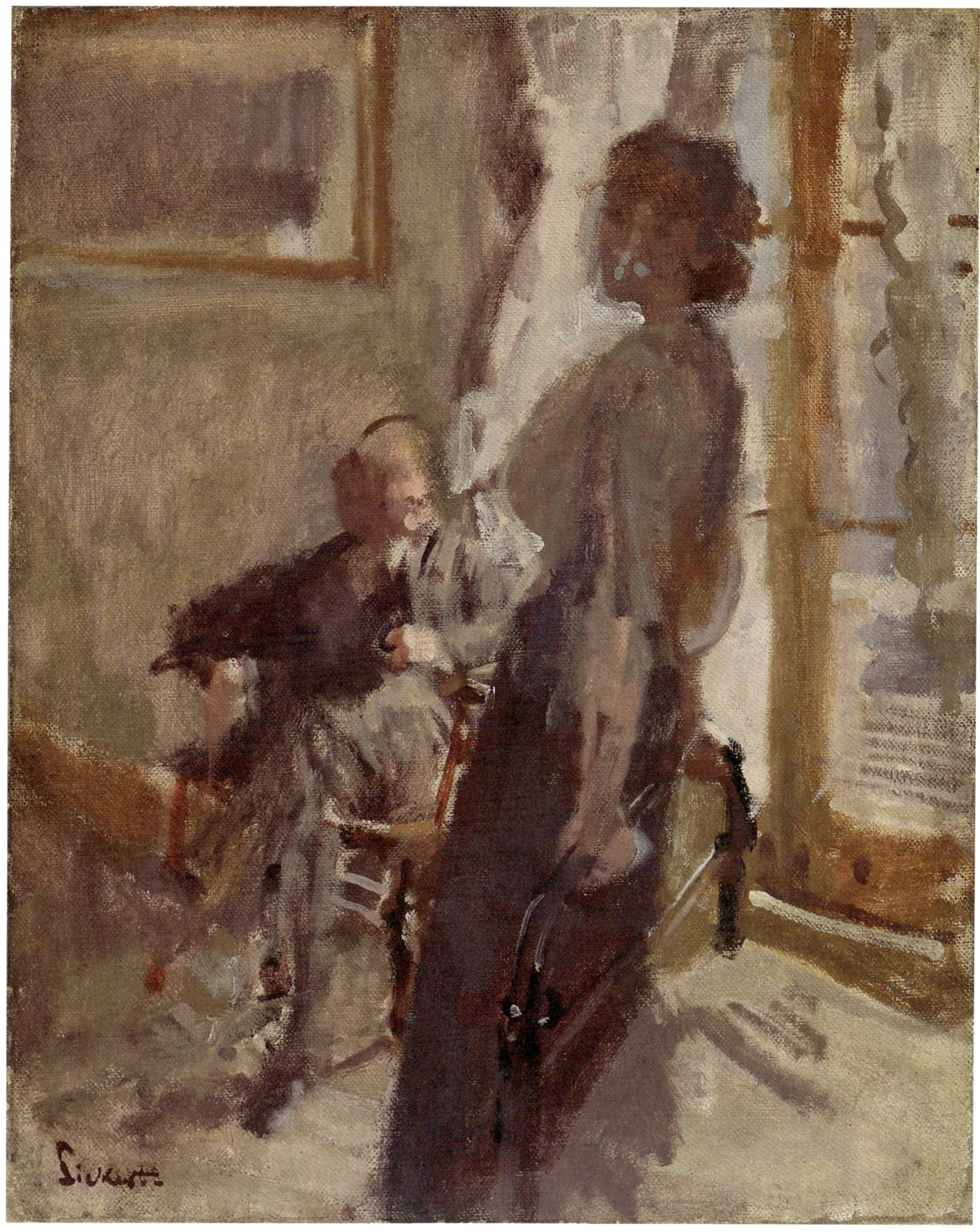

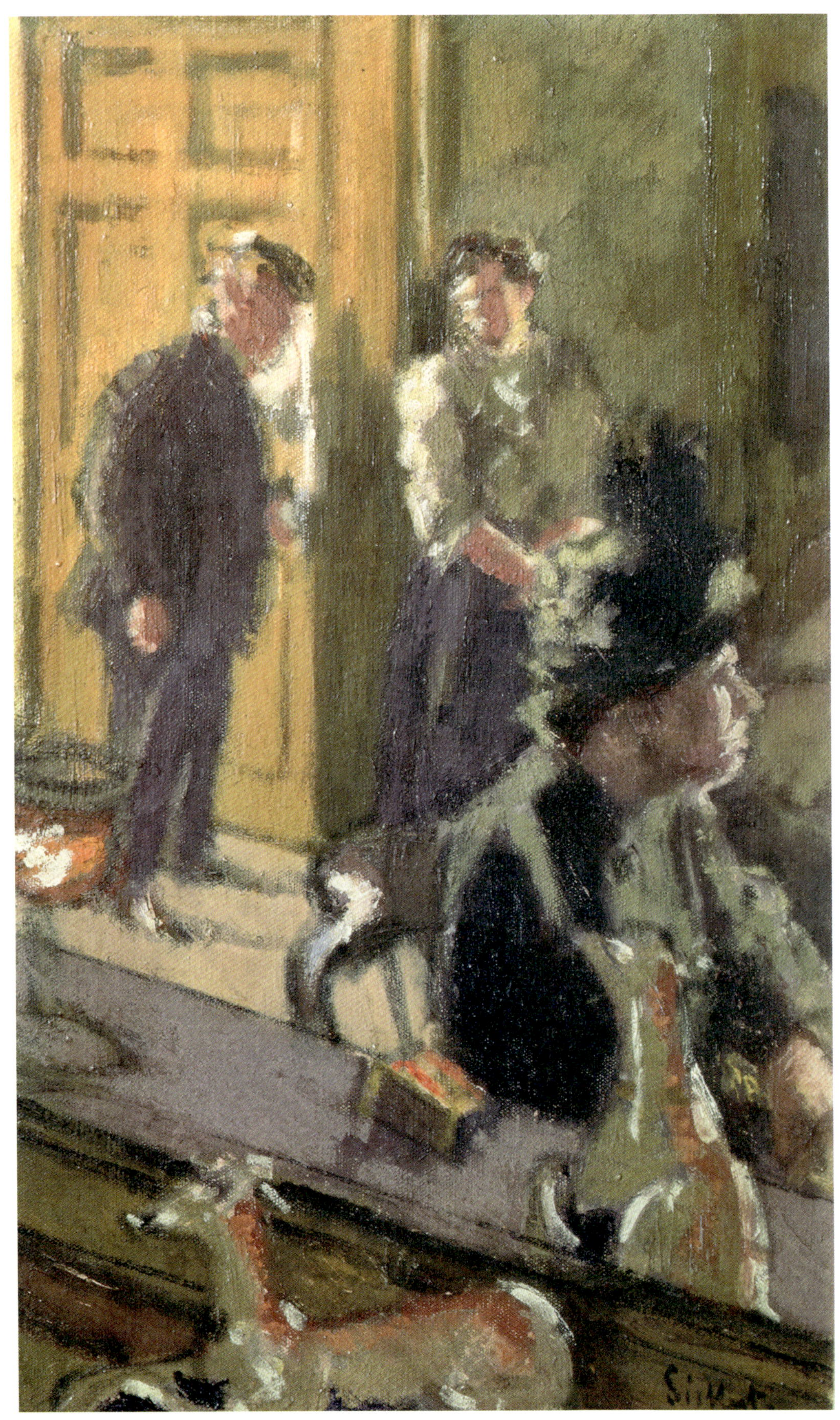

135
A Few Words: Off to the Pub c.1912
Oil paint on canvas
Collection of Margo and Nicholas Snowman

136
Off to the Pub 1911
Oil paint on canvas
Tate

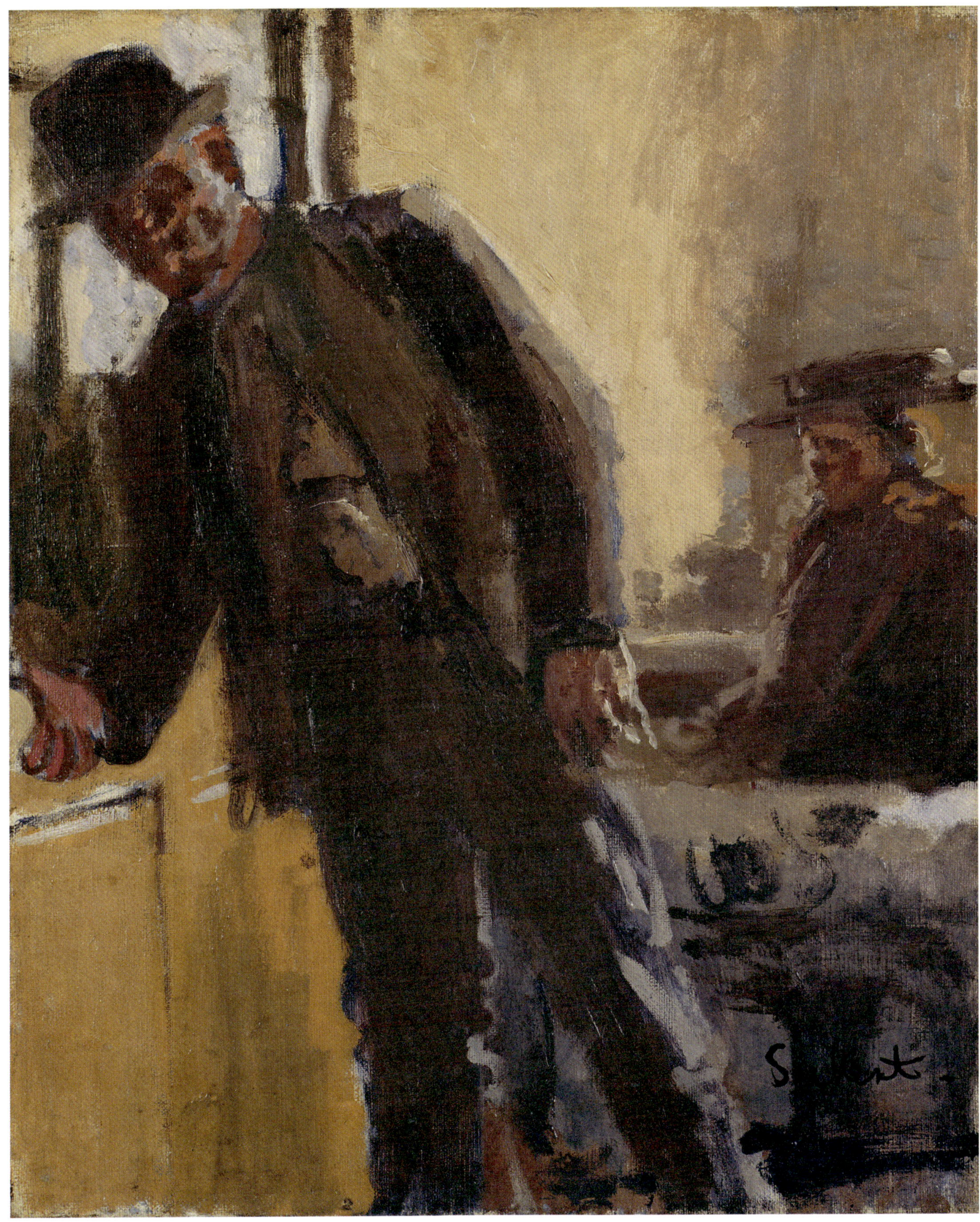

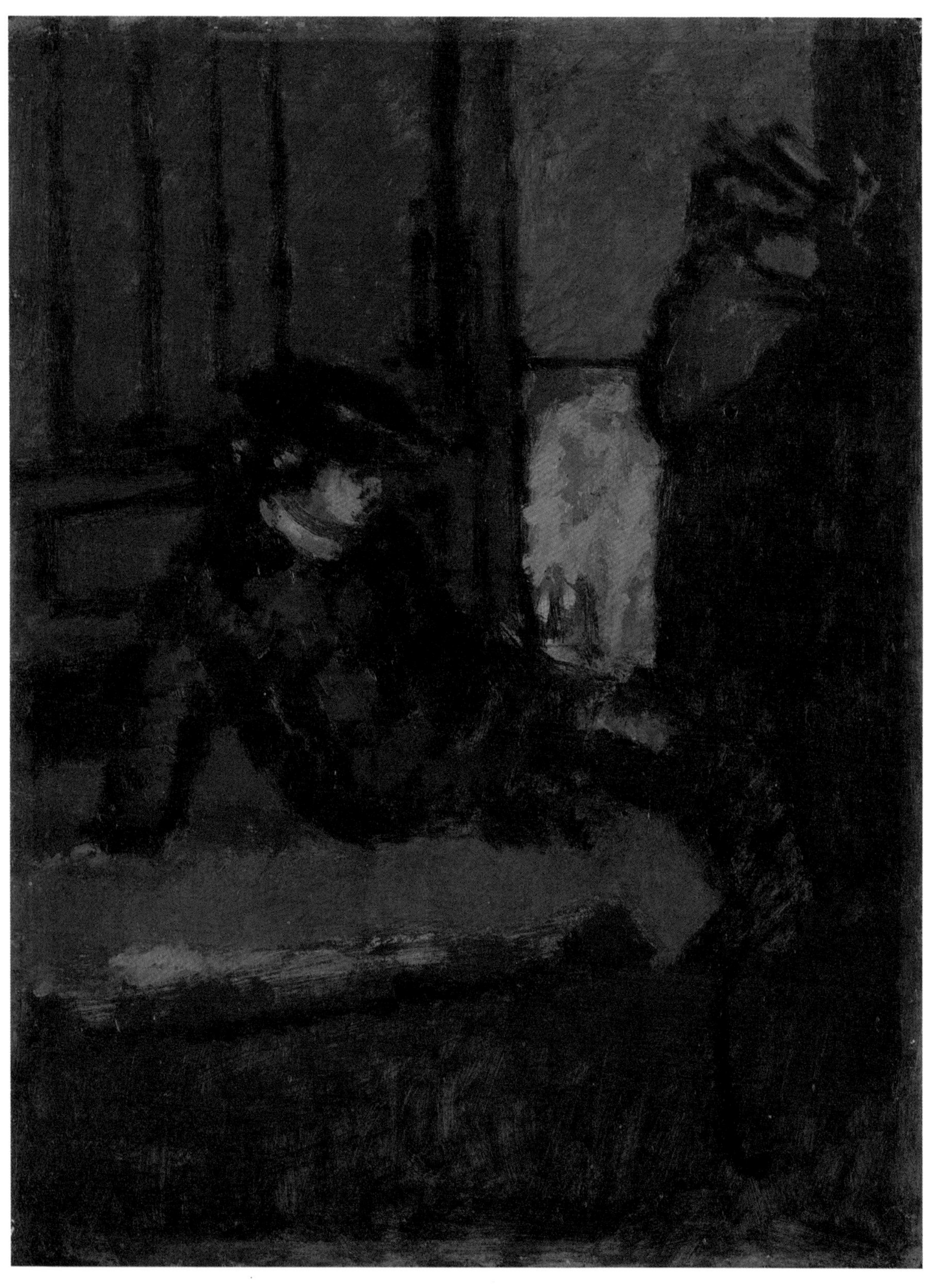

137
Two Coster Girls
c.1907–8
Oil on panel
Government Art Collection

138
Flower Girl 1911
Oil paint on canvas
Private collection

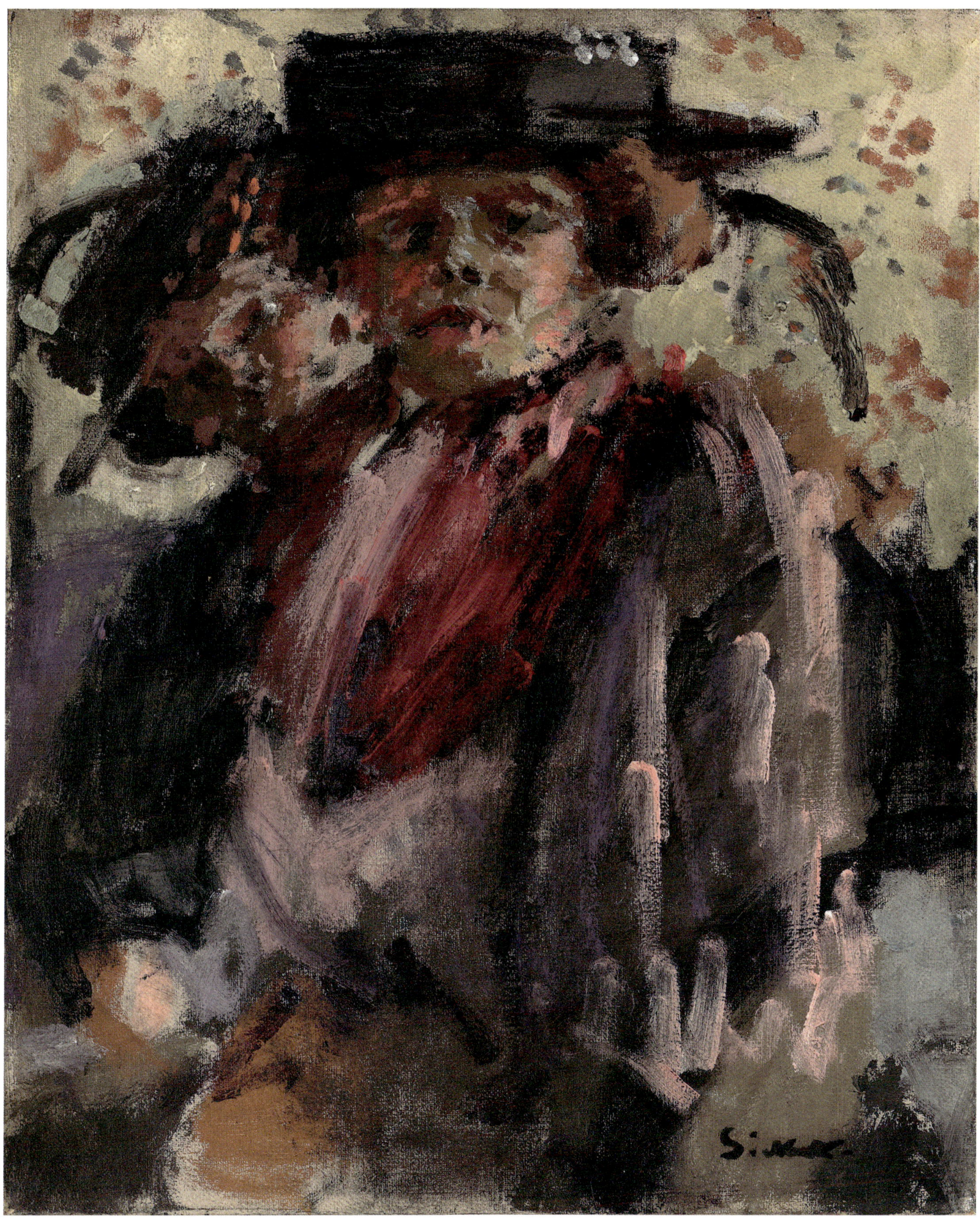

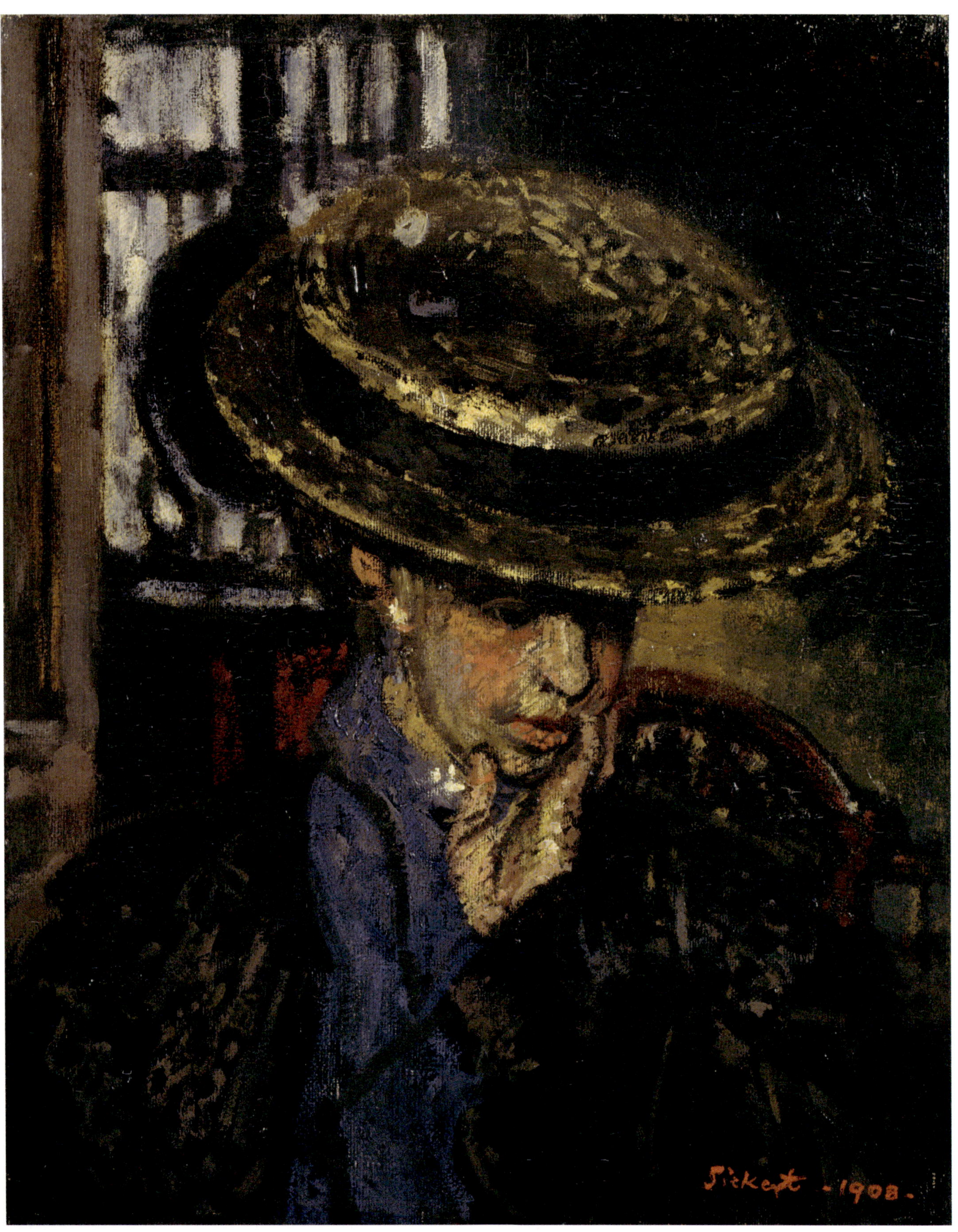

Sickert - 1908.

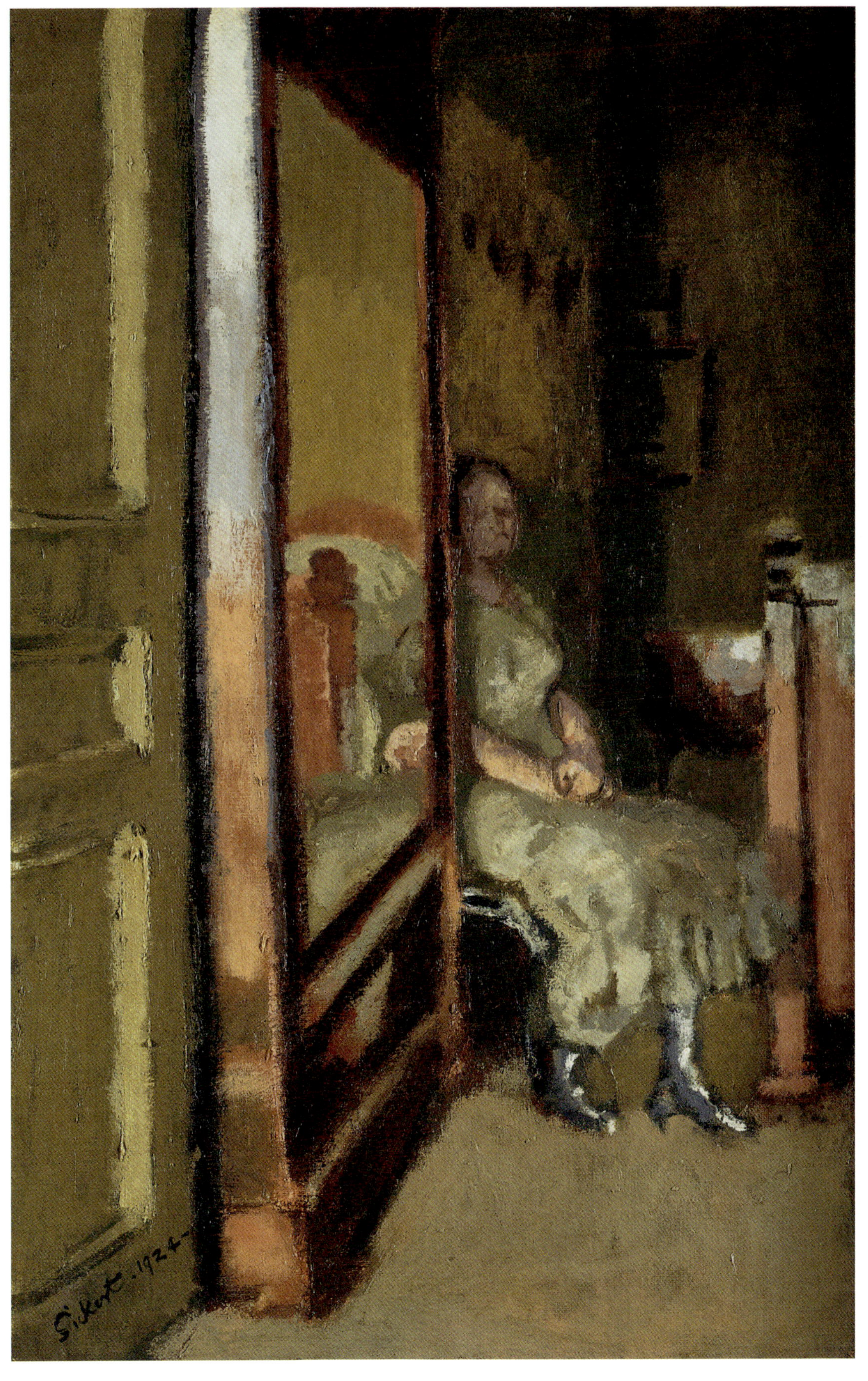

139
L'Américaine 1908
Oil paint on canvas
Tate

140
L'Armoire à Glace 1924
Oil paint on canvas
Tate

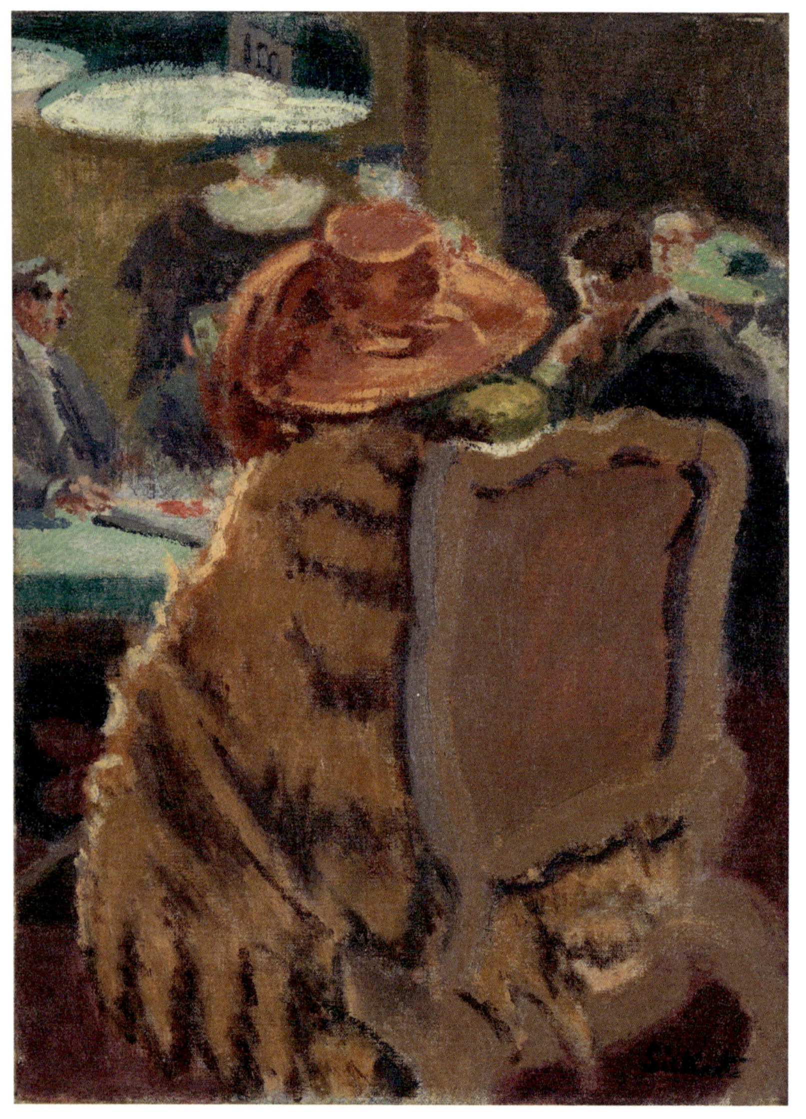

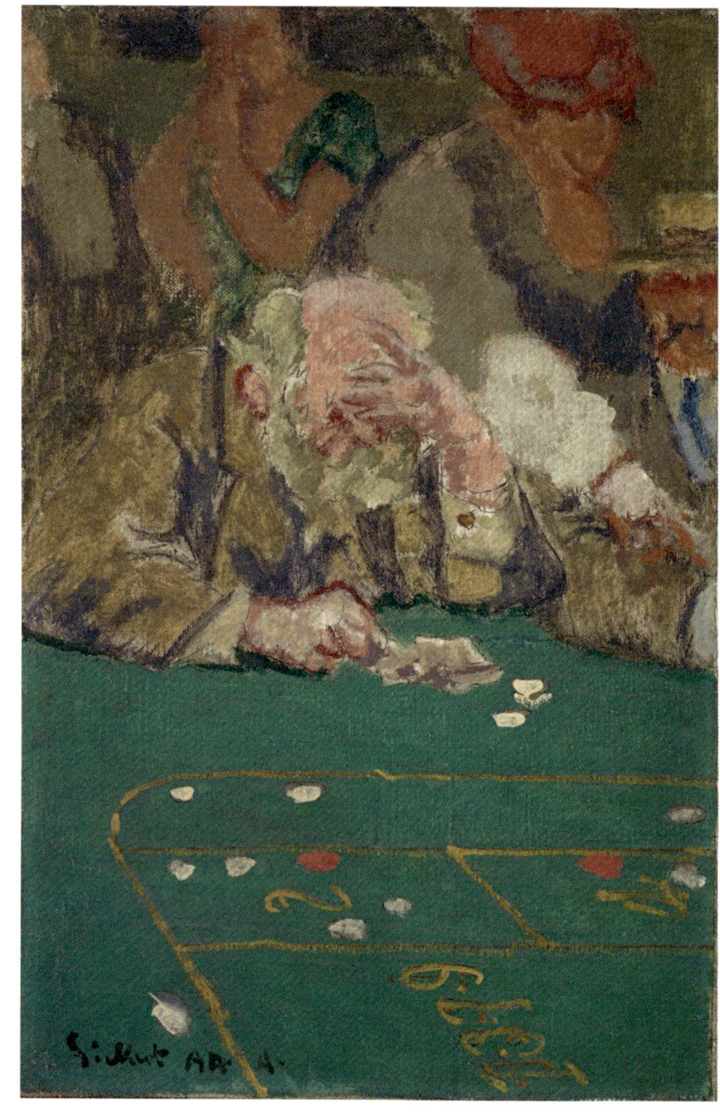

141
*Baccarat – the Fur
Cape* 1920
Oil paint on canvas
Tate

142
The System 1924–6
Oil paint on canvas
National Galleries of
Scotland

143
Baccarat 1920
Oil paint on canvas
Private collection c/o
Grant Ford Limited

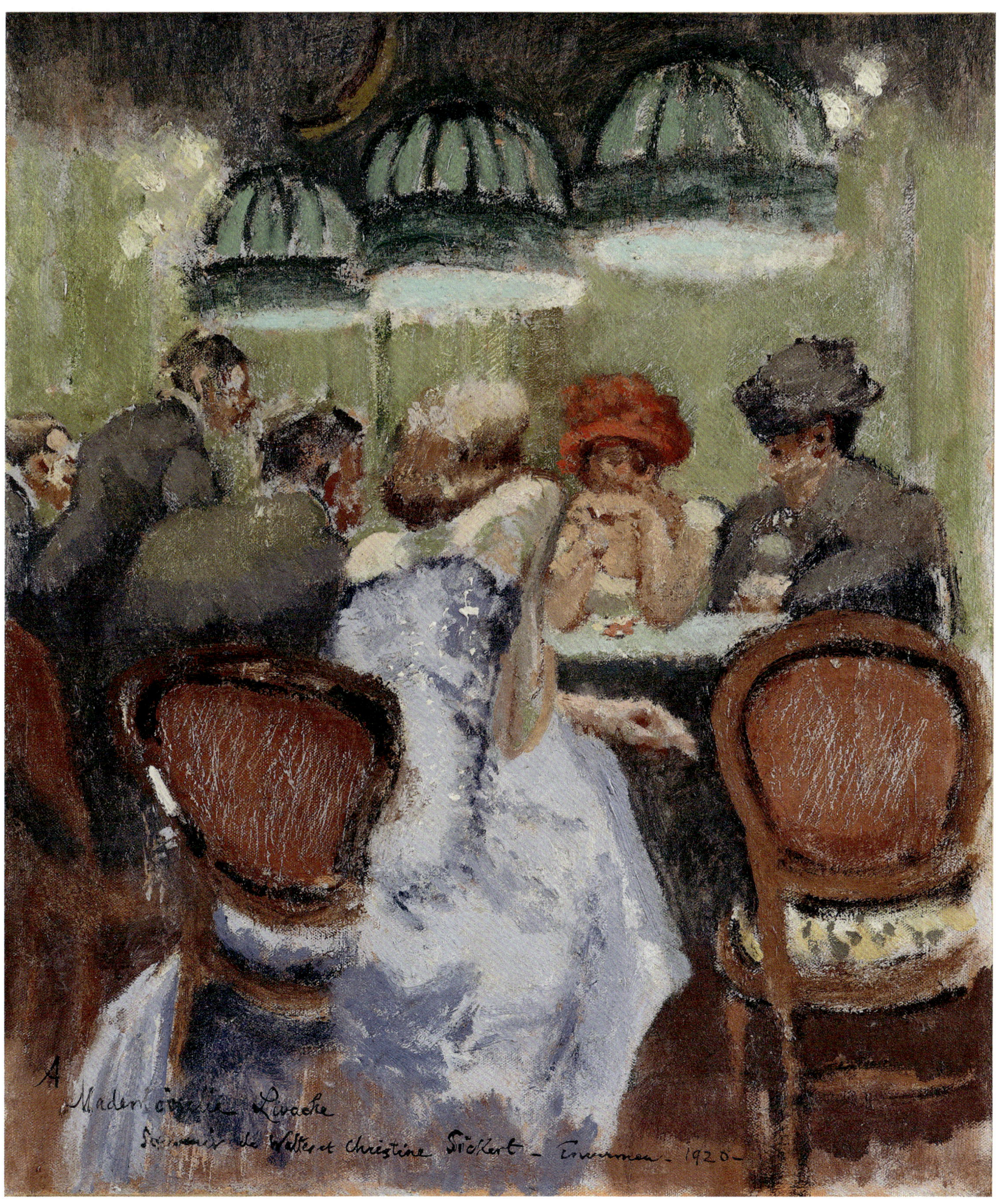
A
Mademoiselle Livache
Souvenir de Walter et Christine Sickert — Envermeu — 1920

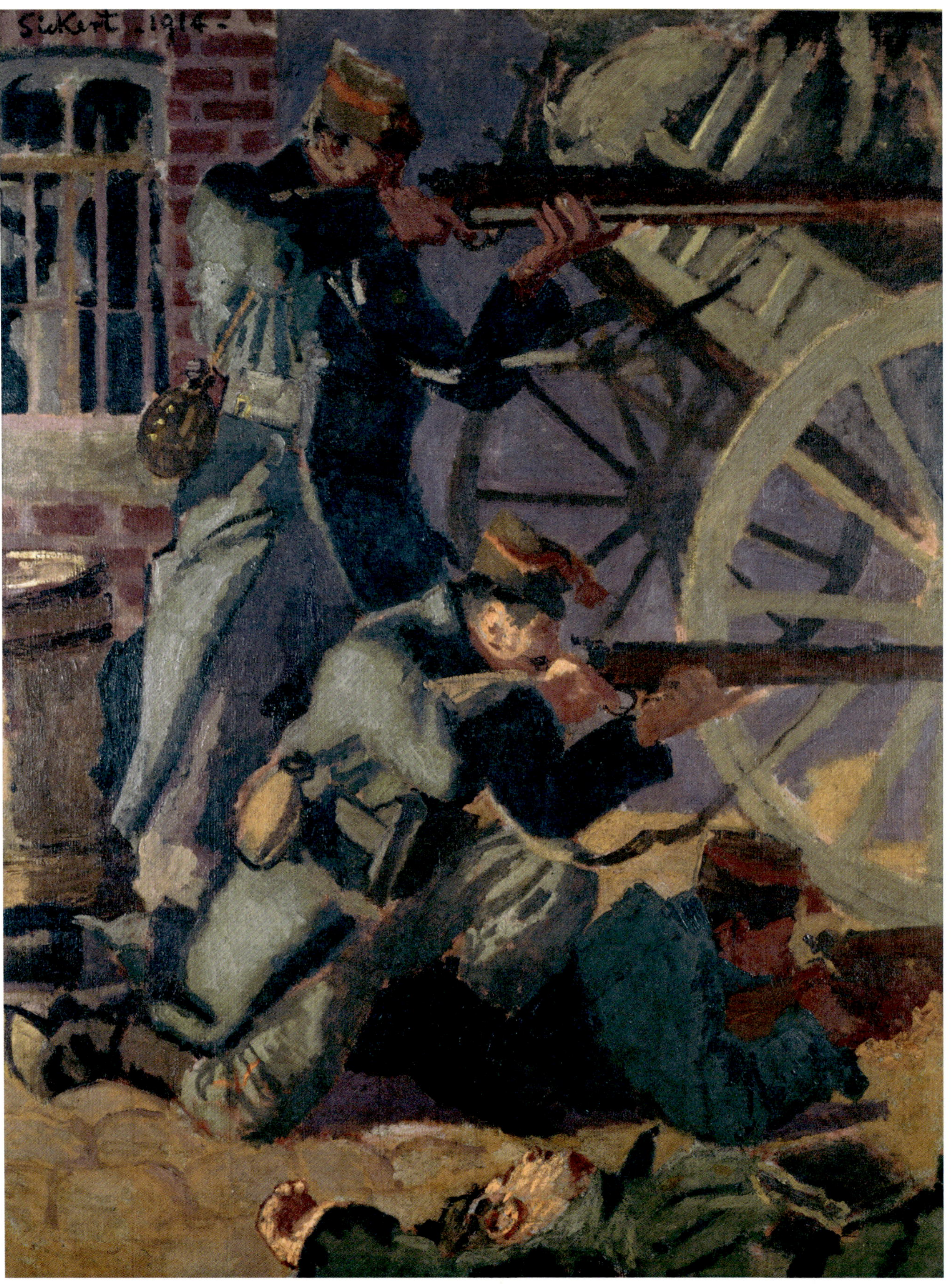

Sickert .1914.

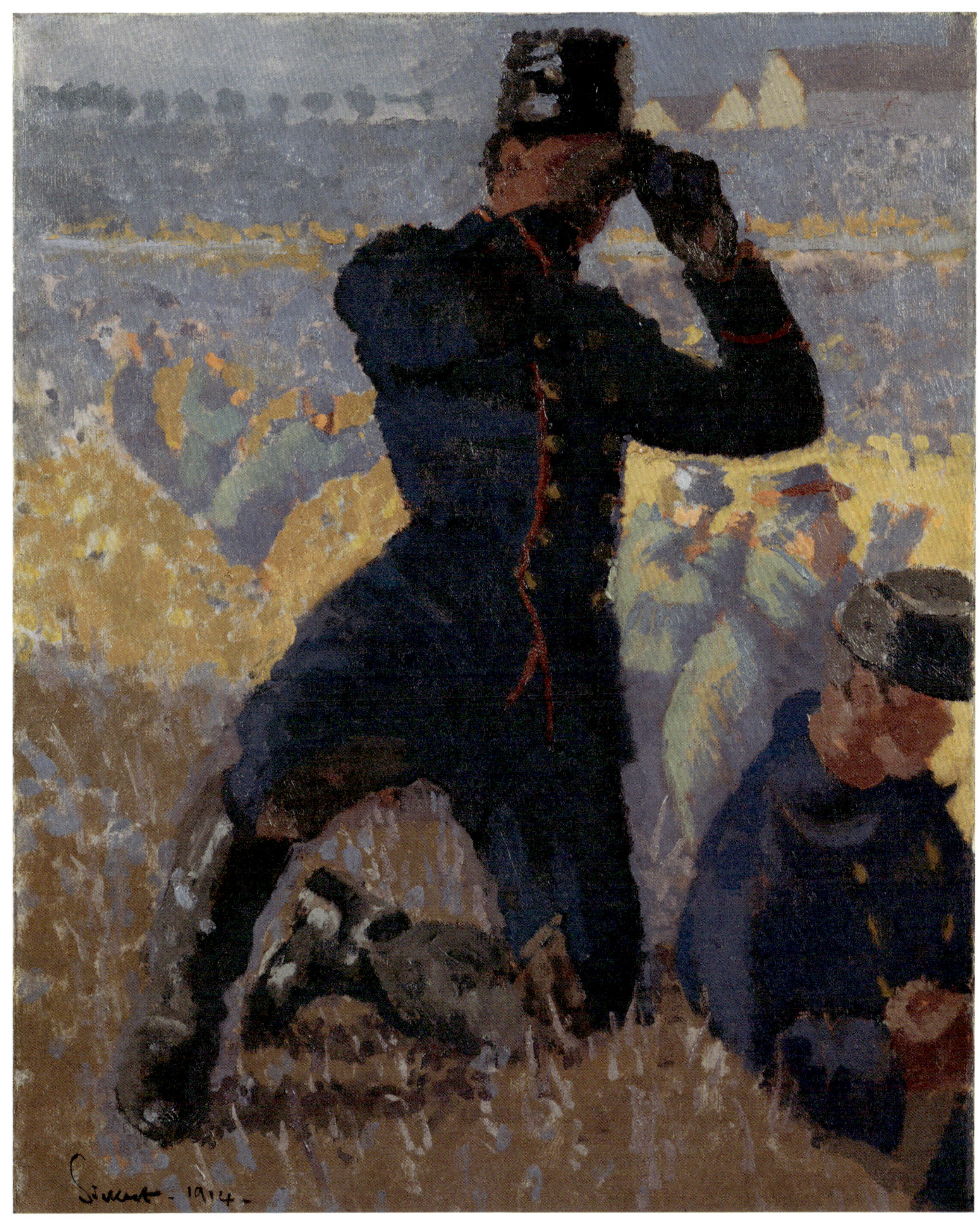

144
*Soldiers of King Albert
the Ready* 1914
Oil paint on canvas
Sheffield Museums Trust

145
The Integrity of Belgium
1914
Oil paint on canvas
Government Art Collection

TRANSPOSITION: THE FINAL YEARS

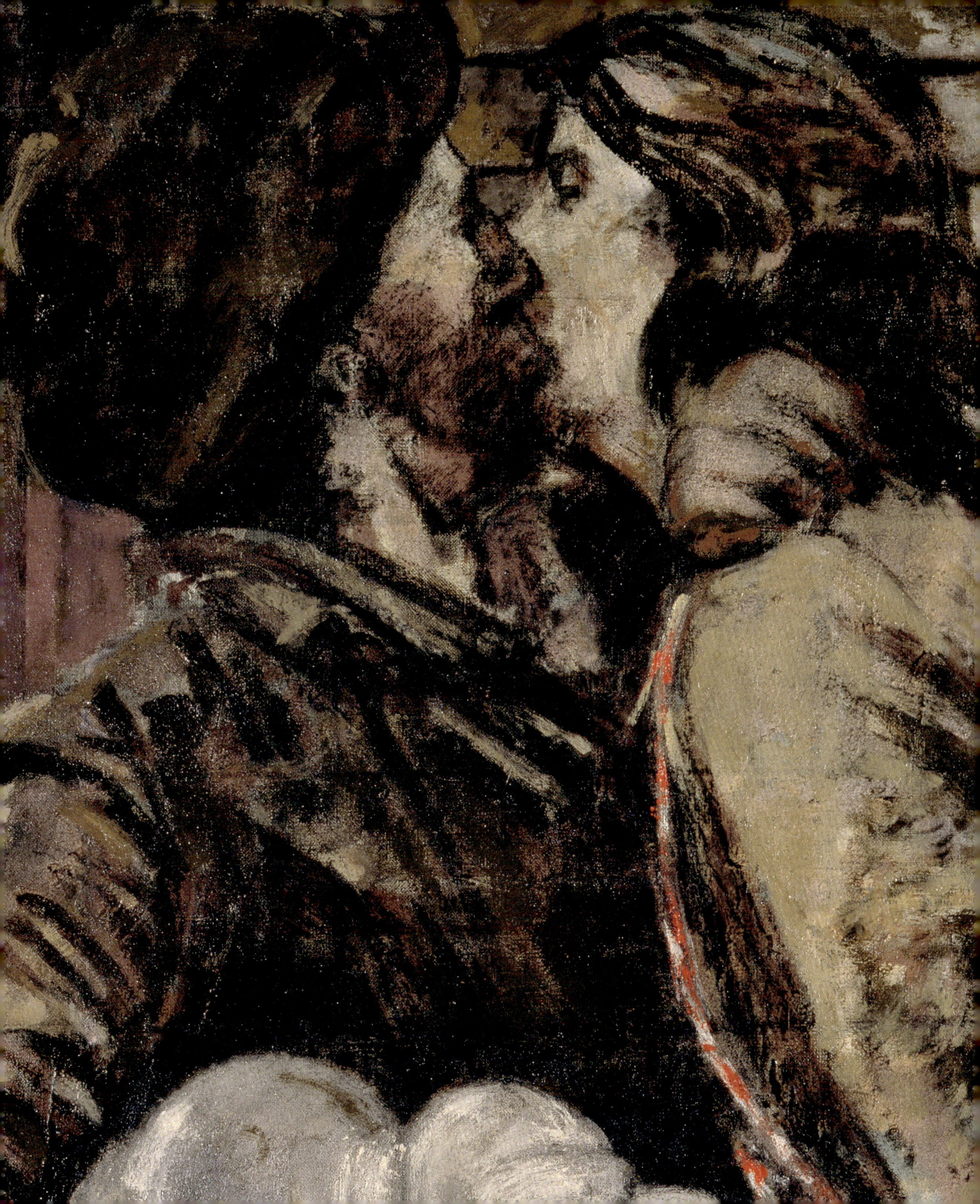

SAM ROSE

FINAL YEARS AND ECHOES

For many of his early admirers, Sickert's late works proved impossibly strange.[1] Why would an artist known for close observation of scenes from life turn to newspaper photographs and Victorian prints as source material? Why would the careful arrangement of harmonies reminiscent of his sometime teacher Whistler be replaced by washed-out colours or jarring arrays of high-keyed tones? Why, in short, would a well-established artist – respected, even if a touch outdated – change his style and subject matter so dramatically?

In supporting Sickert's earlier work, the Bloomsbury critics Clive Bell and Roger Fry had long regarded Sickert's public persona and pronouncements about his own work as little more than the avant-garde façade expected of an artist of his generation (see fig.40). True, Sickert might disrupt an elegant restaurant with bawdy music hall songs, shout 'God Damn Christianity' when passing a band of cornet-playing salvationists in the street, install French-style floor-pan lavatories in his home to bemuse his guests, or hang a print of Landseer's *Monarch of the Glen* in his studio 'pour emmerder Roger Fry'.[2] But for these critics Sickert's 'infallible painter's instinct' meant that, even as he claimed to love Victorian illustration and anecdotal artworks, he could not help 'with an almost pathetic

fatality doing what is right': producing paintings that transformed his subjects into purely aesthetic arrangements of tones and colours.[3] In Sickert's later work, however, his broader aims were harder to deny, as he began to inscribe the very surface of his paintings with titles and reference to his sources in newspaper photographs and Victorian prints. It seemed to Fry and Bell that eccentricity, or even senility, had finally gotten the better of the artist. Other supporters of Sickert's early work were even more direct in their concern for Sickert's mental state, implying that he had never quite recovered from a mental and emotional breakdown of the 1920s that followed the death of his second wife Christine Angus at the beginning of the decade.

Oddly enough, then, it was also at this exact moment that Sickert rose to truly widespread fame and popular success. In the 1920s Sickert followed his old New English Art Club colleagues in election as associate then full member of the Royal Academy, an event that one newspaper described as a surprise that 'could not have been greater had Trotsky been embraced by the Carlton Club'.[4] The works Sickert submitted often challenged the norms of the Academy (including portraits such as that of Walter Lumsden, no.148); and, while they were occasionally rejected, they were also regularly the most discussed and admired paintings on show. Tied to provocations such as this, Sickert's new position gained him a level of newspaper publicity that, in the words of recent historians, 'has to be traced through contemporary newspaper columns to be believed', and would 'astonish the public of today'.[5] By 1930, the *Daily Mail* was calling Sickert 'our greatest living artist'.[6] And even as the support of the Bloomsbury critics slipped away, Virginia Woolf's brilliant and brilliantly unusual piece of art writing, *Walter Sickert: A Conversation* of 1934, poked fun at those same critics, living in their world of pure aesthetic sensations that blinded them to the rich array of viewing possibilities to be found in Sickert's work.

Sickert's 'later years' have sometimes been dated to the period in Dieppe and London that followed the death of Angus, but are more often linked to the artist's spring 1927

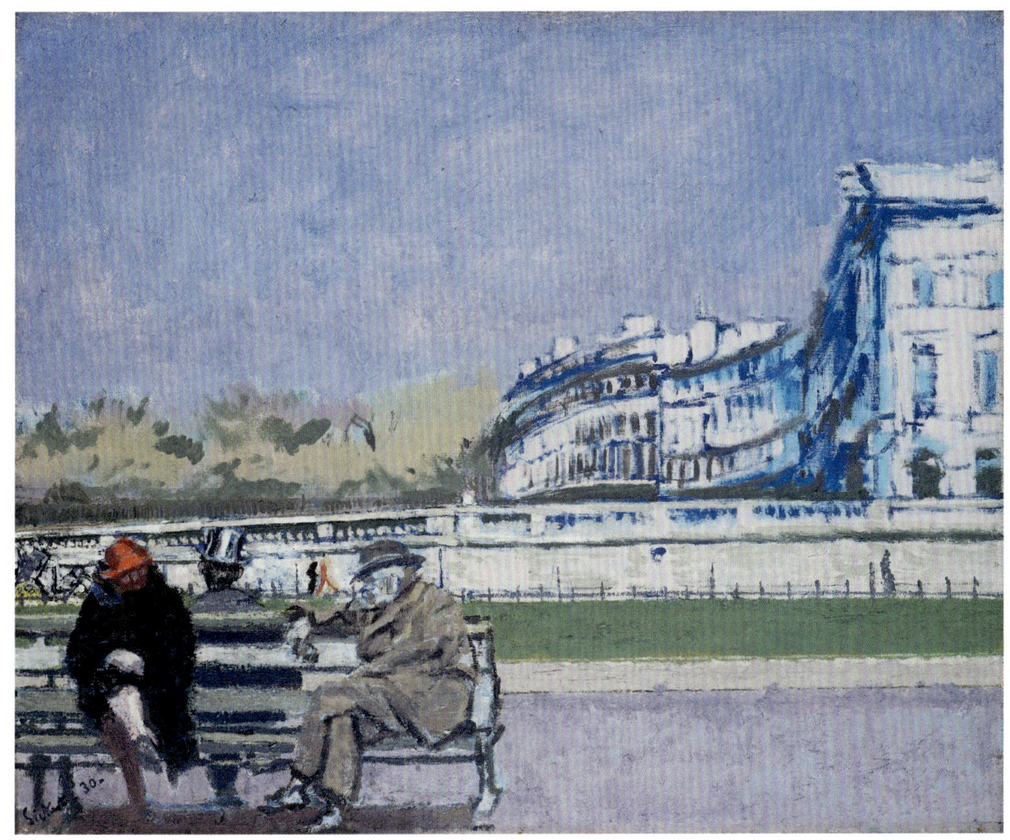

Fig.39
The Front at Hove (Turpe Senex Miles Turpe Senilis Amor) 1930, oil paint on canvas, 63.5 × 76.2, Tate

return to London from Brighton. Sickert had recently metamorphosed professionally from 'Walter Sickert' to 'Richard Sickert', and now he seemed to signal a new start with a series of partial self-portraits as Lazarus. From this point on, he would largely drop the characteristic subject pictures drawn from city life, turning instead to photographs culled from newspapers for his engagement with contemporary events, and to Victorian prints for his series of 'Echoes'.

Though some critics saw a dramatic shift in the look of the works produced at this moment, Sickert's methods continued to follow the same procedure he had perfected in the mid-1910s. Working from a squared-up drawing or print, the painter would transfer the composition, build up a broad tonal underpainting, then, when dry, add final touches as boldly and freely as possible. As Sickert jokingly summed up the method when enlisting Clive Bell's son Quentin to his cause:

> … *mon petit*, it's dead easy, there's nothing to it. You look through old copies of the *Illustrated London News*, or *Punch*, or better still some paper like *Judy*, something the bloody critics will never have heard of, find a cut that you like, square it up, paint it in monochrome using white and ultramarine and then let it dry for two or three weeks. When it is quite hard take an old silk handkerchief … then take some linseed oil and rub down the picture until the surface is quite smooth. Then, using a very restricted palette you paint the thing, but swiftly with rare and discreet touches, like a girl using lipstick.[7]

Rather than a strict reproduction, each stage of this method provided a new opportunity for the mediation and transformation of the source. Working over the squared-up armature that removed the painter-from-life's need to check against or 'collaborate with' their subject, Sickert could – layer by layer – produce extraordinary abstractions and deviations from his subject matter. In works such as *Sir Hugh Walpole* (see no.147) or *The Front at Hove (Turpe Senex Miles Turpe Senilis Amor)* (fig.39 and no.11), for instance, a large and barely gradated patch of underpainting could be left as it was to stand for much of a face or a body to which the patch itself bore little resemblance. The procedure equally allowed the final layers of the painting to float almost entirely free of the earlier layers, with bold strokes of often non-naturalistic colour especially flagrant in performing their double duty as parts of the scene and as abstract patterning across the picture surface (as in the yellow light on Walpole's lapel and shoulder, or the vivid blue that flows from top right into *The Front at Hove* and delineates details of architecture and figures along the way).

Aiding the freedom of Sickert's later works was another element of the working procedure he developed in the 1910s, in which the famed observer of modern life now definitively rejected what he called 'the nonsensical theory of painting direct from nature'.[8] Having toyed with the use of photography as a supplement to drawings since at least the 1890s, Sickert fully embraced it in the 1920s, declaring to Cicely Hey in 1924 that 'artists must use cameras'.[9] Sometimes Sickert would have photographs produced himself, as in the 'Raising of Lazarus' staged in his studio with Sickert atop a ladder posing as Christ above a life-size lay figure that he had arranged to have wrapped in a shroud by a local undertaker. More often, and far more controversially for some, the source image was as pre-formed as photographs and prints found in newspapers and magazines. An irony of Sickert's post-1913 method, as Wendy Baron has pointed out, was that new heights of painterly freedom and abstraction were attained via a technique so systematised 'as to make the execution of a painting almost mechanical'.[10] In drawing on photographs and prints, Sickert also quite literally introduced the mechanical into his procedure, flouting the conventions of authorship that he undermined further in the 1930s when his wife Thérèse Lessore increasingly contributed not just to preparatory squaring and underpainting but to the later stages of his works.

The newspaper-photograph-paintings and 'Echoes' are some of the most unusual and fascinating works of art made in Britain in the interwar years. For later writers on pop art, these showed a prescient understanding of the role that art could play in reckoning with contemporary mass culture, layering and multiplying reproduction and authorship in ways generally thought anathema to easel painting. Sickert certainly recognised the plays with reuse and authorship, sometimes suggesting that his works were intended to creatively translate his sources, and at other times joking that 'It's such a good arrangement: Cruikshank and Gilbert do all the work, and I get all the money!'[11] But though he was later proclaimed as a proto-pop-artist, Sickert's distance from the 1960s should be clear from the fact that where Roy Lichtenstein turned to a Donald Duck cartoon, Sickert, born in 1860, turned as naturally to wood engravings by and after John Gilbert and Adelaide Claxton.

Nostalgia for a distant past inevitably plays a part in these paintings, but the works seem to be driven just as much by fascination with the possibilities that derived from wrenching anachronistic scenes into the twentieth century. Could these nineteenth-century images be made modern, not just recovered in a backwards-facing gesture but given a contemporary form that endowed them with a power and relevance distinctly of the interwar moment? The exploitation of art's capacity to at once exist across and collapse times has grown even more striking as these paintings age, with Sickert's works bringing the Victorian era into the modern, the modern to the Victorian, and both of these together into our own present.

Wedded as they were to a narrow set of artistic ideals, in retrospect it is no wonder that Sickert's early supporters found his later works not only deeply strange but troubling too. These were and remain works that were undoubtedly modern and experimental, but were so in ways that did not fit the critics' tidy stories about the nature of Sickert's oeuvre, and even the direction and nature of modern art as a whole. The works' strangeness in this sense remains of great value. Looking back on Sickert's career as a whole in light of the later works, and as Virginia Woolf recognised at the time, it seems all the clearer that he had always aimed to produce work that playfully escaped the confines of any one single artistic tradition, critical programme, or mode of viewing.

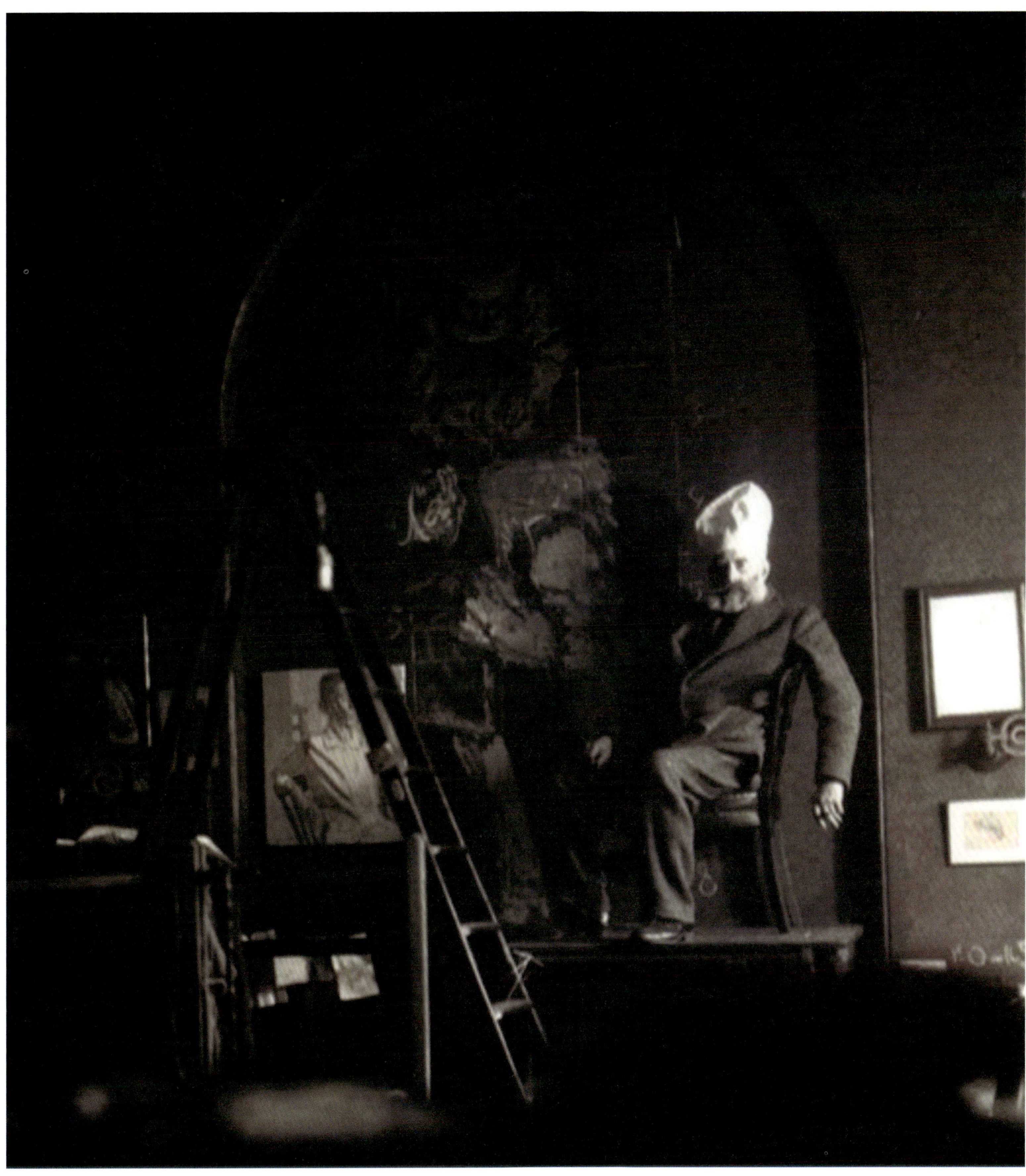

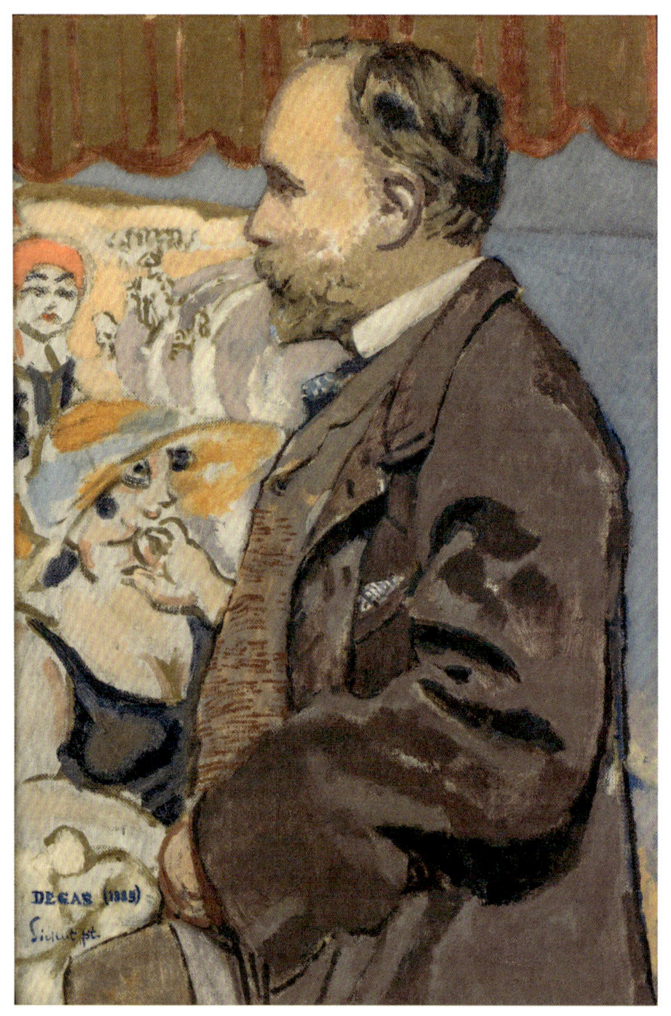

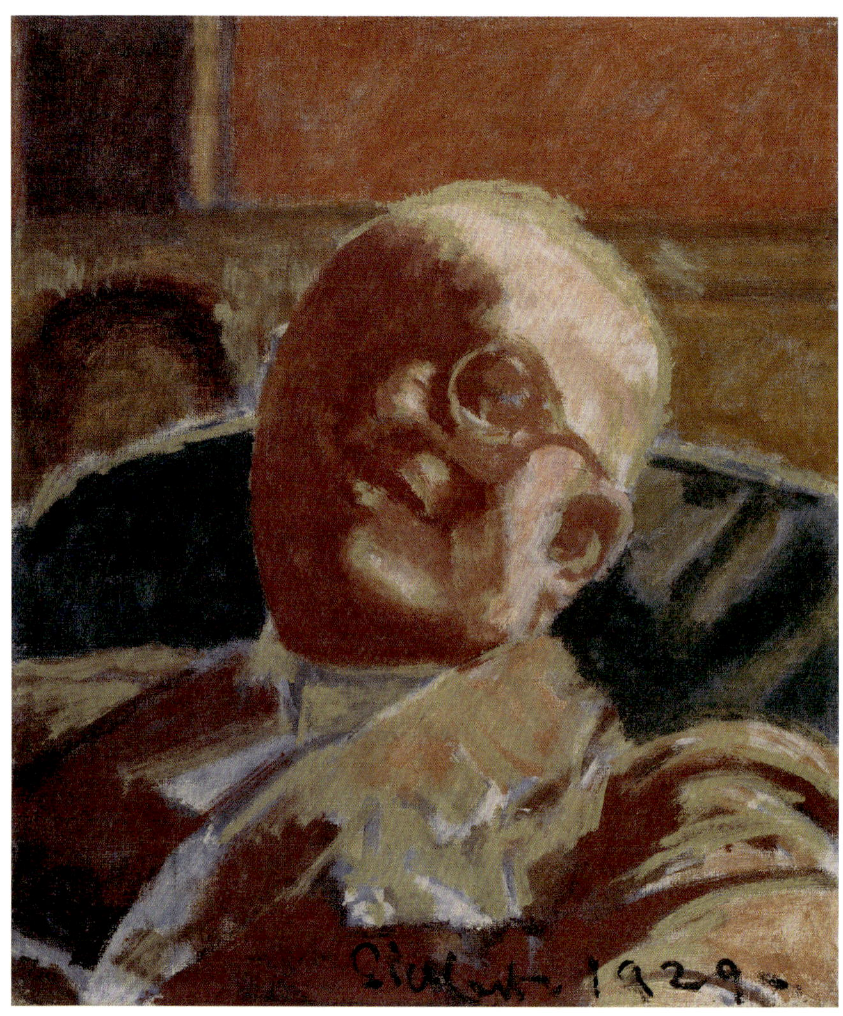

146
Portrait of Degas in 1885
c.1928
Oil paint on canvas
Ministère de l'Europe et
des Affaires étrangères

147
Sir Hugh Walpole 1929
Oil paint on canvas
Glasgow Life (Glasgow
Museums) on behalf of
Glasgow City Council

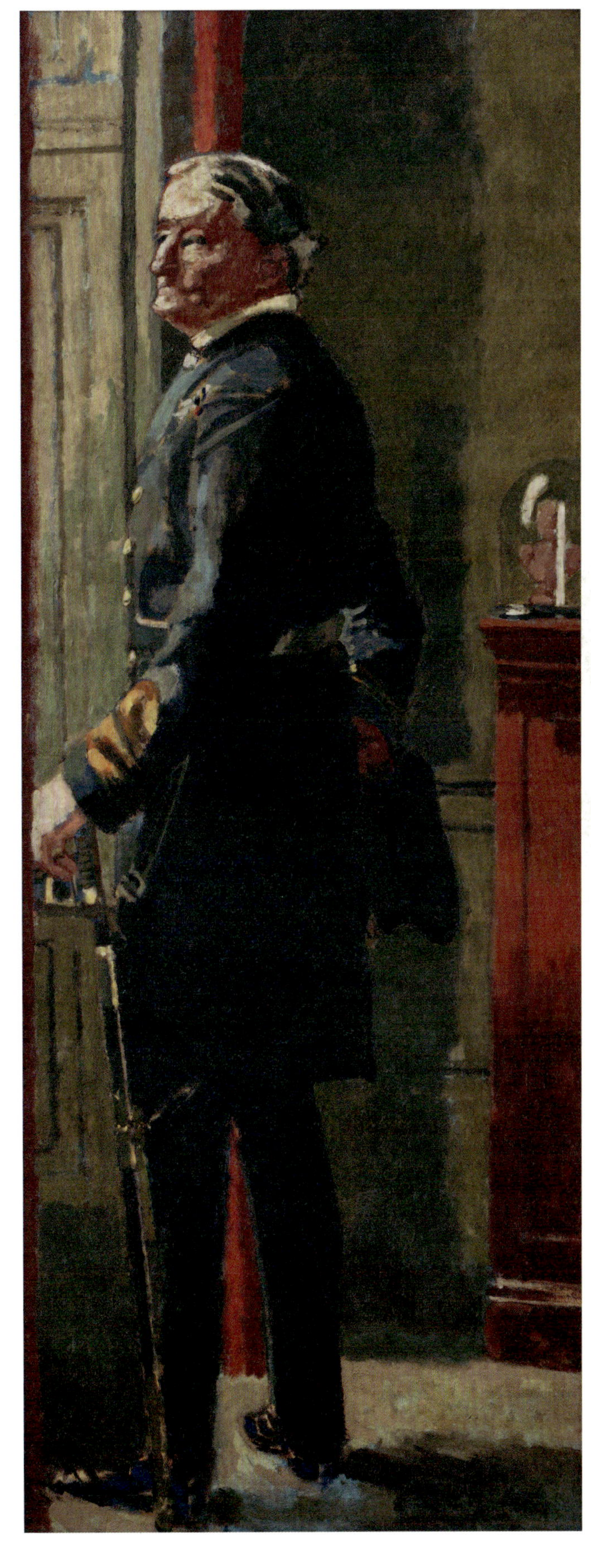

148
Rear Admiral Lumsden
C.I.E., C.V.O. 1927–8
Oil paint on canvas
Private collection, Devon

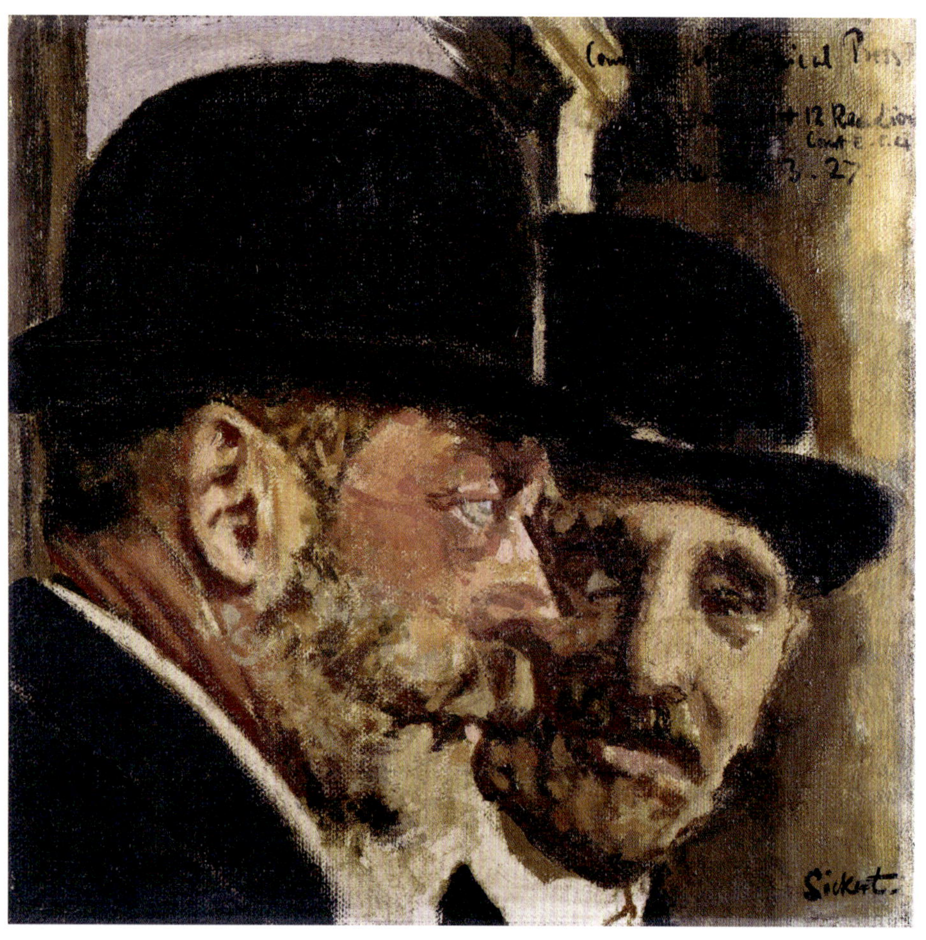

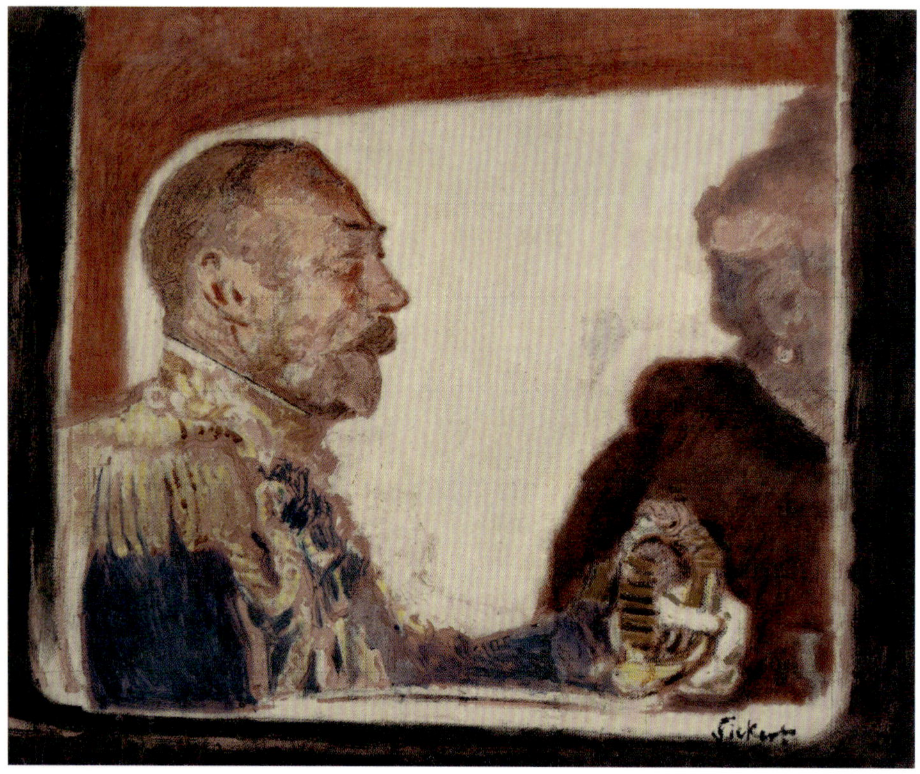

149
*King George V and
his Racing Manager:
A Conversation Piece
at Aintree* c.1929–30
Oil paint on canvas
The Royal Collection /
HM Queen Elizabeth II

150
*King George V and
Queen Mary* 1935
Oil paint on canvas
Private collection

151
From 'The Names Make
News, Snappy Snarls',
Daily Express, 24 July
1936

152
HM King Edward VIII 1936
Oil paint on canvas
Private collection

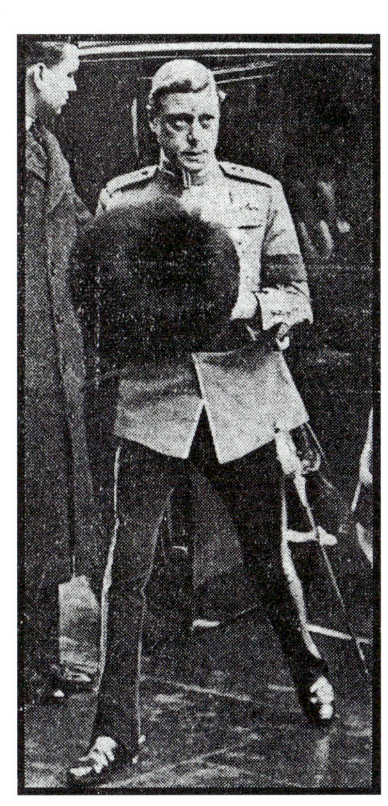

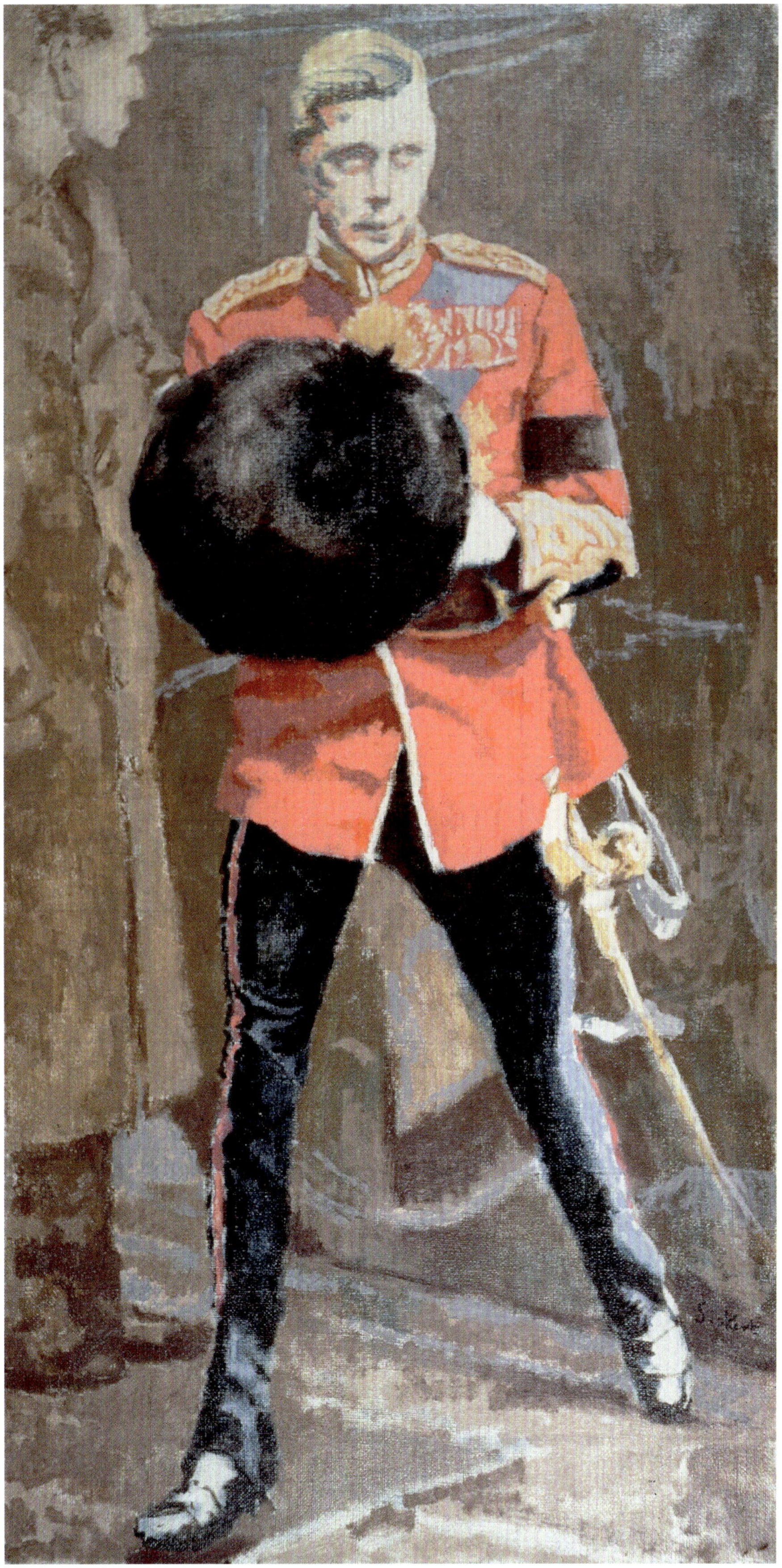

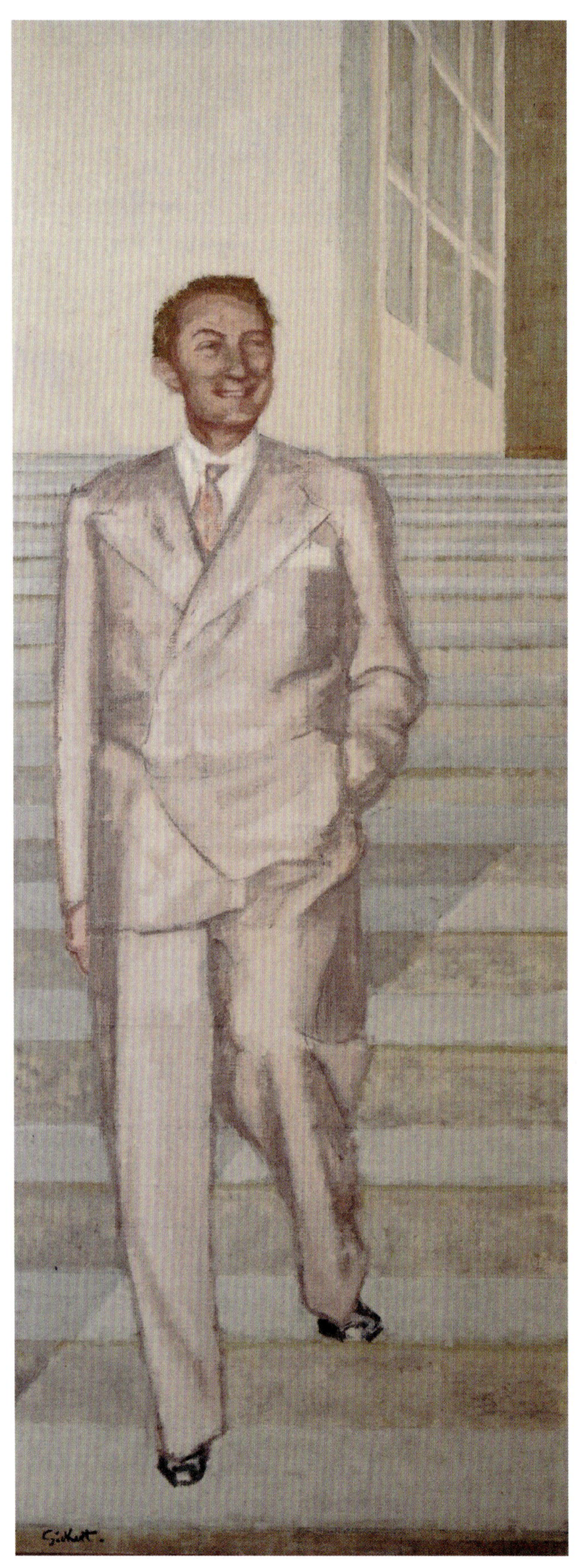

153
Alexander Gavin
Henderson, 2nd Lord
Faringdon c.1935
Oil paint on canvas
Faringdon Collection Trust

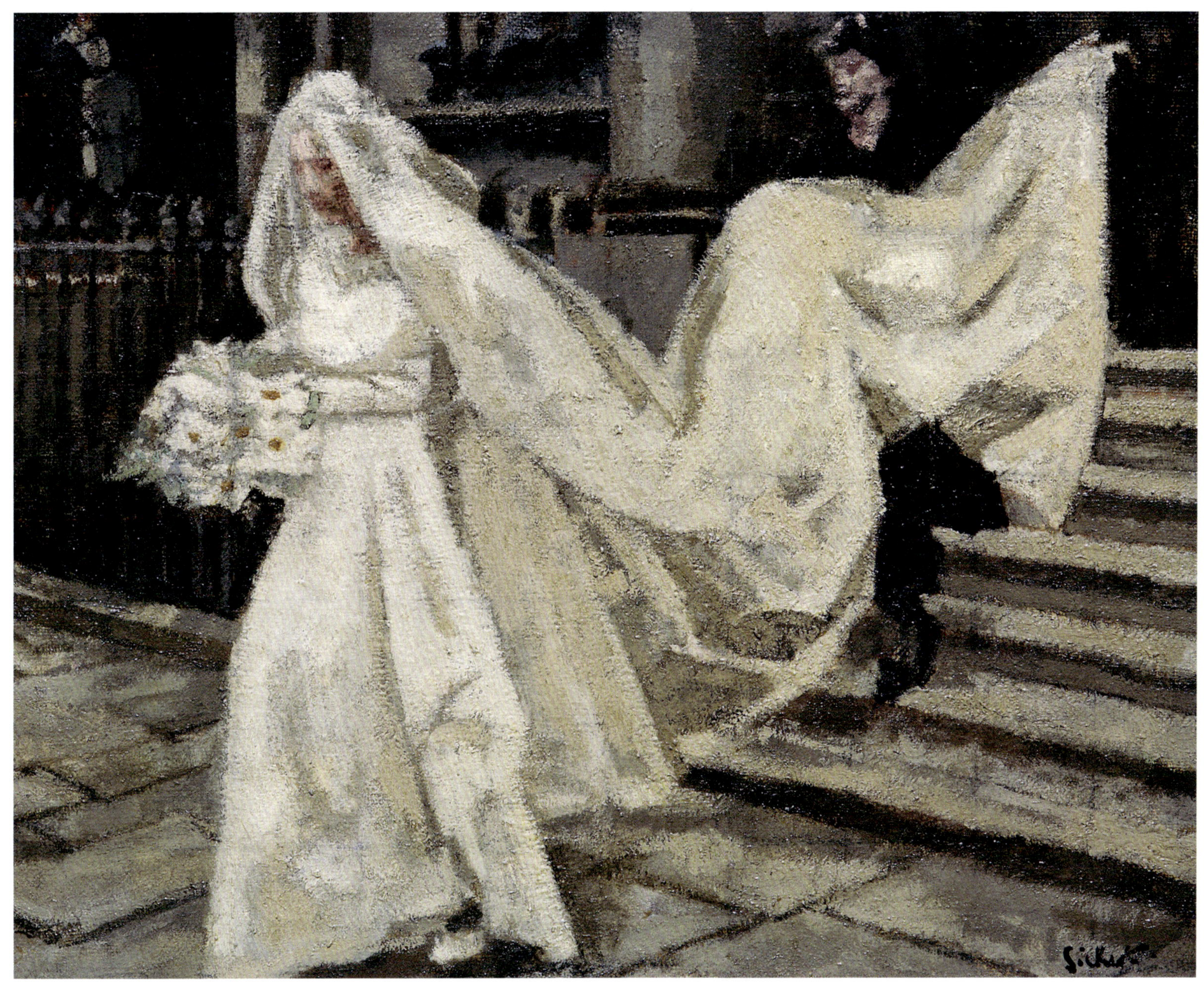

154
Pimlico c.1937
Oil paint on canvas
Aberdeen City Council
(Art Gallery & Museums
Collections)

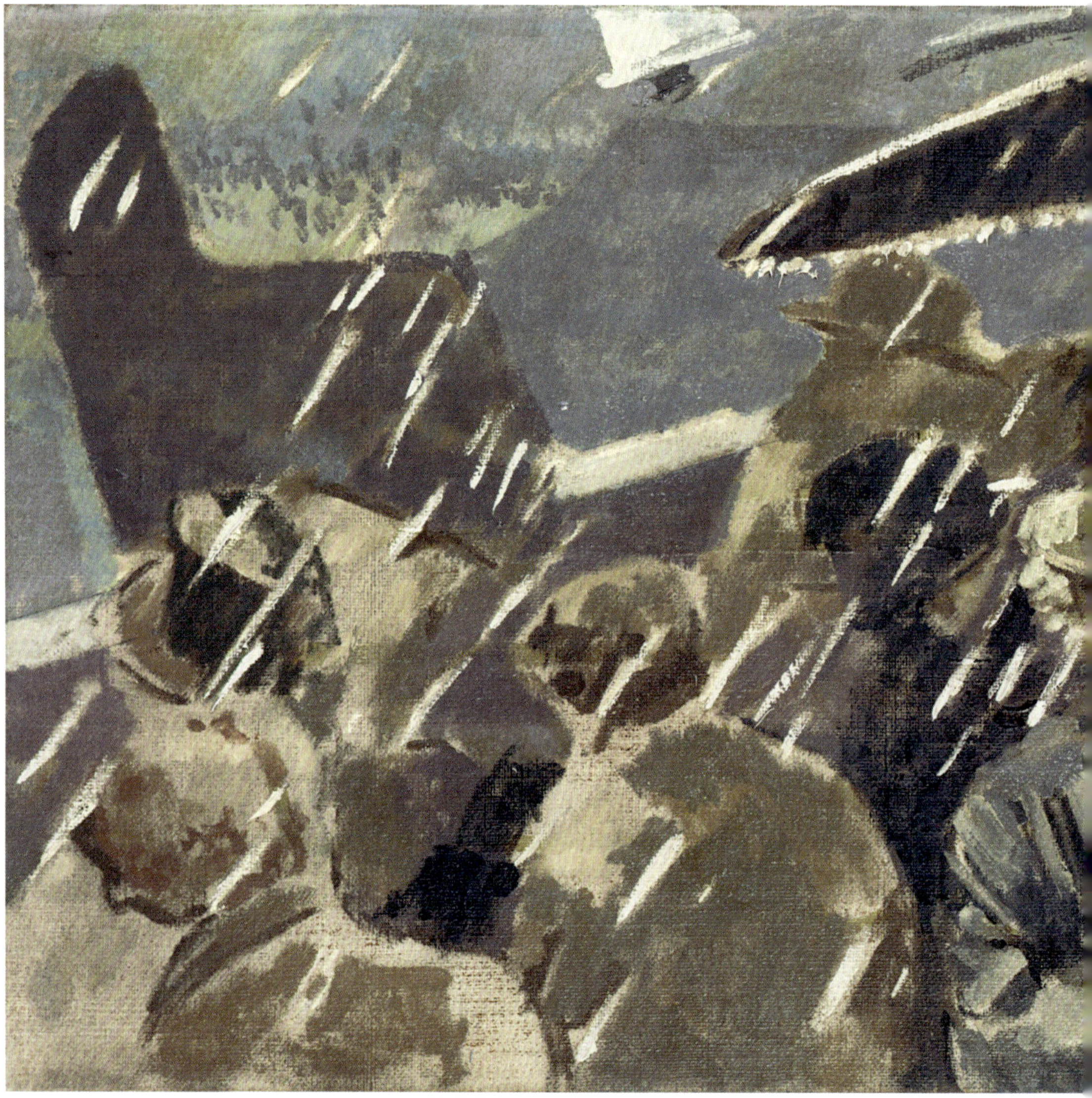

155
Miss Earhart's Arrival 1932
Oil paint on canvas
Tate

156
'Welcome "Lady Lindy"!',
Daily Sketch, 23 May 1932

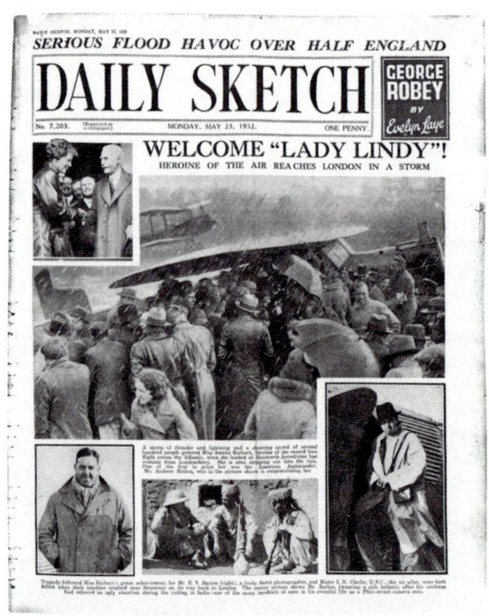

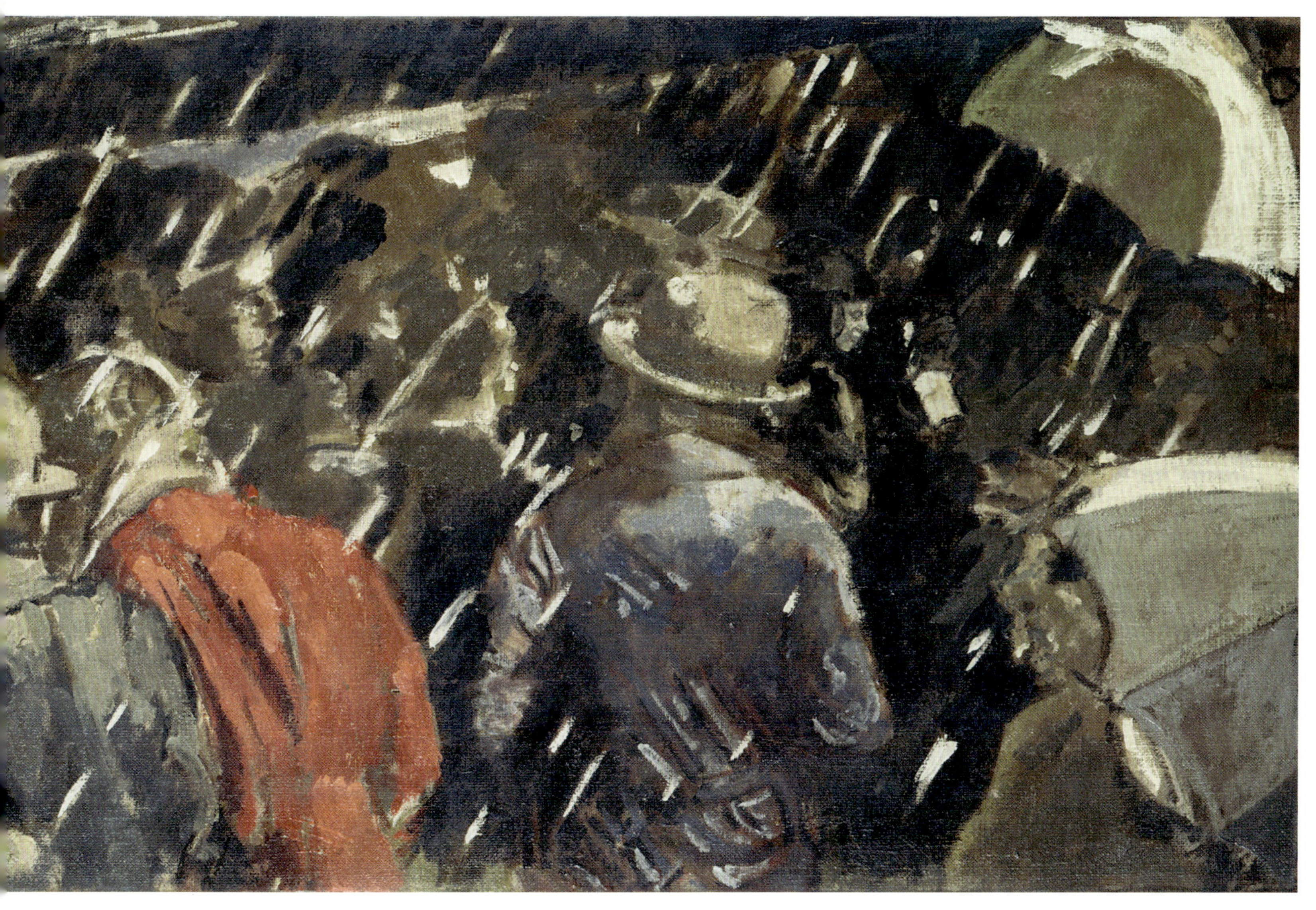

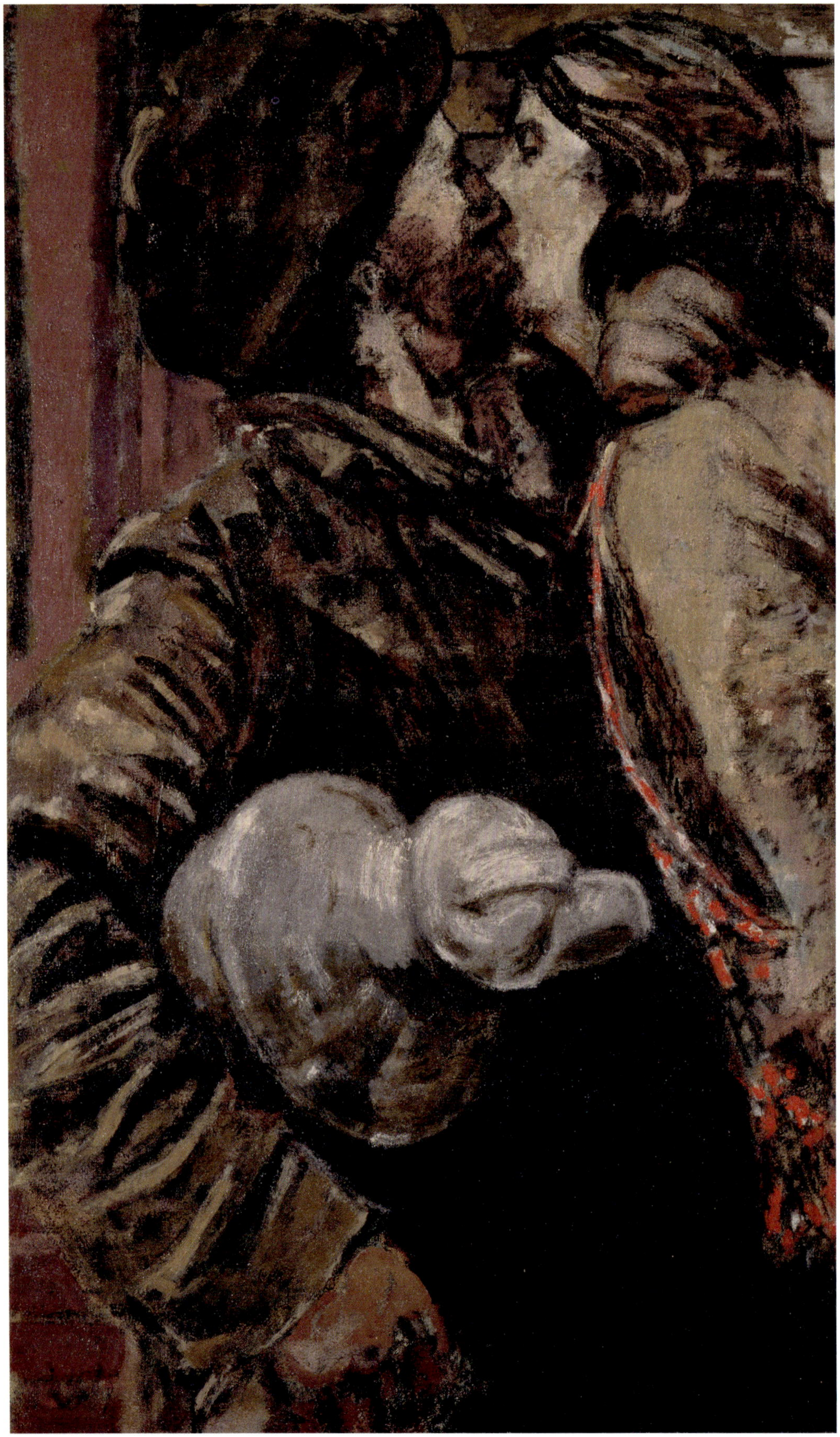

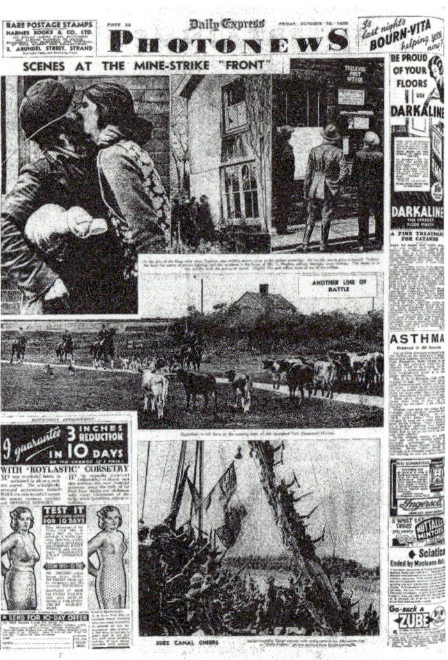

157
The Miner c.1935–6
Oil paint on canvas
Birmingham Museums
Trust on behalf of
Birmingham City Council

158
'Scenes at the
Mine-Strike "Front"',
Daily Express,
18 October 1935

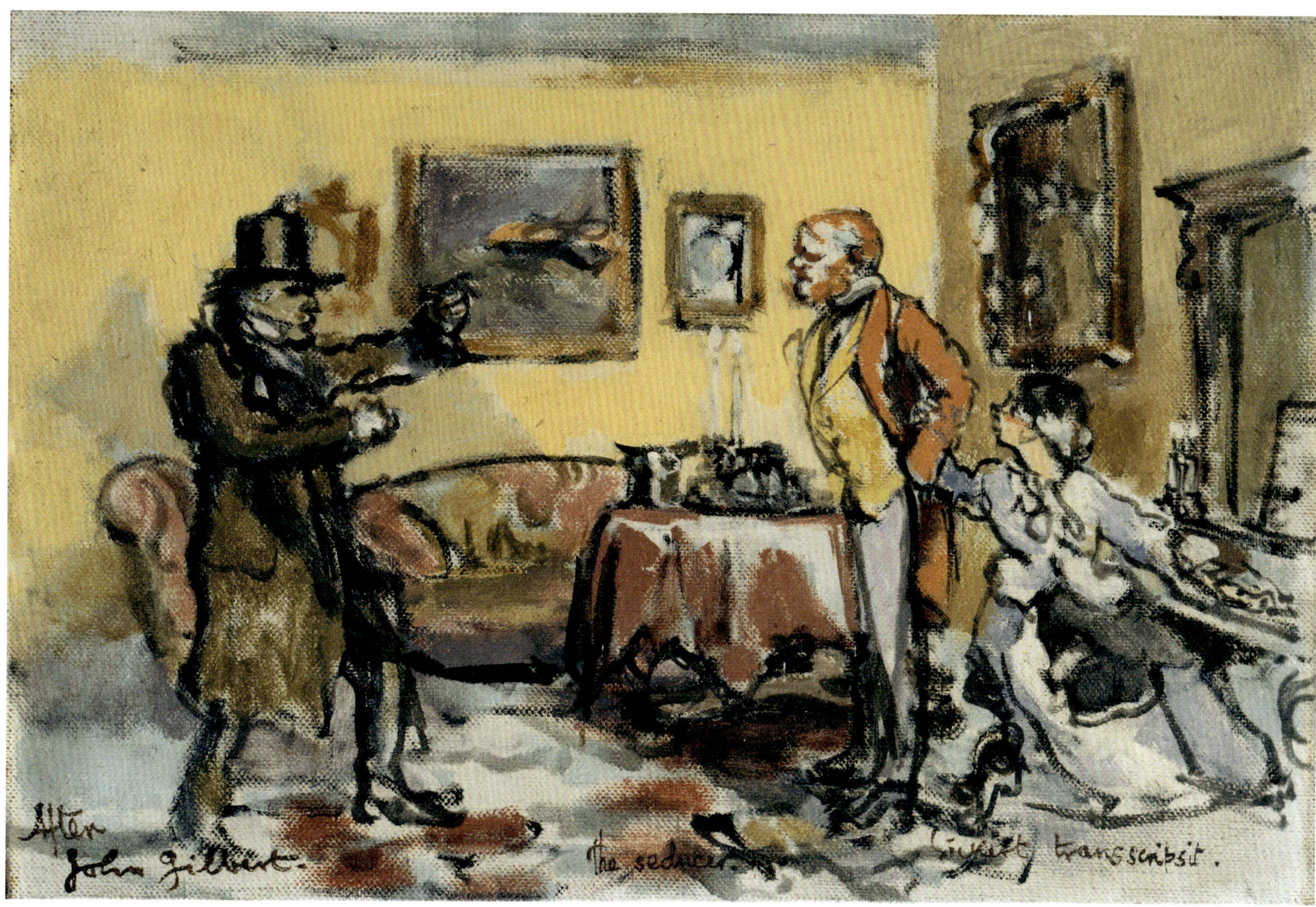

159
'The Unexpected Return
of Rigdon Few', *The
London Journal*, 14 June
1856

160
The Seducer
c.1929–30
Oil paint on canvas
Tate

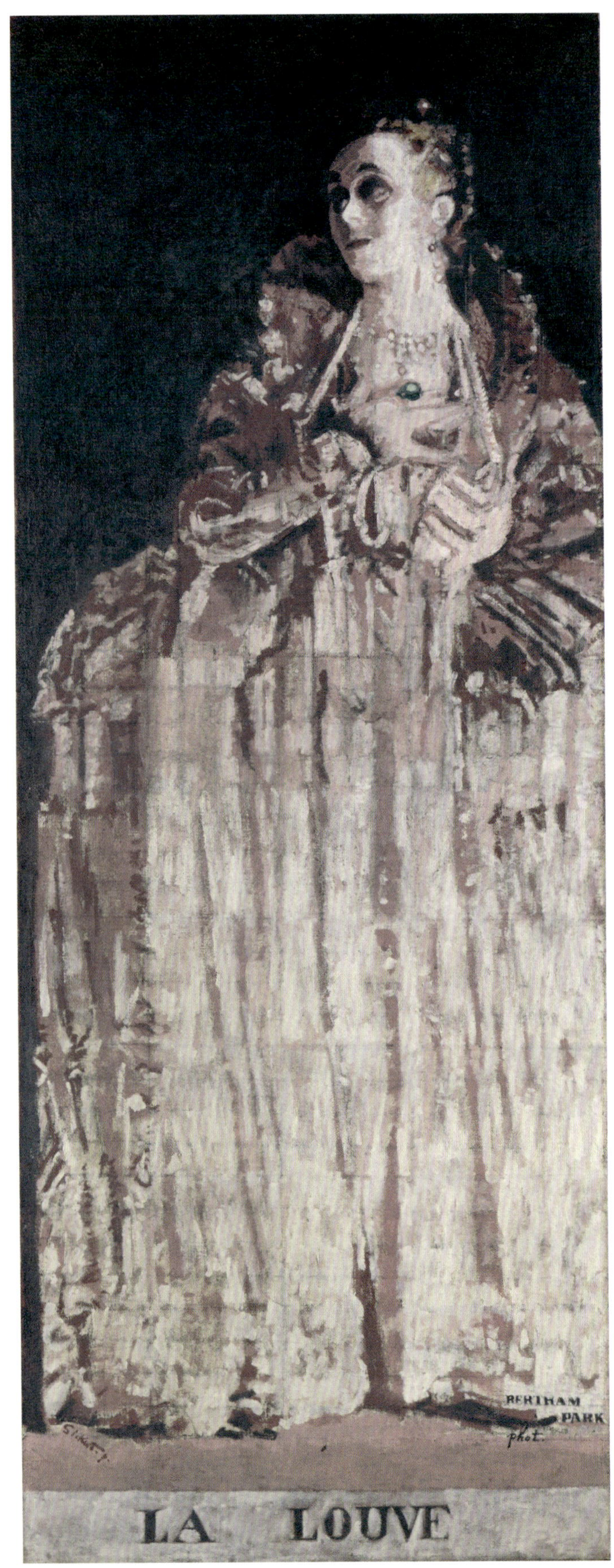

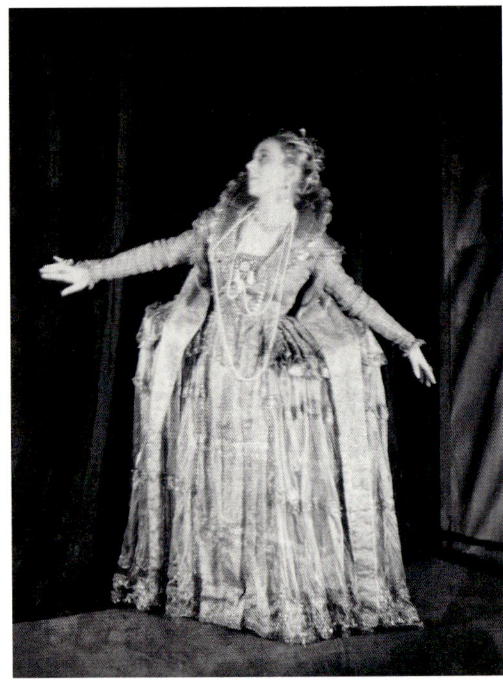

161
*Miss Gwen Ffrangcon-
Davies as Isabella of
France* 1932
Oil paint on canvas
Tate

162
Gwen Ffrangcon-Davies
as Queen Isabella, in
Edward II at The Phoenix
Society, Regent Theatre,
London, 1923

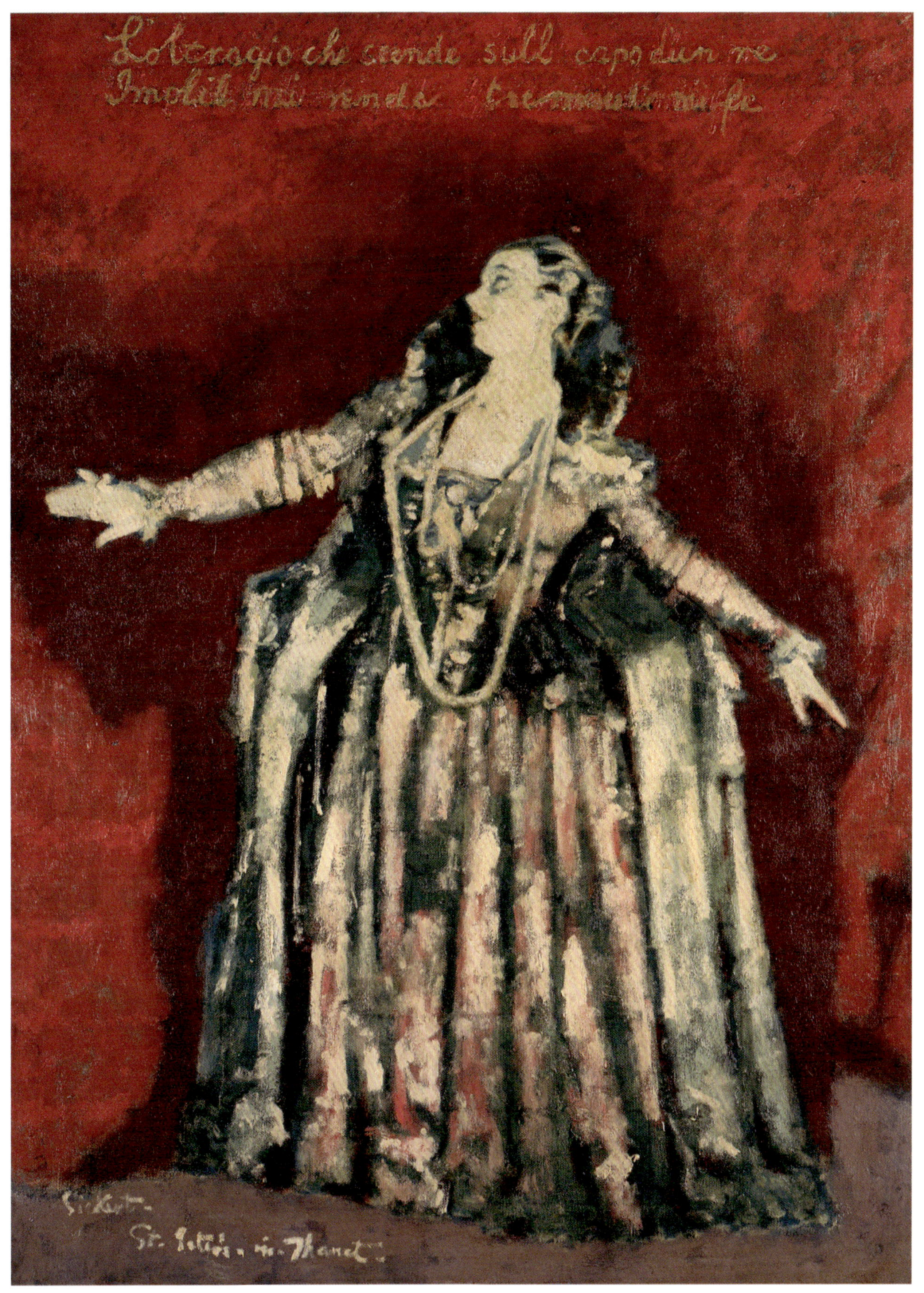

163
Gwen Again 1935–6
Oil paint on canvas
Private collection

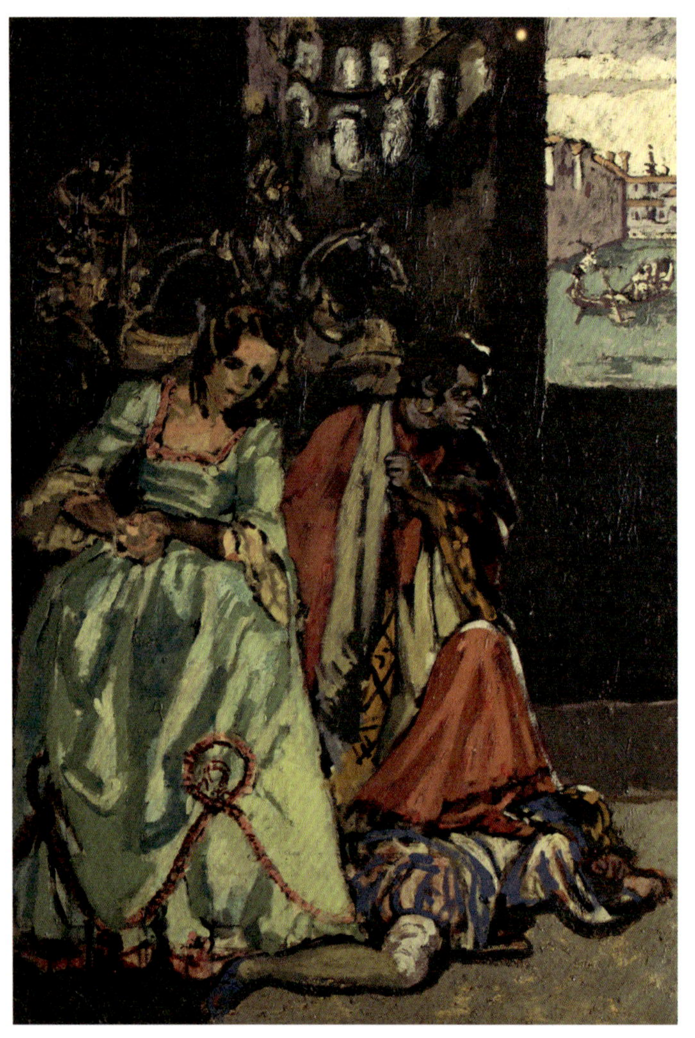

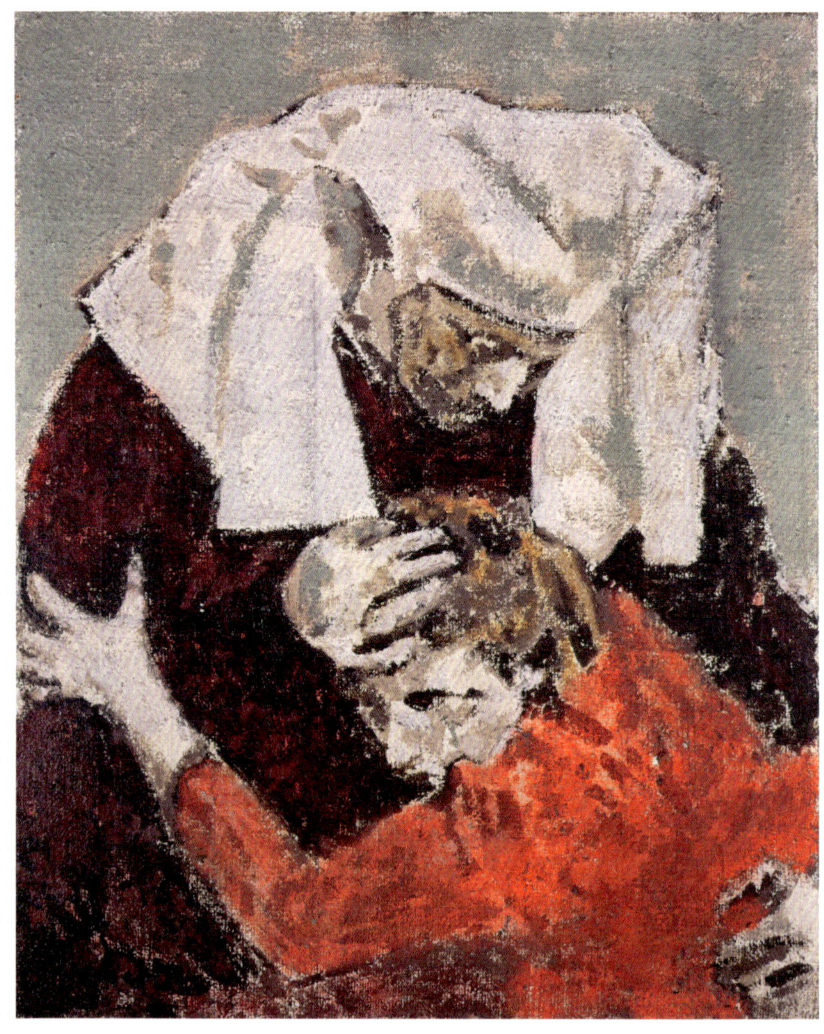

164
Variation on 'Othello'
c.1933–4
Oil paint on canvas
Bristol Culture: Bristol
Museums & Art Gallery

165
Juliet and her Nurse
c.1935–6
Oil paint on canvas
Leeds Art Fund

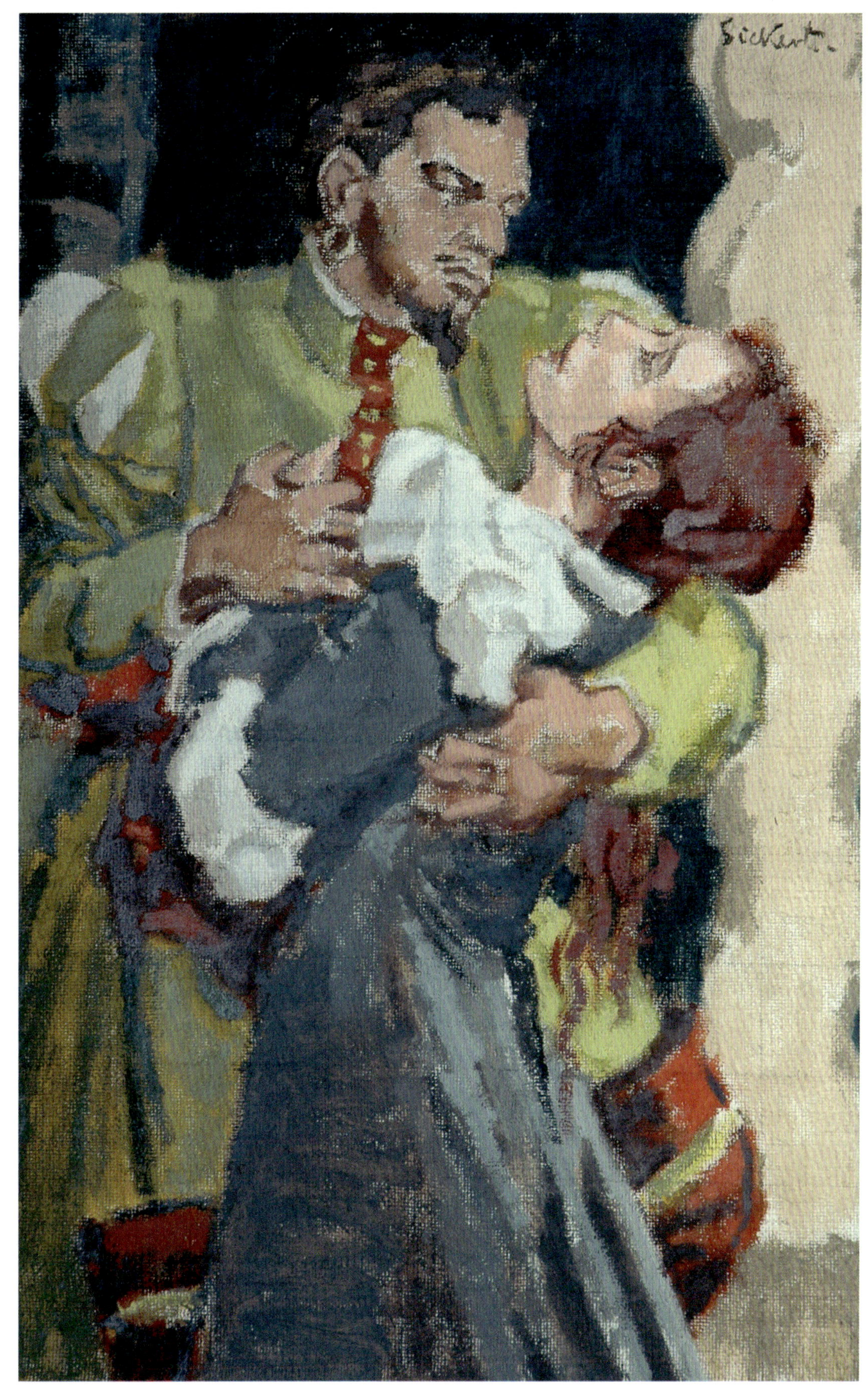

166
'The Taming of the Shrew'
c.1937
Oil paint on canvas
Courtesy of Bradford
Museums and Galleries

167
'An Art English Girls
Know Best', *Evening
News*, 5 November 1927;
still from *A Little Bit of
Fluff*, British International
Pictures, 1928

168
High-Steppers c.1938–9
Oil paint on canvas
National Galleries
of Scotland

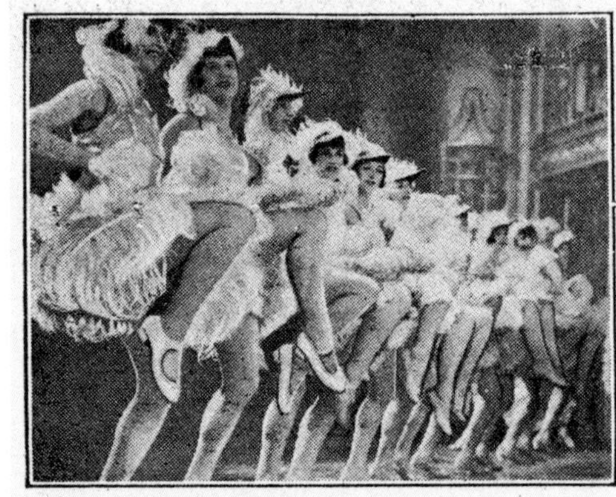

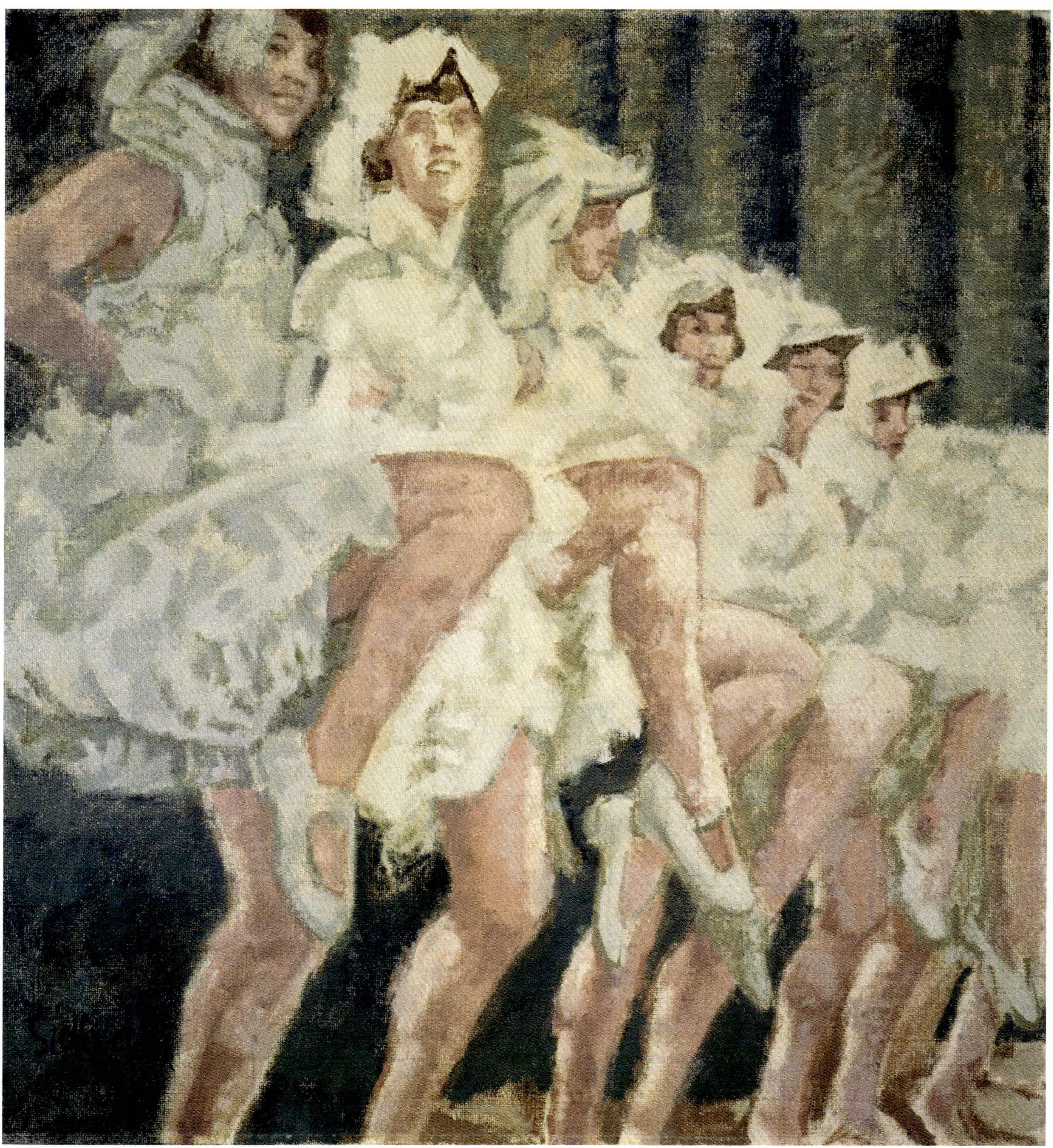

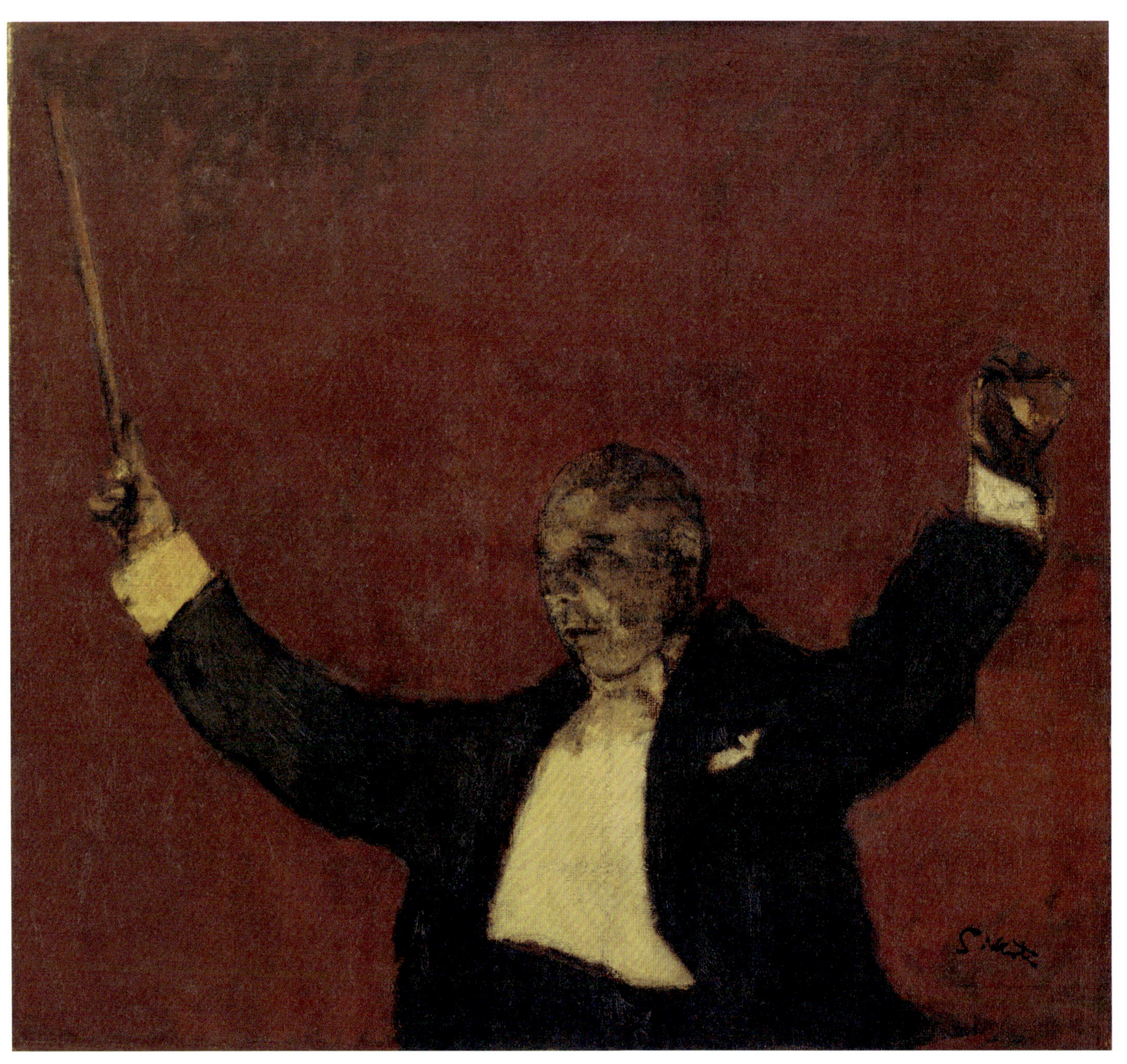

169
*Sir Thomas Beecham
Conducting* 1938
Oil paint on burlap
The Museum of Modern
Art, New York

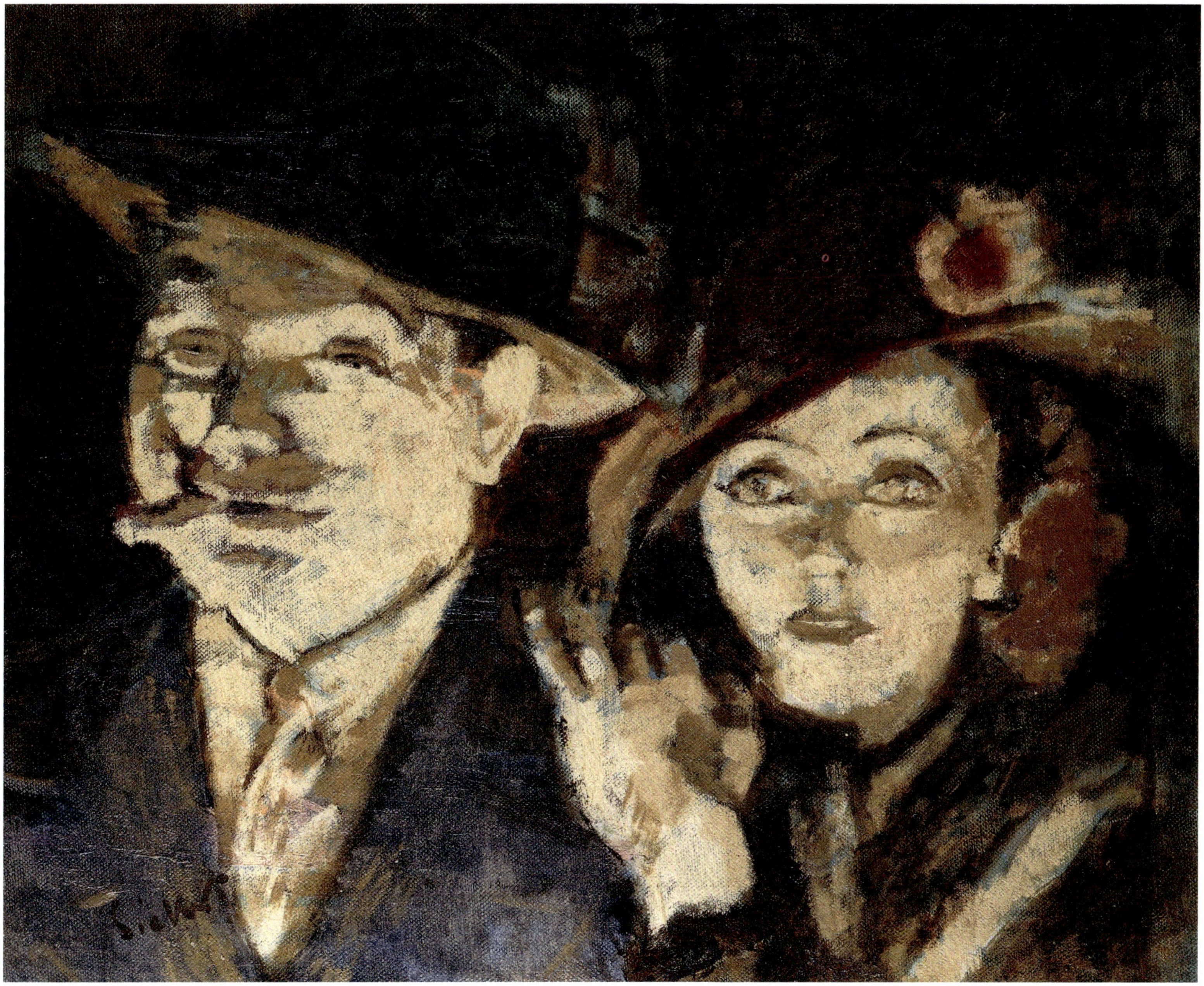

170
Jack and Jill c.1937–8
Oil paint on canvas
Oskowitz Family

171
Bullets or Ballots
lobby card, 1936

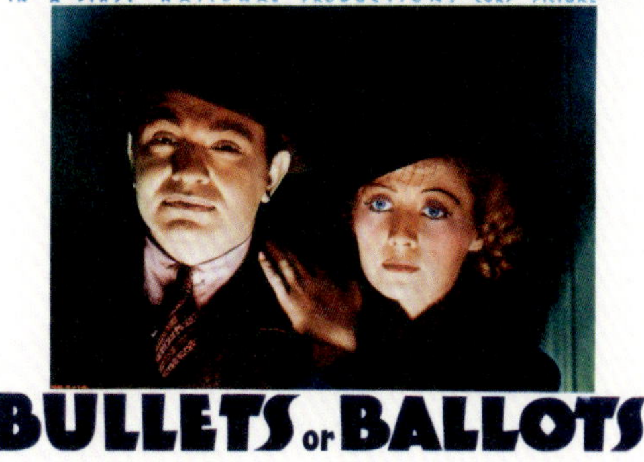

MARTIN HAMMER

EMULATING SICKERT: AUERBACH, BACON, FREUD

Walter Sickert was a major 'influencer', in current parlance. His art has exerted a continuous and varied impact on generations of British artists, from the early twentieth century right through to the present. We will focus here on painters who emerged during the period between Sickert's death in 1942 and the celebrations marking his centenary in 1960.[1] By then, Sickert was something of a national treasure, and his work was widely accessible via exhibitions and illustrated books, and through the filter of his own lively art journalism, brought together in the 1947 volume *A Free House*.[2] Indeed, his prominence could seem oppressive. At the Royal College of Art, according to ex-student David Hockney: 'Sickert was the great god and the whole style of painting in that art school – and in every other art school in England – was a cross between Sickert and the Euston Road School.'[3] The consequence was a good deal of dull and derivative sub-Sickertian painting, which is still produced today. Yet the artist also became a talisman for some of the most inventive postwar British painters, who aspired to forge a new and visceral realism, as an alternative to the more modish approaches of abstraction and appropriation from popular culture.

But how to frame the complex and delicate matter of creative emulation? The following discussion presumes that artistic distinction and originality involve not so much freedom from imitation as a competitive impulse to absorb and fuse the lessons of others into the fabric of one's own work. Such assimilation may end up less self-evident than more passive derivation, and my observations therefore involve some speculation. The other assumption here is that artists may take bearings from the general concerns of an admired contemporary or predecessor, but that they often take inspiration from specific works they have encountered, which somehow meet their own creative needs of the moment.

Sickert's progressive credentials were asserted by the Beaux Arts Gallery in London, run from 1951 onwards by Helen Lessore, the sister-in-law of Sickert's wife Thérèse. In 1953 the gallery mounted a show devoted to Sickert, whose looming self-portrait *The Servant of Abraham* 1929 (see no.8) was a permanent fixture on the premises, and for Lessore a touchstone ('figurative, painterly, the opposite of suave') against which potential young exhibitors might be measured.[4] Those she showcased included the 'Kitchen Sink' painters such as John Bratby and Jack Smith, who espoused an aggressive social realism that temporarily caused a stir; and also the artists later clustered as the 'School of London', such as Francis Bacon, Lucian Freud and Frank Auerbach, whose rise to critical and commercial esteem was reinforced by Lessore's enthusiastic book *A Partial Testament* (1986).[5]

Auerbach had the first of several one-man shows at the Beaux Arts Gallery in January 1956. His work then and since has maintained profound roots in Sickert, mingled with the stimulation Auerbach derived from his sometime teacher David Bomberg, from Chaim Soutine, and from old masters such as Rembrandt, whom Auerbach and his close friend Leon Kossoff studied obsessively in London's National Gallery. Robert Hughes's monograph conveyed Auerbach's recollections of enjoying *A Free House* when he was a student and thereafter, plus his sense that Sickert was 'the one painter of *real* world stature who worked in England in the early part of this century'.[6] That admiration showed through in the work Auerbach produced while a student at the Royal College, as in the heavily worked *E.O.W. Nude* 1953–4 (see fig.41). The wrinkled, viscous texture of the paint may distill his response to Soutine's *Landscape at Céret* (Tate), on show at the Redfern Gallery between December 1953 and January 1954.[7] But Soutine's bold technique seems to have fused in Auerbach's mind with impressions of the audacious Sickert nudes that had recently been shown at the Beaux Arts Gallery. The way Auerbach's reclining nudes loom out of their murky pictorial surroundings recall such Sickerts, framed for Auerbach by their maker's remark that 'perhaps the chief source of pleasure in the aspect of a nude is that it is in the nature of a gleam – a gleam of light and warmth and life'.[8] Likewise, *The Servant of Abraham* provided a template for Auerbach's depictions of heads, such as his 1954 close-up portrait of Leon Kossoff (private collection). For his part, Kossoff recalled being 'knocked out' when he saw this Sickert and *The Raising of Lazarus* 1929–30 at the Beaux Arts, 'two of the most beautiful paintings of our time'.[9]

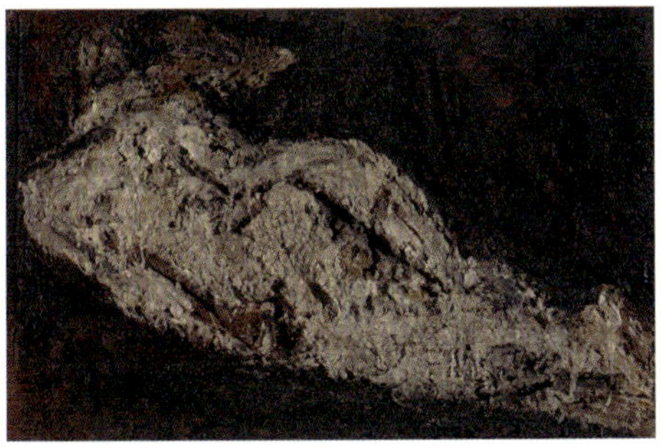

Auerbach has evidently continued to measure his art against Sickert's example. The palette of muted ochres, reds and browns evident in the studio and building-site pictures of the early 1960s is foreshadowed by Sickerts from the Camden Town Group period. Equally, in his views of Mornington Crescent from the late 1960s onwards (see fig.42), Auerbach seems to have had somewhere at the back of his mind Sickert's depictions of Dieppe and London. Even the fact that Auerbach has always used a studio in a dingy part of Camden, close to one of Sickert's own, suggests a strong affinity. Certain views acknowledge in their titles the presence of a statue of Sickert's father-in-law Richard Cobden at a busy road intersection. In sum, Sickert has been a key point of reference within Auerbach's ongoing ambition to fuse visceral painterly surface, evoking the massive substance of reality, with rigorous, often geometric pictorial architecture, and the evocation of subtle and immaterial sensations of light.

Sickert was a significant but perhaps less obvious catalyst for the work of Francis Bacon and Lucian Freud. Their engagement is apparent from the fact that Bacon at some point acquired Sickert's *Granby Street* from c.1912–13 (see no.134), and subsequently gave the picture to Freud.[10] For Bacon, too, the early 1950s was a key moment in his assimilation of Sickert. Rebecca Daniels noted that the conjunction of figure and menacing shadow in Bacon's *Painting* 1950 (see fig.43) was informed by Sickert's drawing *Conversation* 1909 (no.125), a work relating to the Camden Town Murder series which, on the recommendation of Bacon's friend Rodrigo Moynihan, was acquired by the Royal College of Art in early 1950, just before Bacon took over one of the studios for a period.[11] Daniels further argued for the impact of the early Sickerts shown at the Beaux Arts Gallery, immediately preceding Bacon's own show at the gallery in late 1953.[12] Sickert's subdued tonality, and frequent use of vertical shutters and bed as a pictorial framing for solitary figures, look to have fed into Bacons such as *Study for a Portrait* 1953.

The same year saw the creation of Bacon's notorious *Two Figures*, which was thought too controversial for normal display, given its imagery of homosexual love-making (see fig.44). An evident springboard was Eadweard Muybridge's photography of interwoven wrestlers, reinforced by the currency of such imagery in the physique magazines that possessed cult status within the gay community. Yet a specific Sickert may have been a complementary point of reference. Bacon surely encountered Sickert's *La Hollandaise* (see no.120) when it was included in the Redfern Gallery's 'Coronation' exhibition in the summer of 1953. The show included one of Bacon's own 'Head' series, and the two works were listed next to one another in the catalogue.[13] Previously, this now familiar Sickert had languished in obscurity. The notion that contemplating *La Hollandaise* was important for *Two Figures* is supported by the similar ways in which animated marks in the foreground are floated against a dark, tonal ground, and by the broad touches of light paint dragged over the texture of the canvas to describe sheet and pillows. Note, too, the radically blurred treatment of the facial features in each work, and the exaggerated, seemingly random highlights in the modelling of the bodies. Bacon was evidently alert to the sheer boldness and experimentalism of which Sickert was capable, perceiving in *La Hollandaise* a raw sensuality projected not just through illustration but also through

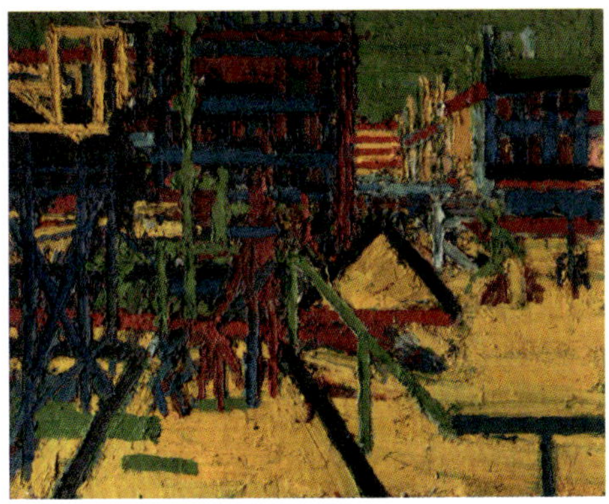

Fig.41
Frank Auerbach, *E.O.W. Nude* 1953–4, oil paint on canvas, 51 × 77, Tate

Fig.42
Frank Auerbach, *Mornington Crescent* 1967, oil paint on board, 121.9 × 147.3, The Metropolitan Museum of Art

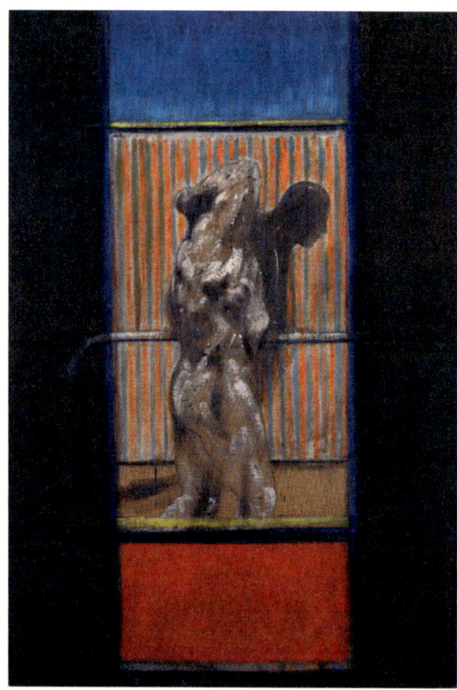

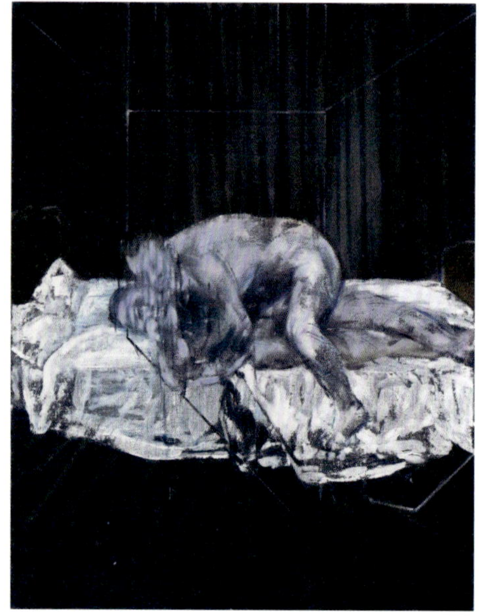

the texture and manipulation of paint, an effect that he proceeded to elaborate in his own picture, grafting stylistic ideas from Sickert onto Muybridge's wrestling imagery.

Their sexually frank treatments of the nude provide the most obvious point of contact between Bacon and Freud. For both, Sickert provided artistic provocation. For instance, *Nude Lying Backwards on Bed* c.1904 was a possible model for Bacon's series of women reclining with their legs up from around 1960, as in Tate's *Reclining Woman* 1961.[14] The inclusion of such pictures in the various centenary exhibitions was symptomatic of a reawakened interest, within an increasingly permissive climate, in Sickert's nudes from before the First World War.[15] These were surely a significant catalyst, too, for the sequence of 'naked portraits' that Freud produced from the late 1960s onwards. The terminology may in itself be a knowing echo of Sickert's essay 'The naked and the Nude' from 1910, which evoked his distaste for the cliched idealisation implicit in the notion of the 'nude'. As the model for a more authentic and inventive approach, Sickert cited the example of Degas, who 'has incessantly chosen to draw figures from unaccustomed points of view'.[16] In his *Naked Girl* from 1966, Freud may at some level have had in mind the pose and sense of the body sinking into the mattress in works by Sickert such as *The Iron Bedstead* c.1906 or *Mornington Crescent Nude* c.1907 (see nos.118 and 119). Equally, the twisted, foreshortened and notably unidealised bodies in, say, the two versions of *Naked Girl Asleep* 1967 and 1968, *Portrait of Rose* 1978–9, and later works such as *Night Portrait* 1985–6 (see fig.45) recall Sickert's explicit but more painterly treatment of the splayed female figure, set off against white sheets, in several works dating from around 1906.

For Bacon, equally, the foreshortened, twisted female body in Sickert's *L'Affaire de Camden Town* (see no.128) provided a template for the naked portraits of Henrietta Moraes from the mid-1960s, and equally for passages in his Crucifixion triptychs of 1962 and 1965, where Sickert's atmosphere of latent violence becomes a dramatic 'bed of crime' (to quote Bacon's favoured phrase).[17] *L'Affaire de Camden Town* is now one of the best-known of Sickert's paintings, but again we may note that it was in France for several decades, and was only given fulsome exposure, and reproduced for the first time, in 1960.[18] Since 1973, the picture has been owned by a private collector who also possesses several major works by Bacon and Freud. Collector and painters were friends, and the acquisition of *L'Affaire de Camden Town* was evidently encouraged by Freud.[19] In this particular Sickert, the reclining nude is of course daringly juxtaposed against a standing male figure, a pictorial conceit which underpinned Freud's *Painter and Model* 1986–7 (see fig.46). In the Freud, the roles are inverted, so that a clothed female painter looms over the naked male, who lies exposed on the battered leather Chesterfield sofa that from the late 1970s often replaced the bed in Freud's exercises in bodily scrutiny.

His reliance on direct observation of the model led Freud to remark that his 'method was so arduous that there was no room for influence', as though his fellow émigré Ernst Gombrich had not shown that observation and representation are always mediated by artistic conventions and preoccupations, which inevitably shape decisions regarding subject matter and treatment.[20] A case in point, to my mind, is the subtle Sickert inspiration in *Large Interior, London W.9* 1973 (see fig.47), where the artist positioned an elderly woman, seated in a quite battered chair, severely dressed and lost in her thoughts, in front of a naked figure lying on her back, her lower half decorously concealed by a brown blanket and her face framed by her arms and gazing contemplatively up at the ceiling. The idea brings to mind Sickert compositions from the pre-war Camden Town series that feature seated males and recumbent naked females. A notable comparison is the Kirkcaldy version of *What Shall We Do for the Rent?* c.1908, which, intriguingly, was exhibited at the Fine Art Society in London in 1973, the year the Freud was created.[21] The pose of Freud's reclining female especially is prefigured, despite Sickert's looser treatment and more intimate scale. The seated figure, also to the right, is male in the Sickert, and registers as lover or husband. Bare floorboards feature in both pictures, though the interior in the Freud is generally more stark and unwelcoming. The light too is harsh and

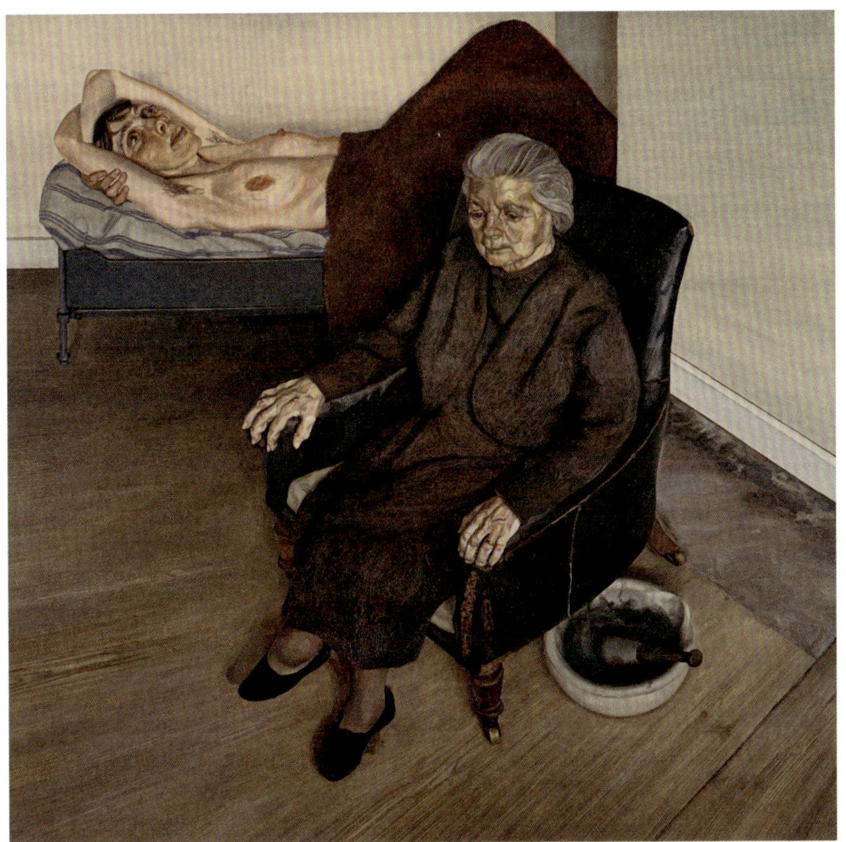

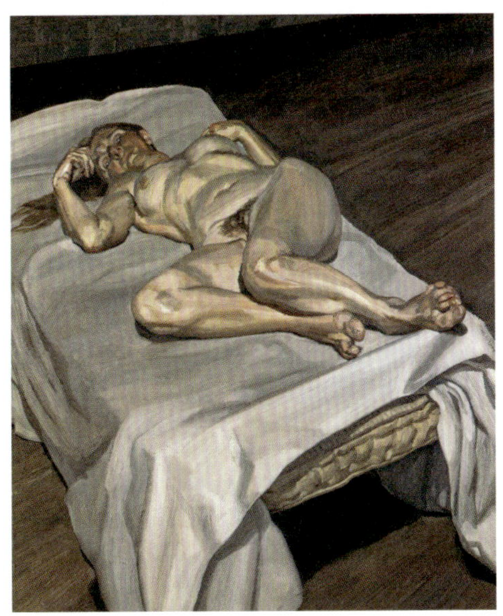

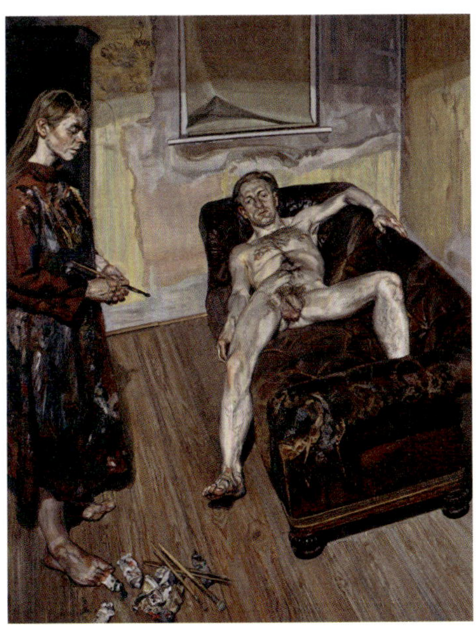

clear, compared to Sickert's soft twilight or dawn effect. Nevertheless, there are enough points of contact to prompt the thought that Freud was gesturing towards *What Shall We Do for the Rent?*

A further juxtaposition may convey Freud's aesthetic and imaginative empathy with Sickert. The predominantly brown, ochre and dirty white palette, the close-up but high viewpoint, the conjunction of frontal and diagonal wall planes, the diagonal orientation of the two older figures, and the atmosphere of psychological dislocation across the generations, combine to suggest an absorption on Freud's part in Sickert's *Ennui* (see no.133), by Sickert's standards an unusually monumental as well as tightly executed and constructed picture. In formal terms, the taut pyramid enclosing Sickert's two figures, notwithstanding their spatial dislocation, corresponds to Freud's configuration of the model's knees containing and offsetting the mother's head and shoulders, while its shape connects visually with the contour of the chair. The obdurate presence of wood, leather, plaster and so

forth seems in each case further to oppress the uncommunicative pairs of individuals. The beer glass on the table in *Ennui* establishes a hard geometric note, offsetting other surfaces and textures, in a manner analogous to Freud's mortar and pestle, likewise an attribute of the older figure. An unmistakable Freud, *Large Interior, London W.9* also ends up looking like a homage to Sickert.

The material assembled here evokes, I hope, the artistic consequences of an enthusiasm for Sickert shared, and doubtless discussed, by Auerbach, Bacon and Freud, three immensely ambitious and original, not to say individualistic, artists. Their engagement with Sickert's art seems to have been productive in diverse ways, and was rooted in opportunistic encounters with specific pictures that they could selectively assimilate and adapt to their own purposes. The key point was made by Sickert himself: 'To the really creative painter … the work of other men is mainly nourishment, to assist him in his own creation.'[22]

ANNA GRUETZNER ROBINS

'CATCH ME IF YOU CAN': SICKERT AND JACK THE RIPPER

Between 31 August and 9 November 1888, five women were brutally murdered in the East End of London by a violent psychopath.[1] In September, a confessional letter to the police signed 'Jack the Ripper' gave the murderer lasting infamy.[2] Hoping that the killer's handwriting would be recognised, a facsimile of the letter and another of a postcard were widely published in the press.[3] Their publication encouraged a number of confessional letters, one of which appeared in a local East End paper. In addition, a young female shop assistant in Bradford and several minors were prosecuted for sending letters. The police destroyed what were clearly hoax letters. Well over 1,500 British newspapers published copies of both documents.[4] Their release upped the intensity of a 'journalistic windfall' that spared few details in a comprehensive serial narrative about poverty, drunkenness, the horrible mutilation of the victims, and a running speculative commentary on the identity of the killer. The established public appetite for fictionalised and sensationalised killing could not get enough of these real-life murders.

There is no proof that Sickert was Jack the Ripper and claims in books written on the subject cannot conclusively be verified, but there is a continuing public fascination with the 'cold case' and Sickert continues to be named as one of the suspects.[5] Sickert had a long-standing fascination with the Whitechapel murders, which he liked to share with his friends and acquaintances. He told his first biographer that once, while walking home at night from a music hall in the East End wearing a long check coat and carrying a little bag, he frightened some young girls who fled 'in terror, yelling "Jack the Ripper, Jack the Ripper!"'[6] He also liked to claim that he inhabited a house where Jack the Ripper once lived. Around 1900, Max Beerbohm wrote that Sickert had 'lodged in Jack the Ripper [sic] house'.[7] In 1907 Sickert took some first-floor rooms in a lodging house at 6 Mornington Crescent, where, apparently, after his landlady told him that a veterinary student whom she believed to be Jack the Ripper had lived in the rooms some twenty years before, he painted *Jack the Ripper's Bedroom* (see fig.51). Around 1930, Sickert told the artist André Dunoyer de Segonzac that 'he lived, I believe, in Whitechapel in the house where the real-life Jack the Ripper lived and told me with much wit, the discerning and edifying life of this monstrous assassin'.[8] This means that Sickert lived in at least two different houses that he believed to have been once inhabited by Jack the Ripper.[9]

Teasing his friends about the identity of Jack the Ripper was part of the game. He told Osbert Sitwell that he had written the name of the veterinary student in a book of Casanova's memoirs that he had borrowed from Albert Rutherston, 'but the book was lost during the bombing of London'.[10] Finally he even claimed to have painted a portrait of the killer.[11]

These accounts could be dismissed as amusing anecdotes, but Jack the Ripper was a significant fantasy figure for Sickert. As the present author's essay on Sickert's identities in self-portraiture has established (see p.16), Sickert's theatrical background meant that he enjoyed acting out roles. The painter Marjorie Lilly, who first came to know him in 1917, stated in an interview that, when thinking about Jack the Ripper, Sickert would 'have a fit'.[12] He would get out his bullseye lantern (a type of lantern carried by the police investigating the murders), donning a red handkerchief and a cap over his eyes (witnesses claimed to have spotted

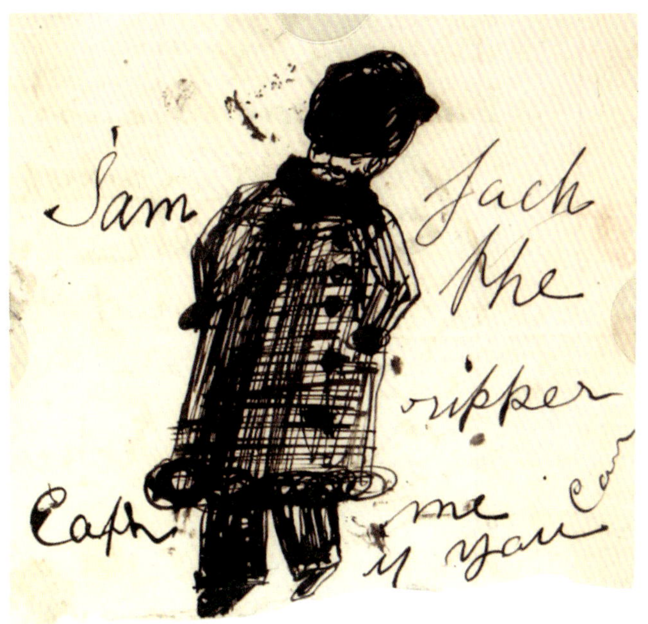

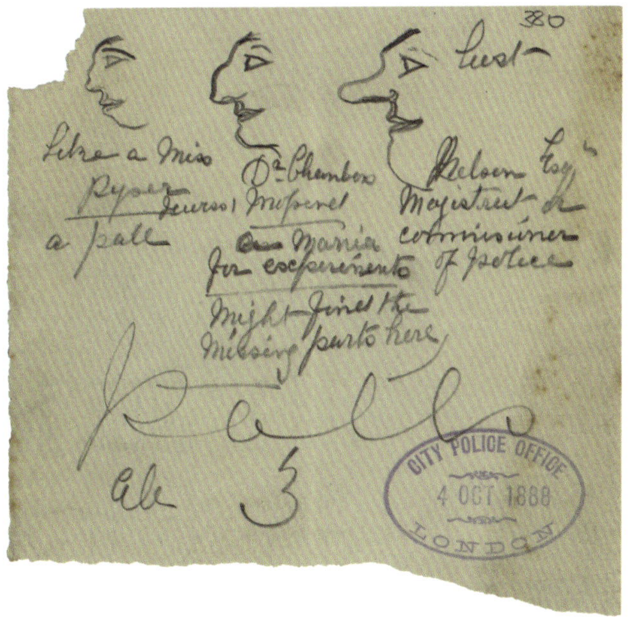

Fig.48
Drawing in black ink on paper pasted on lined paper, made in response to a description given to the police, 19 November 1888, National Archives

Fig.49
Letter with drawing of three heads in profile, received by City of London Police, 4 October 1888, London Metropolitan Archives

Fig.50
Woodcut purporting to be a portrait of Jack the Ripper, printed on a letter dated 12 November 1888, National Archives

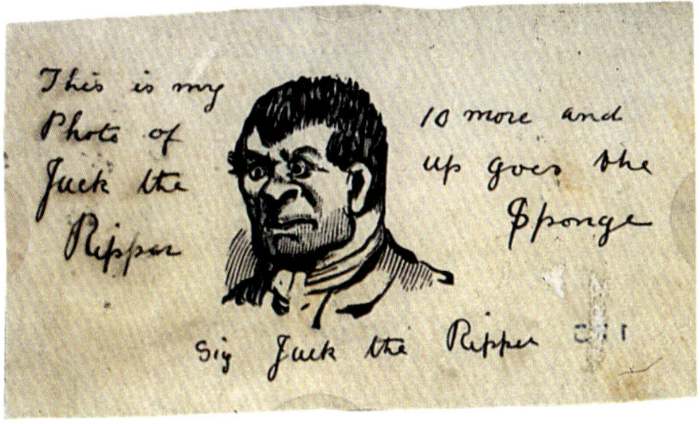

someone they believed to have been Jack the Ripper with these accessories),[13] and even retrieving a 'Gladstone bag' (another accessory) when he made an expedition to the crime area.[14]

Sickert's attachment to Jack the Ripper fit with his well-known performative roles as different characters and historical figures, but his identification with the serial killer went deeper. Many of the letters that were purported to have been written by Jack the Ripper that are now in The National Archives and the London Metropolitan Archives are distinguished by idiosyncratic speech and slang that masks a sophisticated intelligence.[15]

Given the public interest in the subject, in 2002 Tate suggested that 'the internationally respected paper historian, consultant and forensic paper analyst' Peter Bower should look at the letters.[16] In his benchmark study on J.M.W. Turner's papers, Bower had explained that two Turner watercolours were made on 'the same batch' of a quire of writing paper consisting of twenty-four sheets,[17] and that two other watercolours 'were originally parts of the same sheets', and he had reassembled groups of watercolours made from one sheet of paper 'torn down into sixteen irregular sized pieces'.[18]

Using similar research methods, Bower has conclusively shown that the paper of three letters written by Sickert in 1890[19] matches two Jack the Ripper letters of October 1888, including one with a linear arrangement of three female heads in profile (see fig.49)[20] which suggest an awareness of the treatise *The Analysis of Beauty* by Hogarth whom Sickert admired enormously, and the word 'Lust' written next to them.[21] All five letters are written on the same group or quire of twenty-four sheets of Gurney Ivory Laid writing paper, where 'everything matches'. As Bower reports: 'One can only assert that two sheets come from the same batch if everything matches.'[22] Another Ripper letter, signed Nemo,[23] the stage name Sickert used as a young actor, matches a letter from Sickert to the artist William Rothenstein.[24] Bower, however, has been cautious. He suggests, for example, that a music hall sketch by Sickert in the Walker Art Gallery (see no.53) is only a probable match to two Ripper letters in The National Archives.[25] The sketch is part of a large group of music hall studies that Sickert pasted into scrapbooks, but the majority of these – including the Walker drawing – were remounted, which probably affected the paper. Bower's research has not gained public currency in the way that other assertions about Sickert's connection with the crimes have, and it is ironical that Bower's work on Turner's papers and the papers of other artists is accepted, but not his findings about the Ripper letters.[26]

In addition to the paper matches identified by Bower, a group of over forty Jack the Ripper letters – written and illustrated with artists' materials – was examined. Some were finger-painted; others were written with a draughtsman's pen and drawing ink; others were painted with a brush, including an example of what Tate Conservation identified as use of etching ground in which crude doodles representing male figures, some of whom have knives, lean over prostrate female figures.[27] Others have more fully finished illustrations, including one that contains boxing slang, which Tate Conservation identified as a woodcut portrait whose brutish features conform to the perceived notion of 'an anthropologically degenerate individual' (see fig.50).[28] Others were written with black ink (including a caricature of a man in profile), as well as coloured ink, a blue copy pencil (used for copying a drawing for printing), graphite and coloured pencil.[29] Another with the phrase 'catch me if you can' is written in pencil in calligraphic script painted over with a brush in red ink.[30]

Sickert's identification with Jack the Ripper was deeply embedded in his psyche, but it does not mean that he was the killer. The endless press reports undoubtedly incited his interest. He probably made the fine pen and ink drawing of the killer wearing an astrakhan coat, with his chin nestling on the collar (see fig.48),[31] which illustrates a description of a suspicious man published in the press.[32] Together with twelve others, including the one that is a probable match to the Sickert sketch in the Walker Art Gallery, it contains the phrase 'catch me if you can'.[33] We will never know exactly why Sickert wrote these letters. Their confessional character, together with their taunting tone, is troublesome, but they could be part of a complicated game by a very complicated artist, who taunted 'catch me if you can'. He was by no means the only one to confess to a crime that he did not commit.[34]

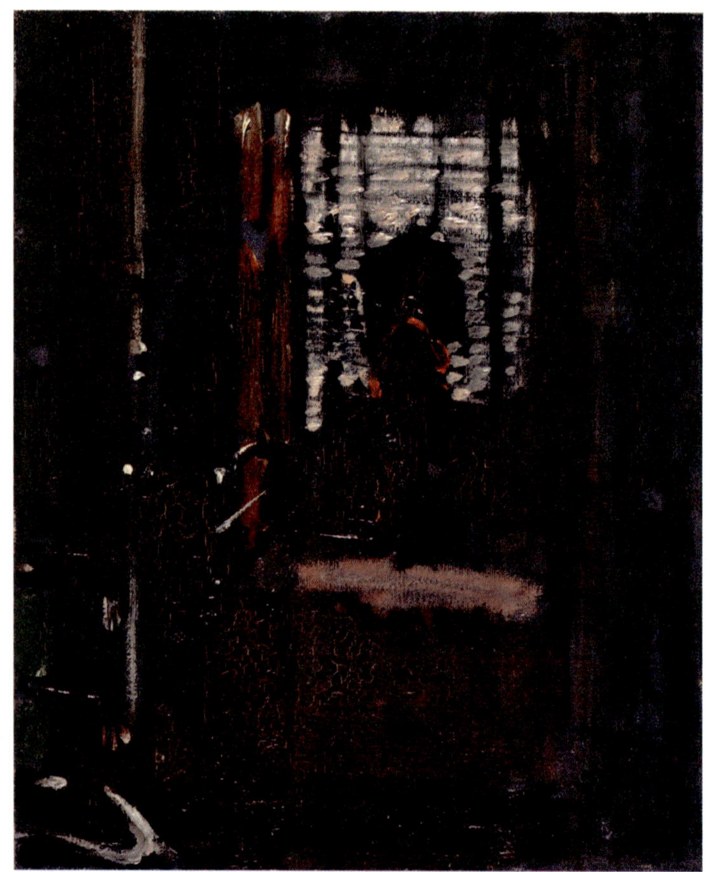

Fig.51
Jack the Ripper's Bedroom 1906–7, oil paint on canvas, 50.8×40.7, Manchester Art Gallery

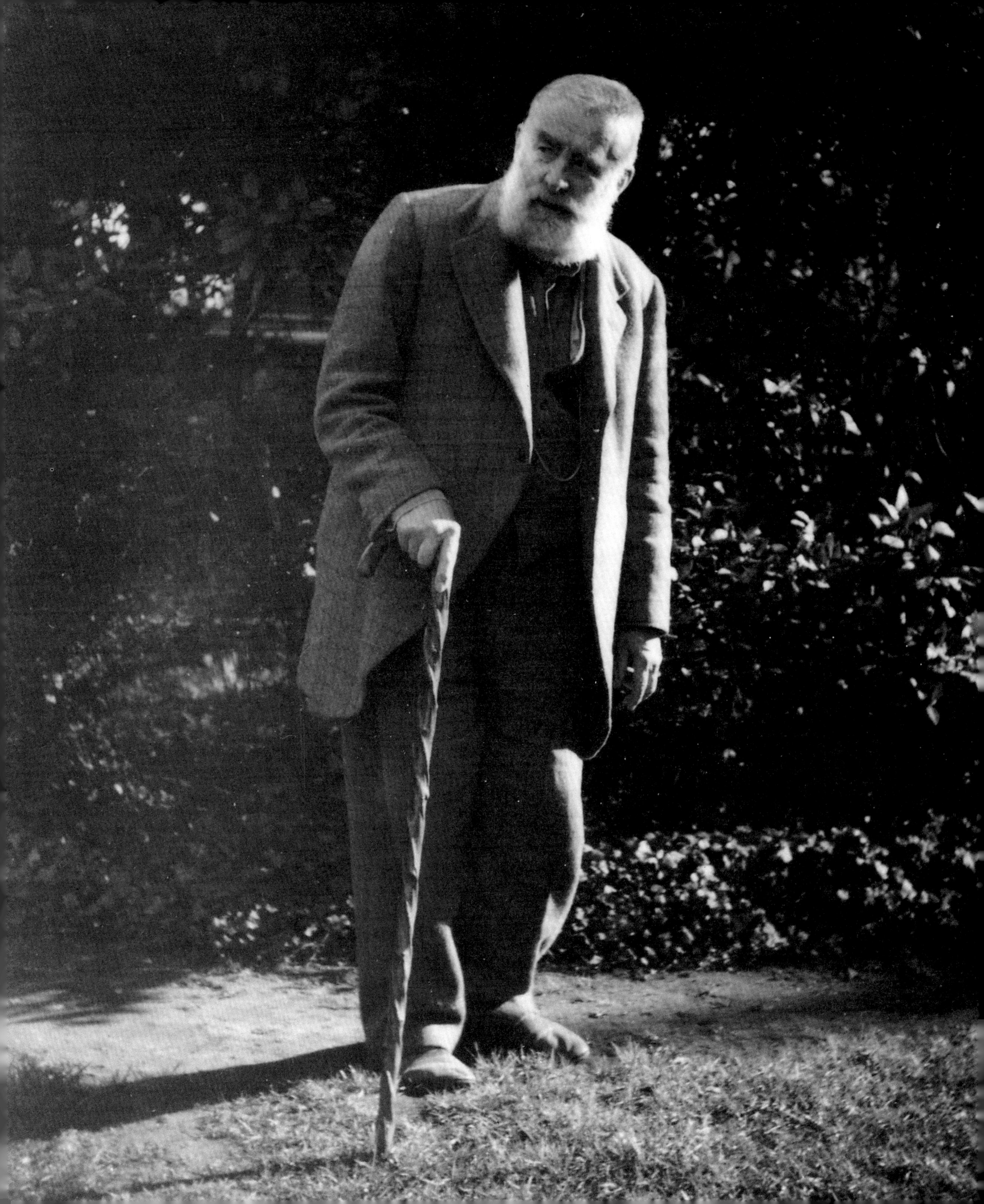

NOTES

INTRODUCTION

1   Sickert, 'Idealism', in *Walter Sickert: The Complete Writings on Art*, ed. Anna Gruetzner Robins, Oxford 2000, pp.228–30.
2   See Robins 2000.
3   See Anna Gruetzner Robins and Richard Thomson, *Degas, Sickert and Toulouse-Lautrec: London and Paris, 1870–1910*, exh. cat., Tate Britain, London 2005.
4   Marjorie Lilly, *Sickert: The Painter and his Circle*, London 1971; Patricia Cornwell, *Ripper: The Secret Life of Walter Sickert*, Seattle 2017.
5   See *Late Sickert: Paintings 1927 to 1942*, Arts Council tour, Hayward Gallery, London, November 1981–January 1982; Sainsbury Centre for the Visual Arts, University of East Anglia, Norwich, March–April 1982; Wolverhampton Art Gallery, April–May 1982. Texts by Frank Auerbach, Richard Morphet, Helen Lessore and Denton Welch, and catalogue of works by Wendy Baron.

THE LOOK OF SICKERT: PAINTING THE SELF

1   Robert Emmons, *The Life and Opinions of Walter Richard Sickert*, London 1941, p.4.
2   Sickert, 'Mural Decoration', *English Review*, July 1912, in *Walter Sickert: The Complete Writings on Art*, ed. Anna Gruetzner Robins, Oxford 2000, p.326.
3   Sickert, 'Two Exhibitions', *Speaker*, 7 Nov. 1896, in Gruetzner Robins 2000, p.109.
4   Simon Houfe, *The Work of Charles Samuel Keene*, Aldershot 1995, p.1.
5   Ibid., p.2.
6   William Rothenstein, *Men and Memories: Recollections of William Rothenstein, 1872–1900*, London 1934, p.167.
7   Sickert met Gauguin in Dieppe in 1885, when he advised him to give up painting, but his opinion of Gauguin's work later changed, and when *Manaò Tupapaú* (now at the Albright-Knox Art Gallery, Buffalo) was among a large number of Gauguin pictures to be exhibited in London, he campaigned for the National Gallery to purchase it.
8   See Alastair Wright, 'Gauguin's Self-Portraits: Egos and Alter Egos', in *Gauguin: Portraits*, ed. Cornelia Homburg and Christopher Riopelle, Ottawa and London 2019, p.24. The 1906 exhibition included *Self-Portrait Dedicated to Carrière* 1888/1889

(National Gallery of Art, Washington); *Autoportrait au chapeau* 1894 (Musée d'Orsay, Paris); *Self-Portrait with Palette*, c.1894 (Private Collection); and *Portrait de l'artiste 'à l'ami Daniel'* 1896 (Musée d'Orsay, Paris).
9   Sickert, letter to Jacques-Émile Blanche, n.d., but around 1900, Ms 7055 168, Institut de France.
10 Louis Vauxcelles, 'Le Salon d'Automne: Supplément', *Gil Blas*, 5 Oct. 1906, in Anna Gruetzner Robins and Richard Thomson, *Degas, Sickert and Toulouse-Lautrec: London and Paris, 1870–1910*, exh. cat., Tate Britain, London 2005, p.180.
11 Sickert, letter to Nan Hudson, probably April 1907, in Wendy Baron, *Sickert: Paintings and Drawings*, New Haven and London 2006, p.70.
12 I take this definition from Monique Kornell, 'écorche', *Grove Art Online*, https://wwwoxfordartonlinecom.lonlib.idm.oclc.org/groveart/view/10.1093/gao/9781884446054.001.0001/oao-9781884446054-e-7000024851?rskey=D4oWZ2, accessed 20 September 2021.
13 Bottom, in William Shakespeare's *A Midsummer Night's Dream*, Act I, Scene 2.
14 Matthew Sturgis, *Walter Sickert: A Life*, London 2005, p.83.
15 Sickert, letter to Ethel Sands, September 1913, TGA 9125/5/63.
16 Marjorie Lilly, *Sickert: The Painter and his Circle*, London 1971, p.17.
17 See Kasia Boddy, *Boxing: A Cultural History*, London 2008, p.82. 'Interpreting Intelligence', in *Punch*, 21 April 1860, illustrates a street urchin secretly buying a copy of a sports paper for a well-dressed 'personnage'.
18 Wendy Baron and Richard Shone (eds.), *Sickert: Paintings*, exh. cat., Royal Academy of Arts, London 1992, p.288.
19 Richard Shone points out that Sickert is leaving [sic] Burlington House, the home of the Royal Academy. See Shone, *W.R. Sickert: Drawings and Paintings, 1809–1942*, London 1990, p.44.
20 Richard Sickert, 'The Epstein Statues in the Strand', *Daily Telegraph*, 11 May 1935, in Gruetzner Robins 2000, pp.677–8.
21 Richard Shone, *From Beardsley to Beaverbrook: Portraits by Walter Richard Sickert*, Bath 1990, p.46, reproduces a 1940 photograph on which the painting is based, but Sickert replaced the background with a bookcase.

THE APPRENTICESHIP YEARS: FROM WHISTLER TO DEGAS

1   Sickert, letter to Whistler [24 March/April 1885], Archives and Special Collections, Glasgow University Library. MS Whistler S67. Published in *The Correspondence of James McNeill Whistler, 1855–1903*, ed. Margaret F. MacDonald, Patricia de Montfort and Nigel Thorp. Online edition, University of Glasgow: http://www.whistler.arts.gla.ac.uk/correspondence, GUW #05423.
2   Sickert, 'L'Affaire Greaves', *The New Age: A Weekly Review of Politics, Literature, and Art*, vol.9, no.7, 15 June 1911, p.160.
3   'An Art Student writes to us as follows', *Pall Mall Gazette*, 7 June 1882, in *Walter Sickert: The Complete Writings on Art*, ed. Anna Gruetzner Robins, Oxford 2000, p.3.
4   'With Wisest Sorrow', *Daily Telegraph*, 1 April 1925, in Gruetzner Robins 2000, p.511.
5   In an article for the *Saturday Review* (26 December 1896), Sickert had questioned the authenticity of lithographs drawn on transfer paper rather than directly onto the lithographic stone. However, the relationship between the two men was already damaged: Whistler disapproved of Sickert's continued association with the painter and collector Sir William Eden, with whom he had quarrelled the previous year.
6   The trial took place in November 1878. For a comprehensive account, see Linda Merrill, *A Pot of Paint: Aesthetics on Trial in Whistler v. Ruskin*, Washington, DC 1992.
7   'Black and White Illustration' (lecture to art students), 30 November 1934, in Gruetzner Robins 2000, p.670.
8   Katy Norris, *Sickert in Dieppe*, exh. cat., Pallant House Gallery, Chichester 2015, p.28.
9   Gruetzner Robins 2000, p.511.
10 Norris 2015, p.28.
11 Wendy Baron, *Sickert: Paintings and Drawings*, New Haven and London 2006, p.160 cat.38.
12 'The Dowdeswell Galleries [Third Notice]', *New York Herald*, 10 April 1889, in Gruetzner Robins 2000, p.32.
13 Ibid.
14 'The New Life of Whistler', *Fortnightly Review*, Dec. 1908, in Gruetzner Robins 2000, p.186.
15 Gruetzner Robins 2000, p.511.
16 David Peters Corbett, *Walter Sickert*, London 2001, p.7.

17 On occasion, Sickert participated literally in Whistler's interrogation of his materials. This often meant failure and copious losses for Whistler, as Sickert later remembered: 'perhaps 30 per cent., and I am putting it pretty high, of the perpendicular six-footers were allowed to remain in existence. I cannot remember how many of these I helped him to cut into ribbons on their stretchers.' See Gruetzner Robins 2000, p.511.

THE MUSIC HALL AND THE 'STAGE-STRUCK' ARTIST

1   Dalya Alberge, 'Quick on the Draw', *The Independent*, 26 Jan. 1993.
2   Tracy C. Davis, 'The Moral Sense of the Majorities: Indecency and Vigilance in Late-Victorian Music Halls', *Popular Music*, vol.10, no.1, The 1890s, Jan. 1991, p.39.
3   See Anna Gruetzner Robins, 'Sickert "Painter-in-Ordinary" to the Music-Hall', in *Sickert: Paintings*, eds. Wendy Baron and Richard Shone, exh. cat., Royal Academy of Arts, London 1992, p.13.
4   Robert Emmons, *The Life and Opinions of Walter Richard Sickert*, London 1941, p.24.
5   Sickert, 'Sadler's Wells', *The Times*, 26 Oct. 1932. Reprinted in Emmons 1941, p.218. See also *Walter Sickert: The Complete Writings on Art*, ed. Anna Gruetzner Robins, Oxford 2002 (first pub. 2000).
6   Matthew Sturgis, *Walter Sickert: A Life*, London 2005, p.22.
7   Mark Aston, 'Walter Sickert: an acting artist at Sadler's Wells', 23 Jan. 2013: https://islingtonblogs.typepad.com/sadlers-wells-archive/2013/01/walter-sickert-an-artiste-at-sadlers-wells.html, accessed 15 March 2021.
8   John Rothenstein, *English Modern Painters*, London 1952, p.33.
9   Sickert, letter to Alfred Pollard, 28 and 29 March 1879. Woudhuysen collection.
10 H.M. Swanwick, *I Have Been Young*, London 1935, p.60.
11 Sickert, letter to Alfred Pollard, 15 April 1880. Woudhuysen collection.
12 *The Standard* (22 June 1880): Classified ads. London; Issue 17448.
13 *The Standard* (24 June 1880): Classified ads. London; Issue 17450.
14 *The Times* (28 June 1880): Classified ads. London.
15 Islington Museums, 'From Munich to Highbury: Walter Sickert and the Sickert family collection in Islington':

20200421waltersickertmunich
displayilhc.pdf (islington.gov.uk),
accessed 12 February 2021.
16 Sturgis 2005, p.110.
17 'The New English Art Club Exhibition:
Arts Club, Hanover Square', *The
Scotsman*, 24 April 1889, in
Gruetzner Robins 2000, p.41.
18 Davis 1991, p.39.
19 See Barry J. Faulk, *Music Hall
and Modernity: The Late-Victorian
Discovery of Popular Culture*,
Athens, OH 2004, p.23.
20 Arthur Symons, letter to Herbert
Horne, 25 May 1892, in *Arthur
Symons: Selected Letters, 1880–
1935*, eds. Karl Beckson and John
M. Munro, Basingstoke and London
1989, p.96 n.7.
21 Anna Gruetzner Robins, *A Fragile
Modernism: Whistler and his
Impressionist Followers*, New Haven
and London 2007, pp.106–7.
22 See 'London Sketches – at a Music
Hall', *The Graphic*, 5 April 1873.
British Library, 19th Century British
Library Newspapers BA320141829.
23 See Alberge 1993.
24 Davis 1991, p.39.
25 Ibid., p.42.
26 Rebecca Daniels, 'Walter Sickert
and Urban Realism: Ordinary Life
and Tragedy in Camden Town',
British Art Journal, vol.3, no.2,
Spring 2002, pp.58–69: https://
www.jstor.org/stable/41614379,
accessed 12 February 2021.
27 *Camden and Kentish Town's and
St Pancras Gazette*, 1 Feb. 1899;
quoted in Jean Aster, 'History of
the New Bedford Theatre, Camden
Town: A Case Study of the Working
Class "Recreational Revolution"
during the Edwardian Era and
beyond', unpublished PhD thesis,
University of London, May 1999,
pp.15–16.
28 Robert Upstone, *Modern Painters:
The Camden Town Group*, exh. cat.,
Tate Britain, London 2008, p.74.
29 Quoted in Gruetzner Robins 1992,
p.13.

**THE MUCH-ABUSED APOSTLE OF
MUSIC-HALL ART: SICKERT AND
THE STAGE**

1 The present essay title, 'The much-
abused apostle of music-hall art',
is taken from this text. Sickert,
'The Gospel of Impressionism:
A Conversation Between Two
Impressionists and a Philistine',
Pall Mall Gazette, 21 July 1890,
in *Walter Sickert: The Complete
Writings on Art*, ed. Anna Gruetzner

Robins, Oxford 2000, p.74. Many
thanks to Anna Gruetzner Robins,
Wendy Baron, Thomas Kennedy, and
Peter Charlton of the British Music
Hall Society.
2 Ibid., p.76.
3 Ibid., p.75.
4 Jerry White, *London in the
Nineteenth Century*, London 2016,
p.280.
5 Robert Emmons, *The Life and
Opinions of Walter Richard Sickert*,
London 1941, pp.47–8.
6 Charles Douglas Stuart and A.J.
Park, *The Variety Stage: A History
of the Music Halls from the Earliest
Period to the Present Time*, London
1895, p.73. By 1898, the Bedford
was rather shabby. Prior to its
demolition, *The Era* noted that
'the old hall, with its inconvenient
approaches and its stuffy entrances,
will be no more'. Anon, 'Music Hall
Gossip', *The Era*, 14 May 1898,
p.19.
7 The title refers to the 'Prompt Side'
and 'Opposite Prompt' wings. The
painting was referred to with this
title in Anon, 'Two Picture Exhibitions
in London', *Leeds Mercury*,
3 Dec. 1889, p.5, and Walter
Armstrong, 'Two Winter Exhibitions',
Manchester Daily Examiner, 5 Dec.
1889, p.12. Wendy Baron notes that
drawings in Donegal's Glebe House
and Gallery identify the Bedford as
the location. Baron also notes that
profile sketches of audience figures,
held in a private collection, have the
inscription by Sickert 'Bedford Jan
19 88'. In contrast, in Manchester
Art Gallery's collection, a drawing
of the unnamed performer's head
features on a sheet of studies by
Sickert, which included Gatti's
music hall subjects. See Wendy
Baron, *Sickert: Paintings and
Drawings*, New Haven and London
2006, pp.176–7.
8 Emmons 1941, p.48.
9 Colin MacInnes, *Sweet Saturday
Night*, London 1967, p.10.
10 Emmons 1941, p.48.
11 Sickert, 'The Gospel of
Impressionism', in Gruetzner Robins
2000, p.76. By the 1880s, due to
ageing buildings and their growing
popularity, many were demolished
to be replaced by larger, grander,
theatre buildings – a fate which
eventually befell the Bedford in
1898. The Bedford manged to retain
something of a mid-nineteenth-
century ambience, probably
the reason Sickert favoured it,
although he preferred its pre-1898
incarnation, 'before the music-halls
had become two-house-a-night wells,

like theatres to look at'. Sickert,
'The Allied Artists' Association', *The
New Age*, 14 July 1910, in Gruetzner
Robins 2000, p.258.
12 On Sickert's paintings at the
'London Impressionist' exhibition,
including *The P.S. Wings in the O.P.
Mirror*. Anon, 'Notes on Current
Topics', *Yorkshire Post and Leeds
Intelligencer*,
7 Dec. 1889, p.6.
13 Anon, 'From Private
Correspondence', *The Scotsman*,
15 April 1889, p.7.
14 Sickert, 'The New English Art Club
Exhibition: Arts Club, Hanover
Square', *The Scotsman*,
24 April 1889, in Gruetzner Robins
2000, p.41.
15 George Moore, 'Degas: The Painter
of Modern Life', *The Magazine of
Art*, Jan. 1890, p.423.
16 Arthur Symons, 'A Spanish Music
Hall' (1892), in Symons, *Cities and
Sea-Coasts and Islands*, New York
1918, p.145.
17 For more on Vesta's life, see Carol
A. Morley, 'The Most Artistic Lady
Artist on Earth: Vesta Victoria',
in *Women in the Arts in the Belle
Epoque: Essays on Influential
Artists, Writers and Performers*,
ed. Paul Fryer, Jefferson, NC 2012,
pp.186–209.
18 Anon, 'London Variety Stage',
The Stage, 28 March 1890, p.16.
19 Further success would follow in
1906 with Fred W. Leigh's 'Waiting
at the Church; or, My Wife Won't
Let Me'.
20 Anon, 'The Playhouses', *Illustrated
London News*, 2 Feb. 1889, p.134.
For more on the instrument, see
Laura Vorachek, 'Whitewashing
Blackface Minstrelsy in Nineteenth-
Century England: Female Banjo
Players in "Punch"', *Victorians:
A Journal of Culture and Literature*,
no.123, Spring 2013, pp.31–51.
21 See cats.55.1 and 55.4 in Baron
2006, p.187.
22 Anon, 'Londoners in Straw Hats',
Huddersfield Chronicle, 6 Aug.
1894, p.4. The inclusion of the hat
also suggests Sickert captured the
hall during the summer. Sickert was
well aware of the value of props.
Discussing Steer's aforementioned
Signorina Zozo in 'Dresdina', he
shrewdly noted: 'Even the hats
of those "Johnnies" in front will be
interesting to posterity.' Sickert,
'The Gospel of Impressionism',
in Gruetzner Robins 2000, p.76.
23 'The London Music Halls', *The
Era*, 21 May 1887, p.17, and 'The
London Music Halls', *The Era*,
23 Jan. 1886, p.10.

24 'Music Halls', *London and Provincial
Entr'acte*, 13 April 1889, p.6.
25 'The Gem of Comedy: Miss Ada
Lundberg'. Advertisement, *The Era*,
22 Nov. 1890, p.28.
26 Edward Ledger (ed.), *The Era
Almanack – Dramatic & Musical*,
London 1878. Quoted in Sam Beale,
*The Comedy and Legacy of Music-
Hall Women 1880–1920: Brazen
Impudence and Boisterous Vulgarity*,
London 2020, p.2.
27 Sickert, 'Impressionism'. Preface
to *A Collection of Paintings by the
London Impressionists at
the Goupil Gallery, London*, 2 Dec.
1889.
See Gruetzner Robins 2000, p.60.
28 Sickert, 'The Allied Artists'
Association', in Gruetzner Robins
2000, p.258.

**BEYOND PORTRAITURE:
SICKERT AND LIFELIKENESS**

1 Sickert, 'Idealism', *Art News*,
12 May 1910.
2 Sickert, 'Future of the Autumn
exhibition', *Liverpool Post and
Mercury*, 21 Oct. 1929.
3 Wendy Baron and Richard Shone
(eds.), *Sickert: Paintings*, exh. cat.,
Royal Academy of Arts, London
1992, p.176.
4 *Virginia Woolf: Collected Essays*,
vol.2, London 1924, p.235.
5 Ibid. Richard Shone suggests that
the generalised landscape might in
fact be based
on a Dieppe seascape.
6 J.W. Goodison, 'Sickert's Use of
Photography', *Burlington Magazine*,
vol.113, no.822, Sept. 1971,
pp.551–2.
7 The artist misspelt the name of
Victor Lecourt, who owned a famous
restaurant near Dieppe, and his
portrait is known in Sickert literature
under his erroneous, exhibited name
as a result.
8 Robert Emmons, *The Life and
Opinions of Walter Richard Sickert*,
London 1941, p.188.
9 Quoted in André Chastel, *Vuillard
1868–1940*, Paris 1946, p.94.
10 Marcia Pointon, *Portrayal and the
Search for Identity*, London 2012,
p.48.
11 Andrew Causey, 'The English
Impressionist', *Illustrated London
News*, 10 Feb. 1968, p.27.
12 Sickert, 'The Study of Drawing',
The New Age,
16 June 1910, pp.156–7.
13 *Le tose* means 'the girls' in Venetian
dialect.

**'FULL OF APPEAL –
SAD – WAN – TOUCHING':
SICKERT'S 'PICTURESQUE' WORK**

1 Sickert, letter to Florence Humphrey, 1898, in Wendy Baron, *Sickert: Paintings and Drawings*, New Haven and London 2006, p.37.
2 Accounts differ as to whether Sickert travelled to Dieppe in the summer or winter of 1898. I concur with Matthew Sturgis, who cites correspondence between Sickert's associates Max Beerbohm and Reggie Turner, placing Sickert in the town at the end of August. See Sturgis, *Walter Sickert: A Life*, London 2005, p.263.
3 Sickert, letter to Florence Humphrey, 1899, in Baron 2006, p.37.
4 The possibility that Sickert employed photography as source material for his architectural landscapes has been speculated. Robert Upstone puts forward a convincing case for the influence of stereoscopic photographs on Sickert's Venetian scenes, but ultimately concludes that any direct use is 'suggestive rather than definitive'. See Upstone, *Sickert in Venice*, exh. cat., Dulwich Picture Gallery, London 2009, pp.57–63. For a discussion of the impact of touristic picture postcards on Sickert's Dieppe paintings, see Katy Norris, *Sickert in Dieppe*, exh. cat., Pallant House Gallery, Chichester 2015, pp.76–8.
5 This dynamic is detailed in letters Sickert wrote to Constance Hulton. The letters are variously quoted in Baron 2006, pp.45–7.
6 Jacques-Émile Blanche, *Portraits of a Lifetime*, London 1937, p.45.
7 Sickert likely saw an exhibition of Monet's Rouen Cathedral series at Durand-Ruel's gallery in 1895 while en route to Venice. He was a close associate of Camille Pissarro when the impressionist was based in Dieppe painting his series of St Jacques in the summer of 1901, and was undoubtedly directly influenced by him. Although in later years Sickert was ambivalent about Monet's approach to working in series, he continued to hold Pissarro in high regard. See commentary on Monet's painting of the Ducal Palace, Venice, in Walter Sickert, 'French Pictures at Knoedler's Gallery', *Burlington Magazine*, July 1923, and later appraisal of Pissarro's contribution to modern painting in Sickert, 'Camille Pisarro (1830–1903)' at Leicester Galleries, June 1931. Both articles are reprinted in *Walter Sickert: The Complete Writings on Art*, ed. Anna Gruetzner Robins, Oxford 2000, pp.463 and 611.
8 Sickert, letter to Ethel Sands, 1915, in Baron 2006, p.45.
9 There is a wealth of scholarship relating to Sickert's London subjects. See essays by Richard Shone, 'Walter Sickert, the Dispassionate Observer', and Anna Gruetzner Robins, 'Sickert "Painter-in-Ordinary" to the Music-Hall', in *Sickert: Paintings*, eds. Wendy Baron and Richard Shone, exh. cat., Royal Academy of Arts, London 1992; 'Walter Sickert: The Camden Town Murder and Tabloid Crime', in Lisa Tickner, *Modern Life & Modern Subjects: British Art in the Early Twentieth Century*, London 2000; and Barnaby Wright (ed.), *Walter Sickert: The Camden Town Nudes*, exh. cat., Courtauld Gallery, London 2008. In recent years, this imbalance has been addressed by two separate exhibitions focusing on Venice and Dieppe. See Upstone 2009 and Norris 2015.
10 This approach builds upon recent scholarship examining Sickert's identity as an internationalist artist. See Anna Gruetzner Robins, 'Walter Sickert and the Language of Art', in *Internationalism and the Arts in Britain and Europe at the Fin de Siècle*, ed. Grace Brockington, Oxford 2009, and Sophie Hatchwell, '"Acquiring a Foreign Accent": Painting as Cosmopolitan Language in Edwardian Art Writing', in *Imagined Cosmopolis: Internationalism and Cultural Exchange, 1870s–1920s*, ed. Charlotte Ashby et al., Oxford 2019.
11 Upstone 2009, pp.24–7.
12 Sickert had two major solo exhibitions in Paris while living in France, the first at Durand-Ruel Gallery in December 1900 and the second at Bernheim-Jeune in June 1904. He also exhibited at the Salon des Indépendants and Salon d'Automne. In 1903, he exhibited at the annual Glaspalast show in Munich and the Biennale in Venice within the French sections. Sickert remained aloof from the International, although he exhibited two Venetian pictures with the society in 1905, two years after Whistler's death.
13 Richard Shone, 'Sickert in Dieppe Exhibition Review', *Burlington Magazine*, vol.157, no.1353, Dec. 2015, pp.872–3.
14 Jean, Lady Hamilton, quoted in Sturgis 2005, p.335.
15 Baron 2006, pp.37–8.
16 Ibid.
17 Blanche 1937, p.49.

SICKERT AND FRANCE

1 Sickert, 'Alphonse Legros', *The Speaker*, 10 April 1897, in *Walter Sickert: The Complete Writings on Art*, ed. Anna Gruetzner Robins, Oxford 2000, pp.155–7.
2 Sickert, 'Memories of Edgar Degas', 1917, in *Degas: The Painter of Modern Life. Memories of Degas by George Moore and Walter Sickert*, London 2011, p.76. The butterfly motif, which here refers to Whistler, was chosen by the artist as a sort of stylised signature which he used on his works.
3 Sickert, 'Impressionism', *The New Age*, 30 June 1910, in Gruetzner Robins 2000, pp.253–4.
4 Sickert, 'New Wine', *The New Age*, 21 April 1910, in Gruetzner Robins 2000, pp.218–19.
5 François Fosca, 'Walter-Richard Sickert', *L'Amour de l'art*, no.11, Nov. 1930, p.445.
6 Wendy Baron, *Sickert: Paintings and Drawings*, New Haven and London 2006, p.56.
7 Giampaolo Nuvolati, 'Le flâneur dans l'espace urbain', *Géographie et cultures* [Corps urbains], no.70, 2009, pp.7–20.
8 Gruetzner Robins 2000, p.XXIX.
9 Charles Baudelaire, *Le Peintre de la vie moderne*, 1863, coll. Litteratura. com, p.11.
10 Sickert, letter to Sir William Eden, 15 November 1901, in Anna Gruetzner Robins and Richard Thomson, *Degas, Sickert and Toulouse-Lautrec: London and Paris, 1870–1910*, exh. cat., Tate Britain, London 2005, p.156.
11 Sickert, letter to Sir William Eden, 15 November 1901, in Denys Sutton, *Walter Sickert: A Biography*, London 1976, p.109.
12 Anna Gruetzner Robins, 'Sickert and the Paris Art World', in Gruetzner Robins and Thomson 2005, p.178.
13 Arsène Alexandre, 'Les Petites exposition', *Le Figaro*, 7 June 1904, p.4.
14 Robert de Tanlis, *Lemeur*, 21 January 1907, in Matthew Sturgis, *Walter Sickert: A Life*, London 2005, pp.372–3.
15 Paul Jamot, 'Exposition Sickert', *La Chronique des arts et de la curiosité*, 19 Jan. 1907, p.19.
16 Louis Vauxcelles, 'Le Salon d'Automne, Supplément', *Gil Blas*, 17 Oct. 1905, pp.1–2.
17 Gustave Geffroy, 'Le Salon d'Automne', *Le Journal*, 22 Oct. 1905, p.5.
18 Louis Vauxcelles, 'Le Salon d'Automne, Supplément', *Gil Blas*, 30 Sept. 1908, p.2.
19 Raymond Bouyer, *Le Bulletin de l'art*, 19 Jan. 1907.
20 Félix Monod, 'Supplément chronique. Un peintre Anglais: M. Walter Sickert', *Art et Décoration*, July 1909, p.3.
21 Fosca 1930, p.445.
22 It is also worth mentioning the small group of paintings by Sickert gathered after the war by the collector Georges Bemberg and on display since 1994 at the Fondation Bemberg, Toulouse.

SICKERT AND THE NUDE

1 W.B. Richmond, letter to Robert Ross, in Margery Ross (ed.), *Robert Ross: Friend of Friends* (1952), pp.215, 196–7, quoted in Matthew Sturgis, *Walter Sickert: A Life*, London 2005, pp.424, 722 n.20.
2 Sickert, 'On the Conduct of a Talent', *The New Age*, 11 June 1914, in *Walter Sickert: The Complete Writings on Art* (an invaluable resource), ed. Anna Gruetzner Robins, Oxford 2000, pp.376–8 (p.377, italics original).
3 I include here paintings of a nude woman with a clothed man, discussed by Wendy Baron in her essay on the 'conversation pieces' (see p.166).
4 The shoe – more like a little low-heeled boot with a cuff, its tongue hanging forward towards the toe – is outlined in a related drawing, *Nude on a Couch* (Princeton University Art Museum), reproduced in Wendy Baron, *Sickert: Paintings and Drawings*, New Haven and London 2006, cat.191.1. I am, like all writers on Sickert, indebted to the scholarship of Wendy Baron.
5 Sturgis 2005, pp.264–5.
6 Baron 2006, p.49, calls the shoe 'voluptuous'; the Daxer & Marschall auction site calls it 'flamboyant'; Baron, in Barnaby Wright (ed.), *Walter Sickert: The Camden Town Nudes*, exh. cat., Courtauld Gallery, London 2007, p.29, calls it 'flashy and coquettish'.
7 There are kicked-off shoes in other works by Sickert: see Baron 2006, cats.344 and 344.1, and Anna Gruetzner Robins, *Walter Sickert: Drawings. Theory and Practice: Word and Image*, Aldershot 1996, figs.30, 31 and 32. Did Sickert know the pink-lined shoe abandoned with underclothes in Henri Gervex's scandalous *Rolla* (1878)? Gervex later claimed that it was Degas who told him to 'put a corset on the floor!' See Hollis Clayson, *Painted Love: Prostitution in French Art of the Impressionist Era*, New York 1992, p.88.
8 In early 1904, Sickert wrote to the artist Jacques-Émile Blanche that the dismal weather had driven him indoors: 'I can't stand being frozen'. Quoted in Baron 2006, p.49.
9 Sickert, 'The New English and After', *The New Age*, 2 June 1910, in Gruetzner Robins 2000, p.242. In 1965, the Musée des Beaux-Arts in Rouen told Wendy Baron that *Vénitienne allongée à la jupe rouge* was 'trop scabreux' – too improper or obscene – for public display. See Baron 2006, p.54 n.14.
10 Sickert was a prolific writer on art, both entertaining and provocative. He wrote a weekly column for *The New Age* from April to September 1910. 'The naked and the Nude' (21 July) is reprinted in Gruetzner Robins 2000, pp.260–4. *The New Age* (1894–1938) was an important source on modern art and literature during the editorship of A.R. Orage (1907–22).
11 Kenneth Clark, *The Nude: A Study*

of Ideal Art [1956], Harmondsworth 1960, Chapter I, 'The Naked and the Nude', pp.1–25. In his opening lines, Clark distinguishes the naked body ('huddled and defenceless') from the nude ('balanced, prosperous and confident … the body re-formed'). See Lynda Nead's commentary in *The Female Nude: Art, Obscenity and Sexuality*, London and New York 1992, pp.12–16.

12 Sickert, 'The naked and the Nude', in Gruetzner Robins 2000, p.261. In 'living picture' music hall turns, women in close-fitting, flesh-coloured bodices and tights enacted scenes from painting and sculpture.

13 Sickert, 'The Study of Drawing', *The New Age*, 16 June 1910, in Gruetzner Robins 2000, pp.247–8.

14 Sickert, 'The naked and the Nude', in Gruetzner Robins 2000, p.262.

15 In spring 1883, Sickert, then a pupil and assistant in Whistler's studio, took Whistler's *Arrangement in Grey and Black No. 1* (commonly known as *Portrait of the Artist's Mother*) to Paris for exhibition at the Salon. He carried letters of introduction to Manet (who was too ill to see him but asked his brother Eugène to show Sickert his paintings) and to Degas (who invited him to his studio, initiating a friendship of thirty years). See Sturgis 2005, p.110.

16 I am indebted to essays by Anna Gruetzner Robins, 'The Greatest Artist the World has Ever Known' and 'Sickert and the Paris Art World', in Gruetzner Robins and Richard Thomson, *Degas, Sickert and Toulouse-Lautrec: London and Paris, 1870–1910*, exh. cat., Tate Britain, London 2005, pp.51–93, 155–201. Sickert exhibited at the Salon d'Automne every year from 1905 to 1909, and had solo shows with his dealers Durand-Ruel in 1900 and then Bernheim-Jeune in 1904, 1907 and 1909.

17 Sickert, 'Idealism', *Art News*, 12 May 1910; 'The Study of Drawing', *The New Age*, 16 June 1910; 'The naked and the Nude', *The New Age*, 21 July 1910, in Gruetzner Robins 2000, pp.228–30, 247–9, 260–4. Sickert showed *The Camden Town Murder Series, No. 1* and *The Camden Town Murder Series, No. 2* at the first Camden Town Group exhibition in June 1911.

18 For a useful précis, see David Hayes, 'A History of Camden Town 1895–1914', in Helena Bonett, Ysanne Holt, Jennifer Mundy (eds.), 'The Camden Town Group in Context', Tate Research Publication, May 2012, https://www.tate.org.uk/art/research-publications/camden-town-group/david-hayes-a-history-of-camden-town-1895-1914-r1104374, accessed 13 August 2021. See also Wendy Baron, 'Camden Town Recalled', in *Camden Town Recalled*, exh. cat., Fine Art Society, London 1976, pp.2–15.

19 The mass production of metal beds began in England in the 1840s and reached a peak between 1860 and 1890. An unsigned article on the 'Metallic Bedstead Trade of Birmingham' in the *Furniture Gazette*, vol.24, Nov. 1886, p.363, gives the price of a basic iron bed as five or six shillings. At least Sickert's models would have been relatively comfortable. Degas's model Alice Michel complained that he demanded difficult and painful poses, 'where one had to arch one's back or tighten one's muscles to the tips of one's fingers'. Quoted in Heather Dawkins, 'Frogs, Monkeys and Women: A History of Identifications Across a Phantastic Body', in *Dealing with Degas: Representations of Women and the Politics of Vision*, ed. Richard Kendall and Griselda Pollock, London 1992, pp.212–13.

20 Virginia Woolf, *Walter Sickert: A Conversation*, London 1934, pp.17–18.

21 'Voici d'abord une série de nus, peints au crépuscule, parmi [le] désordre pauvre des chambres garnies d'hôtels. Ce sont des filles, affalées sur le lit défait, des filles au corps flêtri, fatigué[e]s par les dures besognes de la prostitution.' Louis Vauxcelles, 'La Vie artistique: Exposition Walter Sickert à Félix Fénéon', *Gil Blas*, 12 Jan. 1907, p.2. Quoted in Gruetzner Robins and Thomson 2005, pp.178, 215 n.42.

22 Hollis Clayson argues that prostitution appealed to male 'painters of modern life' because it marked the intersection of two widespread views of modernity: the modern as 'temporary, unstable and fleeting' and the modern social relation as 'more and more frozen in the form of the commodity'. Clayson 1992, p.9.

23 I am grateful to the owners for allowing access to this painting, and to Dr Robert Travers for facilitating my visit.

24 See Baron 2006, pp.321–2, for the dating of this painting and its possible identification with *Le grand miroir,* exhibited at Bernheim-Jeune in 1907 and 1909.

25 Sickert was seeing Degas 'a good deal', and Bonnard's paintings at the Salon d'Automne included *Le Cabinet de Toilette*. On the Paris nudes, see Baron 2006, p.63, and on Degas p.67 ns.1, 3. Anthea Callen claims that the sight of a woman bathing was available to a bourgeois man only through a financial transaction with either a prostitute or an artist's model (wives bathed in private). Callen, 'Degas' Bathers: Hygiene and Dirt – Gaze and Touch', in Kendall and Pollock 1992, pp.176–7.

26 Sickert, undated letter to Nan Hudson [1907], quoted in Baron 2006, pp.70, 78 n.9. His 'typical lodgings first-floor' is furnished with an iron bedstead, a chest of drawers, an oval dressing mirror with curved supports, a bedside chair, and a wash stand with basin and chamber pot. In *Mornington Crescent nude, contre jour* 1907, the light is filtered through slatted blinds. (Sickert had a fondness for contre-jour effects, and in 1902 had purchased on his wife's behalf Degas's silhouetted *Woman at a Window* 1871–2.)

27 Baron 2006, p.71.

28 Barnaby Wright discusses the truncated torso, the 'casket-like' bed, and Rebecca Daniels's suggestion that the painting is linked to the Camden Town Murder series, in Wright 2007, p.78.

29 T.J. Clark, *The Painting of Modern Life: Paris in the Art of Manet and his Followers* [1984], London 1985, p.133. Soon after the Salon opened in 1865, Manet's *Olympia* was rehung above the spectators' eyeline, reducing the impact of Olympia's challenging gaze. See Charles Bernheimer, 'Manet's Olympia: The Figuration of Scandal', *Poetics Today*, vol.10, no.2, Summer 1989, pp.255–77 (p.257).

30 Louis Vauxcelles, 'Le Salon d'Automne: Supplément', *Gil Blas*, 5 Oct. 1906, p.2, in Gruetzner Robins and Thomson 2005, p.178.

31 In 1912, against a gathering tide of critical opinion, Sickert maintained that 'the whole field of natural "genre" pictures … is waiting to be re-tilled'. Sickert, 'The Old Ladies of Etching-needle Street', *English Review*, Jan. 1912, in Gruetzner Robins 2000, pp.288–96 (p.295).

32 Wyndham Lewis, 'Modern Art', *The New Age*, 2 April 1914, p.703. His letter was a spirited response to Sickert's article 'On Swiftness' the week before (26 March 1914, reprinted in Gruetzner Robins 2000, pp.346–9), in which he described quasi-cubist work by Lewis, Gaudier and Epstein as 'Pornometric'. 'We hear a great deal about non-representative art. But while the faces of the persons suggested are frequently nil, non-representation is forgotten when it comes to the sexual organs' (p.347).

33 There is a civilian variant, *The Sick Child* c.1915.

34 *Daily Telegraph*, unsigned review, 11 January 1911, p.12.

35 P.G. Konody, 'The Carfax Gallery', *Observer*, 12 May 1912, p.6. (Konody confirms Sickert's 'sincerity'.)

36 A.J. Finberg, 'Art and Artists. The Camden Town Group and Others', *The Star*, 10 Dec. 1912, quoted in Baron 2006, p.375.

37 Claude Phillips, 'The Camden Town Group', *Daily Telegraph*, 17 Dec. 1912, p.14. For selected reviews of the three Camden Town Group exhibitions, see 'The Camden Town Group in Context', Tate Research Publication, May 2012, https://www.tate.org.uk/art/research-publications/camden-town-group/reviews-and-articles-r1106679, accessed 15 August 2021.

38 David Peters Corbett, '"Gross Material Facts": Sexuality, Identity and the City in Walter Sickert, 1905–1910', *Art History*, vol.21, no.1, March 1998, pp.45–64 (p.49). Quoting for my own purposes I have not done justice to Corbett's argument.

39 Wendy Baron notes that Sickert 'picked his models casually, almost never using professionals'. He recalled Blanche, probably the model for *Woman Washing her Hair* 1906, as 'the thinnest of the thin like a little eel, and exquisitely shaped, with red hair'. Baron 2006, pp.128, 324.

40 According to Marjorie Lilly, Sickert was at a party with George Moore and Max Beerbohm when they fell to discussing Moore's favourite type of woman: 'They asked me what I like best and I said, my own particular brand of frump.' Lilly, *Sickert: The Painter and his Circle*, London 1971, p.28. Marie Hayes, Sickert's erstwhile charwoman, was the model for *Jack Ashore*, along with 'Hubby', his studio factotum. Comparing a drawing for *Jack Ashore* with other studies of Marie, Anna Gruetzner Robins suggests that Sickert has 'wilfully enlarged' her breasts; see Gruetzner Robins 1996, p.34.

41 Clark 1960, p.87. 'The body is not one of those subjects which can be made into art by direct transcription – like a tiger or a snowy landscape' (p.3).

42 Sickert, 'Idealism', in Gruetzner Robins 2000, pp.228–30 (p.229). Raphael and workshop, *The Loggia of Psyche,* Villa Farnesina, Rome (1517–18).

43 Sickert, 'Goosocracy', *The New Age*, 12 May 1910, in Gruetzner Robins 2000, pp.230–2 (p.230). He refers to the 'supergoose' in 'The naked and the Nude', in Gruetzner Robins 2000, p.261.

44 Woolf 1934, pp.18, 20.

45 Sickert, 'The Language of Art', *The New Age*, 28 July 1910, in Gruetzner Robins 2000, pp.264–7 (p.266).

THE MODERN CONVERSATION PIECES

1 'A Monthly Chronicle. Maurice Asselin', *Burlington Magazine*, vol.28, no.153, Dec. 1915. Asselin (1882–1947) was a French painter and Sickert's closest friend during the first two years of the war. For a time, they shared Sickert's Red Lion Square studio, and Asselin acted as joint host at 8 Fitzroy Street 'At Homes'. Sickert painted two portraits of Asselin (see Wendy Baron, *Sickert: Paintings and Drawings*, New Haven and London

2006, p.429, cats.453 and 453.1).

2 Identified by Anna Gruetzner Robins, in *Walter Sickert: The Complete Writings on Art*, ed. Gruetzner Robins, Oxford 2000, p.396, as *The Strode Family* c.1738 (Tate Britain, London).

3 I have not traced the whereabouts of Asselin's painting, *La Robe grise*.

4 Degas deposited the painting for sale at Galerie Durand-Ruel, Paris, in 1905.

5 The wedding night from Émile Zola's *Thérèse Raquin* is the most popular suggestion.

6 See Susan Sidlauskas, 'Resisting Narrative: The Problem of Edgar Degas's *Interior*', *Art Bulletin*, vol.75, no.4, Dec. 1993, pp.671–96 (p.679 n.36).

7 It is not known whether Sickert saw Bonnard's painting before 1908 when it was sold from the collection of its first owner, Thadée Natanson.

8 The influence of this French painter (1861–1942) secured Sickert the promise of his first one-man exhibition with Bernheim-Jeune.

9 French author (1869–1951), who won the Nobel Prize for Literature in 1947.

10 French writer, art critic, collector and journalist (1853–1945).

11 In a BBC broadcast interview with Stanley Smith on 18 August 1960, Jeanne Daurmont recalled the meeting shortly after she and her sister had arrived in England. She claimed she had been a milliner, her sister a charwoman. Sickert's paintings suggest a racier lifestyle.

12 This was the title under which the painting was exhibited at Bernheim-Jeune in January 1907, and again at the London Goupil Gallery Salon in spring 1922.

13 Baron 2006, p.316, cat.264.2 – a sketch made to show his friend Mrs Swinton the paintings he was doing over the Easter 1906 week.

14 Woolf constructed *Walter Sickert: A Conversation* (London 1934) as a dinner-table discussion of Sickert's exhibition at Agnews in 1933.

15 Ibid., p.16.

16 See *The P.S. Wings in the O.P. Mirror* (no.36).

17 See *Little Dot Hetherington at the Bedford Music Hall* (no.40).

18 Sickert, letter to Ethel Sands and Nan Hudson, 1908, TGA 9125/5/36, misdated in Tate Archive to August–September 1911.

19 Nan Kivell was appointed Managing Director of the Redfern Gallery in 1922. Under his auspices, the gallery exhibited many works by Sickert, including his early work, in the 1930s.

20 Rebecca Daniels considered the resemblance of Wood as published in the trial reports with the man in Sickert's paintings, in 'Walter Sickert and Urban Realism: Ordinary Life and Tragedy in Camden Town', *British Art Journal*, vol.3, no.2, Spring 2002, pp.58–69.

21 *The Observer*, 18 June 1911.

22 Sickert, 'A Critical Calendar', *English Review*, March 1912. Robert Smythe Hichens (1864–1950) was a prolific and popular contemporary novelist.

23 This exhibition of Sickert drawings took place at the Carfax Gallery in January 1911.

24 'We stay together.'

25 The original title, *Summer in Naples*, was possibly a mischievous allusion by Sickert to Cézanne's *L'Après-midi à Naples*. For a fuller explanation of this suggestion first made by Matthew Sturgis, see Baron 2006, p.375.

26 The painting was bought by Félix Fénéon on behalf of Paul Signac, from the sale of Sickert's work organised by Bernheim-Jeune in June 1909.

27 'Wellington House Academy' in memory of the school of that name, attended by Charles Dickens, once housed at this address.

28 The bust of the boxer Tom Sayers also appears in Sickert's self-portrait (see no.5).

29 Degas's mother, Célestine Musson, was a Creole from New Orleans.

30 The title is taken from Terence, *Andria*, Act III, Scene 3: 'Amantium irae amoris integratio est' (lovers' quarrels are a part of love).

31 See the catalogue of 'Studies and Etchings by Walter Sickert' at the Carfax Gallery, March 1913.

32 *Daily Telegraph*, 29 Oct. 1915.

33 'The Language of Art', *The New Age*, 28 July 1910.

FINAL YEARS AND ECHOES

1 This essay is indebted to the scholarship of Wendy Baron, Anna Gruetzner Robins, Richard Shone, David Peters Corbett, Rebecca Daniels and Merlin Seller. I also draw on Sam Rose, '"With an almost pathetic fatality doing what is right": Late Sickert and his Critics', *Art History*, vol.37, no.1, Feb. 2014, pp.126–47.

2 Quentin Bell, 'Some Memories of Sickert', *Burlington Magazine*, vol.129, no.1009, April 1987, pp.226–31.

3 Roger Fry, 'Samples of Modern British Art', *New Statesman and Nation*, 21 Nov. 1931, p.641; Roger Fry, 'Walter Sickert A.R.A.', *New Statesman*, 17 Jan. 1925, p.417.

4 *Manchester City News*, 22 Nov. 1924, as quoted and discussed in Rose 2014, p.134.

5 Richard Shone, *Walter Sickert*, Oxford 1988, p.102; Malcolm Easton (ed.), *Sickert in the North*, Hull 1968, p.iii.

6 For this quotation and other contemporary praise, see David Peters Corbett, *Walter Sickert*, London 2001, p.71.

7 Bell 1987, p.231.

8 Note in Sickert's personal copy of Arthur Fish, *John Everett Millais*, London 1924, Courtauld Institute of Art, Book Library, Sickert Collection, quoted and discussed in Rose 2014, p.135.

9 Quoted in Wendy Baron, *Sickert: Paintings and Drawings*, New Haven and London 2006, p.118.

10 Ibid., p.98.

11 Osbert Sitwell (ed.), *A Free House! Or The Artist as Craftsman: Being the Writings of Walter Richard Sickert*, London 1947, p.liii.

EMULATING SICKERT: AUERBACH, BACON, FREUD

1 This essay draws on Martin Hammer, '"Mainly Nourishment": Echoes of Sickert in the Work of Francis Bacon and Lucian Freud', *Visual Culture in Britain*, vol.14, no.1, 2013, pp.87–100; 'After Camden Town: Sickert's Legacy since 1930', in Helena Bonett, Ysanne Holt, Jennifer Mundy (eds.), 'The Camden Town Group in Context', Tate Research Publication, May 2012, https://www.tate.org.uk/art/research-publications/camden-town-group/martin-hammer-after-camden-town-sickerts-legacy-since-1930-r1104349, accessed 16 August 2021. The latter also includes a valuable Sickert exhibition listing: 'Walter Richard Sickert, Bibliography', in https://www.tate.org.uk/art/research-publications/camden-town-group/walter-richard-sickert-bibliography-r1104380.

2 Osbert Sitwell (ed.), *A Free House! Or The Artist as Craftsman: Being the Writings of Walter Richard Sickert*, London 1947.

3 *David Hockney by David Hockney*, London 1976, p.34.

4 Andrew Forge, 'Helen Lessore and the Beaux Arts Gallery', in *Helen Lessore and the Beaux Arts Gallery*, exh. cat., Marlborough Fine Art, London 1968, p.6.

5 Helen Lessore, *A Partial Testament: Essays on Some Moderns in the Great Tradition*, London 1986.

6 Robert Hughes, *Frank Auerbach*, London 1989, pp.87–8.

7 See Martin Hammer, 'Found in Translation: Chaim Soutine and English Art', *Modernist Cultures*, vol.5, no.2, Nov. 2010, p.230.

8 Sickert, 'The naked and the Nude' (1910), in Sitwell 1947, p.324.

9 James Hyman, *The Battle for Realism: Figurative Art in Britain during the Cold War, 1945–1960*, New Haven and London 2001, p.224 n.138.

10 Rebecca Daniels, 'Francis Bacon and Walter Sickert: "Images which Unlock Other Images"', in *Francis Bacon: New Studies*, ed. Martin Harrison, Gröningen 2009, p.84.

11 Ibid., pp.63–5.

12 Ibid., p.82.

13 *The Redfern Gallery Coronation Exhibition*, exh. cat., Redfern Gallery, London 1953, nos.48 and 49.

14 Daniels 2009, pp.82–5.

15 See Barnaby Wright (ed.), *Walter Sickert: The Camden Town Nudes*, London 2007.

16 Sickert, 'The naked and the Nude' (1910), in Sitwell 1947, p.324.

17 Discussed in Martin Hammer, *Francis Bacon and Nazi Propaganda*, London 2012, p.207.

18 For this and other exhibition histories, see the Catalogue Raisonné in Wendy Baron, *Sickert: Paintings and Drawings*, New Haven and London 2006.

19 Catherine Lampert, email to author, 25 August 2012.

20 Cited in Sebastian Smee, *Lucian Freud*, Cologne 2007, p.4.

21 Baron 2006, cat.344.

22 Sickert, 'Risi-Bisi' (1912), in Sitwell 1947, p.176.

'CATCH ME IF YOU CAN': SICKERT AND JACK THE RIPPER

1 For a compassionate account of these women's lives, see Hallie Rubenhold, *The Five: The Untold Lives of the Women Killed by Jack the Ripper*, London 2019.

2 The letter, dated 25 September 1888 (National Archives, MEPO 3/142ff.2), was believed to have been the first letter signed 'Jack the Ripper'. However, in the 1980s, a letter dated 17 September 1888 (National Archives, MEPO 3/142ff.27), which also has this signature, was discovered after being filed incorrectly.

3 The letter with the salutation 'Dear Boss' (dated 25 September 1888) and the postcard (postmarked 1 October 1888), both of which were signed 'Jack the Ripper', were sent to the Central News Agency. The postcard has disappeared, but a facsimile is reproduced in Stewart P. Evans and Keith Skinner, *Jack the Ripper: Letters from Hell*, Stroud 2001, p.30.

4 See, for example, 'Jack the Ripper – Facsimile of the Blood Smeared Postcard and Letter', *Evening News*, 4 Oct. 1888, p.4.

5 Stephen Knight's *Jack the Ripper: The Final Solution* (London and New York 1976), Jean Overton Fuller's *Sickert and the Ripper Crimes* (Oxford 1990), and Patricia Cornwell's *Portrait of a Killer: Jack the Ripper – Case Closed* (New York and London 2002) and *Ripper: The Secret Life of Walter Sickert* (Seattle 2017) all link Sickert to the crimes of Jack the Ripper.

6 Robert Emmons, *The Life and Opinions of Walter Richard Sickert*, London 1941, p.49. Matthew Sturgis cites this incident without reference,

and describes the young women as 'tarts'; see Sturgis, *Walter Sickert: A Life,* London 2005, p.160.

7   Max Beerbohm, cited in Richard Shone, *From Beardsley to Beaverbrook: Portraits by Walter Richard Sickert*, Bath 1990, p.14. Shone dates the notebook to 'around 1896', but this is too early because on the same page of this undated notebook (now held in the New York Public Library) Beerbohm refers to the death of Oscar Wilde, who died in 1900. On the other hand, David Cecil appears to suggest a date of around 1900; see Cecil, *Max: A Biography*, London 1964, p.204. It may be that the conversation took place in summer 1901, when Beerbohm and Sickert saw each other in Dieppe.

8   'Il habita, je crois, à White Chapel dans la maison où vécut "Jack l'Éventreur" et me raconta, avec beaucoup d'esprit, la vie discrète et édifiante de ce monstreux assassin [*sic*].' André du Segonzac, letter to Denys Sutton, 16 November 1968, Sutton 4669, Box 37, University of Glasgow.

9   Sturgis 2005, p.535, suggests that Segonzac confused the Whitechapel address with the Mornington Crescent address. However, three people who knew Sickert claimed that he either owned or lived in a house in the East End. Sturgis cites Ethel Sands and Marjorie Lilly, who remembered that Sickert had 'an uneasy interlude at some queer place in Aldersgate' and a builder who did some work on a house 'in – or off – Petticoat Lane' (p.737 n.43).

10 Osbert Sitwell, *A Free House! Or The Artist as Craftsman. Being the Writings of Walter Richard Sickert*, London 1947, p.xl.

11 Keith Baynes, letter to Denys Sutton, Sutton Papers, University of Glasgow.

12 Marjorie Lilly, interviewed by John Woodeson, c1723/48, British Library.

13 Marjorie Lilly, *Sickert: The Painter and his Circle*, London 1971, p.15.

14 Ibid., p.19.

15 There are over three hundred extant letters, ranging in date from September 1888 to October 1896. Some of these confessional letters were sent to the press, but the majority were sent to Scotland Yard or local police stations. A proportion of these are missing their envelopes.

16 http://www.fondazionefedrigoni.it/en/567/paper_industry_gold_medal_2018_peter_bower

17 Peter Bower, *Turner's Later Papers*, London 1999, p.50.

18 Ibid., p.109.

19 The letters were written from his mother's address, 12 Pembroke Gardens, London, and are as follows: Walter Sickert to Miss Case, n.d., but probably 1890 (British Library, Add.50956 f.109), and two undated letters from Sickert to D.C. Thomson (David Croal Thomson Papers, Getty Research Institute Library). The latter two can be dated to June 1890 because they discuss the publication of Thomson's *The Barbizon School of Painters: Corot, Rousseau, Diaz, Millet, Daubigny, etc.*, London, June 1890, for which Sickert made an etching (Thomson was the manager of the London branch of the Goupil Gallery).

20 The letter was received by the City of London Police, 4 October 1888, London Metropolitan Archives CLA/048/CS/02/380.

21 The other Ripper letter is postmarked 31 October 1888, National Archives, MEPO 3/142ff.508–9.

22 Peter Bower, cited in Cornwell 2017, p.249, which discusses Bower's findings in greater detail; see pp.247–53.

23 CLA/048/CS/02/367.

24 Sickert, letter to William Rothenstein, n.d., Rothenstein Papers, Houghton Library, Harvard University, Ms Eng 1148(1367)/38. The address – '127 Cheyne Walk', a small room at the shabby end of the street, which Sickert used as a studio from late in 1893 – is written above the printed address of 10 Glebe Studios, where Sickert had a teaching studio in autumn 1890. The drawing and scribbled calculations on the letter were probably added at an earlier date.

25 The first letter is dated 22 July 1889, and the second was received 23 September 1889. National Archives, MEPO 3/142/337 and MEPO 3/142/393.

26 For example, to dispute Bower's findings, Sturgis 2005, p.640, cites the authority of 'Documentary Evidence Ltd.', but this does not appear to be a registered company; see https://find-and-update.company-information.service.gov.uk.

27 Letter dated 29 November 1889, National Archives, MEPO 3/142ff.433. Tate Conservation was given permission to take a scrapping for testing.

28 Letter dated 12 November 1888, National Archives, MEPO 3/142/175. The woodcut is annotated '10 more and up goes the sponge' and 'This is my photo of Jack the Ripper'.

29 Anne Driesse, Conservator, Harvard Art Museums, conducted further examination of these materials. See Cornwell 2017, pp.239–41.

30 The letter is dated 17 October 1889, but not signed; cited and reproduced in Evans and Skinner 2001, pp.286–7.

31 Letter postmarked 19 November 1888, National Archives, MEPO 3/142/76.

32 See, for example, 'A Strange Story', *St James Gazette*, 14 Nov. 1888.

33 The letter, in purple pencil, is dated 22 July 1889, National Archives, MEPO 3/142/337. See also n.22.

34 For a discussion of a number of instances where people confessed to crimes that they did not commit, see Peter Brooks, *Troubling Confessions: Speaking Guilt in Law and Literature*, Chicago and London 2000.

LIST OF EXHIBITED WORKS

All works are by
Walter Richard Sickert
(1860–1942)
unless otherwise stated.
Information is correct
at time of publication but
is subject to change.

Walter Richard Sickert 1860–1942
Self-Portrait 1882
Pen and ink on paper
17.1 × 10.8
Islington Local History Centre

Walter Richard Sickert 1860–1942
Self-Portrait c.1896
Oil paint on canvas
45.7 × 35.6
Leeds Museums and Galleries. Gift
from Miss Ellen M. Heath, 1942

Walter Richard Sickert 1860–1942
Self-Portrait. The Painter in his Studio
1907
Oil paint on canvas
50.8 × 61
Art Gallery of Hamilton, Ontario, Canada

Walter Richard Sickert 1860–1942
Self-Portrait. Juvenile Lead 1907
Oil paint on canvas
51 × 45.8
Southampton City Art Gallery

Walter Richard Sickert 1860–1942
Self-Portrait: The Bust of Tom Sayers
1913
Oil paint on canvas
61 × 50.3
The Ashmolean Museum, University of
Oxford. Presented by the Christopher
Sands Trust, 2001

Walter Richard Sickert 1860–1942
Self-Portrait. Lazarus Breaks his Fast
c.1927
Oil paint on canvas
76.2 × 63.5
Private collection

Walter Richard Sickert 1860–1942
The Servant of Abraham 1929
Oil paint on canvas
61 × 50.8
Tate. Presented by the Friends of the
Tate Gallery 1959

Walter Richard Sickert 1860–1942
*The Front at Hove (Turpe Senex Miles
Turpe Senilis Amor)* 1930
Oil paint on canvas
63.5 × 76.2
Tate. Purchased 1932

Walter Richard Sickert 1860–1942
Self-Portrait in Grisaille 1935
Oil paint on canvas
68.5 × 25.4
National Portrait Gallery, London; Given
by Sir Alec Martin through the Art Fund,
1943

Walter Richard Sickert 1860–1942
Reading in the Cabin 1940
Oil paint on canvas
44 × 80
Corsham Court Collection

Walter Richard Sickert 1860–1942
Six Pence Three Farthings 1884
Etching, brown ink on paper
9.9 × 13.8
The Syndics of the Fitzwilliam Museum,
University of Cambridge

Walter Richard Sickert 1860–1942
The Acting Manager 1884
Etching, printed in black-brown ink
on wove paper
23.6 × 23.3 (plate), 33 × 32.6 (sheet)
The Ashmolean Museum, University of
Oxford. Purchased, 1963

James Abbott McNeill Whistler
1834–1903
A Shop 1884–90
Oil paint on wood
13.9 × 23.3
The Hunterian, University of Glasgow

Walter Richard Sickert 1860–1942
White Violets c.1884
Oil paint on panel
22.9 × 14.6
The Courtauld, London
(Samuel Courtauld Trust)

Walter Richard Sickert 1860–1942
Venice, The Little Lagoon, after Whistler
c.1884
Drypoint, black carbon ink on paper
10.1 × 6.9
The Syndics of the Fitzwilliam Museum,
University of Cambridge

Walter Richard Sickert 1860–1942
The Burning of the Japanese Exhibition
1885
Etching, black carbon ink on paper
33.1 × 23.2
The Syndics of the Fitzwilliam Museum,
University of Cambridge

Walter Richard Sickert 1860–1942
Shop Front, The Laundry 1885
Pencil, pen and ink on paper
18.4 × 26
Islington Local History Centre

Walter Richard Sickert 1860–1942
The Laundry Shop 1885
Oil paint on panel
38.8 × 24.8
Leeds Museums and Galleries.
Bought 1937

Walter Richard Sickert 1860–1942
The Butcher's Shop, Dieppe 1885
Oil paint on panel
36 × 48.5
York Museums Trust (York Art Gallery).
Presented by the Very Reverend Milner
White, Dean of York, 1951

Walter Richard Sickert 1860–1942
La Saison des Bains, Dieppe 1885
Oil paint on panel
31.8 × 23.2
Brooklyn Museum, Gift of Ferdinand
Gottschalk, 18.37

Walter Richard Sickert 1860–1942
*The End of the Act, or The Acting
Manager* c.1885–6
Oil paint on canvas
61 × 50.8
Private collection

Walter Richard Sickert 1860–1942
A Shop in Dieppe 1885–9
Oil paint on canvas
35 × 26.7
The Hunterian, University of Glasgow

Walter Richard Sickert 1860–1942
Seascape c.1887
Oil paint on wood
23.7 × 14.3
National Galleries of Scotland.
Bequeathed by Dr Dorothea Walpole and
Mr R.H. Walpole 1963

Walter Richard Sickert 1860–1942
The Red Shop (or The October Sun)
c.1888
Oil paint on panel
26.7 × 35.6
Norfolk Museums Service (Norwich
Castle Museum & Art Gallery),
bequeathed by H.B. Broadbent 1949

James Abbott McNeill Whistler
1834–1903
The Bathing Posts, Brittany 1893
Oil paint on wood
16.6 × 24.3
The Hunterian, University of Glasgow

James Abbott McNeill Whistler
1834–1903
Sketch Portrait of Walter Sickert 1894–5
Oil paint on canvas
45.8 × 35.6
Hugh Lane Gallery

James Abbott McNeill Whistler
1834–1903
The Priest's Lodging, Dieppe 1897
Oil paint on wood
16.5 × 24.3
The Hunterian, University of Glasgow

James Abbott McNeill Whistler
1834–1903
A Shop with a Balcony 1897–9
Oil paint on wood
22.3 × 13.7
The Hunterian, University of Glasgow

James Abbott McNeill Whistler
1834–1903
Shop Front: Dieppe 1897–9
Pen, brown ink, chalk, watercolour and
gouache on brown paper laid down on card
27.4 × 17.8
The Hunterian, University of Glasgow

THE MUSIC HALL

Edgar Degas 1834–1917
*The Ballet Scene from Meyerbeer's
Opera 'Robert Le Diable'* 1876
Oil paint on canvas
76.6 × 81.3
Victoria and Albert Museum, London.
Bequeathed by Constantine Alexander
Ionides

Walter Richard Sickert 1860–1942
*Bonnet et Claque. Ada Lundberg at the
Marylebone Music Hall* c.1887
Oil paint on canvas
41.9 × 59.7
Private collection

Walter Richard Sickert 1860–1942
*Sam Collins's Music Hall, Islington
Green* 1888
Pencil, pen and ink on paper
12.5 × 10
Lord and Lady Irvine of Lairg

Walter Richard Sickert 1860–1942
Figures in an Auditorium c.1888
Pencil on lined paper
8.6 × 11.9
National Museums Liverpool,
Walker Art Gallery

Walter Richard Sickert 1860–1942
*Audience with Woman in Hat Seen from
the Back* c.1888
Pencil on paper
8.6 × 11.9
National Museums Liverpool,
Walker Art Gallery

Walter Richard Sickert 1860–1942
Music Hall Gallery with Figures c.1888
Pencil on paper
20.5 × 12.7
National Museums Liverpool,
Walker Art Gallery

Walter Richard Sickert 1860–1942
*Little Dot Hetherington at the Bedford
Music Hall* c.1888–9
Oil paint on canvas
61 × 61
Private collection

Walter Richard Sickert 1860–1942
The P.S. Wings in the O.P. Mirror
c.1888–9
Oil paint on canvas
62.2 × 52
Rouen, Musée des Beaux-Arts

Walter Richard Sickert 1860–1942
The Pit at the Old Bedford c.1889
Oil paint on canvas
20.3 × 25.4
Fondation Bemberg, Toulouse

Walter Richard Sickert 1860–1942
The Sisters Lloyd c.1889
Oil paint on canvas
63.5 × 76.5
Government Art Collection. Purchased
from Leicester Galleries, December
1958

Walter Richard Sickert 1860–1942
Vesta Victoria at the Old Bedford c.1890
Oil paint on canvas
36.8 × 24.1
Burrows Family

Walter Richard Sickert 1860–1942
Minnie Cunningham at the Old Bedford
1892
Oil paint on canvas
76.5 × 63.8
Tate. Purchased 1976

Walter Richard Sickert 1860–1942
Gallery of the Old Bedford c.1894–5
Oil paint on canvas
76.2 × 60.4
National Museums Liverpool,
Walker Art Gallery

Walter Richard Sickert 1860–1942
Gallery of the Old Mogul 1906
Oil paint on canvas
63.5 × 67
Private collection

Walter Richard Sickert 1860–1942
Noctes Ambrosianae 1906
Oil paint on canvas
63.5 × 76.2
Nottingham City Museums & Galleries

Walter Richard Sickert 1860–1942
L'Eldorado c.1906
Oil paint on canvas
49 × 59
The Henry Barber Trust, the Barber
Institute of Fine Arts, University of
Birmingham

Walter Richard Sickert 1860–1942
Théâtre de Montmartre c.1906
Oil paint on canvas
50.8 × 61.6
King's College, University of Cambridge

Walter Richard Sickert 1860–1942
*Gaîté Montparnasse, dernière galerie de
gauche* 1907
Oil paint on canvas
61 × 50
The Ashmolean Museum, University of
Oxford. Presented by the Christopher
Sands Trust, 2001

Walter Richard Sickert 1860–1942
The New Bedford 1907–9
Oil with tempera on canvas
182.9 × 72.4
Leeds Museums and Galleries. Bought
1937

Walter Richard Sickert 1860–1942
Gaîté Montparnasse c.1907
Oil paint on canvas
61.2 × 50.8
The Museum of Modern Art, New York.
Mr. and Mrs. Allan D. Emil Fund, 1958

Walter Richard Sickert 1860–1942
Figures in a Box, Gaîté Montparnasse
c.1907
Chalk, pen and ink, white heightening on
squared-up paper
30.5 × 24.8
National Museums Liverpool,
Walker Art Gallery

Walter Richard Sickert 1860–1942
Man Seated with a Woman Alongside
c.1913–14
Chalk, pen and ink, heightened with
white, on paper
38.1 × 28
National Museums Liverpool,
Walker Art Gallery

Walter Richard Sickert 1860–1942
Brighton Pierrots 1915
Oil paint on canvas
63.6 × 76.8
Tate. Purchased with assistance from
the Art Fund and the Friends of the Tate
Gallery 1996

Walter Richard Sickert 1860–1942
*Drawing of a theatre/music hall
audience [Vernet's café-concert, Dieppe]*
c.1919–20
Ink on paper
30.3 × 20.3
Tate. Presented by Mrs Andrina Tritton,
December 1981

Walter Richard Sickert 1860–1942
*Drawing of a man in top hat and coat
tails on stage [Vernet's café-concert,
Dieppe]* c.1919–20
Pencil on paper
35 × 22.9
Tate. Presented by Mrs Andrina Tritton,
December 1981

Walter Richard Sickert 1860–1942
*Drawing of a man in hat and jacket on
stage [Vernet's café-concert, Dieppe]*
c.1919–20
Pencil on paper
38 × 25.5
Tate. Presented by Mrs Andrina Tritton,
December 1981

Walter Richard Sickert 1860–1942
Drawing of a ballerina pirouetting
c.1919–20
Pencil on paper
37 × 23.5
Tate. Presented by Mrs Andrina Tritton,
December 1981

Walter Richard Sickert 1860–1942
The Trapeze 1920
Oil paint on canvas
63.5 × 80.6
The Syndics of the Fitzwilliam Museum,
University of Cambridge

Walter Richard Sickert 1860–1942
Brass and Wind Instrumentalists c.1922–3
Pencil, pen and ink on paper
38 × 18.7
National Museums Liverpool,
Walker Art Gallery

Walter Richard Sickert 1860–1942
String Players in a Women's Orchestra
c.1922–3
Pencil on paper
25 × 18.7
National Museums Liverpool,
Walker Art Gallery

Walter Richard Sickert 1860–1942
Eugene Goosens Conducting c.1923–4
Oil paint on canvas
40.7 × 66
Daniel Katz Ltd, London

Walter Richard Sickert 1860–1942
Vernet's, Dieppe 1925
Oil paint on canvas
61 × 50.8
frame: 78.5 × 67.2 × 8.5
The Syndics of the Fitzwilliam Museum,
University of Cambridge

Walter Richard Sickert 1860–1942
Studies of Dancing Couples n.d.
Pencil on paper
38.1 × 27.6
National Museums Liverpool,
Walker Art Gallery

BEYOND PORTRAITURE

Walter Richard Sickert 1860–1942
Blackbird of Paradise c.1892
Oil paint on canvas
66.4 × 48.3
Leeds Museums and Galleries.
Bought 1945

Walter Richard Sickert 1860–1942
Aubrey Beardsley 1894
Tempera on canvas
76.2 × 31.1
Tate. Purchased with assistance from
the Art Fund 1932

Walter Richard Sickert 1860–1942
Israel Zangwill c.1896–8
Oil paint on canvas laid on board
61 × 50.8
National Galleries of Scotland.
Purchased 1959

Walter Richard Sickert 1860–1942
Le Châle Vénitien 1903–4
Oil paint on canvas
45.7 × 38.1
Ivor Braka

Walter Richard Sickert 1860–1942
La Giuseppina against a Map of Venice
c.1903–4
Oil paint on canvas
50.8 × 40.6
Mr and Mrs Michael Hughes

Walter Richard Sickert 1860–1942
Two Women on a Sofa – Le Tose
c.1903–4
Oil paint on canvas
45.7 × 53.3
Tate. Bequeathed by Sir Hugh Walpole
1941

Walter Richard Sickert 1860–1942
Jeanne. The Cigarette 1906
Oil paint on canvas
50.8 × 40.6
Lent by The Metropolitan Museum of
Art, Bequest of Mary Cushing Fosburgh,
1978 (1979.135.17)

Walter Richard Sickert 1860–1942
Mrs Swinton 1906
Oil paint on canvas
76.2 × 63.5
The Syndics of the Fitzwilliam Museum,
University of Cambridge

Walter Richard Sickert 1860–1942
The Mantelpiece c.1906
Oil paint on canvas
76.2 × 50.8
Southampton City Art Gallery

Walter Richard Sickert 1860–1942
Girl at a Window, Little Rachel 1907
Oil paint on canvas
50.8 × 40.6
Tate. Accepted by HM Government in lieu of
tax and allocated to the Tate Gallery 1991

Walter Richard Sickert 1860–1942
The New Home 1908
Oil paint on canvas
50.8 × 40.6
Ivor Braka

Walter Richard Sickert 1860–1942
Jacques-Émile Blanche c.1910
Oil paint on canvas
61 × 50.8
Tate. Purchased 1938

Walter Richard Sickert 1860–1942
Harold Gilman c.1912
Oil paint on canvas
61 × 45.7
Tate. Presented by the Trustees of the
Chantrey Bequest 1957

Walter Richard Sickert 1860–1942
Victor Lecourt 1921–4
Oil paint on canvas
81.3 × 60.5
Manchester Art Gallery, George Beatson
Blair bequest, 1941

Walter Richard Sickert 1860–1942
Cicely Hey 1923
Oil paint on canvas
75.8 × 35.5
The Whitworth, The University of
Manchester

THE URBAN ENVIRONMENT

Walter Richard Sickert 1860–1942
The Theatre of the Young Artists 1890
Oil paint on canvas
52 × 65
The Atkinson, Southport

Walter Richard Sickert 1860–1942
L'Hôtel Royal, Dieppe c.1894
Oil paint on canvas
50.2 × 61
Sheffield Museums Trust

Walter Richard Sickert 1860–1942
The Lion of St Mark c.1895–6
Oil paint on canvas
90.2 × 89.8
The Syndics of the Fitzwilliam Museum,
University of Cambridge

Walter Richard Sickert 1860–1942
Santa Maria del Carmelo c.1895–6
Oil paint on canvas
38.5 × 45.5
The Ashmolean Museum, University of
Oxford. Presented by the Christopher
Sands Trust, 2001

Walter Richard Sickert 1860–1942
*The Façade of St Mark's. Red Sky at
Night* c.1895–6
Oil paint on canvas
45.4 × 61
Southampton City Art Gallery

Walter Richard Sickert 1860–1942
*St Mark's, Venice (Pax Tibi Marce
Evangelista Meus)* 1896
Oil paint on canvas
90.8 × 120
Tate. Bequeathed by General Sir Ian
Hamilton GCB, GCMG, DSO 1949

Walter Richard Sickert 1860–1942
St Mark's, Venice 1896–7
Oil paint on canvas
100.5 × 151
Courtesy of the British Council
Collection

Walter Richard Sickert 1860–1942
Les Arcades et La Darse c.1898
Oil paint on canvas
50.8 × 67
Fondation Bemberg, Toulouse

Walter Richard Sickert 1860–1942
The Façade of St Jacques 1899–1900
Oil paint on canvas
41.2 × 33.2
Rouen, Musée des Beaux-Arts

Walter Richard Sickert 1860–1942
The Façade of St Jacques 1899–1900
Oil paint on canvas
53.8 × 45.3
The Whitworth, The University of
Manchester

Walter Richard Sickert 1860–1942
The Horses of St Mark's 1901–6
Oil paint on canvas
54.6 × 45.7
Bristol Culture: Bristol Museums &
Art Gallery

Walter Richard Sickert 1860–1942
The Façade of St Jacques 1902
Oil paint on canvas
130.8 × 105
Private collection

Walter Richard Sickert 1860–1942
Le Grand Duquesne 1902
Oil paint on canvas
131.6 × 104.8
Manchester Art Gallery

Walter Richard Sickert 1860–1942
The Façade of St Jacques 1902–3
Pencil and oil paint on canvas
61 × 51
Private collection

Walter Richard Sickert 1860–1942
Bathers, Dieppe c.1902
Oil paint on canvas
131.5 × 104.6
National Museums Liverpool,
Walker Art Gallery

Walter Richard Sickert 1860–1942
The Fair at Night c.1902–3
Oil paint on canvas
129.5 × 97.2
Touchstones Rochdale Art Gallery,
Link4Life. Ogden Bequest purchase, 1942

Walter Richard Sickert 1860–1942
The Façade of St Jacques 1907
Oil paint on canvas
66.5 × 54.3
Pallant House Gallery, Chichester
(On Loan From a Private Collection 1995)

Walter Richard Sickert 1860–1942
*Rue Notre Dame des Champs, Paris.
Entrance to Sargent's Studio* 1907
Oil paint on canvas
61.2 × 50.8
The Ashmolean Museum, University of
Oxford. Presented by the Christopher
Sands Trust, 2001

Walter Richard Sickert 1860–1942
Rowlandson House – Sunset 1910–11
Oil paint on canvas
61 × 50.2
Tate. Bequeathed by Lady Henry
Cavendish-Bentinck 1940

Walter Richard Sickert 1860–1942
Celebrations, Dieppe 1914
Oil paint on canvas
90 × 63.5
Private collection. Courtesy of PIANO
NOBILE, London

Walter Richard Sickert 1860–1942
Café des Arcades (or Café Suisse)
c.1914
Oil paint on canvas
54.6 × 38.1
Leeds Museums and Galleries. Bought
1942

Walter Richard Sickert 1860–1942
Queens Road Station, Bayswater
1915–16
Oil paint on canvas
62.3 × 73
The Courtauld, London
(Samuel Courtauld Trust)

Walter Richard Sickert 1860–1942
Maple Street 1916
Oil paint on canvas
76.8 × 51.1
Lent by The Metropolitan Museum of
Art, Gift of Emma Swan Hall, 1998
(1998.451.2)

Walter Richard Sickert 1860–1942
Nuit d'Amour c.1920
Oil paint on canvas
90.2 × 69.8
Manchester Art Gallery. Purchased with
the aid of a grant from the Heritage
Lottery Fund and with the assistance of
the National Art Collections Fund and
Friends and Patrons and Associates of
Manchester Art Galleries

Walter Richard Sickert 1860–1942
The Garden of Love or Lainey's Garden
c.1927–8
Oil paint on canvas
81.9 × 61.6
The Syndics of the Fitzwilliam Museum,
University of Cambridge

Walter Richard Sickert 1860–1942
Easter c.1928
Oil paint on canvas
66.1 × 77.2
Courtesy of Board of Trustees of
National Museums NI

THE NUDE

Edgar Degas 1834–1917
Après le bain, femme nue couchée
1885–90
Pastel on paper mounted at the edges
by the artist on board
49 × 88
David and Ezra Nahmad Collection

Pierre Bonnard 1867–1947
Femme assoupie sur un lit 1899
Oil paint on canvas
96.4 × 105.2
Paris, Musée d'Orsay, acquired 1947

Walter Richard Sickert 1860–1942
The Little Bed 1902
Pencil and chalk on paper
15.7 × 28.2
University of Reading Art Collection
UAC/10520

Walter Richard Sickert 1860–1942
Fille Vénitienne Allongée 1903–4
Oil paint on canvas
37.5 × 46.2
Rouen, Musée des Beaux-Arts

Walter Richard Sickert 1860–1942
Cocotte de Soho 1905
Pastel on millboard
62 × 50
Private collection

Walter Richard Sickert 1860–1942
Le Lit de Fer 1905
Pastel on buff paper
33 × 50.1
Private collection

Walter Richard Sickert 1860–1942
Nude Stretching: La Coiffure 1905–6
Pastel on paper
71 × 55
Private collection

Walter Richard Sickert 1860–1942
Woman Washing her Hair 1906
Oil paint on canvas
45.7 × 38.1
Tate. Bequeathed by Lady Henry
Cavendish-Bentinck 1940

Walter Richard Sickert 1860–1942
La Maigre Adeline 1906
Oil paint on canvas
46 × 38.4
Lent by The Metropolitan Museum of
Art, Bequest of Scofield Thayer, 1982
(1984.433.24)

Walter Richard Sickert 1860–1942
Le Lit de Cuivre c.1906
Oil paint on canvas
40.9 × 50.9
Loaned by the Royal Albert Memorial
Museum & Art Gallery, Exeter City Council

Walter Richard Sickert 1860–1942
Nuit d'Été c.1906
Oil paint on canvas
50.8 × 40.6
Private collection

Walter Richard Sickert 1860–1942
The Studio: The Painting of a Nude c.1906
Oil paint on canvas
75 × 49
Property of a European Collector.
Courtesy of PIANO NOBILE, London

Walter Richard Sickert 1860–1942
La Hollandaise c.1906
Oil paint on canvas
51.1 × 40.6
Tate. Purchased 1983

Walter Richard Sickert 1860–1942
The Iron Bedstead c.1906
Oil paint on canvas
39.5 × 50
Private collection, courtesy Hazlitt
Holland-Hibbert

Walter Richard Sickert 1860–1942
Mornington Crescent Nude c.1907
Oil paint on canvas
45.7 × 50.8
The Syndics of the Fitzwilliam Museum,
University of Cambridge

Walter Richard Sickert 1860–1942
A Consultation 1907–8
Chalk, heightened with white on faded
green paper
24.5 × 24.5
Lord and Lady Irvine of Lairg
Lucian Freud 1922–2011
Naked Portrait 1972–3
Oil paint on canvas
61 × 61
Tate. Purchased 1975

MODERN CONVERSATION PIECES

Walter Richard Sickert 1860–1942
The Camden Town Murder c.1907–8
Oil paint on canvas
64.5 × 62
Daniel Katz Family Trust

Walter Richard Sickert 1860-1942
Two Coster Girls c.1907–8
Oil on panel
35.5 × 26
Government Art Collection. Purchased
from the Fine Art Society, May 1979

Walter Richard Sickert 1860–1942
L'Américaine 1908
Oil paint on canvas
50.8 × 40.6
Tate. Bequeathed by Lady Henry
Cavendish-Bentinck 1940
(Petit Palais only)

Walter Richard Sickert 1860–1942
Persuasion. La Belle Gâtée c.1908
Black chalk, heightened with white on
violet – faded to buff – paper
26.7 × 20.3
Bristol Culture: Bristol Museums &
Art Gallery

Walter Richard Sickert 1860–1942
The Camden Town Murder, or *What Shall
We Do for the Rent?* c.1908
Oil paint on canvas
25.6 × 35.6
Yale Center for British Art, Paul
Mellon Fund

Walter Richard Sickert 1860–1942
Woman Seated at a Window c.1908–9
Oil paint on canvas
52 × 40
Private collection
(Petit Palais only)

Walter Richard Sickert 1860–1942
Conversation 1909
Black chalk, heightened with white,
pen and ink on buff paper
33.7 × 23.5
Royal College of Art Collection

Walter Richard Sickert 1860–1942
L'Affaire de Camden Town 1909
Oil paint on canvas
61 × 40.6
Private collection

Walter Richard Sickert 1860–1942
Dawn, Camden Town c.1909
Oil paint on canvas
50.6 × 40.2
Private collection, courtesy Hazlitt
Holland-Hibbert
Walter Richard Sickert 1860–1942
Flower Girl 1911
Oil paint on canvas
38.1 × 30.5
Private collection

Walter Richard Sickert 1860–1942
Off to the Pub 1911
Oil paint on canvas
50.8 × 40.6
Tate. Presented by Howard Bliss 1943

Walter Richard Sickert 1860–1942
The Prussians in Belgium c.1912
Oil paint on canvas
50.5 × 40.5
Private collection, courtesy Hazlitt
Holland-Hibbert

Walter Richard Sickert 1860–1942
A Few Words: Off to the Pub c.1912
Oil paint on canvas
50.8 × 30.5
Collection of Margo and Nicholas
Snowman

Walter Richard Sickert 1860–1942
Jack Ashore 1912–13
Oil paint on canvas
36.8 × 29.8
Pallant House Gallery, Chichester
(Wilson Gift through the Art Fund 2006)

Walter Richard Sickert 1860–1942
Granby Street c.1912–13
Oil paint on canvas
51 × 41
Private collection

Walter Richard Sickert 1860–1942
The Integrity of Belgium 1914
Oil paint on canvas
92.5 × 71.5
Government Art Collection. Purchased
from Phillips, 5 November 1991

Walter Richard Sickert 1860–1942
Soldiers of King Albert the Ready 1914
Oil paint on canvas
211.5 × 166.4
Sheffield Museums Trust

Walter Richard Sickert 1860–1942
Ennui c.1914
Oil paint on canvas
152.4 × 112.4
Tate. Presented by the Contemporary
Art Society 1924

Walter Richard Sickert 1860–1942
Baccarat 1920
Oil paint on canvas
55.2 × 45.7
Private collection c/o Grant Ford Limited

Walter Richard Sickert 1860–1942
Baccarat – the Fur Cape 1920
Oil paint on canvas
59.1 × 41.9
Tate. Bequeathed by Lady Henry
Cavendish-Bentinck 1940

Walter Richard Sickert 1860–1942
L'Armoire à Glace 1924
Oil paint on canvas
61 × 38.1
Tate. Purchased 1941
Walter Richard Sickert 1860–1942
The System 1924–6
Oil paint on canvas
61.2 × 38.8
National Galleries of Scotland. Accepted
by HM Government in lieu of Inheritance
Tax and allocated to the Scottish
National Gallery of Modern Art 2009

TRANSPOSITION: THE FINAL YEARS

Walter Richard Sickert 1860–1942
Rear Admiral Lumsden C.I.E., C.V.O.
1927–8
Oil paint on canvas
245 × 91.5
Private collection, Devon
Walter Richard Sickert 1860–1942
Portrait of Degas in 1885 c.1928
Oil paint on canvas
79 × 57
Ministère de l'Europe et des Affaires
étrangères

Walter Richard Sickert 1860–1942
Sir Hugh Walpole 1929
Oil paint on canvas
76.2 × 63.5
Lent by Glasgow Life (Glasgow
Museums) on behalf of Glasgow City
Council. Purchased, 1947

Walter Richard Sickert 1860–1942
*King George V and his Racing Manager:
A Conversation Piece at Aintree*
c.1929–30
Oil paint on canvas
46.4 × 46.4
The Royal Collection / HM Queen
Elizabeth II

Walter Richard Sickert 1860–1942
The Seducer c.1929–30
Oil paint on canvas
42.5 × 62.5
Tate Collection

Walter Richard Sickert 1860–1942
*Miss Gwen Ffrangcon-Davies as Isabella
of France* 1932
Oil paint on canvas
245.1 × 92.1
Tate. Presented by the Art Fund, the
Contemporary Art Society and C. Frank
Stoop through the Contemporary Art
Society 1932

Walter Richard Sickert 1860–1942
Miss Earhart's Arrival 1932
Oil paint on canvas
71.7 × 183.2
Tate Collection

Walter Richard Sickert 1860–1942
Variation on 'Othello' c.1933–4
Oil paint on canvas
110 × 73
Bristol Culture: Bristol Museums &
Art Gallery

Walter Richard Sickert 1860–1942
Variation on Peggy 1934–5
Oil paint on canvas
57.8 × 71.8
Tate. Bequeathed by Dame Peggy
Ashcroft 1992
(Petit Palais only)

Walter Richard Sickert 1860–1942
King George V and Queen Mary 1935
Oil paint on canvas
63.5 × 75.5
Private collection

Walter Richard Sickert 1860–1942
Gwen Again 1935–6
Oil paint on canvas
140 × 97
Private collection

Walter Richard Sickert 1860–1942
*Alexander Gavin Henderson, 2nd Lord
Faringdon* c.1935
Oil paint on canvas
231 × 85
Faringdon Collection Trust

Walter Richard Sickert 1860–1942
The Miner c.1935–6
Oil paint on canvas
127.6 × 76.8
Lent by Birmingham Museums Trust on
behalf of Birmingham City Council

Walter Richard Sickert 1860–1942
Juliet and her Nurse c.1935–6
Oil paint on canvas
76.2 × 61
Leeds Art Fund. On loan to Leeds
Museums and Galleries. Bought 1937

Walter Richard Sickert 1860–1942
HM King Edward VIII 1936
Oil paint on canvas
180 × 90
Private collection

Walter Richard Sickert 1860–1942
Pimlico c.1937
Oil paint on canvas
60.8 × 73.4
Aberdeen City Council (Art Gallery &
Museums Collections)

Walter Richard Sickert 1860–1942
'The Taming of the Shrew' c.1937
Oil paint on canvas
101.5 × 62
Courtesy of Bradford Museums and
Galleries

Walter Richard Sickert 1860–1942
Jack and Jill c.1937–8
Oil paint on canvas
62 × 75
Oskowitz Family

Walter Richard Sickert 1860–1942
Sir Thomas Beecham Conducting 1938
Oil paint on burlap
98.5 × 104.5
The Museum of Modern Art, New
York. Bertram F. and Susie Brummer
Foundation Fund, 1955

Walter Richard Sickert 1860–1942
High-Steppers c.1938–9
Oil paint on canvas
132 × 122.5
National Galleries of Scotland.
Purchased 1979

PICTURE CREDITS

INDEX